About the Author

Eric Ecklund is an instructor in both Management and Computer Technology at Cambria-Rowe Business College in Johnstown, Penn., where he teaches courses ranging from Small Business Management and Marketing to Network Administration and Advanced Web Design. He is the author of *Windows XP: A Professional Approach* (Glencoe/McGraw-Hill, 2002) and wrote the instructor's manuals for *Survey of Operating Systems* (McGraw-Hill/Osborne, 2003) and *Introduction to PC Hardware and Troubleshooting* (McGraw-Hill/Osborne, 2003), which are two of the other books in the Mike Meyer's Computer Skills series. He also served as peer reviewer for *Survey of Operating Systems* and has reviewed and helped edit several other management and computer texts published by various divisions of McGraw-Hill.

Eric earned a B.S. degree and Pennsylvania teaching certificate from the University of Pittsburgh and an M.B.A. degree from Seton Hill College.

About the Tech Editor

John Cronan was introduced to computers when he was in college, more than 25 years ago. John first became involved in writing and editing computer-related materials in the early 1990s. In the ensuing years, he has worked on dozens of books and software product manuals, additionally performing technical reviews of other authors' works in the course of operating his own technical writing and editing business. John recently authored *Microsoft Office Excel 2003 QuickSteps* and co-authored *Microsoft Office Access 2003 QuickSteps*. Other recent books he has worked on and published by McGraw-Hill/Osborne include *Windows Server 2003: A Beginner's Guide* (Matthews) and *FrontPage 2003: The Complete Reference* (Matthews). John and his wife, Faye, (and cat, Little Buddy) live in historic Everett, Wash.

About the Peer Reviewers

This book was greatly influenced by the dedicated group of teachers and subject-matter experts who reviewed this book and whose suggestions made it so much better. To them we give our heartfelt thanks.

Fred Bisel (CCIE written, CCNP, CCDP, CCAI, MCSE 4.0/2000) is an instructor and system administrator at Craven Community College in New Bern, N.C. He holds a B.S. in mathematics from East Kentucky University and an M.A. in education from East Carolina University. He is an accomplished banjo performer and recently placed second at the Teluride (Colorado) and MerlFest (North Carolina) banjo contests.

Kevin Carpenter (MCSE 4.0/2000) has a B.A. and M.A. in English from Iowa State University, where he taught freshman English for four years. Kevin has worked for Heald College in San Francisco as the IT Program Manager.

CJ Gray is currently a computer network systems instructor for Pittsburgh Technical Institute. He has also been a technical trainer for New Horizons Computer Learning Center, where he specialized in MCSE training, and CoManage Corporation. He currently holds MCSE, MCSA, Security+, Linux+, A+, and Network+ certifications.

Winston H. Maddox is Assistant Professor and Department Chair of the Information Technology programs in the Business and Technology division of Mercer County Community College, West Windsor, N.J. Winston specializes in teaching introductory and advanced courses and concepts in operating system architecture, networking, programming, and applications. Winston has certified with Novell and Microsoft. Winston holds an M.A. from Bowling Green State University and a B.A. from the University of Hartford.

Rajiv Malkan is a Professor of Computer Technologies and Business at Montgomery College in Conroe, Tex. He has 25 years of experience in teaching business and computer-related courses at different institutions and 11 years of experience as an instructional division leader. He holds a B.A. in Chemistry and Physics from University of Bombay, and also holds the equivalent of an M.A. in Textile Management from Bombay, India. He also holds a M.A. in Computer Science from Florida Institute of Technology and an M.B.A. from Phillips University.

Walter G. Merchant, Jr. (Ph.D., MCSE, MCP, SCNA, CCNA, CNA) has 28 years of professional networking experience using systems from mainframe to LAN/WAN applications. Previous experience includes CIO for international software development/networking organization, Project Manager for software development company, and for the last four years he has been employed as a College Professor at ECPI College of Technology teaching Sun Solaris, Red Hat Linux, HP-AIX UNIX, Windows XP/2000 Professional/Server/Advanced Server, Windows NT v3.51/4.0, Novell 4.11/5.0, and Network Routing using Cisco 2500/2501 series routers. He has more than 15 years of teaching experience at various colleges and institutes. He holds a B.S. in Computer Science, M.S. in Education, M.S. in Computer Science, and a Ph.D. in Management Information Systems.

■ Acknowledgments

My first acknowledgement has to go to Kathleen Sutterlin for getting me started down the road that led me to here. When Kathleen worked as the McGraw-Hill representative to Cambria-Rowe Business College, she got me started working on reviews and helping with technical edits and even helped me land my first text project. Since this is my first opportunity to thank her in print, I wanted to be sure that she got top billing. She deserves it.

I also owe a debt of gratitude to Chris Johnson, the Sponsoring Editor. It was Chris who, after seeing my work on peer reviews and instructor's manuals, asked me to write this text. He played a huge role in helping me develop and shape the concept for this book and I greatly look forward to working on future projects under him. His support and encouragement, which he always finds time to provide in spite of his busy schedule, make the job of an author much easier than it might otherwise be.

Laura Stone, my Developmental Editor, fulfilled the promise of her title beyond my wildest expectations. By collecting, condensing, and helping to interpret the wonderful feedback of the peer reviewers, she helped me revise and refine each chapter until it was clear, concise, and complete. All this while maintaining her sense of humor, and tolerating mine, which is truly an admirable achievement!

John Cronan, my Technical Editor, did a wonderful job of checking my facts, figures, concepts, and procedures. His attention to detail, and his technical expertise, are without peer. He not only ensured that everything I said was checked and double-checked, but he also brought a unique and valuable perspective to the job that frequently helped me to explain difficult concepts in a better way.

Carolyn Welch, Lisa Wolters-Broder, and Mark Karmendy made up the Project Editorial team and really cracked the whip to move each chapter through copy edit and layout. I'm still amazed at how quickly everything started to move once they got involved and I thank them collectively and individually for their help in ironing out those last few wrinkles.

Robert Campbell, the Copy Editor, and Linda Medoff, the Proofreader, deserve my thanks for helping me to hide my average grammar and spelling skills and for knowing what I wanted to say even when my late night typing said something completely different!

I also want to thank my illustrators, Melinda Lytle and Kathleen Edwards, for taking my child-like concept drawings and transforming them into true works of art. In a similar vein, I want to thank the whole Composition and Layout team for making Melinda and Kathleen's art and my words fit so handsomely on the printed page.

■ *I dedicate this book to my parents, Robert and Dawn Ecklund, who always told me I could and never doubted I would.*

Finally, I also need to thank those who didn't work on the book, but made it possible for me to do so. I'd like to thank my wife, Charlotte, and my daughters, Lauren and Anna, for their patience, support, and love during this project. I really couldn't have done it without them around me. I also appreciate the support of my friends and co-workers at Cambria-Rowe Business College who were always nice enough to ask how the project was going and tolerated me on those grumpy mornings when I got a chapter finished at 5 AM! Lastly, I'd like to thank my students, past, present, and future, who were constantly on my mind as I wrote this book. I wrote it for them, and for students everywhere like them. May it bring them knowledge and lead them to success.

CONTENTS AT A GLANCE

Chapter 1 ■ **Welcome to the Evolution: Windows Server 2003**   1

Chapter 2 ■ **Getting Started: Installing Windows Server 2003**   28

Chapter 3 ■ **A Net Improvement: Configuring Network Services and Protocols**   74

Chapter 4 ■ **Preparing to Serve: Understanding Microsoft Networking**   108

Chapter 5 ■ **Directory Assistance: Administration Using Active Directory Users and Computers**   136

Chapter 6 ■ **A Place for Everything: Storage Management**   170

Chapter 7 ■ **Preparing for Output: Printer Configuration and Management**   202

Chapter 8 ■ **Crowd Control: Controlling Access to Resources Using Groups**   232

Chapter 9 ■ **Traffic Control: Monitoring and Managing Server Performance**   258

Chapter 10 ■ **From Here to There: Remote Installation of the Windows XP Professional Client**   294

Chapter 11 ■ **The Best Policy: Managing Computers and Users Through Group Policy** 324

Chapter 12 ■ **From There to Here: Server Management Using Remote Desktop for Administration** 354

■ **Glossary** 379

■ **Index** 391

TABLE OF CONTENTS

Preface xiv
Introduction xvii

Chapter 1
■ Welcome to the Evolution: Windows Server 2003 1

The Evolution of Windows Server 2003   1
  Windows for Workgroups   1
  Windows NT   4
  Windows 2000   8
Introducing the Windows Server 2003
  Family   11
  Windows Server 2003
    Standard Edition   12
  Windows Server 2003
    Enterprise Edition   12
  Windows Server 2003
    Datacenter Edition   13
  Windows Server 2003 Web Edition   14
What's New and Improved in Windows
  Server 2003?   15
  Improved Benefits   15
  What Is .NET Anyway?   16
  New Features   17
Meeting the System Requirements   19
  Minimum Requirements   19
  Recommended Requirements   21
Chapter 1 Review   22

Chapter 2
■ Getting Started: Installing Windows Server 2003 28

Checking Hardware Compatibility   29
  Using the Microsoft Windows
    Upgrade Advisor   29
  Using the Windows Upgrade Advisor . . .   29
  The Hardware Compatibility List
    and the Windows Server Catalog   31
  Using the Online Hardware
    Compatibility List   32
  Using the Windows Server Catalog   34
Choosing an Installation Method   37
  Attended Installation   37
  Unattended Installation   37
  Other Installation Options   39
Preparing to Install Windows
  Server 2003   40
  Upgrade or Clean Installation?   40
  Partitioning   42
  File System   42
  Licensing   44
  Server Name   44
  Initial Password   46
  Network Settings   46
  Creating an Installation Plan
    for Windows Server 2003   47
Installing and Activating Windows
  Server 2003   48
  Performing an Attended Installation   48
  Performing an Attended Installation
    of Window Server 2003   49
  Testing the Installation   55

Updating Windows Server 2003 58
   Using Windows Update 58
   Running Windows Update 59
   Update Categories 61
   Configuring Windows Update 63
Troubleshooting Common
   Installation Problems 64
   Can't Install 64
   Installation Aborts 65
   Post-Installation Problems 65
Chapter 2 Review 67

Chapter 3
▪ A Net Improvement: Configuring
Network Services and Protocols 74

Understanding Basic TCP/IP Concepts 75
   Addressing 75
   Verifying TCP/IP Configuration 81
Configuring TCP/IP 82
   Dynamic Versus Static IP Addressing . . . 82
   Changing Connection Properties 82
   Configuring a Static IP Address 83
Setting Up DHCP 85
   DHCP Benefits 86
   Installing DHCP, DNS, and WINS 87
   Configuring DHCP 89
   Adding a New DHCP Scope 90
Setting Up DNS and WINS 94
   The Difference Between DNS and WINS . . . 94
   Configuring DNS 95
   Configuring DNS and Activating
     DNS and WINS Options in the
     DHCP Server 96
   Client Configuration 101
Chapter 3 Review 102

Chapter 4
▪ Preparing to Serve: Understanding
Microsoft Networking 108

Identifying the Logical Structures
   of Microsoft Networks 109
   Domains 109
   Trees 111
   Forests 112
   Organizational Units and Sites 113
Active Directory Features in Windows
   Server 2003 115
   Basic Benefits of Active Directory 115
   New Features of Active Directory 117
Creating a Domain by Installing
   Active Directory 118
   Planning the Active Directory
     Installation 118
   Installing Active Directory
     on a Stand-Alone Server 120
   Raising the Domain and Forest
     Functional Level 127
   Raising Domain and Forest
     Functionality Levels 128
Chapter 4 Review 131

Chapter 5
▪ Directory Assistance: Administration
Using Active Directory Users and
Computers 136

Identify Active Directory Objects 137
   Computer 137
   User 139
   Contact 141
   Group 141
   Organizational Unit 142
   Printer and Shared Folder 143
Create Objects Using Active Directory
   Users and Computers 143
   The Active Directory Users
     and Computers Interface 144

Exploring Active Directory Users
    and Computers 144
The Initial Active Directory
    Containers and Objects 148
Creating Common Active
    Directory Objects 150
Creating Computer Accounts,
    User Accounts, and
    Organizational Units 151
Managing Objects Using Active Directory
    Users and Computers 154
Object Properties 154
Basic Active Directory Users and
    Computers Object Management 159
Moving and Editing Objects in Active
    Directory Users and Computers 159
Chapter 5 Review 165

Chapter 6
■ A Place for Everything: Storage Management 170

Basic Disks Versus Dynamic Disks 171
Capabilities and Limitations of
    Basic Disks 171
Advantages of Dynamic Disks 172
When to Use Dynamic Disks 172
Converting Basic Disks to
    Dynamic Disks 173
Using Volumes to Manage Storage 175
Volumes That Grow 175
Volumes That Improve Performance . . . 176
Volumes That Improve Reliability 177
Creating Volumes on Dynamic Disks 179
Using Windows Backup 185
Backup Options 185
Features and Shortcomings
    of Windows Backup 186
Performing a Backup and Restore
    with Windows Backup 188
Backing Up and Restoring a Volume
    with Windows Backup 189

Troubleshooting Storage 193
Disk Errors 193
Failing Disks with Mirrored Volumes . . . 195
Poor Performance 195
Chapter 6 Review 197

Chapter 7
■ Preparing for Output: Printer Configuration and Management 202

Installing a Printer 203
Connection Options 203
Data Handling Options 205
Installing a Locally Connected,
    Nonremote Printer 206
Installing a Locally Connected Printer . . . 207
Configuring and Sharing Print Devices . . . 212
Configuring Print Device Properties 212
Sharing a Printer 214
Managing Printers and Print Jobs 218
Managing Printers 218
Creating a Printer Pool 220
Managing Print Jobs 222
Troubleshooting Common Printer
    Problems 225
Problem: Users Cannot Print
    to a Network Printer 225
Problem: Pages of Nonsense Characters
    Print Instead of Document 225
Chapter 7 Review 227

Chapter 8
■ Crowd Control: Controlling Access to Resources Using Groups 232

Windows Server 2003 Group Accounts 233
Group Scope and Membership Rules 233
Best Practices for Using
    Group Accounts 234
Creating and Managing
    Group Accounts 237

Manage Folder, File, and Printer Access . . . 242
   Share Permissions 242
   Creating and Sharing a Folder
      and Setting Share Permissions 244
   NTFS Permissions 246
   Setting NTFS Permissions and
      Demonstrating Inheritance 249
   Printer Permissions 251
Troubleshooting Share and Access
   Control Problems 252
   Check Both Share and NTFS
      Permissions 252
   Use the Effective Permissions Utility . . . 253
   Check Group Membership 253
   Check Special Permissions 253
Chapter 8 Review 254

Chapter 9

**■ Traffic Control: Monitoring and
Managing Server Performance** 258

Server Monitoring Using Task Manager . . . 259
   Opening and Exploring Task Manager . . . 259
   Monitoring and Managing
      with Task Manager 264
   Working with Task Manager 266
Server Monitoring and Alerts Using
   the Performance Console 268
   Using System Monitor to
      Monitor Server Performance 268
   Using System Monitor 271
   Using Performance Logs and Alerts . . . 273
   Creating a Counter Log 275
   Configuring an Alert 282
Monitoring Event Logs 285
   The Application, Security,
      and System Logs 285
   Monitoring Event Logs 287
Chapter 9 Review 290

Chapter 10

**■ From Here to There: Remote
Installation of the Windows XP
Professional Client** 294

Configuring a Server for Remote
   Installation Services 295
   Remote Installation Services
      Function and Requirements 295
   Installing Remote Installation
      Services 297
Configuring Remote Installation
   Services 298
   Operating System Considerations 298
   Configuring RIS and Creating a
      Windows XP Professional
      Flat Image 300
   Additional RIS Configuration Settings . . . 303
   Advanced RIS Configuration 306
Performing a Remote Installation of
   Windows XP Professional 309
   RIS Client Requirements 309
   Installing an OS to a Client Machine
      Using RIS 311
Creating an Image from a Reference
   Computer 314
   RIPrep Images 314
   Creating a RIPrep Image of a
      Reference Computer 316
   Installing from a RIPrep Image 319
Chapter 10 Review 320

Chapter 11

**■ The Best Policy: Managing Computers
and Users Through Group Policy** 324

Understanding the Capabilities
   of Group Policy 325
   Group Policy Tools 325
   Group Policy Settings Categories 327

Creating a New Group Policy Object
and Opening the Group Policy
Object Editor 330
Managing Security Using Group Policy 333
Security Settings 333
Software Restriction Policies 334
Modifying Security and Software
Restriction Policies 335
Managing Users' Environments Using
Group Policy 337
Scenarios for Using
Administrative Template Settings 339
Modifying the Administrative
Template Policies 340
Managing Group Policy Implementation
and Interaction 342
How Group Policy Is Applied 342
Analyzing Group Policy Interactions 344
Using RSoP and Modifying Group
Policy Priority 344
Chapter 11 Review 349

Remote Desktop for Administration
Limitations 358
Enabling Remote Connections to
Windows Server 2003 360
Configuring and Creating a Remote
Desktop Connection 361
Remote Desktop Connection Options 361
Configuring a Remote Desktop
Connection 365
Using Remote Desktop for
Administration Sessions 368
Managing Remote Desktop Connections . . . 369
Modifying Sessions Settings at the Server . . 369
Managing Current Sessions 371
Configuring and Managing Remote
Desktop for Administration Sessions
from the Server 372
Chapter 12 Review 375

■ **Glossary** 379
■ **Index** 391

Chapter 12
■ From There to Here: Server Management Using Remote Desktop for Administration 354

Describing Basic Remote Desktop for
Administration Concepts 355
Benefits of Terminal Server 355
Benefits of Remote Desktop for
Administration 356

■ Information Technology Skill Standards and Your Curriculum

Students in today's increasingly competitive IT career market are differentiated not only by their technical skills, but also by their communication, problem solving, and teaming skills. More and more, these professional skills are the ones that guarantee career longevity and success. The National Workforce Center for Emerging Technologies (NWCET) and McGraw-Hill Technology Education have partnered in an effort to help you build technical *and* employability skills in the classroom.

Skill standards–aligned curriculum is becoming a *de facto* requirement for schools everywhere in the United States today. Programs are required to be standards aligned in order to show clearly that students are being taught and assessed consistently and to an agreed upon set of skill and content standards. For those programs preparing students to enter the workforce, skill standards provide an excellent skeleton upon which to build courses.

Research has shown improved learning and retention of knowledge when learning takes place in a rich learning context. Students that learn in a real-world context are also better equipped to transfer their skills to the real world. IT skill standards provide the kind of real-world data that educators can use. Educators can draw from the skill standards to develop contextually rich assignments that help students to situate their learning in specific work contexts with complex and real-world problems to solve.

IT skill standards provide a common language between industry and education so that building bridges between these two groups can be more efficient. The more industry recognizes what educational programs are doing, the easier it is for education to gain industry support. Schools that use a skill standards–aligned program are better prepared to gain support from industry for technical advisory boards, student internships, job shadows, faculty internships, and a host of other support resources.

IT skill standards provide increased portability of skills because of the common language. Other institutions can clearly identify the content and skills that graduates of a skill standards–aligned curriculum have acquired. Programs that are skill standards based will effectively oil the wheels of articulation between programs that traditionally may have difficulty agreeing on what has been taught and assessed.

NWCET and McGraw-Hill in Partnership

NATIONAL WORKFORCE CENTER *for* **EMERGING TECHNOLOGIES**

McGraw-Hill Technology Education and the NWCET have partnered with the goal of helping IT educators meet these demands by making the IT skill standards more easily available and ready to use. McGraw-Hill Technology Education and the NWCET have developed four different products that will help you to address the IT skill standards in your Security+ programs and courses:

- A summary crosswalk that highlights the IT skill standards addressed by the McGraw-Hill *Introduction to Windows Server 2003* textbook:

Chapter 1	Chapter 2	Chapter 3
A5—Research technical alternatives and analyze technical options	C2—Implement new system configuration	C2—Implement new system configuration

Chapter 4	Chapter 5	Chapter 6
C2—Implement new system configuration	C1—Plan and system configuration	C2—Implement new system configuration F4—Perform system back ups and restore data

Chapter 7	Chapter 8	Chapter 9
C2—Implement new system configuration	C1—Plan and system configuration C2—Implement new system configuration	E4—analyze system performance to baseline F5—Troubleshoot and maintain client, server and network systems

Chapter 10	Chapter 11	Chapter 12
C3—Perform workstation configuration and software loading	C2—Implement new system configuration G3—Implement and enforce system and user security requirements	F5—Troubleshoot and maintain client, server and network systems

- A detailed crosswalk listing Technical Knowledge, Employability Skills, and Performance Indicators addressed by the compliant curriculum (textbook, lab manual, and learning activities in the instructor pack CD)

- Twelve skill standards–based activities with associated assessment tools

- A training document that helps instructors understand and use the features of teaching a skill standards–aligned curriculum

NWCET Background and Mission

In 1995, the National Science Foundation (NSF) designated and funded the NWCET as a National Center of Excellence in Advanced Technological Education. The Center was created to advance IT education and improve the supply, quality, and diversity of the IT workforce.

The National Workforce Center for Emerging Technologies has since become a leader in new designs for Information Technology (IT) education developing products, services, and best practices that provide timely, relevant, and lasting solutions to meet the needs of IT educators and the IT workforce. The NWCET translates the rapidly changing demands of the technology workplace into programs, curricula, courseware, and assessments that prepare students for current and future IT careers.

The NWCET is perhaps best known for its IT skill standards. Skill standards provide an agreement of what is expected to be successful in a given career area. They provide a validated, industry-derived framework upon which educators can build curricula. Using industry skill standards as the foundation for curricula will result in a closer alignment between educational programs and workplace expectations, and result in a better-skilled workforce.

To support new and innovative IT programs and degrees, the NWCET (www.nwcet.org) provides other professional development opportunities for high school teachers and community college and university faculty. The Educator-to-Educator Institute (E2E) (http://e2e.nwcet.org), the training branch of the NWCET, is dedicated to helping IT educators achieve excellence in IT instruction. CyberCareers (www.cybercareers.org) is a web site oriented toward middle and high schools students and teachers and provides a wide variety of career education materials such as job descriptions and an IT Interest Inventory.

INTRODUCTION

■ What Will You Learn?

In this book, you'll learn about Windows Server 2003: Microsoft's latest network server operating system. You'll learn about the evolution of Microsoft operating systems that led to the development of this new addition, and how Windows Server 2003 improves on what had come before. You'll learn how to install the operating system and configure it for use on a Microsoft network as a domain controller. You'll learn how to use the operating system to share resources with network computers, and how to manage that access using Windows Server 2003's security features. You'll then learn how to use a variety of tools to monitor and manage the functioning of the server and the network. You'll also learn how to use Windows Server 2003 to remotely install Windows XP Professional on network client machines, as well as how to manage those computers from the central server. Finally, you'll learn how to access and remotely manage a Windows Server 2003 server from another computer.

This book is organized into 12 chapters:

- Chapter 1, *Welcome to the Evolution: Windows Server 2003*, gives you an overview of what operating systems preceded Windows Server 2003 and introduces you to the new and improved features Microsoft's latest operating system offers. This will help you to understand why Windows Server 2003 is an important new edition to the Windows family.

- Chapter 2, *Getting Started: Installing Windows Server 2003*, takes you step-by-step through the process of getting Windows Server 2003 installed on a computer system. You'll learn about the various hardware requirements and how to check the compatibility of your hardware. You'll also learn about the various methods of installation that are available.

- Chapter 3, *A Net Improvement: Configuring Network Services and Protocols*, shows you how to configure a computer running Windows Server 2003 for use on a network. You'll set up the server to use TCP/IP networking and configure it to provide several important services to the rest of the network.

- Chapter 4, *Preparing to Serve: Understanding Microsoft Networking*, helps you understand the various organizational structures of a Microsoft network, and the role Active Directory plays in creating and managing such networks. You'll also learn how to install and configure Active Directory in Windows Server 2003, thus creating a new domain controller and a new network.

- Chapter 5, *Directory Assistance: Administration Using Active Directory Users and Computers*, explains how Active Directory is used to administer Microsoft domain-based networks. You'll learn how to use the Active Directory Users and Computers tool to create user accounts, computer accounts, groups, and other network objects. You'll also learn how to work with and manage such objects after their creation.

- Chapter 6, *A Place for Everything: Storage Management*, shows you how to manage disk storage in Windows Server 2003. You'll learn the difference between basic and dynamic disks and learn how to create a variety of volumes for the storage of data. You'll also learn how to back up data and troubleshoot storage problems.

- Chapter 7, *Preparing for Output: Printer Configuration and Management*, covers network printing. You'll learn how install and configure printers for network use as well as how to manage printers and print jobs. You'll also learn various troubleshooting techniques for addressing printing problems.

- Chapter 8, *Crowd Control: Controlling Access to Resources Using Groups*, shows you how to manage access to network resources. You'll learn how to use user accounts and groups in conjunction with share and NTFS permissions to control who can access resources and what they can do with them.

- Chapter 9, *Traffic Control: Monitoring and Managing Server Performance*, examines the tools and techniques for day-to-day server and network management. You'll learn how to use Task Manager, the Performance console, and event logs to monitor a variety of performance measurements.

- Chapter 10, *From Here to There: Remote Installation of the Windows XP Professional Client*, shows you how to configure Windows Server 2003 to act as a Remote Installation Services server. You'll learn how to create images of operating systems and reference computers and install them to remote machines over the network.

- Chapter 11, *The Best Policy: Managing Computers and Users Through Group Policy*, introduces you to basic group policy concepts. You'll learn how group policy can be used to remotely manage both users and computers over a network. You'll also learn how group policy settings are configured and applied.

- Chapter 12, *From There to Here: Server Management Using Remote Desktop for Administration*, shows you how to manage a Windows Server 2003 computer from remote locations. You will learn how to configure remote connections using Remote Desktop for Administration and how to manage and use those connections.

About the CD-ROM

The CD included with this text is a 180-day evaluation copy of Windows Server 2003 Enterprise edition. With this CD, you can install the operating system on any compatible computer and fully experience every aspect of Windows Server 2003 covered in this text. Simply follow the installation instructions in Chapter 2 and you're good to go! This copy of the operating system is fully functional in every way and is included, at no extra cost to you, to give you the hands on experience you need to become skilled in using Microsoft's latest network operating system.

■ You Will Learn to...

We don't want to simply give you an encyclopedia of information because we don't want you to feel like you're standing in front of an information fire hose! Rather, you will find that this book presents just the key points about working with Windows Server 2003, and will help guide you as you continue to explore the operating system. This book is designed to teach you basic skills that you'll need in order to be successful as you begin working with Microsoft networks and server operating systems.

Walk and Talk Like a Pro

Each chapter starts with a list of learning objectives. These are followed by lucid explanations of each topic supported by a real-world, on-the-job scenario and enhanced by liberal use of graphics and tables. To give you hands-on experience and help you "walk the walk," each chapter contains detailed Step-by-Step tutorials and short Try This! exercises that enable you to practice the concepts. To help you "talk the talk," each chapter contains definitions of important terms, summarized in a Key Terms list and compiled into a Glossary at the end of the book. Be ready for a Key Terms Quiz at the end of each chapter!

Troubleshoot Like a Pro

While there is quite a bit of useful information in this book, a single book simply can't give you everything you need to know about Windows Server 2003. In addition to providing you with a solid introduction to the operating system, we'll also give you some of the tools that will help you help yourself, which is a valuable skill whether you're on the job or working at home. For example, we'll show you how to use the help files and perform updates to your new operating system, and we'll teach you how to use the Internet to find even more information that will help you with potential troubleshooting problems.

Think Like a Pro

We've also included Inside Information sidebars, which provide insight into some of the subtleties of working with Windows Server 2003 networks, and Cross Checks that help you understand how the various features of Windows Server 2003 work together. Notes and Tips are sprinkled throughout the chapters, and Warnings help prevent mishaps (or an emotional meltdown). At the end of each chapter, a Key Terms Quiz, Multiple-Choice Quiz, and Essay Quiz help you measure what you've learned and hone your ability to present information on paper. The Lab Projects challenge you to independently complete tasks related to what you've just learned.

■ Resources for Teachers

Teachers are our heroes, to whom we give our thanks and for whom we have created a powerful collection of time-saving teaching tools. These tools are available on CD-ROM:

- An Instructor's Manual that maps to the organization of the textbook

- ExamView® Pro testbank software, which generates a wide array of paper or network-based tests, and features automatic grading

- Hundreds of questions, written by experienced IT instructors

- A wide variety of question types and difficulty levels, allowing teachers to customize each test to maximize student progress

- Engaging PowerPoint® slides on the lecture topics

- A crosswalk that highlights the IT skill standards addressed by the McGraw-Hill *Introduction to Windows Server 2003* textbook

- A training document that helps instructors understand and use the features of a skill standards–aligned curriculum

- Twelve skill standards–based activities with associated assessment tools

Welcome to the Evolution: Windows Server 2003

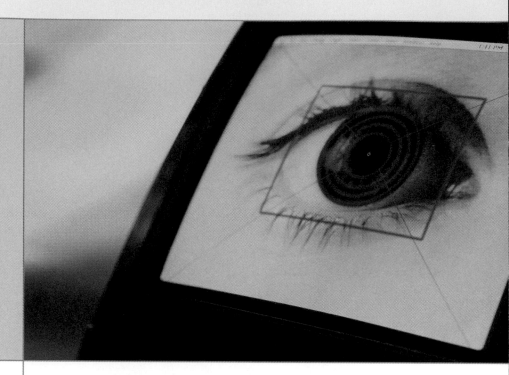

"As for the future, your task is not to foresee but to enable it."
—Antoine de Saint-Exupéry

In this chapter, you will learn how to:

- **Describe the evolution of Windows Server 2003**
- **Describe the members of the Windows Server family**
- **Describe the improved benefits and new features of Windows Server 2003**
- **Identify the server hardware requirements**

Can you think of anything that changes faster than computer technology? It's really amazing to think about how much things have changed since personal computers first appeared on the scene around 20 years ago. Take computer networks as an example.

In the early days of computer networks, it was enough to connect a few computers together as equals so that they could share each other's files and other resources such as printers. Today's businesses require networks that offer robust security, exceptional reliability, and powerful centralized management functions. These changing needs have been the driving force behind the evolution of network operating systems like Microsoft Server 2003.

In this chapter we'll introduce Microsoft's latest network operating system, Microsoft Server 2003. We'll begin by examining the evolutionary steps that led up to this powerful new offering. We'll explore the different versions of Windows Server 2003 that have been created to meet different network needs and we'll take a look at what's new and improved. Finally, we'll prepare for installing Windows Server 2003 by identifying the operating system's hardware requirements.

The Evolution of Windows Server 2003

I've chosen to describe Windows Server 2003 as an evolutionary, rather than a revolutionary, product for a very good reason. Like any piece of software, each new network operating system builds upon those products that have come before. As hardware and the needs of users change, so must the operating system accommodate those changes. By spending a little time discussing the predecessors of Windows Server 2003, we can begin to understand the forces that shaped its development. We'll be taking a look at three of these earlier operating systems: Windows for Workgroups; Windows NT; and Windows 2000. On to the history lesson!

Windows for Workgroups

Networking certainly didn't start with Windows for Workgroups, but it sure got a lot easier. Prior to its release in 1992, networking a DOS or Windows computer required the user to manually add on the appropriate networking components to the operating system. In addition, it was usually necessary to run some type of specialized networking software on a network server that centrally managed access to resources. Building, maintaining, and even using networks required quite a bit of specialized training. This was a definite stumbling block for many smaller businesses that could have benefited from being networked but didn't have the resources to make it happen. With the Windows for Workgroups operating system, setting up and using small networks was a simple matter of a couple of quick clicks.

- The Windows for Workgroups 3.11 Splash screen

The most revolutionary aspect of Windows for Workgroups was that it had the built-in ability to be both a **client** and a **server** at the same time on the same network. That made it easy for users to access shared resources on a network (as clients) and share resources from their machines (as servers).

It's possible to write entire books about the three operating systems that form the most direct ancestry of Windows Server 2003. In fact, it's been done! However, we're going to limit our discussion of these earlier operating systems to examining some of the major evolutionary trends in network operating systems. Keep in mind that our primary topic will be Windows Server 2003. This background information is only meant to set the stage for understanding the process that led to Windows Server 2003's development. If you want to skip the historical background, for now, you could begin with the next section, titled "Introducing the Windows Server 2003 Family."

There were actually two versions of Windows for Workgroups released by Microsoft. Windows for Workgroups 3.1 was released in October 1992, and Windows for Workgroups 3.11 was released a little more than a year later. As the minor change of version number suggests, the changes were mostly minor refinements and bug fixes. The two versions may be considered the same for the purposes of our discussion.

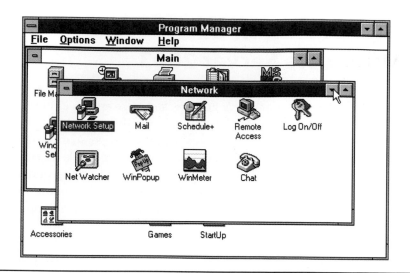

• The Windows for Workgroups Desktop with the Network Window open

For example, a user could send documents to a printer connected to another computer while making a folder on their computer accessible to other users on the network. This type of network, where each machine can act as a file and print server to its peers, is often called a **peer-to-peer** network. A small peer-to-peer network is depicted in Figure 1.1.

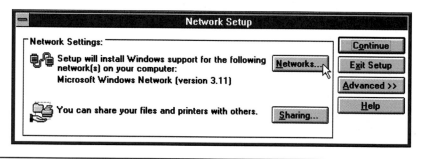

• Network Setup dialog box for Windows for Workgroups 3.11

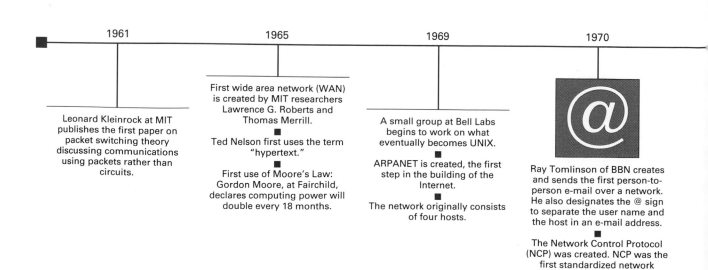

1961
Leonard Kleinrock at MIT publishes the first paper on packet switching theory discussing communications using packets rather than circuits.

1965
First wide area network (WAN) is created by MIT researchers Lawrence G. Roberts and Thomas Merrill.
■
Ted Nelson first uses the term "hypertext."
■
First use of Moore's Law: Gordon Moore, at Fairchild, declares computing power will double every 18 months.

1969
A small group at Bell Labs begins to work on what eventually becomes UNIX.
■
ARPANET is created, the first step in the building of the Internet.
■
The network originally consists of four hosts.

1970
Ray Tomlinson of BBN creates and sends the first person-to-person e-mail over a network. He also designates the @ sign to separate the user name and the host in an e-mail address.
■
The Network Control Protocol (NCP) was created. NCP was the first standardized network protocol used by ARPANET.

Computers

Printer

Microsoft's term "workgroup" is essentially synonymous with the term "peer-to-peer networking" and is still used today in modern Microsoft network operating systems to describe such networks.

● **Figure 1.1**   A peer-to-peer network

Although Windows for Workgroups was a very popular operating system with both business and home users, it did suffer from a few problems that prevented it from being the be-all, end-all network operating system. However, you really can't blame Microsoft. The troubles lie in the inherent nature of peer-to-peer networks.

The first problem is that peer-to-peer networks are terribly ineffective once the network exceeds seven to ten computers. As networks began to grow, it became clear that centralized management was going to be important. The management problems inherent in peer-to-peer networks become clear when you consider the second problem area for Windows for Workgroups: the way users accessed resources.

When a user wanted to share a folder with other users of a Windows for Workgroups network, they were able to assign a password to that particular folder. When another user would access that resource, they were required to type in the correct password. Even if there were only five computers on the network, as depicted in Figure 1.2, if each was sharing a single folder with a unique password, a user would have to keep track of five different passwords! Of course, users could choose not to set a password, but then anyone on the network could access the folder.

To be completely fair, the way sharing was handled wasn't unique to Windows for Workgroups. In fact, the method described is still common to-

Windows for Workgroups also provided for easy connection to most of the server-based networks in existence at the time of its release. This made it possible for organizations running larger networks to easily allow client machines to both access server-managed resources and share resources directly with each other.

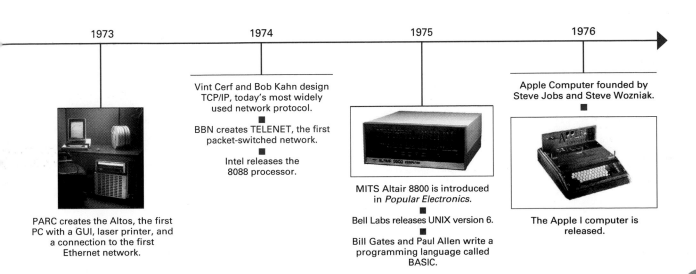

1973 — PARC creates the Altos, the first PC with a GUI, laser printer, and a connection to the first Ethernet network.

1974 — Vint Cerf and Bob Kahn design TCP/IP, today's most widely used network protocol.
■ BBN creates TELENET, the first packet-switched network.
■ Intel releases the 8088 processor.

1975 — MITS Altair 8800 is introduced in *Popular Electronics*.
■ Bell Labs releases UNIX version 6.
■ Bill Gates and Paul Allen write a programming language called BASIC.

1976 — Apple Computer founded by Steve Jobs and Steve Wozniak.
■ The Apple I computer is released.

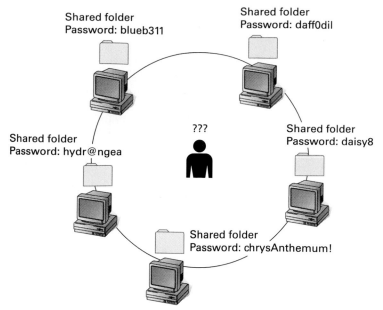

Shared folder
Password: blueb311

Shared folder
Password: daff0dil

Shared folder
Password: hydr@ngea

???

Shared folder
Password: daisy8

Shared folder
Password: chrysAnthemum!

● Figure 1.2 Five shared folders with unique passwords on a peer-to-peer network

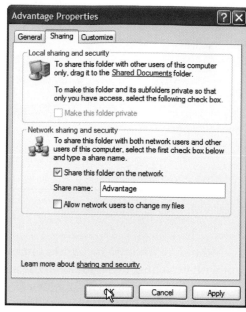

● Figure 1.3 Sharing a folder on a Windows XP computer in a peer-to-peer network

day on peer-to-peer networks because there's no easy way for a peer-to-peer network to maintain a central user database. Without a way to set access levels for individual users, the only solution is to set a password and distribute it to the right users. However, Windows XP even did away with that, as you can see in Figure 1.3, by removing the option for setting a password entirely! Thus we have the third major weakness of Windows for Workgroups: the nature of peer-to-peer networks prevented, and still prevents, users from having sufficient control over security.

Windows NT

Microsoft never intended for Windows for Workgroups to be the single solution for all networks. It was a product that filled a particular niche: the need for easy peer-to-peer networking. A year prior to the release of Windows for

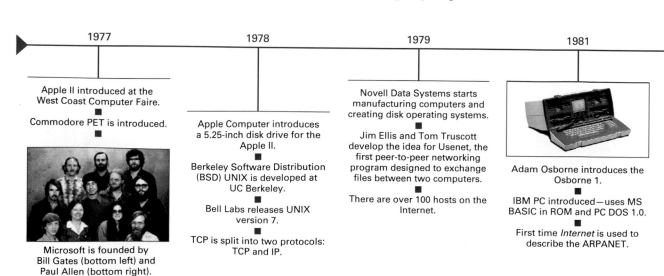

1977

Apple II introduced at the West Coast Computer Faire.
■
Commodore PET is introduced.
■

Microsoft is founded by Bill Gates (bottom left) and Paul Allen (bottom right).

1978

Apple Computer introduces a 5.25-inch disk drive for the Apple II.
■
Berkeley Software Distribution (BSD) UNIX is developed at UC Berkeley.
■
Bell Labs releases UNIX version 7.
■
TCP is split into two protocols: TCP and IP.

1979

Novell Data Systems starts manufacturing computers and creating disk operating systems.
■
Jim Ellis and Tom Truscott develop the idea for Usenet, the first peer-to-peer networking program designed to exchange files between two computers.
■
There are over 100 hosts on the Internet.

1981

Adam Osborne introduces the Osborne 1.
■
IBM PC introduced—uses MS BASIC in ROM and PC DOS 1.0.
■
First time *Internet* is used to describe the ARPANET.

Workgroups, Microsoft announced work on a new operating system. By July 1993 Windows NT, the first Windows operating system to be independent of DOS, was on the market.

Windows NT was truly a revolutionary product for Microsoft. It not only was completely independent of DOS, it was also better suited to take advantage of the increased processor power and RAM capacities that had started to appear in personal computers. There were actually many improvements and new features introduced with Windows NT, but for our purposes, it's the improvements that lead us to Windows Server 2003 that are most important.

Windows NT was the first Microsoft operating system to be released as separate server and workstation products. The importance of this is two-fold. On one hand, Microsoft was clearly acknowledging the need for a specially designed server operating system for **client/server networks**. In a client/server network, even though client machines may still share resources, there are one or more central server machines that manage the network and are the primary agent for sharing resources out to the clients. Although NT still supported peer-to-peer networking, it was clearly designed for networks built around central servers. NT Server could provide the type of centralized control of resources and security necessary for networks to grow beyond small **workgroups**. On the other hand, the workstation product enabled tighter integration of client machines with the rest of the network. This level of integration continues today in desktop operating systems such as Windows XP Professional. Client/server networks that consist of client and server operating systems that "understand" each other intimately are able to achieve exceptional levels of security both over the network and locally at the client machines.

One example of the improved security offered by NT Server and Workstation was the **Security Accounts Manager (SAM)**. The SAM was a database of user security accounts that was used to **authenticate**, or verify, the identity

• The Windows NT Server 4.0 Splash screen and logon prompt

There were actually eight different versions of Windows NT (counting both server and workstation products). In addition to the different versions, Microsoft released numerous operating system updates, called Service Packs, which were used to fix problems and add functionality. The end result is a myriad of different implementations of the Windows NT operating system! The only change that really matters to our discussion is that with Windows NT 4.0 Server and Workstation, Microsoft adopted the now-familiar user interface found in Windows 9x (95 and 98) products. Prior to that, Windows NT resembled Windows for Workgroups.

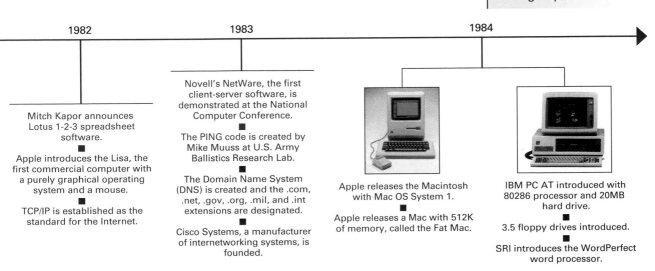

1982

Mitch Kapor announces Lotus 1-2-3 spreadsheet software.
∎
Apple introduces the Lisa, the first commercial computer with a purely graphical operating system and a mouse.
∎
TCP/IP is established as the standard for the Internet.

1983

Novell's NetWare, the first client-server software, is demonstrated at the National Computer Conference.
∎
The PING code is created by Mike Muuss at U.S. Army Ballistics Research Lab.
∎
The Domain Name System (DNS) is created and the .com, .net, .gov, .org, .mil, and .int extensions are designated.
∎
Cisco Systems, a manufacturer of internetworking systems, is founded.

1984

Apple releases the Macintosh with Mac OS System 1.
∎
Apple releases a Mac with 512K of memory, called the Fat Mac.

IBM PC AT introduced with 80286 processor and 20MB hard drive.
∎
3.5 floppy drives introduced.
∎
SRI introduces the WordPerfect word processor.

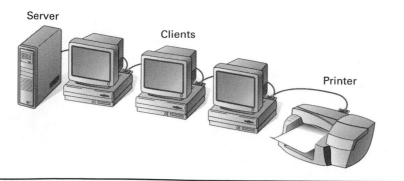

Server

Clients

Printer

• A client/server network

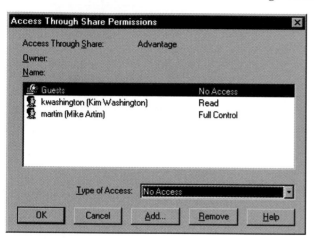

Access Through Share Permissions

Access Through Share: Advantage
Owner:
Name:

Guests	No Access
kwashington (Kim Washington)	Read
martim (Mike Artim)	Full Control

Type of Access: No Access

OK   Cancel   Add...   Remove   Help

• Setting Share Level Permissions by User Account in Windows NT

of, users at both the local client and network levels. At the client level, the SAM enhanced security by allowing only users with pre-existing accounts on the computer to log on. At the network level, user accounts were maintained in a server-based SAM forming what Microsoft called a **domain**. The domain SAM was the central management tool that allowed both the server and client machines to selectively grant **permissions**, or types of access, to shared resources according to who the user was, allowing far greater flexibility than the scheme used by Windows for Workgroups.

Another huge improvement introduced by Windows NT was a new **file system**, called **NT File System (NTFS)**. A file system is simply a method for reading, writing, storing, and otherwise manipulating files stored on disk drives. Unlike the **file allocation table (FAT)** file system used by DOS, NTFS introduced an extensive set of local permissions that controlled what a user could do with any particular file or folder stored on an NTFS-formatted hard drive. Coupled with the permissions for shared resources, which controlled access over the network, these local permissions allowed for extremely fine-grained control over what users could and could not do with what they accessed.

It's not easy to find a lot of flaws in Windows NT. By the time Microsoft had released the last version (Windows NT 4.0) and the numerous Service Packs for it, the company had created a very solid and stable network operating system. Just how good was Windows NT? Consider that Microsoft is still making a major push to get Windows NT network administrators to upgrade to Windows Server 2003. That's a big deal because Windows NT was already supposed to be

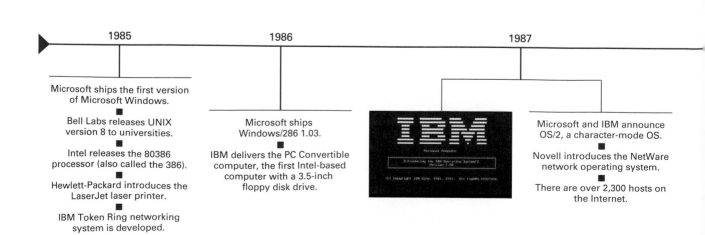

1985	1986	1987

Microsoft ships the first version of Microsoft Windows.

Bell Labs releases UNIX version 8 to universities.

Intel releases the 80386 processor (also called the 386).

Hewlett-Packard introduces the LaserJet laser printer.

IBM Token Ring networking system is developed.

Microsoft ships Windows/286 1.03.

IBM delivers the PC Convertible computer, the first Intel-based computer with a 3.5-inch floppy disk drive.

Microsoft and IBM announce OS/2, a character-mode OS.

Novell introduces the NetWare network operating system.

There are over 2,300 hosts on the Internet.

"old news" *back at the start of 2000* when Windows 2000 Server was released! A significant number of network administrators simply figured "if it ain't broke…." However, it makes sense that there must have been some weak areas, or we wouldn't be about to talk about Windows 2000 in the next couple of paragraphs and Windows Server 2003 for a solid dozen chapters!

It turns out that Windows NT's greatest weakness was probably behind the reluctance of some administrators to upgrade. Windows NT could be a real pain in the neck to administer. The tools provided to network administrators did the job but were frequently confusing and far from intuitive. My personal theory is that Windows NT administrators are scared to death that they'll have to relive the agonizing learning curve they underwent to master NT! On the other hand, I think I agree with them somewhat. If an administrator really has mastered Windows NT and has their network fine-tuned and performing well, it sure seems logical to hold the course. However, those administrators are going to have to change eventually: on January 29, 2003, Microsoft announced that by July 1, 2003, Windows NT server would no longer be offered for sale through any channel. By January 1, 2005, all support for Windows NT will also be discontinued.

There is one other area that was lacking in Windows NT. As good as the security system was, the original version of NTFS still stored files "in the clear." What that means is that an unauthorized person could compromise sensitive information if they managed to gain access to a logged-on administrator account, learned an administrator account password, or somehow managed to bypass Windows NT's permissions. I know that sounds as if it might take some skill, but it actually requires nothing more than a bootable floppy disk, physical access to the server, and time! Booting from a floppy bypasses all of those fancy SAM databases and access permissions in a matter of minutes. As organizations of all types, including the government, became more dependent on networks, this type of exposure became a critical concern.

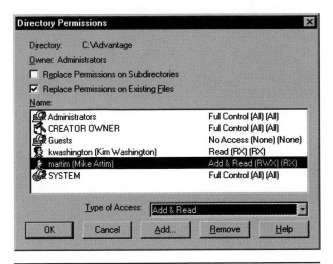

- Setting Folder Level Permissions by User Account in Windows NT

You will work extensively with user security accounts, permissions for shared resources, and NTFS permissions in later chapters. For now, just focus on the basic concept, and we'll pick up the nitty-gritty details later!

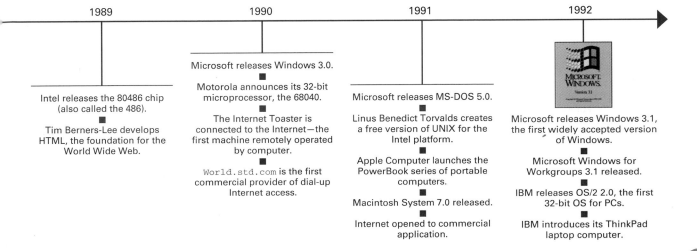

1989

Intel releases the 80486 chip (also called the 486).
■
Tim Berners-Lee develops HTML, the foundation for the World Wide Web.

1990

Microsoft releases Windows 3.0.
■
Motorola announces its 32-bit microprocessor, the 68040.
■
The Internet Toaster is connected to the Internet—the first machine remotely operated by computer.
■
World.std.com is the first commercial provider of dial-up Internet access.

1991

Microsoft releases MS-DOS 5.0.
■
Linus Benedict Torvalds creates a free version of UNIX for the Intel platform.
■
Apple Computer launches the PowerBook series of portable computers.
■
Macintosh System 7.0 released.
■
Internet opened to commercial application.

1992

Microsoft releases Windows 3.1, the first widely accepted version of Windows.
■
Microsoft Windows for Workgroups 3.1 released.
■
IBM releases OS/2 2.0, the first 32-bit OS for PCs.
■
IBM introduces its ThinkPad laptop computer.

Windows 2000

Shortly after Microsoft released version 4.0 of Windows NT in 1996, the company started development of the next version, which was to be named Windows NT 5.0. By the time this new version was released in the beginning of 2000, the name had been changed to Windows 2000. Although the name had changed, it's clear from its origins that Windows 2000 was really nothing more than a continued refinement of Windows NT. However, those refinements were quite significant and heavily foreshadow what we will see in Windows Server 2003.

Unlike Windows NT or Windows for Workgroups, Windows 2000 is still a viable choice and, in fact, is likely to be the operating system in use for businesses that might upgrade to Windows Server 2003. Many businesses have been and will be carefully analyzing the strengths and weaknesses of Windows 2000 Server as they decide whether or not to upgrade to Windows Server 2003. Although Windows 2000 started out as the next version of Windows NT, the changes that were made resulted in some truly significant improvements.

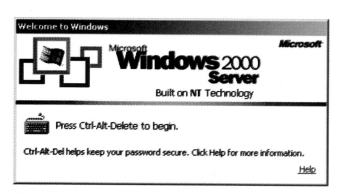

• The Windows 2000 Server logon prompt

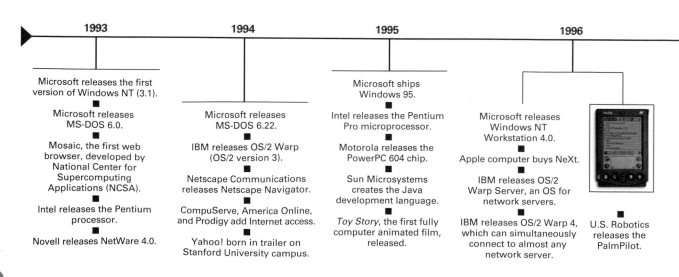

1993	1994	1995	1996
Microsoft releases the first version of Windows NT (3.1).		Microsoft ships Windows 95.	
Microsoft releases MS-DOS 6.0.	Microsoft releases MS-DOS 6.22.	Intel releases the Pentium Pro microprocessor.	Microsoft releases Windows NT Workstation 4.0.
Mosaic, the first web browser, developed by National Center for Supercomputing Applications (NCSA).	IBM releases OS/2 Warp (OS/2 version 3).	Motorola releases the PowerPC 604 chip.	Apple computer buys NeXt.
	Netscape Communications releases Netscape Navigator.	Sun Microsystems creates the Java development language.	IBM releases OS/2 Warp Server, an OS for network servers.
Intel releases the Pentium processor.	CompuServe, America Online, and Prodigy add Internet access.	*Toy Story*, the first fully computer animated film, released.	IBM releases OS/2 Warp 4, which can simultaneously connect to almost any network server.
Novell releases NetWare 4.0.	Yahoo! born in trailer on Stanford University campus.		U.S. Robotics releases the PalmPilot.

You probably recall that a major weakness of Windows NT was that it was terribly difficult to master and use to administer networks. I don't think there's any doubt that Microsoft took that problem into consideration when it developed what is probably the best new feature in Windows 2000: Active Directory.

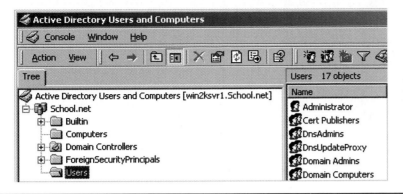

• The Active Directory Users and Computers window

Active Directory is essentially a central database that allows for easy management of user accounts, client machines, printers, other network servers, other networks, and just about anything else that might be part of the network. Active Directory not only replaces the SAM of Windows NT, it also improves upon it by centralizing both security and management. Active Directory makes the jobs of administrators, especially those working with large networks, easier by several orders of magnitude.

Another management improvement is the new **Microsoft Management Console (MMC)**. Where Active Directory focuses on managing the network and its components, MMC provides a central, consistent, yet customizable interface with which to manage the actual server and client computers. Properly utilized, both Active Directory and MMC can save network administrators a lot of frustration and a lot of time. Take it from me that saving time and frustration are at the top of the list of things administrators want to do!

Microsoft also addressed the security issue present in Windows NT. Windows 2000 introduced an updated version of the NTFS file system: NTFS5. NTFS5 directly addresses the problem of files being stored "in the clear" by making it possible to encrypt files and folders. Encrypted files and

As you might have guessed after our mention of the various Windows NT versions, Microsoft also released more than one Windows 2000 product. However, these were not improved versions released over time, but rather different editions released at more or less the same time that were intended to meet different needs. There were actually three different editions of the server operating system and one edition for client machines. The desktop operating system intended for clients was called Windows 2000 Professional. The Server operating systems consisted of Windows 2000 Server, Windows 2000 Advanced Server, and Windows 2000 Datacenter Server. The differences between the three are unimportant for this discussion, but we'll see later that this practice of releasing different editions has continued with the release of Windows Server 2003.

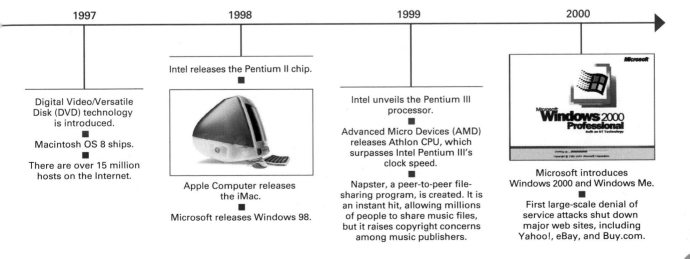

| 1997 | 1998 | 1999 | 2000 |

Intel releases the Pentium II chip.

Digital Video/Versatile Disk (DVD) technology is introduced.

Macintosh OS 8 ships.

There are over 15 million hosts on the Internet.

Apple Computer releases the iMac.

Microsoft releases Windows 98.

Intel unveils the Pentium III processor.

Advanced Micro Devices (AMD) releases Athlon CPU, which surpasses Intel Pentium III's clock speed.

Napster, a peer-to-peer file-sharing program, is created. It is an instant hit, allowing millions of people to share music files, but it raises copyright concerns among music publishers.

Microsoft introduces Windows 2000 and Windows Me.

First large-scale denial of service attacks shut down major web sites, including Yahoo!, eBay, and Buy.com.

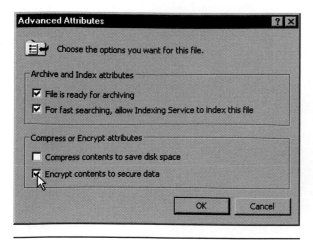

• Encrypting a file in Windows 2000

Now that two versions of the NTFS file system exist, it is best to refer to the prior version as NTFS4 and the new version as NTFS5.

We will be discussing elements like Active Directory, MMC, and NTFS5, at great length later in the text. For now, just try to understand the basics of each feature and what it added to the functionality of Windows 2000 as a network operating system. Those concepts that seem confusing at this point will make much more sense later on. Trust me!

folders are completely useless to anyone other than the user that encrypted them, no matter how they are accessed. Without someone's logging on as that user, the file is essentially gibberish. This feature alone makes Windows 2000 a valuable upgrade for businesses that work with sensitive data.

NTFS5 also added another important feature known as *disk quotas.* Through the use of disk quotas, administrators can now directly control how much hard drive space is used by any particular user account. This gives administrators the ability to more accurately manage valuable storage space without depending on voluntary compliance by users. Speaking as a bit of a "disk hog," I can personally attest to just how quickly a user like myself can consume more than his fair share of a server's hard drives!

Since Windows Server 2003 should address any lack in Windows 2000, it's difficult to discuss its shortcomings without getting ahead of ourselves. However, even prior to the product announcement for Windows Server 2003, users of Windows 2000 already had some suggestions on areas that needed to be improved. These suggestions tend to concern two main areas: ease of use and the interface.

No matter how much beta, or advanced, testing a product undergoes, there's nothing like putting it in the hands of the consumer to really find the "rough spots." In spite of the improvements that Active Directory and the MMC offer to network and server administrators, many still found the new tools to be a bit difficult to work with. Microsoft made clear very early in the development process that this problem would be addressed for Windows Server 2003. By the time you finish this text, you should be able to draw your own conclusions as to how well they did!

The interface concerns may seem a bit trivial at first. The problem is that the interfaces of Windows 2000, and for that matter, the later versions of Windows NT, were essentially still the old Windows 95 interface with some very minor improvements. In spite of the old saying that "the clothes make the man," the same really can't be said of network operating systems and their interfaces. However, the interface did look dated in comparison with the desktop operating systems in use on client machines. There were also

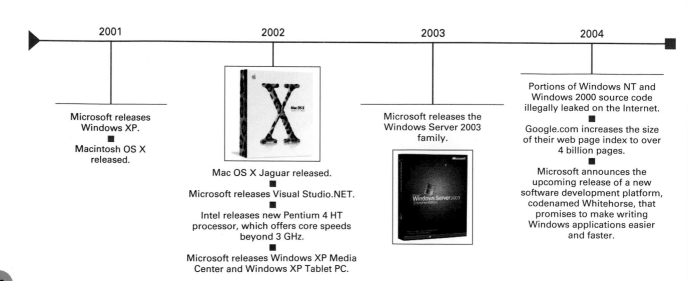

2001 — Microsoft releases Windows XP.
■
Macintosh OS X released.

2002 — Mac OS X Jaguar released.
■
Microsoft releases Visual Studio.NET.
■
Intel releases new Pentium 4 HT processor, which offers core speeds beyond 3 GHz.
■
Microsoft releases Windows XP Media Center and Windows XP Tablet PC.

2003 — Microsoft releases the Windows Server 2003 family.

2004 — Portions of Windows NT and Windows 2000 source code illegally leaked on the Internet.
■
Google.com increases the size of their web page index to over 4 billion pages.
■
Microsoft announces the upcoming release of a new software development platform, codenamed Whitehorse, that promises to make writing Windows applications easier and faster.

some features that had begun to appear on those client operating system interfaces that could be useful in a server operating system. All in all, a "face-lift" certainly couldn't hurt!

■ Introducing the Windows Server 2003 Family

As mentioned earlier, Windows 2000 was the first product for which Microsoft began releasing several different editions of its server software. This was done to accommodate the sometimes widely different demands businesses put on their networks. The same strategy has been used for the Windows Server 2003 family, with one minor change.

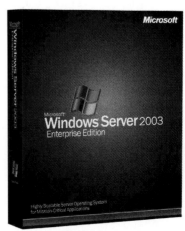

Box shot reprinted with permission from Microsoft Corporation

Windows 2000 offered three server editions (Standard, Advanced, and Datacenter) and one desktop operating system for client machines (Professional). The Windows Server 2003 family consists of four different server products (Standard, Enterprise, Datacenter, and Web) but does not offer a client operating system. That role is currently best filled by either Windows 2000 Professional or Windows XP Professional. In fact, Windows XP is actually based on much of the same code as Windows Server 2003!

Let's take a look at the four members of the Windows Server 2003 family and how they differ. We'll briefly discuss what each offers in terms of the hardware capabilities and offered services and then characterize the target market for each edition.

Windows Server 2003 Standard Edition

The Standard Edition of Windows Server 2003 is an ideal choice for most small to medium-sized networks. In terms of various services, Standard Edition is missing only a few of the specialized services found in the more powerful editions. The most significant differences are found in the hardware capabilities of the different versions. Even then, the capabilities of Standard Edition are more than sufficient to meet most business's needs.

The Standard Edition of Windows Server 2003 is built to run on the current crop of 32-bit processors, such as the Intel Xeon processor. The maximum RAM capacity is a full 4GB, as long as the server supports a RAM bank of that size. If the server supports **symmetric multiprocessing (SMP)**, a technology that allows a computer to run more than one processor, it is possible to run Standard Edition on up to four processors simultaneously. This allows businesses to upgrade a network by adding processors (if the server supports it), rather than replacing or adding servers. These capabilities are essentially identical to the older Windows 2000 Standard Edition Server, thus making this edition a good choice for businesses currently running that operating system.

Windows Server 2003 Standard Edition offers the full suite of services needed by most small to medium-sized networks. In addition to basic services such as Active Directory, file services, print services, and various management services, Standard Edition also offers extensive support for Internet connectivity and security. The only areas in which the Standard Edition of Windows Server 2003 is lacking services are those that specifically support the operation of large networks.

The target market for Windows Server 2003 Standard Edition is primarily small businesses or department-level business units. Businesses that plan to utilize their networks for internal file and print services, Internet access, and basic application services may find Standard Edition well suited to their needs.

Windows Server 2003 Enterprise Edition

The Enterprise Edition of Windows Server 2003 was specifically designed for those networks that had grown, or were planning to grow, beyond the capacity provided for in Standard Edition. Microsoft describes Enterprise Edition as being "highly **scalable**," which means it is capable of easily adapting to increased demands. The additional capabilities of Enterprise Edition directly reflect this focus on large or growing networks.

One of the major differences between Standard Edition and Enterprise Edition is that the latter provides support for the 64-bit Intel Itanium processor by offering separate 32- and 64-bit versions of the operating system. This relatively new processor family was specifically designed for extremely processor-intensive tasks like those found on some large networks. In addition to supporting this new class of processor, Enterprise Edition also doubles the number of processors usable on an SMP server to eight. In terms of RAM capacities, when running the 64-bit processor version, Enterprise Edition supports up to 64GB of RAM. If the 32-bit version is running, that maximum is a still significant 32GB. Finally, to reduce server downtime, the 32-bit version of Enterprise Edition supports **Hot Add Memory**, which is the ability to add or replace RAM without shutting down the server. This allows a business to maximize its ability to provide constant, reliable access to the server.

The biggest modification to available services in Enterprise Edition is the addition of specialized functions needed by large networks. Among these the most important is support for server **clustering**. Clustering refers to linking multiple servers together in such a way that they can share the processing and/or network communication load. Clustering can also improve network reliability by enabling one or more servers in a cluster to be taken offline without disrupting the network. In addition to clustering, Enterprise Edition also provides some improved directory services to help coordinate resources across large networks.

Even small businesses that are planning for significant future growth may find that Windows Server 2003 Enterprise Edition is a wise first choice due to its scalability. Businesses that depend on their networks for e-commerce or other business-critical activities should also consider Enterprise Edition for the various features such as clustering that can enhance performance and reliability. Finally, due to the greatly enhanced RAM maximums and support for 64-bit processors, any business that uses its network for processor-intensive tasks should look to Enterprise Edition as a possible solution.

The evaluation copy of Windows Server 2003 included with this text is the Enterprise Edition. As such, the Enterprise Edition has been used to create the screen shots throughout the text that illustrate various procedures and features of the operating system. However, the great bulk of what we will cover will apply just as readily to Standard Edition and Datacenter Edition. I'll point out any exceptions to this as we go along.

Windows Server 2003 Datacenter Edition

Windows Server 2003 Datacenter Edition addresses the needs of those businesses that, quite simply, cannot be without their networks for even a moment. In addition to certain hardware enhancements, Microsoft also offers a comprehensive support system with this edition called the Windows Datacenter High Availability Program. Through this support program, businesses will receive the critical support necessary to ensure network reliability. This support will be provided by a Datacenter Support Provider (DSP), who will be available 24 hours a day, seven days a week, 365 days a year to handle any problems and coordinate support from Microsoft and the server vendor if necessary.

Windows Server 2003 Datacenter Edition provides the same support for 64-bit processors as Enterprise Edition does by offering separate 32- and 64-bit versions. The 32-bit version of Datacenter Edition is capable of supporting 32 SMP processors and 64GB of RAM. The 64-bit version is capable of supporting 64 SMP processors and up to 512GB of RAM.

The services available in Datacenter Edition are essentially those available in Enterprise Edition with one noticeable lack. Datacenter Edition does not support some of the Internet connectivity services supported by the

Due to the special-purpose nature of Web Edition, we will not be dealing with it in this text beyond this chapter.

other editions. In organizations using Datacenter Edition, these services would typically be taken over by specialized servers.

As mentioned earlier, the Datacenter Edition is designed for those businesses that cannot afford even a momentary disruption in their networks. It's also the ideal solution for networks that handle enormous amounts of data. Businesses such as large financial institutions and e-commerce companies are prime candidates for this, the most powerful operating system in the Windows Server 2003 family.

Windows Server 2003 Web Edition

As we've mentioned, the Windows 2000 Server family also included a Standard Edition (Server), an Enterprise Edition (Advanced Server), and a Datacenter Edition (Datacenter Server). However, there was no parallel to the new Windows Server 2003 Web Edition. This brand new product is specifically designed to fill the role of a dedicated web server for organizations that wish to take control of their own web hosting needs.

Since web page serving and hosting is not a processor- or RAM-intensive process, Web Edition doesn't need to support the same RAM and processor levels as the other members of the Windows Server 2003 family. Web Edition supports only 32-bit processors running up to 2GB of RAM. This edition also supports up to two SMP processors.

Microsoft has pared down the services offered in Web Edition to create a product that provides all the services needed for its specialized task without the overhead of unneeded services. In fact, all of the features of Web Edition are present in the other editions. Think of Web Edition as a special-purpose tool designed solely for the task of hosting web sites and serving up web pages.

Web Edition is specifically intended to be an inexpensive option for those businesses that want a dedicated web server. Although the other editions of Windows Server 2003 can certainly perform the same role, they are a bit of overkill if hosting web sites and serving up web pages is all you need to do! By paring down the feature set, Microsoft was able to significantly lower the price of Web Edition compared to the others. The retail price of Web Edition is about 60 percent less than the price of Standard Edition. As such, this product is not really an alternative to the other three editions, but rather, a completely new class of product.

☑ Cross Check

The Windows Server 2003 Family

We've discussed many of the differences between the various versions and editions of Windows Server 2003. Review the material we've covered and answer these questions:

1. How would you describe, in your own words, the target market for the four editions (Standard, Enterprise, Datacenter, and Web)?

2. Imagine a specific business for which each edition would be appropriate. Describe that business and identify the edition they would choose and why.

What's New and Improved in Windows Server 2003?

As you might expect from an evolutionary product, Windows Server 2003 offers the same basic features of its predecessors while adding some improved benefits and some brand new features as well. In the following sections, we'll introduce and explain the most important benefit improvements and new features. Since some of these improvements and innovations can get a little technical, I'm going to describe them in pretty general terms for now. We'll dig deeper later.

Improved Benefits

When compared to Windows 2000 and Windows NT, there are several areas where there have been significant improvements in Windows Server 2003. Rather than try and list them all, I'll give you my top five.

It's Faster

According to Microsoft's testing, Windows Server 2003 is at least twice as fast as Windows NT *on the same hardware!* Although there isn't a big difference in performance when compared to Windows 2000, both Enterprise and Datacenter Editions of Windows Server 2003 now have support for more RAM and SMP processors than was offered under Windows 2000.

It's More Reliable

The holy grail of computer networks is the server that never crashes and the network that is never down. Although it's pretty darn tough to prevent every possible situation that can bring a network to its knees, Microsoft has added many enhancements to Windows Server 2003 that significantly improve reliability.

It's Easier to Manage

Even with the improvements Windows 2000 made over Windows NT, there were still some areas that needed some tweaking. In our earlier discussion about Windows 2000, I mentioned that both Active Directory and the MMC (Microsoft Management Console) were generally thought to need some work. Well, they sure got it! While it will take a while to get feedback from users on how much they like the improvements, Microsoft certainly put forth an effort to make these and many other management tools easier and more intuitive to use.

It's More Secure

Every silver lining has its cloud. The growth of the Internet and progress in computer technology has brought us a lot of good but has also exposed our computer networks to increasingly numerous and sophisticated attacks. When you consider that businesses now depend on their networks more than ever, you can see why security is such an important topic. With Windows Server 2003, Microsoft introduces numerous enhancements to security against threats both internal and external.

It's More Connected

Windows Server 2003 is a continuation of Microsoft's efforts at more closely integrating its operating systems with the Internet. In addition to Internet connectivity, this latest operating system does a better job of connecting clients to networks, administrators to servers, and even networks to networks. In fact, Windows Server 2003 is the first operating system to fully integrate Microsoft's new **.NET** (pronounced "dot net") initiative. What is .NET, you ask? Well, that's a good question and I've got an answer, but it's going to take a little explaining. Let's take a little side trip.

What Is .NET Anyway?

I promised you I'd explain this .NET thing and I'm going to give it my best shot. However, you've got to understand something: *Microsoft has been having a hard time explaining .NET!* Perhaps a little background is in order.

Windows 2002 Server Becomes Windows .NET Server Becomes Windows Server 2003

When Microsoft first announced a name for its new server product in June 2001, it announced it as Windows 2002 Server. That name made a lot of sense considering they were planning to release it during 2002 and the previous product was Windows 2000. However, by September 2001, the name had changed to Windows .NET Server and then, by August 2002, to Windows .NET Server 2003. That last change just reflects the acknowledgment that the product wouldn't be out until 2003. But what is .NET and why isn't .NET part of the operating system's name anymore?

The answer to the first question (I told you I'd tell you!) is that .NET is a system for connecting—*everything*. That's basically what it comes down to. Microsoft defines the term on its web site as, ". . .a set of Microsoft technologies for connecting information, people, systems, and devices." The idea is to establish a system that allows all of these entities to share information and services easily without necessarily being part of the same network or even geographically close to each other. Users and computers would be able to share information and understand each other with less hassle and configuration than is now necessary. Devices like web-enabled cell phones, handheld computers, and networks of all types would be able to connect and communicate with ease.

If you're still having trouble understanding exactly what .NET is supposed to do, don't worry. You're not alone. Microsoft has found it to be very difficult to get people to understand exactly what they're talking about with .NET. Part of the problem was that they confused the issue a bit by using .NET in the name of a lot of other new products that weren't clearly related to each other. In fact, they had so much trouble giving .NET a real "identity" in people's minds that they decided it was a bit too early to slap the name on their latest operating

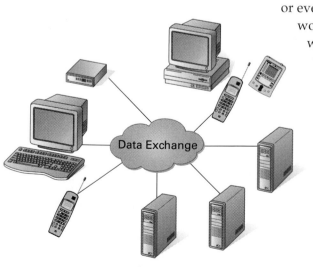

• The .NET Initiative

system. That's where the name Windows Server 2003 comes in. .NET is still part of Windows Server 2003; Microsoft hasn't abandoned it. They've just decided to change their branding strategy for now.

For what it's worth, I think you'll be hearing a lot more about .NET in coming years. Once there is a larger installed base of operating systems and software applications that support .NET technologies, people will begin to see and understand how much .NET can improve the exchange of information. I still remember a lot of people who didn't see any use to "that Internet thingy." Time will tell.

Try This!

Find Out What's Behind .NET

You can learn more about .NET and the technologies behind it on Microsoft's web site. To complete this task, you will need a computer with an Internet connection and a web browser. Try this:

1. Point your browser to `www.microsoft.com/net/basics/`. Click the link labeled The Basic Elements of .NET.

2. Read the information that describes the elements of .NET and the components of .NET-connected software.

3. Use your browser's Back button to navigate back to the page from the first step.

4. Click the link labeled What are Web services?

5. Read the information, paying special attention to the section under the header An Example: How Web Services Connect Applications.

 In addition to the features listed in this section, you'll also find that Windows Server 2003 offers a user interface similar to that used by Windows XP. Since most of these changes are simply cosmetic, you'll have no problem finding your way around, even if you haven't used Windows XP. However, it is a nice change from the older Windows 95–based interface, and I must admit, I think it looks quite good!

New Features

You already know about one of the new features in Windows Server 2003 from the little side trip we just finished. However, in addition to .NET there are many other new features, both big and small, to be found in Windows Server 2003. Rather than try to discuss them all, I've chosen some personal favorites to share with you here. These four new features are straightforward enough to understand without already being a network administration expert. In addition, I think they are excellent examples of how Windows Server 2003 offers new benefits to both users and network administrators.

Folder Redirection of My Documents

It's just a fact of life that client computers crash more often than servers. Servers are specifically designed to ensure exceptional reliability and are built to withstand heavy use. As good as client machines get, they just aren't as dependable as most servers. Add to that the fact most users store their files on their client computer's hard drive, and you have a potential problem.

Users almost always have been able to save to the server in network situations. In fact, most server operating systems, Windows Server 2003 included,

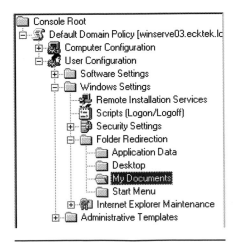

• Configuring Folder Redirection for the My Documents folder

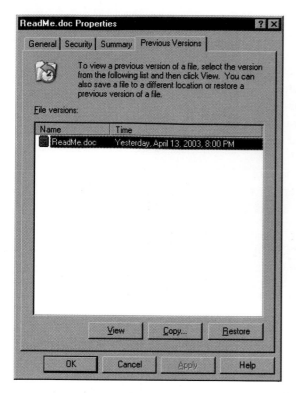

• **Figure 1.4**   Restoring a previous version of a file

create for each user a home directory on the server for just that purpose. However, most applications default to the My Documents folder on the local machine and most users are accustomed to saving their files there. **Folder Redirection of My Documents** allows network administrators to automatically send all files saved to My Documents to a My Documents folder in the user's home directory. This occurs with no user intervention and puts the files on the safest, most dependable system on the network. It also makes the next two features even more valuable.

Shadow Copies of Shared Folders

Shadow Copies of Shared Folders is a truly nifty new feature that benefits both network administrators and users. This technology enables users to retrieve previous versions of files easily and without administrator intervention. That means that if a user has accidentally deleted or modified a file, they can immediately recover from the mistake themselves. Not only does this improve productivity for network users, it also decreases the amount of time network administrators have to spend responding to individual requests for file recovery. In addition, prior to Shadow Copy, files could be restored only from the latest backup. Shadow Copy stores file revisions with every file write, allowing for users to select, as shown in Figure 1.4, exactly which version of a file they wish to restore. Since the My Documents folder can be redirected to the user's home directory, every file the user saves can potentially take advantage of Shadow Copy. This compounding of benefits continues as we look at the next new feature.

Open File Backup

Backing up files is an essential task on any network server. By making copies of all crucial data files, businesses can return to operation quickly after incidents that destroy or damage the data stored on the server. However, backups have always been a bit of a hassle for network administrators because they had to be done when users weren't using the server. In the past, backup technologies could not back up files that were currently opened by users. This relegated backups to the wee hours of the morning, which presented a problem to those businesses that ran 24 hours a day!

Windows Server 2003 now allows for an **open file backup**. By making use of the technology behind Shadow Copy, the included backup utility can now back up all files, including those that are currently in use. This not only allows backups to be run at more convenient times, it also allows them to be run more frequently. Since there is no need to wait until all files are closed, administrators can run backups at several times during the day to ensure that the very latest information is available for restoration if needed. Additionally, since the My Documents folder can now be redirected to the server, all user documents can be included in these backups, thus protecting the work of individual users and not just the data they intentionally saved to the server.

Software Restriction Policies

Let's face it; there are certain software packages that shouldn't be running on a business network. I'm not talking about just games, but any program

Of course, users could back their files up on their own, but most users don't do it often enough. By redirecting users' files to the server, enabling Shadow Copy, and backing up using open file backups, Windows Server 2003 allows the whole process to be centralized and automated so that the chance of losing data is minimized.

A complete list of Windows Server 2003 features is available at Microsoft's web site at http://www.microsoft.com/windowsserver2003/. Click the Features Highlights Sorter link under Quick Links to choose which edition and which feature category you are interested in.

that has a negative effect on productivity, security, or network performance and stability. Programs like music-downloading applications can slow down network communications, while other programs, especially those downloaded from the Web, may contain viruses or other malicious code.

Software restriction policies allow administrators to prevent certain applications from being run on network computers. This allows administrators to improve the security of the network and, in some cases, improve the stability of client machines. I know from personal experience that most of the problems I run across on client machines are due to a number of ill-behaved programs that users download from the Internet. Eliminating the ability of those programs to run helps out both the user and the administrator quite a bit!

If your personal computer is acting "funny," you might want to try uninstalling some of those applications you may have downloaded from the Internet. You'd be surprised at just how much trouble some programs can cause!

Cross Check

The New Features of Windows Server 2003

We've discussed several new features that can be found in Windows Server 2003. Review the material, if necessary, and answer the following questions:

1. How do these features benefit users of the network?
2. How do these features benefit network administrators?
3. How do these features benefit the business as a whole?

■ Meeting the System Requirements

Earlier in this chapter we discussed some of the new maximum capabilities of Microsoft Server 2003 as they applied to RAM and SMP processors. In addition to those maximums, each edition of Windows Server 2003 also has certain minimum hardware requirements that *must* be met and certain recommended requirements that *should* be met to achieve acceptable server performance.

Minimum Requirements

For the most part, the minimum requirements for each edition of Windows Server 2003 do vary a bit. However, the minimum requirements for both the Standard Edition and the Web Edition are the same. Considering that Web Edition is essentially a pared-down version of Standard Edition, this should come as no surprise.

Standard Edition and Web Edition Minimum Requirements

Both the Standard Edition and the Web Edition require a CPU with at least a 133 MHz clock speed. This requirement can be met easily by the majority of the early Intel Pentium processors and many other compatible processors made by companies such as AMD (Advanced Micro Devices). However, this minimum is quite low and likely to provide very unsatisfactory performance under even minimal server loads. Both editions require only a single CPU. Although they support SMP, as mentioned earlier in this chapter, they do not require it.

Inside Information

Total Cost of Ownership

Businesses have to consider the total effect of what they do on their bottom line. One way they do this is by trying to calculate the TCO (total cost of ownership). But what does TCO mean and how does it apply to Windows Server 2003?

Imagine you need to buy a car. On one hand, you have an old junker that a friend will let you have for $500. On the other hand, you have a brand new car that the dealer is selling for $10,000. Which one would you buy? Which one has better gas mileage? Which one is more likely to need frequent repair? Answering questions like those is how you consider the TCO.

Several of the Windows Server 2003 features we've discussed try to reduce the total cost of ownership for a network. For instance, by saving the IT (Information Technology) department time by reducing the need to support users, the company should save money on overtime. By reducing lost work time due to lost files, the company should increase productivity, and thus profits. As we continue to study Windows Server 2003, look for other ways it helps reduce the TCO of a network.

Inside Information

Server-Class Computers

I did a little research to see how hard it was to find a computer that meets the minimum requirements we've discussed. A quick check of three major online retailers of computer systems turned up three systems (one each) that would run the Web, Standard, and 32-bit Enterprise Editions of Windows Server 2003 just fine. The surprising thing is that each one was under $500! However, there's more to a server than just a CPU, some RAM, and a sizeable hard drive.

Real server-class computers are engineered to provide exceptional reliability and ease of management. In addition to being assembled from top-quality components, everything from the power supply to the motherboard is designed with the special needs of a network server in mind. So what would a server-class computer cost that met our requirements? Well, after a little more shopping I came up with an answer. The cheapest server-class computers came in at between two and four times what the equivalent client-class computer cost. The only change I made to the system requirements was to add support for at least two SMP processors. When you consider that a single server might serve 50, 100, or more clients, that's not too much of a premium to pay.

The RAM requirement for these two editions is set at an absolute minimum of 128MB. Depending on how the server will be employed, this amount may suffice for some time. For simple file servers, RAM is not always a critical component. However, most networks will find this minimum to be too low. However, if the motherboard has the capacity, RAM is easily added as needed.

A minimum of 1.5GB of hard drive space is required for both the Standard and the Web Editions of Windows Server 2003. This relatively small amount would really only allow for the installation of the operating system and not much else. There really is no maximum amount of storage, since new drives and new technologies are being introduced almost daily. The simple fact of the matter is that, when it comes to servers, you can never have too much storage!

Enterprise Edition Minimum Requirements

You might remember I mentioned that Enterprise Edition is available in both 32-bit and 64-bit versions. As you might have guessed, the different versions have different minimum CPU requirements. What you might not have guessed is that other requirements also change depending on which version is being run.

The 32-bit version of Enterprise Edition requires the same 133 MHz minimum processor as the Web and Standard Editions. However, the minimum for the 64-bit version is 733 MHz, which just happens to be the speed of the slowest of the Intel Itanium processors! As was the case earlier, SMP processors, while supported, are not required for either the 32- or 64-bit version of Enterprise Edition.

The RAM requirements for both the 32- and 64-bit versions of Enterprise Edition are set to the same 128MB minimum stated for Web Edition and Standard Edition. Although the operating system will install and run at this level, businesses that saw the need for the more powerful Enterprise Edition will certainly want to go with at least the recommended levels (which we will discuss in the following section).

Interestingly enough, the minimum hard drive space requirements for the 32-and 64-bit versions are different. This is due to the need to install special 64-bit code applications, as well as some 32-bit code, when using the 64-bit version. The minimum requirement for the 32-bit version of Enterprise Edition is still 1.5GB. The 64-bit version requires a minimum of 2GB.

Datacenter Edition Minimum Requirements

Minimum requirements for Datacenter Edition of Windows Server 2003 really aren't much to be concerned about. That's because the only way to purchase Datacenter Edition is, as you may remember, from an authorized OEM selling servers that are certified as compatible by Microsoft and already have the OS installed. However, for the purposes of comparison to the other editions, let's take a look at what the stated minimums are.

The 32-bit version of Datacenter Edition requires a bit more processor than the other editions call for. The stated minimum is a 400 MHz CPU. The 64-bit version still requires the same 733 MHz minimum called for by Enterprise Edition. One significant change is that both versions of Datacenter Edition require a minimum of eight SMP processors installed.

The minimum RAM requirements take a huge leap for Datacenter Edition, which is not surprising, considering the need to support a minimum of eight SMP processors. In fact, the minimum requirement is four times that of the other editions, which gives us 512MB.

The minimum hard drive space for Datacenter Edition is exactly the same as it was for Enterprise Edition. The 32-bit version requires 1.5GB, while the 64-bit version needs at least 2GB.

Recommended Requirements

In most cases, the minimum requirements for each edition of Windows Server 2003 are theoretical minimums at best. Most network administrators would quickly find that following those requirements would not provide acceptable levels of performance. Let's take a look at what Microsoft actually recommends for each edition.

Standard Edition and Web Edition Recommended Requirements

Microsoft recommends that servers be equipped with at least a 550 MHz processor and 256MB of RAM when running either of these editions. Depending on server load, even these recommendations could still be too low.

Enterprise Edition and Datacenter Edition Recommended Requirements

The recommended CPU clock speed for both the 32- and 64-bit versions of both editions is merely 733 MHz. However, there is a significant difference between the RAM recommendations, again due to the need to support eight SMP processors under the Datacenter Edition. Enterprise Edition recommends the same 256MB of RAM as was recommended for both Standard Edition and Web Edition. The recommendation for Datacenter Edition is a full 1GB. Please see Table 1.1 for a summary of the minimum requirements and Table 1.2 for the recommended hardware requirements for all editions and versions. Where appropriate, maximums appear in parentheses in Table 1.2.

Table 1.1	Minimum Hardware Requirements for All Members of the Windows Server 2003 Family			
Edition	**Processor**	**RAM**	**Disk Space**	**SMP**
Web Edition Minimum	133 MHz	128MB	1.5GB	1
Standard Edition Minimum	133 MHz	128MB	1.5GB	1
Enterprise Edition Minimum	133 MHz/32-bit 733 MHz/64-bit	128MB	1.5GB/32-bit 2GB/64-bit	1
Datacenter Edition Minimum	400 MHz/32-bit 733 MHz/64-bit	512MB	1.5GB/32-bit 2GB/64-bit	8

Table 1.2	Recommended Hardware Requirements for All Members of the Windows Server 2003 Family, with Maximums in Parentheses			
Edition	**Processor**	**RAM**	**Disk Space**	**SMP**
Web Edition Recommended	550 MHz	256MB (max. 2GB)	N/A	N/A (max. 2)
Standard Edition Recommended	550 MHz	256MB (max. 4GB)	N/A	N/A (max. 4)
Enterprise Edition Recommended	733 MHz	256MB (max. 32GB/32-bit) (max. 64GB/64-bit)	N/A	N/A (max. 8)
Datacenter Edition Recommended	733 MHz	1GB (max. 64GB/32-bit) (max. 512GB/64-bit)	N/A	N/A (max. 32)

Chapter 1 Review

■ Chapter Summary

After reading this chapter and completing the Try This! exercises, you should understand the following facts about Windows Server 2003.

Describe the Evolution of Windows Server 2003

■ Windows Server 2003 evolved from the operating systems that came before it: Windows for Workgroups, Windows NT, and Windows 2000.

■ Windows for Workgroups made setting up and using small networks much simpler than had previously been possible. Computers running Windows for Workgroups were able to act as both clients and servers on the same peer-to-peer network.

■ Windows for Workgroups suffered from the limitations of peer-to-peer networks, which are difficult to manage and use once they begin to grow beyond seven to ten computers.

■ Windows NT was the first Windows operating system to be completely independent of DOS. It was also the first Microsoft operating system to be released as both a server and a workstation product.

■ Windows NT offered improved security through the SAM, or Security Accounts Manager. At the network level, the SAM became the basis for the domain, the central management unit for Microsoft networks.

■ Windows NT introduced the NTFS, or NT File System, which permitted the setting of local permissions on files or folders.

■ Most people found Windows NT difficult to master and administer. Windows NT also lacked sufficient security measures to protect files stored on the hard drive from unauthorized access.

■ Windows 2000 was essentially the latest version of Windows NT with additional refinements.

■ Windows 2000 introduced Active Directory; the MMC, or Microsoft Management Console; NTFS5, which enabled file encryption; and disk quotas. These tools collectively addressed the shortcomings of Windows NT.

Describe the Members of the Windows Server Family

■ Windows Server 2003 is available in four different editions: Standard Edition; Enterprise Edition; Datacenter Edition; and Web Edition.

■ Standard Edition runs on 32-bit processors, can take 4GB of RAM, and supports up to four SMP processors at once.

■ Standard Edition offers Active Directory, file and print services, management services, and Internet connectivity and security. It is targeted at small businesses or department-level business units.

■ Enterprise Edition offers both a 32-bit version and a 64-bit version that runs on the Intel Itanium processor. Both versions accept up to eight SMP processors. The 64-bit version supports up to 64GB of RAM. The 32-bit version supports up to 32GB of RAM and also supports Hot Add Memory.

■ Enterprise Edition supports the additional service of server clustering. It is targeted at businesses that depend on their networks for e-commerce or other business-critical activities.

■ Datacenter Edition offers the Windows Datacenter High Availability Program, which provides support through a Datacenter Support Provider. Datacenter Edition is available only with the purchase of a certified server from a licensed OEM, or original equipment manufacturer.

■ Datacenter Edition also offers both a 32-bit and 64-bit version. The 32-bit version supports 64GB of RAM and up to 32 SMP processors. The 64-bit version supports 512GB of RAM and up to 64 SMP processors.

- Datacenter Edition offers all of the features of Enterprise Edition with the exception of some Internet connectivity services. It is targeted at businesses that cannot afford disruption of their network operations.

- Web Edition supports 32-bit processors running up to 2GB of RAM and up to two SMP processors.

- Web Edition offers a pared-down set of services found in the other editions that focus on hosting web sites and serving up web pages. It is intended as an inexpensive option for businesses that want to run their own web server.

Describe the Improved Benefits and New Features of Windows Server 2003

- Windows Server 2003 is at least twice as fast as Windows NT and supports more RAM and SMP processors than Windows 2000 in certain editions. It is more reliable, easier to manage, and more secure than previous operating systems.

- Windows Server 2003 is the first operating system to fully integrate Microsoft's .NET initiative. .NET is a set of technologies that should greatly ease the ability of servers, clients, networks, and other devices and entities to communicate with each other and share data without extensive hassle and configuration.

- Windows Server 2003 offers new features such as redirection of users' My Documents folder, Shadow Copies of Shared Folders, Open File backups, and software restriction policies.

Identify the Server Hardware Requirements

- Both Standard Edition and Web Edition require a 133 MHz processor, 128MB of RAM, and 1.5GB of hard drive space. Microsoft recommends a 550 MHz processor and 256MB of RAM for both editions.

- Enterprise Edition 32-bit requires a 133 MHz processor, 128MB of RAM and 1.5GB of hard drive space. Enterprise Edition 64-bit requires a 733 MHz 64-bit processor, 128MB of RAM, and 2GB of hard drive space. Microsoft recommends a 733 MHz processor and 256MB of RAM for both versions.

- Datacenter Edition 32-bit requires a 400 MHz processor, 512MB of RAM, 1.5GB of hard drive space, and eight SMP processors. Datacenter Edition 64-bit requires a 733 MHz 64-bit processor, 512MB of RAM, 2GB of hard drive space, and eight SMP processors. Microsoft recommends a 733 MHz processor and 1GB of RAM for both versions.

■ Key Terms

.NET *(16)*

Active Directory *(9)*

authenticate *(5)*

client *(1)*

client/server network *(5)*

clustering *(13)*

domain *(6)*

file allocation table (FAT) *(6)*

file system *(6)*

Folder Redirection of My Documents *(18)*

Hot Add Memory *(13)*

Microsoft Management Console (MMC) *(9)*

NT File System (NTFS) *(6)*

open file backup *(18)*

peer-to-peer network *(2)*

permissions *(6)*

scalable *(12)*

Security Accounts Manager (SAM) *(5)*

server *(1)*

Shadow Copies of Shared Folders *(18)*

shares *(6)*

software restriction policies *(19)*

symmetric multiprocessing (SMP) *(12)*

workgroup *(5)*

■ Key Terms Quiz

Use the Key Terms list to complete the sentences that follow. Not all terms will be used.

1. In a _____ , one or more central computers manage the network and are the primary agent for sharing resources out to the clients.

2. Windows Server 2003's _____ feature means that the server can be backed up even while users are still working and all files will still be backed up.

3. Windows 2000 introduced a new version of _____ that allowed for files to be encrypted.

4. Windows NT uses its Security Accounts Manager (SAM) to _____ users.

5. The Datacenter Edition of Windows Server 2003 not only supports _____ processors, it requires that at least four be present in a system that can support at least eight.

6. In an effort to improve the ease with which network administrators could manage their networks, Windows 2000 introduced Active Directory and _____.

7. Both Enterprise Edition and Datacenter Edition support _____, which means that multiple servers can act as one, thus sharing the load and increasing reliability.

8. NTFS provides for the setting of _____ that allow one to specify who can access a resource and what they can do with it.

9. A workgroup is simply another name for a _____.

10. Windows Server 2003 allows network administrators to set _____, which can prevent certain programs from being run on the network.

■ Multiple-Choice Quiz

1. Which of the following is sometimes referred to as a shell for DOS, rather than an actual operating system, because it required DOS to run?

   a. Windows Server 2003
   b. Windows 2000
   c. Windows NT
   d. Windows for Workgroups

2. What is the realistic upper limit (in terms of computers) for a peer-to-peer network?

   a. One to three
   b. Three to four
   c. Four to seven
   d. Seven to ten

3. Which of the following was described as being targeted at small businesses or department-level business units?

   a. Windows Server 2003 Standard Edition

   b. Windows Server 2003 Enterprise Edition
   c. Windows Server 2003 Datacenter Edition
   d. Windows Server 2003 Web Edition

4. Which operating system was the first from Microsoft to be released in both server and workstation versions?

   a. Windows Server 2003
   b. Windows 2000
   c. Windows NT
   d. Windows for Workgroups

5. The process of creating a file that cannot be read, even if it is accessed, by anyone not possessing the correct password is

   a. Authentication
   b. Encryption
   c. Integration
   d. Clustering

6. Which of the following did *not* have a corresponding product in the Windows 2000 family?

   a. Windows Server 2003 Standard Edition

   b. Windows Server 2003 Enterprise Edition

   c. Windows Server 2003 Datacenter Edition

   d. Windows Server 2003 Web Edition

7. Windows Server 2003 Datacenter Edition recommends _____ RAM.

   a. 128MB

   b. 256MB

   c. 512MB

   d. 1GB

8. On a properly configured Windows Server 2003–based network, users can retrieve previous versions of files that have been damaged or deleted thanks to

   a. Open file backup

   b. Shadow Copies of Shared Folders

   c. Folder redirection of My Documents

   d. Active Directory

9. The 64-bit versions of both Windows Server 2003 Enterprise Edition and Datacenter Edition were designed to run on the Intel

   a. Titanium

   b. Ideanimum

   c. Itanium

   d. Xenon

10. Windows Server 2003 Web Edition costs approximately how much less than the Standard Edition?

    a. 20%

    b. 40%

    c. 60%

    d. 80%

11. Which edition of Windows Server 2003 cannot be purchased in a store?

    a. Standard Edition

    b. Enterprise Edition

    c. Datacenter Edition

    d. Web Edition

12. Active Directory replaced the

    a. NTFS

    b. SMP

    c. SAM

    d. DSP

13. The ability to run more than one processor at once is referred to as

    a. NTFS

    b. SMP

    c. SAM

    d. DSP

14. Which edition variant supports the Hot Add Memory Feature?

    a. Enterprise Edition 32-bit

    b. Datacenter Edition 32-bit

    c. Enterprise Edition 64-bit

    d. Datacenter Edition 64-bit

15. Under the Windows Datacenter High Availability Program, service is provided through a/an

    a. NTFS

    b. SMP

    c. SAM

    d. DSP

■ Essay Quiz

1. You are the owner of your own business and the business's sole employee. You've decided to start promoting your business over the Internet, and you've decided you'd rather maintain the web site yourself, rather than pay someone else to do it. Choose which edition of Windows Server 2003 you would use. Write a paragraph or two explaining and justifying your choice.

2. You are in charge of choosing the new network operating system for your employer's network. Your company is a small 20-person operation. You primarily use your network for printing, e-mail, and Internet access. Choose which edition of Windows Server 2003 you would recommend. Write a paragraph or two explaining and justifying your choice.

3. You are in charge of choosing the new network operating system for your employer's network. Your company is small but growing. Your company does much of its business on the corporate web site, which you host and maintain internally. Because your current server is in great shape, you've decided to keep it and just upgrade the operating system. Choose which edition of Windows Server 2003 you would recommend. Write a paragraph or two explaining and justifying your choice.

4. Try your hand at explaining .NET in your own terms. Try to imagine what the benefits will be. Feel free to research .NET further before answering the question.

5. You've been asked to prepare a presentation for the VP of Finance at your company. Your presentation is supposed to justify to the VP the expense of upgrading your Windows NT network to Windows Server 2003. Like most people in her position, your VP is solely concerned with how each decision affects the bottom line. How will you persuade the VP to okay the expenditure? Write down your arguments and make sure you can support them.

Lab Projects

• Lab Project 1.1

1. Use the Internet to search for reviews of Windows Server 2003. Although it really doesn't matter if the reviews are of Standard Edition, Enterprise Edition, or Datacenter Edition, try to avoid reviews that focus on Web Edition. Also avoid any reviews or information from the Microsoft web site. Choose two reviews that specifically compare Windows Server 2003 with either Windows NT or Windows 2000. Using your own words, summarize the points made in the reviews, both positive and negative.

2. Compare your summary to what we've discussed in this chapter. Prepare a brief paper that highlights anything new that you learned about in the reviews.

3. Meet in groups of two or three and compare your findings. Discuss this question: are the reviews generally favorable or not? Why?

• Lab Project 1.2

1. Interview three-to-five people who work with networked computers on a regular basis. You might interview classmates, family members, neighbors, your instructors, or just about anybody. However, choose only one person from each network environment. Try to determine whether their network is a peer-to-peer network or a client/server network. Ask them what the five biggest benefits are that they receive from being on the network. Try to make sure that the benefits are directly related to being networked, as opposed to those benefits that might come from just having access to a computer.

2 Summarize the benefits your interviewees share with you, being sure to note whether the benefit was experienced on a peer-to-peer network or a client/server network. Which network seemed to convey the most benefits to the users?

3 Meet in groups of two to three and share your results. Make a note of any new benefits the members of your group may have heard that you did not. Continue to track whether the benefit was experienced on a peer-to-peer network or a client/server network.

4 Given the findings of the group, what do you think are the three greatest benefits of being on a network? Are those benefits particular to whether the network is peer-to-peer or client/server? Share your conclusions with your instructor and group if asked.

Getting Started: Installing Windows Server 2003

*"It's a job that's never started
that takes the longest to finish."*

—J.R.R. Tolkien

In this chapter, you will learn how to:

- **Check hardware compatibility**
- **Choose an installation method**
- **Make pre-installation decisions**
- **Install and activate Windows Server 2003**
- **Update Windows Server 2003**
- **Troubleshoot Windows Server 2003 installations**

If you really want to learn an operating system, there is no better method than jumping in and "getting your hands dirty." However, before you can do that, you've got to get it installed! Fortunately, installing Windows Server 2003 isn't rocket science, but it does require a little planning.

Even client operating systems intended for individual computers require the user to do a little research and make some decisions before beginning installation. When dealing with network operating systems, these decisions are even more important because they lay the groundwork for a stable and useful network. For instance, we have to be sure that the server we are going to install the operating system on is fully compatible and meets at least the minimum hardware requirements. There are also several options available as to the method of installation, each with its own pros and cons, and a few post-installation tasks that complete the whole process.

In this chapter, we'll go through the entire installation process for Windows Server 2003. We will begin by checking the compatibility of our hardware and then move on to a discussion of the various decisions that need to be made before installation begins, including what method of installation to use. We will perform an actual installation of the operating system using one of those methods and activate it using Microsoft's Product Activation. Finally, we'll check for, and install, any product updates and discuss troubleshooting strategies for common installation problems.

■ Checking Hardware Compatibility

Unless you are buying a new server with Windows Server 2003 preinstalled, you'll need to know how to install the OS on an existing server. Whether you plan to start from scratch or upgrade a current installation of Windows NT or 2000 Server, there's a little more to worry about than just knowing the minimum requirements for the CPU and RAM. From our discussion in Chapter 1, you know the minimum and recommended requirements for Windows Server 2003. However, all hardware is not created equal! In order to increase your chances of a painless installation, you should check out the compatibility of *all* of your hardware with the new operating system before you begin. Fortunately, there are several easy ways to do this.

> A piece of hardware might be incompatible with a particular operating system for any number of reasons. It might depend on software that cannot run properly under the new OS, or it might work in a nonstandard way that could destabilize the system. Regardless of the reason, it sure is easier to find out your video card or hard drive won't work *before* you start the lengthy installation process!

Using the Microsoft Windows Upgrade Advisor

The easiest way to check hardware compatibility is through the Microsoft **Windows Upgrade Advisor** utility, which can be run from the installation CD. The user can run this check before the operating system is installed (in fact, it's a good idea) to detect and fix any problems before beginning the process. However, one limitation of this utility is that it will not work properly if the computer is currently running an operating system that cannot be directly upgraded to Windows Server 2003, such as Windows 98 or Windows XP. We'll talk more about which OSs can be upgraded to Windows Server 2003 a little later in this chapter. For now, let's take a look at our current hardware using this simple tool.

Step-by-Step 2.1

Using the Windows Upgrade Advisor

Since operating systems work so closely with computer hardware, it shouldn't be surprising to hear that they tend to be very particular about what hardware they will and will not work with. Even a computer with exactly the right type of processor, plenty of RAM, and sufficient free hard drive space could still have significant problems when installing a new operating system due to incompatible hardware. The problem could be as simple as a device that needs a new driver, which is the program that tells the operating system how to talk to the device. However, it can be as severe as a piece of hardware that can actually crash the operating system unless it is first removed. To top it all off, even pre-existing applications and operating systems can cause problems when installing an upgraded operating system.

In this Step-by-Step you will make sure no problems exist by using the installation CD for Windows Server 2003 to check your existing hardware and/or software for compatibility with the operating system. You will then report your findings to your instructor.

To complete this Step-by-Step, you will need

- A lab computer running either Windows NT 4.0, Windows 2000 Server, or Windows Server

2003. A computer with a clean hard drive and a bootable CD-ROM drive may also be used

- The Windows Server 2003 installation CD

Step 1

If your lab computer is already running one of the listed operating systems, boot the computer and insert the installation CD into the lab computer's CD-ROM drive after it has finished booting. If the setup program does not start automatically within a few moments, open My Computer, right-click the CD-ROM drive icon, and choose Autoplay. If that should fail to work, double-click the CD-ROM drive icon and then double-click the Setup file. After using one of these methods, the Microsoft Windows Server 2003 family dialog box should appear.

If your lab computer has a clean hard drive (no operating system installed), boot the computer and immediately place the installation CD in the drive. If your computer will not boot from the CD, see your instructor for help.

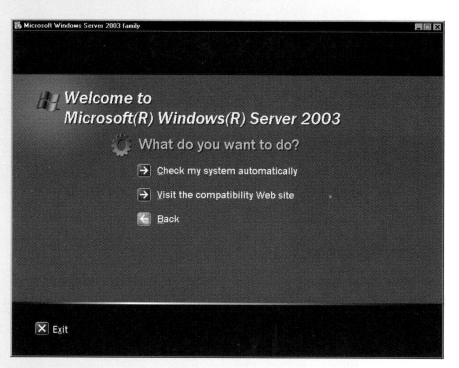

Step 2

When the opening screen of the setup program appears, click the link titled Check system compatibility. On the next screen, click Check my system automatically. Wait for the system check to be concluded.

Tip: If a Get Updated Setup Files dialog box appears after you click Check my system automatically, click the Next button to download the files. However, if your computer is not connected to the Internet, you can usually skip this step safely. Once the files are downloaded, you should be able to continue to the next step.

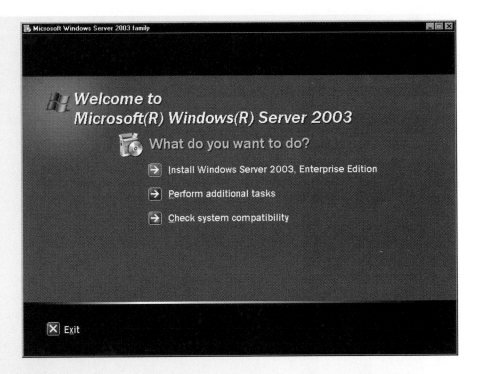

If there are any incompatibilities listed when the Report System Compatibility dialog box appears, click the entries and click Details to learn more about the issues that were discovered. Make a note of any incompatibilities that are reported to you. When you have investigated each of the incompatibilities, click Finish. You should be back at the second screen of the setup program.

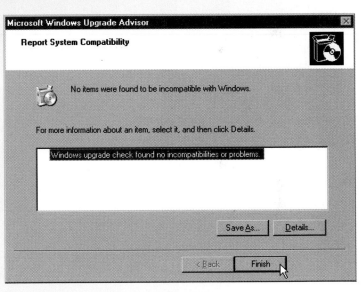

Summarize your findings for your instructor and submit them. Leave your computer on with the second dialog box displayed for the next exercise.

The Hardware Compatibility List and the Windows Server Catalog

What do you do if you want to check the compatibility for a computer that is running Windows 98, XP, or another OS that doesn't qualify for upgrading? What about checking the compatibility of hardware you haven't yet installed, or even purchased? The best bet

Run the Windows Upgrade Advisor from the Command Line

Windows Server 2003 frequently provides a way to run various utilities by typing out commands as opposed to clicking buttons or selecting from a menu. This is done to allow administrators to automate certain tasks using scripts, which are essentially files containing sequences of typed commands. The Windows Upgrade Advisor is one of those utilities that can be run from a typed command. To complete this task, you will need a computer that either is running Windows Server 2003 or can be upgraded to Windows Server 2003 and the Windows Server 2003 installation CD. Try this:

1. Insert the installation CD. If Autoplay brings up the Microsoft Windows Server 2003 family dialog box, click the Exit button in the lower-left corner.

2. Click Start and click Run.

3. In the text box, type **d:\i386\winnt32.exe -checkupgradeonly** (if your CD-ROM is not drive d:, please substitute the correct letter.)

4. Compare the results to those from Step-by-Step 2.1. They should be the same.

is to check out the compatibility of your hardware at Microsoft's web site. Note that Windows XP also has a new online utility for checking hardware compatibility called the Windows Catalog. To access the Windows Catalog from a Windows XP computer, click Start | All Programs | Windows Catalog. You can also point your browser to http://go.microsoft.com/fwlink/?LinkID=14201.) For Windows 2000, the **Hardware Compatibility List (HCL)** was the tool of choice. The HCL allowed you to search a comprehensive list of products by category and keyword and returned information regarding compatibility with Windows 2000 Windows Me (Millennium edition), and even Windows XP. However, the HCL does not address Windows Server 2003 compatibility. It has been replaced by a new online tool called the **Windows Server Catalog**. Before we discuss this new utility, let's take a quick look at how the HCL works.

Step-by-Step 2.2

Using the Online Hardware Compatibility List

Although the HCL has now been replaced, it's still worthwhile to familiarize yourself with how it works. The HCL remains an effective tool for checking hardware compatibility for Windows 2000 Professional systems and, to a lesser extent, systems that run Windows XP. Since it's likely that you'll eventually work with both Windows 2000 and Windows XP clients on a Windows Server 2003 network, you may still need to refer to this tool. Additionally, taking a look at the HCL will allow you to decide whether the Windows Server Catalog we're about to discuss is an improvement or not.

Note: Since Windows Me was designed specifically for home, you're not likely to run into it in a business environment. However, home users running Windows Me can use the HCL to check hardware compatibility for their operating system.

To complete this Step-by-Step, you will need

- A lab computer with Internet access and a browser

- The identities of one or two pieces of hardware for which to check compatibility. These should be provided by the instructor

Step 1

Using your web browser, go to `http://www.microsoft.com/whdc/hcl/search.mspx`. Keep in mind that, since the HCL is being phased out, this link may change. If the Windows Hardware Compatibility List does not appear, try going to `http://www.microsoft.com` and doing a search for the Windows HCL.

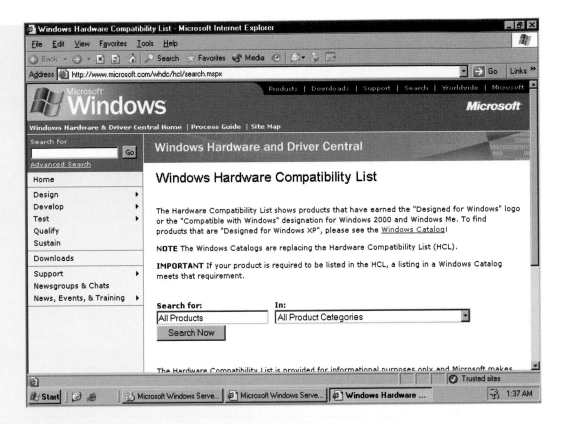

	Step 2

Carefully enter the name (spelling counts!) of one of the products your instructor asked you to research in the Search for text box. Be sure to select the appropriate product category from the In text box. If you are in doubt about what category your product belongs to, ask your instructor. When you have entered the information, click Search Now.

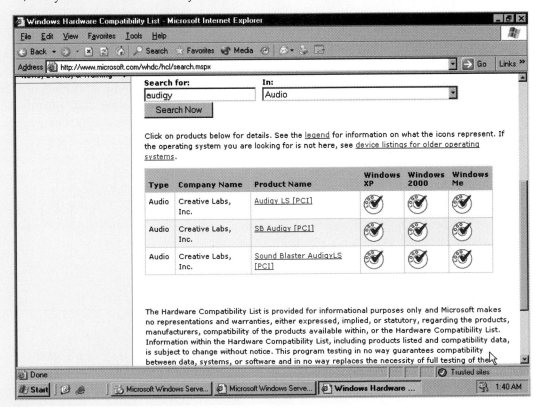

When the results of your search appear, click the listings to see more information. Record the information and then repeat Step 2 for the other product given to you by your instructor. If no results appear, double-check your spelling and try the search again.

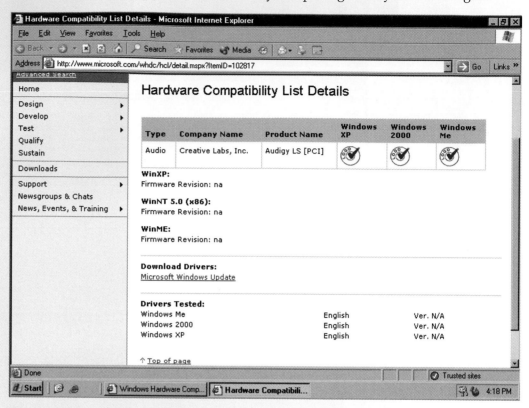

Summarize your findings and submit them to your instructor.

The Windows Server Catalog is also designed to provide information on software compatibility. However, at the time of this writing, this feature had not yet been implemented. The Windows Server Catalog also provides information on compatibility with Windows 2000 server products. However, for information on compatibility with Windows 2000 Professional, you should continue to use the HCL.

The new Windows Server Catalog has several advantages over the now-retired HCL. Quite simply, it's easier to get to, easier to use, and a whole lot nicer looking! You can access the Windows Server Catalog from the setup program on the Windows Server 2003 installation CD, from the All Programs menu of a Windows Server 2003 computer, or directly at http://www.microsoft.com/windows/catalog/server/. As you're about to see in the next Step-by-Step, the Windows Server Catalog offers a simple navigation system that makes it easy to find the compatibility information for a particular piece of hardware or just browse the listings to see what's available. Last, although I'm no graphic design expert, I think you'll find the whole interface to be much more pleasant and engaging than the old HCL utility. Let's give it a try now.

Step-by-Step 2.3

Using the Windows Server Catalog

The Windows Server Catalog is more than just a place to check the compatibility of hardware you already own. Ideally, Microsoft would like administrators to use it as their first destination when considering the purchase of new components and peripherals. This would add value to Microsoft's testing and certifying programs, for which they charge manufacturers a great deal. Manufacturers who undergo the certification process will be better able to recoup their investment if consumers can more easily find their compatible products. Accordingly, Microsoft has tried to make the whole experience of using the Windows Server Catalog a bit more pleasant and "shopping-like" than the dry searches offered by the HCL. The idea is to make it easier to find products that are certified, which will encourage consumers to buy them, which will drive more manufacturers to submit their products to the certification process. After working through this Step-by-Step, you can draw your own conclusions as to how successful they've been.

To complete this Step-by-Step, you will need

- A working computer with Internet access

- The Windows Server 2003 installation CD (optional)

- The identities of one or two pieces of hardware for which to check compatibility. These can be the same pieces used in Step-by-Step 2.2 or others chosen by your instructor

Step 1

While logged on to the computer, insert the Windows Server 2003 installation CD (if you have it) into the CD drive. If the Microsoft Windows Server 2003 family dialog box does not appear within a minute, open My Computer, right-click the CD drive, and choose AutoPlay. When the Microsoft Windows Server 2003 family dialog box appears, click Check system compatibility. On the following dialog box, click Visit the compatibility Web site.

If you do not have access to the installation CD, point your browser to http://www.microsoft.com/windows/catalog/server/.

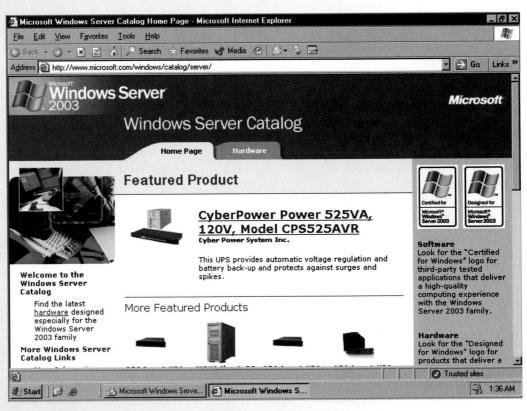

Step 2

Click the tab labeled Hardware at the top of the page. On the left side of the page is a list of hardware categories. Point to the appropriate category for one of your pieces of hardware and, if necessary, click the correct subcategory when it appears to the right of the main category.

Step 3

You may either browse through the pages or search by product name, manufacturer name, or both. Find your first product and look at the right side of the page to see what its status is under Windows Server 2003. Products may have no listing, which indicates they may not work. Products can also be listed as "supported," which means they were not designed for Windows Server 2003 but will work. Ideally, a product's entry will bear the Designed for Microsoft Windows Server 2003 icon, which indicates it has passed rigorous compatibility tests.

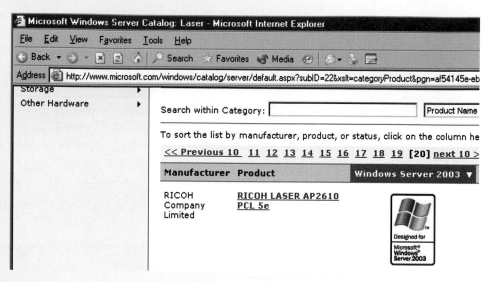

Step 4

Click the entry for your first product to see a more detailed summary of its compatibility, including which specific editions of Windows Server 2003 it is compatible with. Record your findings and research your remaining product.

Step 5

Summarize your findings and submit them to your instructor.

 Cross Check

Checking Hardware Compatibility

Now that you've had a chance to explore the various tools for checking hardware compatibility, take a minute to summarize what you've learned. If you like, review the preceding sections and answer the following questions:

1. Which tool does not provide information on compatibility with Windows Server 2003? What might it still be used for?

2. Which tool replaced the tool from Question 1? In what ways is it different?

3. Which tools are directly accessible from the Windows Server 2003 installation CD?

■ Choosing an Installation Method

Because the company's operating systems are used in so many different environments, Microsoft has typically tried to accommodate as many different installation scenarios as possible. Windows Server 2003 is no exception to this practice. There are several different ways to install the operating system that may prove beneficial in certain situations. Let's take a look at some of the basic variations.

Attended Installation

An **attended installation** simply means that you remain present during the installation process to respond to queries by the installation program. This is probably the most common method used to install any operating system. In fact, it is the method we will use later in this chapter to install our copy of Windows Server 2003. However, along with certain advantages, there are some shortcomings to this method that might make another method preferable.

Benefits of Attended Installations

The primary benefit of an attended installation is that it takes the least amount of preparation. Although it is wise to preplan in several areas (a process we will go through soon), it isn't an absolute requirement. As long as you have a computer that suits the operating system's requirements and a copy of the installation CD, you're good to go! Since this method is also nearly identical to the process of installing client operating systems like Windows 2000 Professional or Windows XP, it is a familiar process even to those who have never installed a server operating system. Of course, this method isn't without its weaknesses.

Potential Problems with Attended Installations

The biggest problem with attended installations is that they are quite time consuming. On most machines, the process will take somewhere around 45 minutes to complete. The time itself isn't really the problem, but there are lengthy periods during the process when all you do is wait for the next prompt to show up! Since it's hard to know exactly when you'll next be asked for your input, you either need to sit through the entire process or keep checking back to see if you need to make a choice or enter information. While this is okay if you've got nothing better to do, it isn't always an efficient use of your time. In some situations, you're better off with an unattended installation.

Unattended Installation

As the name implies, an **unattended installation** does not require your constant presence during the process. By preconfiguring an **answer file**, called unattend.txt, like the one in Figure 2.1, you can start the installation and then leave it to finish on its own. A properly configured answer file contains all of the necessary settings and options you would normally select and enter during an attended installation.

The answer file is normally called unattend.txt, but it can go by other names. If the installation source files to be used during an unattended installation are located on the network, the answer file can be named pretty much anything. However, if the installation files and the answer file will be placed on a CD, the answer file must be named winnt.sif.

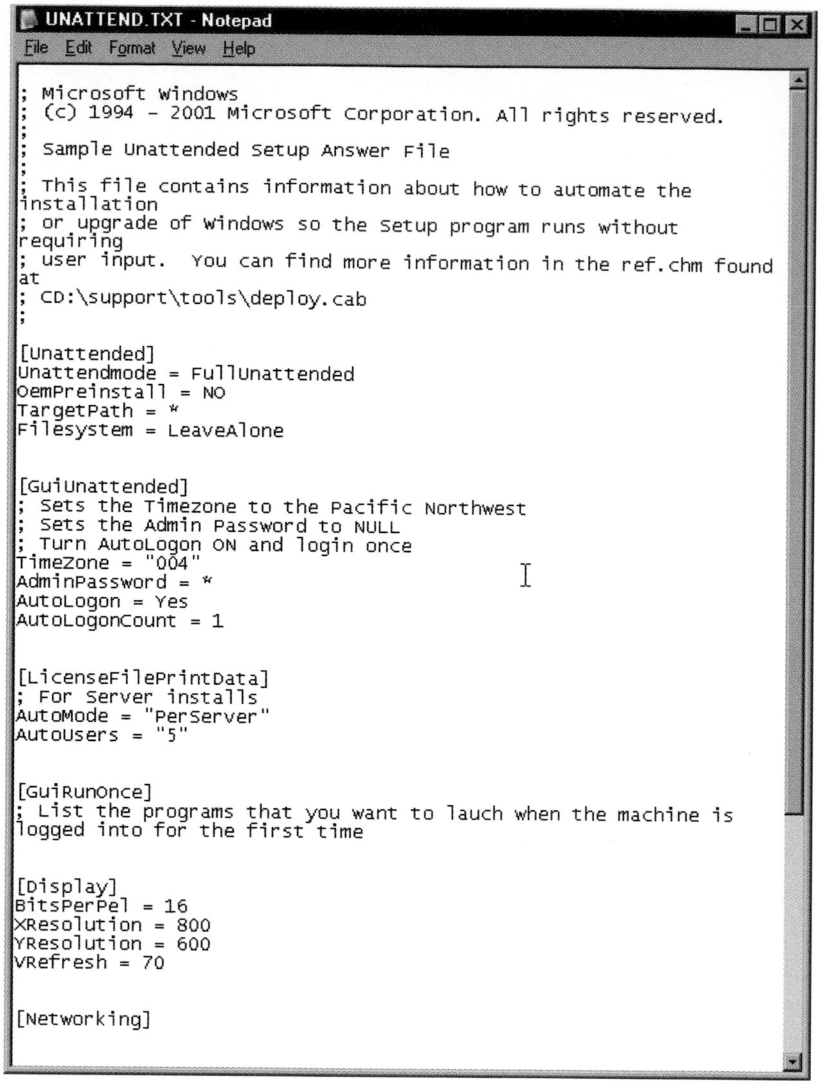

```
UNATTEND.TXT - Notepad                                    _ □ X
File  Edit  Format  View  Help

; Microsoft Windows
; (c) 1994 - 2001 Microsoft Corporation. All rights reserved.
;
; Sample Unattended Setup Answer File
;
; This file contains information about how to automate the
installation
; or upgrade of Windows so the Setup program runs without
requiring
; user input.  You can find more information in the ref.chm found
at
; CD:\support\tools\deploy.cab
;

[Unattended]
Unattendmode = FullUnattended
OemPreinstall = NO
TargetPath = *
Filesystem = LeaveAlone


[GuiUnattended]
; Sets the Timezone to the Pacific Northwest
; Sets the Admin Password to NULL
; Turn AutoLogon ON and login once
TimeZone = "004"
AdminPassword = *
AutoLogon = Yes
AutoLogonCount = 1


[LicenseFilePrintData]
; For Server installs
AutoMode = "PerServer"
AutoUsers = "5"


[GuiRunOnce]
; List the programs that you want to lauch when the machine is
logged into for the first time


[Display]
BitsPerPel = 16
XResolution = 800
YResolution = 600
VRefresh = 70


[Networking]
```

• Figure 2.1   A sample answer file for unattended installations

Benefits of Unattended Installations

As we've already indicated, unattended installations can save you time by allowing you to get on with other work while the installation process is happening. However, this benefit is even greater when you need to install the operating system on more than one machine. If you have to install Windows Server 2003 on several similar servers, you can set up a single answer file and set up all of the machines in the time it would normally take you to install just one copy of the OS. When setting up larger networks, this method becomes invaluable. Unfortunately, those answer files don't just write themselves!

Potential Problems and Solutions for Unattended Installations

In most cases, an unattended installation will not save you much time when setting up a single computer. That's because you have to create an answer file like the one you saw in Figure 2.1 to include all of the correct settings for your computer. In the time it would take to do that yourself, you would likely have been more than halfway through the parts of an attended installation that require your input. It can also be difficult to know exactly what those settings should be without first doing a lot of careful planning and, in most cases, running through at least one attended installation. Even if you know all of the settings and have everything perfectly planned out, a single typo can cause problems, thus wasting more time than was saved. However, if you're really interested in unattended installations, take some time to read the Inside Information sidebar titled "Answer File Aids" and try your hand at Lab Project 2.2 once you've finished the chapter.

In my personal experience, it is rarely necessary to install servers using an unattended install. In most cases, you are only configuring one or two servers at a time, and attended installs aren't too big of a hassle. However, unattended installs are frequently useful when deploying a large number of client operating systems, such as Windows XP or Windows 2000 Professional, so they are still worth knowing about.

Inside Information

Answer File Aids

If you do need to do an unattended installation, there are some tools and other resources that can make the job much easier. If you want to try your hand at creating an answer file using Notepad or another text editor, a help file called ref.chm is available on the Windows Server 2003 CD in the Deploy.cab file. Deploy.cab is located in the Tools subfolder of the Support folder on the installation CD. The ref.chm file is a comprehensive reference that documents every possible setting that can be configured in unattend.txt and several other specialized answer files.

An even more useful resource is the Setup Manager, which is also located in the Deploy.cab file as the file setupmgr.exe. The Setup Manager is an easy-to-use program that walks you through the creation of a basic setup file suitable for most situations. The utility allows you to configure all of the settings you would normally deal with during an attended installation, and it will even set the answer file up for use on multiple machines. As mentioned in the text, you'll find that Lab Project 2.2 at the end of the chapter provides an opportunity to use Setup Manager to create your own unattend.txt answer file. Once you've had the chance to perform an attended install of Windows Server 2003, you can work through the lab to get a feel for what's involved in preparing for an unattended install.

☑ Cross Check

Attended Versus Unattended Installations

Now that you've had a chance to learn about the two basic techniques for installing Windows Server 2003, let's take a minute to summarize what you've learned. If you like, review the preceding sections and answer the following questions:

1. In your own words summarize the process involved in conducting an attended installation and an unattended installation.

2. Describe a situation in which an attended installation would be the best option. When would you want to attempt an unattended installation?

Other Installation Options

There are so many variations on installation methods for Microsoft operating systems that it's hard to cover them all without getting too far off the beaten path. However, there are at least two other handy options I think you should know about.

Network Installations

In some cases, when installing on computers connected to an existing network, it's a good idea to place the installation files on a network share and access them over the network rather than from the CD. To do this, you need to copy the \I386 directory from the installation CD to a shared folder on the network and also place any other needed files (the answer files and device drivers, for instance) in that same folder. That folder should then be mapped to a drive letter on the machine you're installing the OS on. Mapping simply means that you configure the shared network folder to be treated like a drive so the installation program can find its files. This method takes a good bit of planning and advanced work, but it can save time if you have many installations to perform and don't want to run all over creation with a stack of CDs!

It's not a bad idea to keep the \I386 directory handy on the network even if you don't normally do your installations from the network. By keeping the installation files easily accessible, you avoid having to go hunting for a CD if you later add an operating system component you didn't initially install. Just make sure you are in complete compliance with all the terms of your licensing agreement.

Imaged Installations

If you ever need to set up Windows Server 2003 on several identical computers, you may want to make use of a **disk image**. A disk image is exactly what it sounds like: an exact image of a hard drive and all it contains. Disk images allow you to set up one machine, including the operating system and any applications you might want to install, and then make an image of that drive that can be copied to other, identical, computers. Although Windows Server 2003 doesn't make disk images (you need a separate utility for that), it does include some tools that can be used to set up the images and deploy them to other computers. Keep in mind, though, that disk images do require the computers to be identical. You cannot use images to install to many differently configured machines, which limits their usefulness somewhat. However, when you can use them, they can save a ton of time by installing both the OS and the applications all at once.

■ Preparing to Install Windows Server 2003

Although installing Windows Server 2003 isn't a complicated process, doing some preplanning is beneficial. Since the installation program asks the user to make several decisions during the process, making those decisions ahead of time can make the entire installation proceed more quickly. In addition, since some of these decisions can have a significant effect on the final capabilities of the operating system, making the right choices from the start can lead to a more effective server and a better-functioning network. Let's look at each of these decisions in turn.

Upgrade or Clean Installation?

The term **clean installation** refers to installing an operating system on a computer hard drive that has been wiped clean of any prior operating system or data. A clean installation is the recommended approach for any operating system, as it eliminates any chance of incompatibilities with older software and allows the new operating system maximum control over certain aspects of hardware configuration. Doing a clean installation is sort of like redecorating a room by removing everything in it first and starting from scratch. As you can imagine, this process can be more time consuming when it comes time to put everything back, but it does prevent any old problems from carrying over.

The alternative to a clean installation is an **upgrade installation**. During an upgrade installation, the new operating system replaces the existing operating system but preserves existing configuration settings and installed applications and data. The benefit of upgrade installations is that the new operating system is ready to go with minimal time needed to reinstall applications and reconfigure the hardware and the OS.

Windows Server 2003 can, in most cases, be installed as an upgrade to Windows NT 4.0 with Service Pack 5 or later installed, and Windows 2000. However, the recommendation from Microsoft is that Windows Server 2003 be installed using a clean install whenever possible. However, in some cases, the complexity of the existing network and the difficulty involved in reconfiguring the servers make the upgrade option extremely attractive! In situations where the network is simpler or the server in question is new, a clean installation is almost always the better option.

If you do choose to do an upgrade installation, the good news is the actual OS upgrade is ridiculously simple. You start the installation program by logging on to your current operating system and inserting the Windows Server 2003 CD. When the Microsoft Windows Server 2003 family dialog box appears, you choose the install option and click Next when prompted to use the upgrade installation. From there you simply accept the licensing agreement and enter the product key. That's all you've got to do to install the new OS. It's actually a much simpler process than what's required when doing a clean installation. However, there is a catch, as you knew there would be!

Before upgrading the OS of a server that administers a domain-based network, you've got some prep work to do. In such cases, it is necessary to ensure that the network itself, including the Active Directory mentioned in Chapter 1, and all the other key elements of the network are in perfect order and ready for the changeover. You see, when you upgrade a single machine, you only have to worry about one computer and maybe one or two user accounts. When you upgrade a server that administers a domain, you have to consider how the relatively simple change of OS at the server is going to affect the operation of the entire network and all of its clients. *That's* the tricky part about doing an upgrade.

Preparing for an upgrade of one or more domain controllers, which is what servers that administer a domain-based network are called, is best begun by starting the upgrade process as described a few paragraphs back. Shortly after the product key is entered, a dialog box will appear that summarizes any actions that need to be taken before, or even after, upgrading. At a minimum, there are a couple of simple command-line utilities that have to be run to prepare the Active Directory for the change. Additionally, there may be some tips on improving security after the upgrade and instructions on any after-upgrade actions that need to be taken. Once you've made note of the issues, you can cancel the installation, take the necessary actions, and restart the upgrade when everything is in order.

Keep in mind that relatively minor network problems that weren't troublesome under the old OS can become major problems under the new OS. That doesn't mean you should be afraid of upgrades; they can actually save a lot of work. Just take your time, carefully analyze the overall network configuration, and follow the suggestions the installation program provides, before you take those final, simple, installation steps. Additionally, if you do decide to do an upgrade installation, keep in mind that **downgrades** are not supported. What this means is that more powerful editions of previous operating systems, such as Windows 2000 Datacenter Server, may not be "upgraded" to a less-powerful edition of Windows Server 2003, such as Standard Edition or even Enterprise Edition. In this particular case, the only upgrade option is Windows Server 2003 Datacenter Edition.

For a complete list of the available upgrade paths supported by Windows Server 2003, point your browser to `http://www.microsoft.com/windowsserver2003/evaluation/whyupgrade/supportedpaths.mspx` .

Both clean installations and upgrade installations can be performed using either the attended or unattended methods discussed earlier in this chapter. However, upgrade installations are so easy and require so little input on the part of the user that unattended upgrades are relatively uncommon.

Partitioning

If you decide to perform a clean installation of Windows Server 2003, your next decision will be how to partition the hard drive. A hard drive **partition** is a discrete portion of a hard drive, which is used as the underlying structure for the organization of data on the drive. In the case of personal computers, a common practice is to create one large partition, regardless of the size of the drive, and store all data on that partition. Although the same thing can be done on a network server, there are certain advanced storage management techniques that benefit from having some nonpartitioned space available. By leaving some space unpartitioned, it can later be used for various purposes as needed. Space that has already been partitioned is essentially committed and cannot be easily reallocated. We'll discuss some of these advanced storage management techniques in Chapter 6, so we'll certainly want to leave ourselves some room to play!

The Windows Server 2003 installation program allows the user to install the operating system to an existing partition, delete existing partitions, or create new partitions of varying sizes. It's a good idea to decide ahead of time how much of the computer's hard drive should be allocated to the partition Windows Server 2003 will be installed on and how much should be left for later use. You may recall from Chapter 1 that the minimum hard drive space requirements for all editions ranges from 1.5GB to 2.0GB. However, you should never install any version of Windows Server 2003 on such small partitions. The OS itself takes up most of that space, leaving only a few hundred megabytes free. This can prevent you from later doing upgrades to newer versions of the OS and can cause the OS to run poorly. Because of those potential problems (and a healthy dose of "just-in-case!"), I like to set an initial partition size of at least 4GB or more. That ensures I have plenty of space to install the OS and any initial applications and utilities I might need before I get around to allocating the rest of the drive. It also leaves plenty of space for later service packs and other updates that can significantly increase the amount of hard drive space taken by the operating system.

File System

Although partitions form the underlying structure for storing data on a hard drive, they do not provide the actual organizing system. After partitions are created, they must be **formatted**. Formatting is the process that places the file system, which actually organizes the partition and tracks the locations of files, on the drive. The Windows Server 2003 installation program offers two basic alternatives when formatting partitions: NTFS or FAT. I'll tell you now that NTFS is, without a doubt, the way to go. However, let's take a brief look at why that is.

NTFS

As you might recall from Chapter 1, the NTFS file system was first introduced with Windows NT. NTFS offers a number of advantages that are important to a network operating system. For instance, NTFS allows the network administrator to set file- and folder-level access permissions that control not only access, but also what can be done with the files and folders that are accessed. This level of control is essential in most networks.

You might also remember that the current version of NTFS allows files to be encrypted, adding an additional layer of security, and permits selective compression of individual folders to improve storage management. In fact, there are so many benefits to be had from formatting a partition with NTFS, it's hard to imagine why Microsoft still supports the older FAT file system. In all actuality, the reason is pretty simple. The older file system is still available because older operating systems can't directly access NTFS-formatted partitions.

FAT

Although the FAT file system is a less-than-optimal choice when setting up most servers, it is an absolute necessity if you want to be able to boot the server using an older operating system that does not support NTFS and to still access your files. In some cases, administrators like to have the option available to boot into DOS for troubleshooting purposes. However, DOS cannot access a partition formatted in NTFS, so FAT becomes the only available option. The same situation exists if you want to be able to boot the system with Windows 95 or 98, since neither version supports NTFS.

The practice of troubleshooting a server by using older operating systems is not as common as it used to be. In the past, it was sometimes easier to fix problems and recover files from a failed server if you could do so from one of the other OSs. However, Windows Server 2003 provides extensive support for fixing operating system problems by booting from the installation CD and choosing the Recovery Console option depicted in Figure 2.2. Because this option exists, there is little likelihood that you would need to boot into an earlier operating system, and thus there is little reason to use the FAT file system.

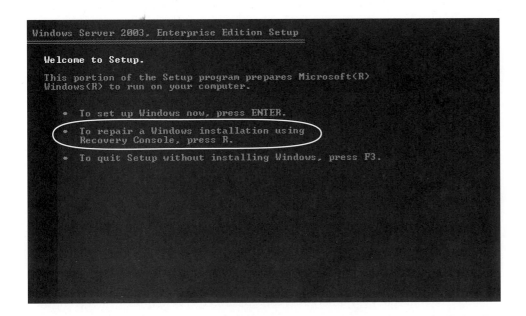

● **Figure 2.2**   Starting the Recovery Console from the installation CD

Chapter 2: Getting Started: Installing Windows Server 2003

Licensing

Microsoft offers two licensing modes for Windows Server 2003, and you must select which mode you are going to use when you install the operating system. The two modes are Per Server and Per Device or Per User. The difference between the two is subtle, but important to understand.

Per-Server Licensing

Per Server licensing is based on the total number of concurrent connections to a particular server. The default option, which matches the number of licenses included with the basic operating system package, is five concurrent connections. This licensing mode can be attractive to smaller networks, since it tends to be a cheaper option. Of course, it requires that the network administrator carefully plan for and monitor the number of concurrent connections to the server, but on smaller networks, that isn't too terribly difficult. The benefit is that more users can make use of the network for a cheaper overall price, as long as only a limited number connect at any one time.

Per-Device or Per-User Licensing

Per Device or Per User licensing used to be called Per Seat licensing. In my opinion, the old name seemed to make more sense. Basically, this licensing mode requires a license for every potential connection to the server (essentially every seat at every computer) but puts no limits on simultaneous connections. This can be advantageous for very large networks where planning for and controlling the number of connections might be impractical. It's also a recommended form of licensing on large networks where client devices connect to more than one server. However, this mode can be more expensive for smaller, simpler networks, and network administrators should plan carefully before deciding which mode makes more sense for their network.

If in doubt as to which mode to choose, select Per Server licensing and set the selector for the number of concurrent connections, as illustrated in Figure 2.3, to the value that matches the number of licenses you've purchased. If, at a later time, you decide you should be using Per Device or Per User licensing, you can change modes. However, you can only make this change one time, and only from Per Server to Per Device or Per User licensing, so be sure of your decision!

Server Name

Choosing the server's name is a deceptively simple decision. For one thing, it is just the name of the computer, and the installation program will even suggest one for us. On top of that, the name can be changed after the installation is complete with little difficulty. However, it is still worth giving this decision some thought because an awful lot depends on the moniker we give our new server!

In order for computers on a network to communicate with each other, it is essential that they all be uniquely identified. The name of each computer is part of its unique identity, and thus no two computers can have the same name. Users and administrators also need to be able to identify individual computers on the network. In those cases, it's not only important that the

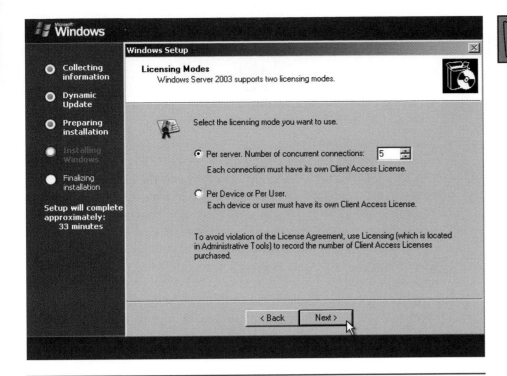

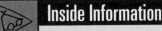
• Figure 2.3   Setting the licensing mode and number of concurrent connections

name be unique, it also helps if it is relatively simple and, well, sensible! As you'll eventually see, the installation program likes to suggest names like "ECKTEK-868MT6KV." Although that may certainly be unique (and how!) it doesn't say much about which machine it identifies, nor is it easy to type!

Of course, we could always go with the suggested name and change it later. It isn't hard to do, as you can see in Figure 2.4. However, as soon as our server is set up, begins to share resources, and becomes an integral part of

• Figure 2.4   Changing the server's name

the network, changes like that are likely to cause problems for other computers that try to access the server. For that reason alone, it makes sense to preplan a simple and sensible name for our server so that we get it right the first time.

Initial Password

If you're anything like me, you can probably think of at least a dozen instances when you need to use a password or personal identification number (PIN) to access an account, a service, a web site, or the like. And, like me, you've probably been tempted to use your dog's name or your birthday or something else easy to type and easy to remember. The problem, of course, is that those easy-to-type and easy-to-remember passwords are also easy for someone else to guess, which can lead to some major problems! Such a password is sometimes called a **weak password**.

Until we can equip our computers with super spy gadgets like fingerprint readers and retinal scanners, we have to depend on our passwords to keep our systems secure. When it comes to network servers, the password for the administrator account is the key to the whole shebang. If somebody can gain access to the server with that password, there isn't anything they can't do! What we want to create is a **strong password**, which is one that is designed to be very difficult to guess.

Creating a strong administrator password is really more of an art than it is a science. We can easily choose complicated strings of meaningless characters that no one will ever guess, but since we'll never remember them, we'll probably end up writing them down somewhere. That's as big a mistake as using Fido's name! What we have to do is choose a password we can remember without writing it down that is still next to impossible to guess. If you wait to choose a password until you are asked during installation, you may find yourself choosing something simple and easy to remember just to get on with the process. Planning the password ahead of time helps avoid that possibility.

Network Settings

The Windows Server 2003 installation program gives you two options for networking settings if it detects a network interface card installed in the server. The first option, called Typical settings, is just that, the typical networking settings used on most networked computers. Typical settings will configure the server to use the TCP/IP protocol suite and to obtain the proper IP address automatically. File and printer sharing will be installed, as will support for logging on to a Microsoft network.

The other available option, Custom settings, allows you to choose exactly which networking protocols and services you wish to run and allows you to configure them on the spot. Although this may be advisable in some situations, these settings are easily modified after installation is complete. In most cases, there is no need to custom-configure network settings during installation, especially if the server will be connecting to an existing network that supports TCP/IP and automatic addressing. I recommend leaving network configuration for later and going with the typical settings.

After configuring the networking settings, the installation program will also ask you to identify the workgroup or domain your computer will be joining. As was the case with the networking settings, this is an option that can be configured after the operating system is installed. However, if you know the name of the workgroup or domain your server will be joining, you may want to have that information handy during the installation process.

The new computer will be able to join the domain only if a computer account has already been created for it or if you are able to enter the username and password of a domain account that is authorized to join computers to the domain. In many cases, it is easier to join a domain after the operating system is installed. If you decide to do that, just leave the default option selected.

 Cross Check

Important Pre-Installation Decisions

We've discussed a number of things that need to be considered before performing an installation of Windows Server 2003. Let's take a moment to think about some of the more important decisions we have to make. If you like, review the preceding sections and answer the following questions:

1. In your opinion, what are three of the most important decisions that should be made prior to installing Windows Server 2003?

2. Explain why the three decisions you've chosen are so important.

Step-by-Step 2.4

Creating an Installation Plan for Windows Server 2003

As you've read, there are a number of decisions to be made prior to beginning an installation of Windows Server 2003. In addition to the decisions you need to make, there are some other pieces of information that you will be asked for during the installation process. This Step-by-Step will help you create a planning document to follow when you actually install the OS later in this chapter. This same planning sheet can be used when setting up automated installations, which we'll be discussing in the next section.

Please consult with your instructor when necessary to obtain the correct information for your lab setup.

Also remember that, in a non-lab situation, this document would have to be well protected prior to installation and destroyed afterward because it will contain your initial administrator password.

To complete this Step-by-Step, you will need

■ A copy of the table printed at the end of this Step-by-Step (see Table 2.1), or a similar form

■ Information from your instructor concerning lab-specific settings

Step 1

Obtain from your instructor the capacity of the hard drive you will be using to install Windows Server 2003. Decide how much space will be allocated to the partition you will create during the installation and record this information in the appropriate place on the planning form. Try to allocate at least 4000MB (roughly 4GB) to this partition while still leaving some space unpartitioned for later use. Be sure to allow at least 1.5GB of space, since this is the minimum space required for the 32-bit versions of any edition of Windows Server 2003.

Step 2

Decide what file system you will use to format the operating system's partition. You can choose between NTFS and FAT, but the NTFS file system will be required for later exercises in this text. You can also choose between a regular format and a quick format. Since the quick format does not thoroughly check the hard drive for errors, you should avoid it unless told otherwise by your instructor. Record your choices on the planning form.

Step 3

While installing Windows Server 2003, you will be asked to enter the 25-character Product Key from the packaging that contained the installation CD. It's a good idea to have this Product Key recorded somewhere safe in case the original packaging should become lost. It's also not a bad idea to record it on your planning form, in large, clear letters and numbers, so that it is easy to read when the time comes to enter it. The case of the letters is not important. Record your Product Key on the planning form.

Step 4

Check with your instructor as to which licensing mode you will be using and record your choice. Since this is a lab situation, you will most likely use the default option, which is Per Server. If you are using the Per Server option, also record the number of concurrent connections you will be configuring. The default option is five.

Step 5

Decide on a computer name for the server and record it in the appropriate place on the planning form. Keep in mind that the name must be unique on the network and should also be brief and descriptive. If necessary, consult with your instructor on this decision and coordinate with the other students in the lab.

Step 6

Choose a strong initial password for the Administrator account. Remember that a strong password is at least six characters long, does not contain any form of the word "administrator," and consists of upper- and lowercase letters, numbers, and special characters. Record your initial password on the planning form but keep in mind that this piece of information must be protected under non-lab conditions.

Step 7

Consult with your instructor as to whether you will be using the typical networking settings or customizing the settings. If you will be using custom settings, ask your instructor for detailed instructions and record them, using additional paper if necessary. Otherwise, record "typical" in the appropriate place on your planning form.

Step 8

If your computer will be joining an existing workgroup, record the name of the workgroup in the appropriate space on your planning form. If your computer will be joining an existing domain, record the name of the domain and the username and password of the domain account that is authorized to join the computer to the domain. Your instructor can provide you with this information.

■ Installing and Activating Windows Server 2003

Now that we've chosen our installation method and finished our preplanning, there's nothing left to stop us from installing Windows Server 2003. Once we get the operating system installed, we'll discuss testing the installation and activating the product with Microsoft.

Performing an Attended Installation

If you haven't yet prepared the Windows Server 2003 Installation Planning Sheet from Step-by-Step 2.4, please do so before beginning the installation process.

In the following Step-by-Step, you are going to install your own copy of Windows Server 2003. You'll be making use of the planning sheet you prepared earlier to do a clean, attended installation using the Windows Server 2003 CD. This is probably the most commonly used installation method and has much in common with the other variations we've discussed.

Table 2.1 **Windows Server 2003 Installation Planning Sheet**

Partition Size (in MB) *Should be a minimum of 1500MB. 4000MB or more recommended.*		**Initial Administrator password** *Follow recommendations for strong passwords.*	
File System for this partition *Should use NTFS. Should not use quick format.*		**Typical or custom networking settings** *Record custom settings if necessary.*	
Product Key *Case does not matter.*		**Enter workgroup name if joining a workgroup**	
Licensing mode and number of concurrent connections *Number of concurrent connections is for Per Server mode only.*		**Enter domain name if joining a domain** *Have ready the username and password of a domain administrator's account authorized to join the computer to the domain.*	
Computer Name *Make sure the name will be unique on the network.*			

Step-by-Step 2.5

Performing an Attended Installation of Window Server 2003

We're going to do an attended, rather than an unattended, installation of Windows Server 2003 because it allows us to talk about each of the required steps as we encounter them. After you've done a couple of attended installations, you'll be comfortable enough with the process that performing unattended installations should be a pretty easy transition. If you've had the opportunity to install Windows 2000 or Windows XP (any version), you'll find that this process is already pretty familiar to you.

To complete this Step-by-Step, you will need

- A fully equipped computer, configured to boot from the CD drive, that has been verified as compatible with Windows Server 2003. Ideally, this computer will meet the recommended requirements for the edition being installed and have a hard drive of 6GB or greater.

- The Windows Server 2003 installation CD

- The Windows Server 2003 Product Key from the CD packaging

- The Windows Server 2003 Installation Planning Sheet from Step-by-Step 2.4

- A connection to a working TCP/IP Windows network with Internet access, preferably providing DHCP support. If DHCP is not running, the instructor will need to provide proper network settings.

Note: This Step-by-Step assumes that you will be doing a completely clean installation and that all existing hard drive partitions will be removed and the disk repartitioned. If this is not the case, please carefully follow your instructor's directions.

Step 1

Insert the Windows Server 2003 installation CD in your CD drive and perform a complete restart of the computer. When the computer restarts, watch for the prompt to press any key to boot from the CD. As soon as you see that prompt, press the SPACEBAR.

Step 2

When the computer boots from the CD, a blue Windows Setup screen will appear and for a couple of minutes the installation program will load a variety of setup files into RAM. Wait until you see the Welcome to Setup screen and press ENTER to begin the Windows setup.

```
Windows Server 2003, Enterprise Edition Setup

    Welcome to Setup.

    This portion of the Setup program prepares Microsoft(R)
    Windows(R) to run on your computer.

        •  To set up Windows now, press ENTER.

        •  To repair a Windows installation using
           Recovery Console, press R.

        •  To quit Setup without installing Windows, press F3.
```

Step 3

When the Windows Licensing Agreement appears, you may read through it by using the PAGE UP and PAGE DOWN keys to navigate. When you are finished reading the agreement, accept it by pressing the F8 key. If you do not agree and press the ESC key, the installation process will terminate, so you really don't have much choice about accepting the agreement!

```
Windows Licensing Agreement

    END-USER LICENSE AGREEMENT FOR 180-DAY
    EVALUATION OF MICROSOFT SOFTWARE

    MICROSOFT WINDOWS SERVER 2003, STANDARD EDITION
    EVALUATION VERSION
    MICROSOFT WINDOWS SERVER 2003, ENTERPRISE EDITION
    EVALUATION VERSION

    PLEASE READ THIS END-USER LICENSE AGREEMENT
    ("EULA") CAREFULLY.  BY INSTALLING OR USING
    THE SOFTWARE THAT ACCOMPANIES THIS EULA
    ("SOFTWARE"), YOU AGREE TO THE TERMS OF THIS
    EULA.  IF YOU DO NOT AGREE, DO NOT USE THE
    SOFTWARE AND, IF APPLICABLE, RETURN IT TO THE
    PLACE OF PURCHASE.

    THE SOFTWARE CONTAINS FUNCTIONALITY THAT
    IS TIME-SENSITIVE AND DESIGNED TO CEASE
    FUNCTIONING AFTER A CERTAIN PERIOD.  PLEASE
    REFER TO SECTION 2.e FOR DETAILS.

    THIS SOFTWARE DOES NOT TRANSMIT ANY
    PERSONALLY IDENTIFIABLE INFORMATION FROM YOUR
    SERVER TO MICROSOFT COMPUTER SYSTEMS WITHOUT
    YOUR CONSENT.

      1. GENERAL.  This EULA is a legal agreement between you (either
```

The next screen you see will display information about any existing partitions that are on the computer's hard drive. Please follow your instructor's directions at this point, but ideally, you will delete all existing partitions and create one new partition of about 4000MB.

```
Windows Server 2003, Enterprise Edition Setup

   The following list shows the existing partitions and
   unpartitioned space on this computer.

   Use the UP and DOWN ARROW keys to select an item in the list.

     •  To set up Windows on the selected item, press ENTER.

     •  To create a partition in the unpartitioned space, press C.

     •  To delete the selected partition, press D.

   16379 MB Disk 0 at Id 0 on bus 0 on atapi [MBR]
         C:  Partition1 [FAT32]              16379 MB ( 16374 MB free)
```

Note: The partitions and the partition sizes you see in the screen shots will be different from what your screen will display. Please use the recommended sizes given in this step or follow your instructor's directions.

To delete an existing partition, highlight it by using the cursor keys and then press D. If this is your only partition, you will be asked to confirm your choice twice by first pressing ENTER and then by pressing L. If this is not your only partition, you may only be asked to press L to confirm. If at any time before pressing L you should change your mind, you can cancel the deletion by pressing ESC. Delete all existing partitions if there is more than one.

Caution: If you delete a partition, you will lose all information stored on that partition. Please check with your instructor before deleting any partitions!

Create a new partition on the unpartitioned space by pressing C. You will then be prompted to enter the size of the partition. The possible minimum and maximum values for this partition will be displayed, and the size will be set to the maximum by default. Do not use the maximum unless told to by your instructor. Backspace over the default value and enter the partition size you recorded on your planning sheet from Step-by-Step 2.4. The partition must be at least 1.5GB, and you should try to leave some space (at least a gigabyte or more) unpartitioned for later use. Press ENTER to create the partition.

After the new partition has been created, make sure it is highlighted and press ENTER to install Windows Server 2003 to this partition.

Select the appropriate file system with which to format the newly created partition. Use the system that you recorded on your planning sheet from Step-by-Step 2.4. This should be the NTFS file system. Do not select the quick format option, as this does not fully examine the hard drive for potential errors. Press ENTER to format the partition with your selected file system.

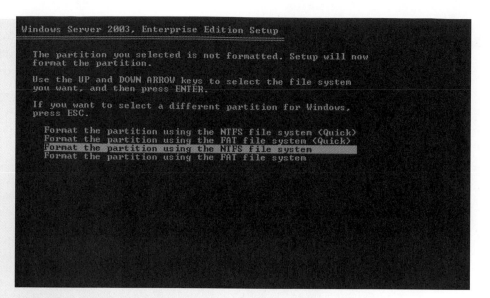

At this point, the installation program will check the drive for errors, set up the file system, and begin to copy over the necessary setup files. Eventually the installation program will reboot the computer and start up in graphical mode to begin the next stage of the installation process.

Step 6

About five minutes after rebooting into graphical mode, the installation program will ask you to confirm your regional settings. Unless you are in a country other than the United States and need support for a non-U.S. keyboard, you should click Next.

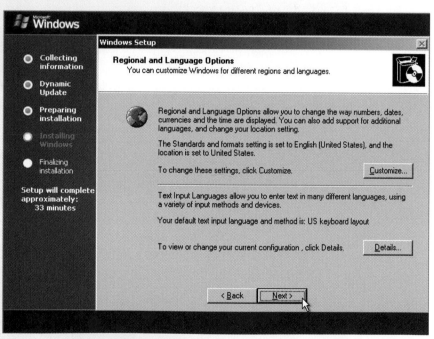

Step 7

When prompted to personalize your software, enter your name, or the name given to you by your instructor. It isn't necessary to enter an organization name, but you may do so. After entering the information, click Next.

Step 8

Carefully enter the 25-character Product Key you recorded on your planning sheet. It is not necessary to move from field to field; just type the key characters in order and they will be put in the correct boxes. When the Product Key is entered correctly, click Next. If you should make a mistake in typing the key, you will receive an error message. Correct the mistake and then click Next.

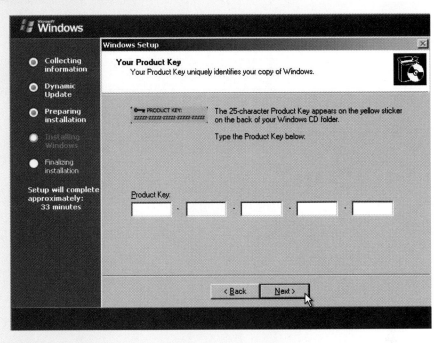

Step 9

Select the licensing mode you recorded on your planning sheet. If you select the Per Server mode, make sure to set the number of concurrent connections correctly. Click Next.

Step 10

Enter the computer name you recorded on your planning sheet. Also enter and confirm your initial password for the administrator account. Click Next.

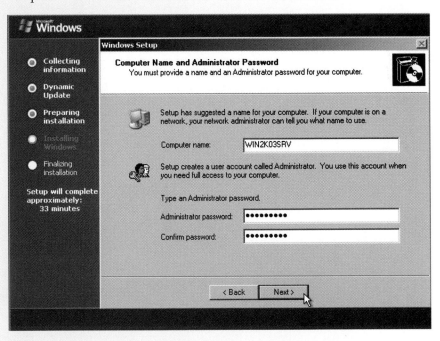

Step 11

If your computer is equipped with a modem, you will be prompted next for your modem dialing information. Make the correct options for your location and click Next. Once you've done that, or if you didn't have a modem, you will next see the Date and Time Settings dialog box. Set the date, time, and time zone, and click Next.

Step 12

After a pause of a few minutes, you will see the Networking Settings screen. Select either the typical or the custom settings as indicated on your planning sheet and click Next.

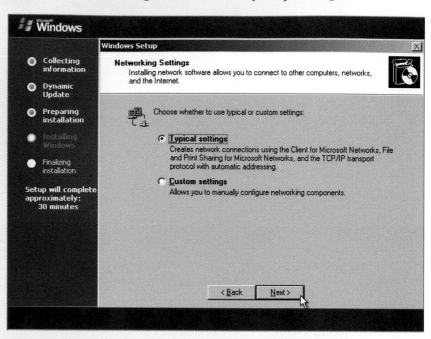

Note: If you select the custom settings, you will be asked to configure your networking components. Please follow your instructor's directions.

Step 13

The final choice you need to make is whether or not this computer will be joining a workgroup or computer domain. If you want to accept the default option, click Next. Otherwise, refer to your planning sheet for your preferred option. Remember that if you choose to join a domain, you will be prompted for the username and password of an account that can join your computer to the domain. In any case, these settings can be changed after the installation is finished.

Step 14

From this point, the installation process can continue without your intervention. After about 20 to 30 minutes, the installation should end with a final reboot of the computer and Windows Server 2003 should start for the first time. When you see the Welcome to Windows logon prompt appear, you'll know you've successfully installed the operating system!

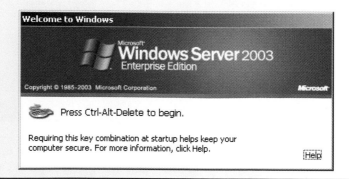

Testing the Installation

Testing the installation of Windows Server 2003 is really pretty easy. The first indication that everything went well is that the system successfully reboots into the new operating system at the end of the installation process. After that, it's a simple matter of logging on and taking a look around.

Logging on to Windows Server 2003

Windows Server 2003 uses the same logon procedure as Windows 2000 did. The logon prompt that appears after the computer boots, as depicted in Figure 2.5, requires the user to press CTRL-ALT-DELETE in order to log on. This keystroke combination is meant to defeat any possible malicious programs that might be trying to record user names and passwords by displaying fake logon prompts.

After you press CTRL-ALT-DELETE, Windows Server 2003 displays the Log On to Windows dialog box shown in Figure 2.6, with spaces to enter the user name and password. Once the user enters the correct user name and password and clicks OK, the computer will finish loading Windows and the desktop will appear. Since no other user accounts have been created at this point, the first logon to Windows would be done using the administrator account and password.

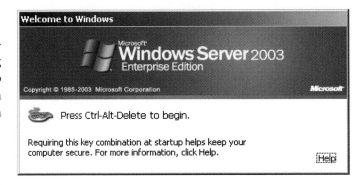

● **Figure 2.5** The Welcome to Windows logon prompt

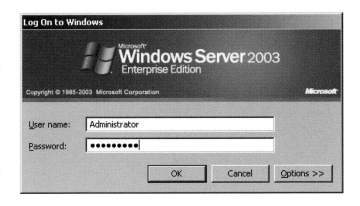

● **Figure 2.6** The Log On to Windows dialog box

 Try This!

Go Exploring!

The first time a new operating system loads, it's completely natural to want to go exploring. Take a moment to poke around the Windows Server 2003 desktop and see what's new. To complete this task, you will need a computer with Windows Server 2003 installed. Try this:

1. If you've not used Windows Server 2003 or Windows XP before, you'll probably be surprised at how empty the desktop is. Click Start and you'll see that the Start menu is also changed from Windows 9x.

2. From the Start menu, you'll notice that Programs is now called All Programs. Point to All Programs and you'll see that the menu still contains the usual groups, such as Accessories and System Tools.

3. You may have noticed that My Computer is now on the Start menu, rather than the desktop. Click My Computer and you'll see that the window looks a little different from both Windows 9x and Windows XP.

4. Continue exploring until you feel you're comfortable with the changes to the interface of the operating system. Make sure to ask questions of your instructor if you run across something you don't understand.

The Options button on the Log On to Windows dialog box controls whether or not the Shutdown button is available when logging on. When the computer is a member of a domain, the Options button will also make it possible to choose between logging on to the local computer or the domain. You'll get a chance to see that function of the Options button in a later chapter.

You can safely close the Manage Your Server window for now. You will be making use of it later in this text.

The first time Windows Server 2003 starts, a special window titled Manage Your Server appears. This window presents a variety of options for configuring the operating system to handle certain server roles. This window will continue to appear at each logon unless the user disables it. Even if it is disabled, the Manage Your Server window may be redisplayed at any time by selecting Start | Administrative Tools | Manage Your Server.

Microsoft Product Activation and Windows Server 2003

Software piracy, or the illicit copying and distribution of software, is a problem that plagues all software companies. Microsoft feels the effects of this issue even more than some, due to the demand for and the nature of their products, and the company has been trying for some time to reduce its exposure to software piracy. The Product Key code that was requested during the installation process was one strategy Microsoft employed. Without the key, you can't install the software. However, the key is easy to copy right along with the CD, and so the overall effect on reducing piracy was slight.

Microsoft Product Activation (MPA) is a relatively new approach to reducing piracy of operating systems, office suites, and other product offerings from Microsoft. Through MPA, products like Windows Server 2003 must be activated within a limited number of days or they will cease to work. Products can only be activated on one computer system, thus eliminating the value of illicit copies of the software. The process works through a combination of codes that identify both the unique copy of the software and the hardware it is being run on and record that information with Microsoft in such a way that later attempts to activate the same software on different hardware will be denied. The recorded information in no way

Try This!

More Information on Product Activation

Since Product Activation is a relatively new concept, it's sometimes a little hard to understand. You can read some additional information on Microsoft's web site about Product Activation and Windows Server 2003. To complete this task, you will need a computer with Internet access and a web browser. Try this:

1. Point your browser to `http://www.microsoft.com/windowsserver2003/techinfo/overview/activation.mspx`.

2. Read the information about Product Activation. Pay special attention to the sections that discuss reactivation. What is the time limit if reactivation is required?

3. Read the section that explains the difference between Product Activation and Registration. What is the difference?

4. If possible, discuss with your classmates and instructor how you feel about Product Activation.

identifies the user, only the copy of the software and the hardware it is installed on. The process is also very easy to go through.

Shortly after installing Windows Server 2003, you will be reminded that you need to activate the software within so many days. The time limit is currently set to 30 days after installation for retail versions of the operating system. During the "grace" period, the software will work normally and is in no way disabled. However, if the product has not been activated by the end of the time period, it will become inaccessible to the user until it is activated.

To activate Windows Server 2003, go to Start | All Programs | Accessories | System Tools | Activate Windows. The Activate Windows window shown in Figure 2.7 will appear, allowing you to choose activation over the Internet or the telephone, or else to defer activation to a later time with periodic reminders. If you choose to activate over the Internet and you have a working connection, the entire process takes a few seconds and requires no other interaction from you. If you choose to activate over the telephone, you will be given a number to call and a 50-digit code that represents your software and your hardware. A Microsoft representative will record your code as you read it and give you a 42-digit activation code that you must enter at your end. Activating by telephone takes about ten minutes, in my experience, and is still relatively hassle-free.

> The grace period for evaluation versions of Windows Server 2003 is only 14 days. The limit for versions distributed through the Microsoft Developers Network (MSDN) is 60 days.

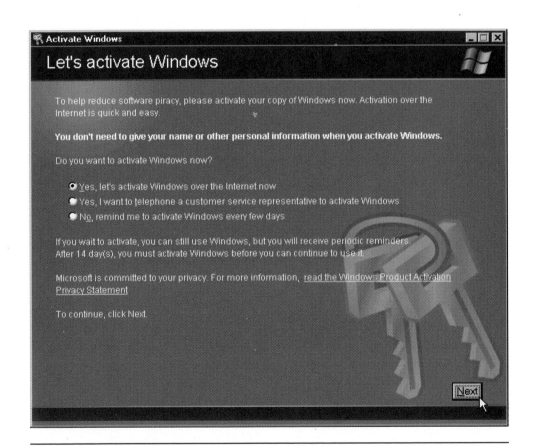

• **Figure 2.7**   Microsoft Product Activation for Windows Server 2003

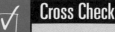
■ Updating Windows Server 2003

It's an inescapable fact of life: operating systems are never perfect nor are they ever quite finished. No matter how hard the developers work at it, it seems impossible to eliminate every bug and close every security loophole. At the same time, the needs of users continue to change after the OS is released, leading to new features, and new hardware comes out that requires new drivers. The long and the short of it is, sooner or later you're going to have to update your operating system.

In the past, updating an operating system was a time-consuming and inefficient process. You had to constantly keep yourself informed with what updates were available from the OS manufacturer as well as the manufacturers of all of your hardware components. You then had to go through the rigmarole of obtaining and installing all of those updates more or less manually. The icing on the cake was, if you go back far enough, you sometimes had to wait for the updates to arrive on disks or CDs because they either weren't available online (I told you we were going back a bit!) or they were too large to download in a reasonable amount of time. Things have gotten better, though, thanks to Windows Update.

Using Windows Update

Windows Update is a web-based service built into the newer Microsoft operating systems that allows for quick and easy checking for updates and installing of updates. Windows Update not only makes it easy to correct critical flaws in the operating system, it also becomes a single point source for new features and updated device drivers that sometimes add new functionality. Let's run our newly installed copy of Windows Server 2003 through Windows Update and see how it works.

Running Windows Update

Although Windows Update can be configured to run automatically, a process we'll cover in a bit, it can also be run on demand. Once we've contacted the Windows Update web site, it will scan our computer and operating system and then report back to us which, if any, updates are currently available for our setup. I know that many people are concerned about privacy on the Internet, and the idea of allowing a web site to scan your system might sound a little intrusive. Actually, the scan is completely anonymous and no personal information is being collected. Microsoft *cannot* identify who you are through Windows Update. The scan is merely checking to see what you've got so that it can tell you what you need. Have no fear.

To complete this Step-by-Step, you will need

- A computer with Windows Server 2003 installed and Internet access

- Administrator-level access to the computer. You may use the administrator account that was created during installation

Step 1

Start the computer and log on as the administrator. Click Start | All Programs | Windows Update. In a few seconds, an Internet Explorer window should open and the Windows Update web site should load. Maximize the window if necessary.

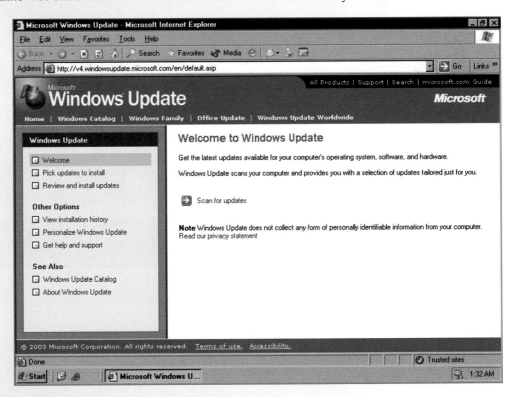

Step 2

Click the Scan for updates link and wait for the scan to complete. You should see a progress percentage near the top of the screen on the right-hand pane. The scans usually don't take very long, even on slower connections.

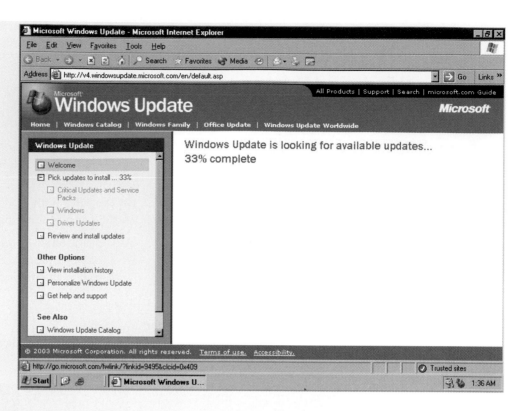

When the scan is finished, you will see information on the right-hand side of the screen reporting the general nature of your results. More detailed information is available by clicking the available update categories on the left-hand pane. The three categories are Critical Updates and Service Packs; Windows Server 2003 family; and Driver Updates. If a number other than a zero appears after one of these categories, you can click the link to display the details of the updates in the left-hand pane.

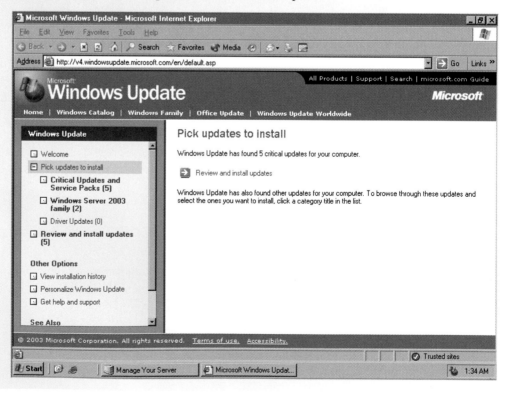

Step 4

Once you've reviewed an update, you can click Add to select it as an update you would like to download and install. Be aware that some updates must be installed separately from other updates. These are usually clearly marked as such, and you will be informed if you try to select them with other updates. After selecting all of the updates you want to install from each of the categories, you can click the Review and install updates link.

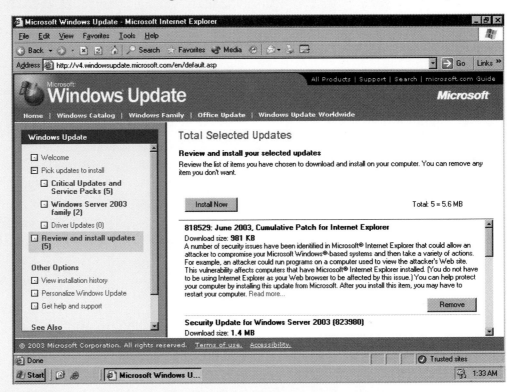

Caution: Since some updates can be quite large and take a long time to download and install, do not install any updates in the next step without specific permission from your instructor. After reviewing the updates, simply close the Internet Explorer window.

Step 5

If you were ready to install the updates you selected, you would normally click Install Now to begin the process. Do not install any updates at this time unless told to by your instructor. Keep in mind that some updates require a reboot of the system after they have been installed. Because of this, it is a good idea to save all open files and shut down all other running programs before beginning the Windows Update process. Unless you are installing updates, you may now close the Internet Explorer window.

Update Categories

You may have noticed in Step-by-Step 2.6 that there were three different categories of updates listed. In reality, there are actually at least four categories of updates that you might encounter, so we should probably take a moment to define what they are.

Try This!

The Windows Update Privacy Policy

If you are one of those folks I mentioned that have some concerns about Windows Update and privacy, you might want to read the Windows Update Privacy Statement. You can access this statement through Windows Server 2003's Help and Support. To complete this task, you will need a computer with Windows Server 2003 installed. Try this:

1. Click Start, and then click Help and Support.

2. In the search box, type **Windows Update Privacy Statement** and then click the white arrow with the green background that appears to the right of the search box.

3. After the search is complete, click the second link listed under Help Topics. This link should be labeled Windows Update Privacy Statement: Windows Automatic Updating.

4. Read the statement to find out what kind of information is collected by the Windows Update process. Pay special attention to the discussion of the Globally Unique Identifier (GUID).

5. If possible, discuss with your classmates and your instructor how you feel about Windows Update and your privacy after reading this statement.

Critical Updates

Although critical updates are listed with service packs, they are actually two separate types of updates. A **critical update** is an update that addresses a security flaw or a problem that could result in serious data loss or system failure. In most cases, critical updates are exactly that: updates that address critical areas of concern that need to be addressed as soon as possible. It's a good practice to scan regularly for critical updates and install them as soon as possible.

Service Packs

Service packs aren't technically updates. A **service pack** is actually a collection of many different updates, improvements, and sometimes additions to the operating system that is released after extensive testing. Service packs are major updates to an operating system and are typically numbered and released periodically throughout the life of the operating system. In most cases, installing service packs is a good idea and may even be necessary in order to use certain applications or to upgrade the operating system to the next version.

Windows Server 2003 Family

The update category Windows, which is renamed Windows Server 2003 family after the Windows Update scan is complete, usually includes minor refinements and additions to the operating system. This is also the category where new components or new versions of components are made available. For example, if Microsoft updates Internet Explorer, the new version would be listed in this category. Most updates in this category are optional but can add new features or improvements to existing features.

Driver Updates

A **driver update** is an improvement to the software programs that allow hardware components, such as video cards and printers, to communicate with the operating system. Not all driver updates will be listed here, but those that are have been tested as compatible with the operating system you are running. Installing updated device drivers is almost always a good idea.

Configuring Windows Update

In addition to running Windows Update manually, the utility can also be configured to scan for updates according to a schedule and even download and install them automatically. To access the configuration settings for Windows Update, click the Start button, right-click My Computer, select Properties, and click the Automatic Updates tab.

The Automatic Update Settings

The first setting you'll notice on the Automatic Updates tab is a check box that says Keep my computer up to date. This check box allows Windows Update to check for and install updates to its own software before downloading and installing any updates you might select. It's generally a good idea to leave this option selected, as these updates can improve the efficiency with which Windows Update does its job.

The Settings section of the Automatic Updates tab provides three options for how Windows Update goes about getting and installing updates.

Notify Before Downloading The first option places Windows Update into a more-or-less manual mode. The utility will still receive information from Microsoft when you are connected to the Internet about available updates, and you will be informed that new updates are available. However, from that point on, the process will be similar to running Windows Update the way we did in Step-by-Step 2.6.

Download Updates and Notify Before Installing This option allows Windows Update to transfer the update files to your computer as they become available but enables you to review them and choose which you actually want to install. This option can be quite a time-saver to those who have an "always-on" connection to the Internet, since even the largest updates will be almost immediately available for installation because they've been downloaded in the background.

Automatically Download and Install The last option allows the user to schedule when updates should be downloaded and installed. This option will automatically install all available updates and automatically reboot the system if the updates require it. I am personally not a big fan of this method because I tend to leave web pages I plan to look at and files I am working on open on my computer overnight. When this option is selected, I find that my windows and files have been closed and the computer rebooted while I was not looking! Call me a control freak, but I like to know when my computer is going to restart. Although I've never actually lost data while using this method, I tend to avoid it anyway.

■ Troubleshooting Common Installation Problems

Although most installations of Windows Server 2003 go off without a hitch, things do happen. Most installation problems are relatively easy to fix, and most aren't due to anything serious. Let's take a look at some troubled individuals and what their problems, and solutions, might be.

Can't Install

Both Robert and his buddy Drew have been trying to install Windows Server 2003 on different computers. Robert's been trying to install his as an upgrade to his Windows XP Professional system so that he can retain all of his programs and settings. However, the installation program keeps displaying a message that says he can't do that. Drew wants to do a clean installation on his Windows 98 machine, but each time he inserts the installation CD and starts his computer, he ends up back on his old operating system.

Unsupported Upgrade Path

Windows Server 2003 can be used to upgrade some previous versions of Windows but not all. In Robert's case, even though he is using a very recent operating system, the Windows Server 2003 upgrade path does not support it. Only Microsoft network operating systems are supported for upgrades. In addition, as mentioned in the section "Upgrade or Clean Installation?" earlier in this chapter, there is a limitation as to which versions can be used to upgrade to each edition.

CD Drive Is Not Bootable

If we can correctly assume that Drew's installation CD is not defective and his computer is otherwise compatible with Windows Server 2003, we can fix his problem pretty easily. One possibility is that his computer is not properly configured to allow booting from the CD drive. His computer may not support bootable CDs (which would be pretty unlikely if the computer was otherwise compatible), or he may need to reconfigure his system BIOS to allow for it.

The other possible problem is one of human error. Most computers require the user to press a key to get the machine to boot from the CD drive. If

For more information on upgrade paths, point your browser to http://www.microsoft.com/windowsserver2003/evaluation/whyupgrade/supportedpaths.mspx on the Internet.

The term BIOS stands for Basic Input/Output System. A computer's BIOS controls the computer during the boot process, before the operating system loads, and also plays an important role in allowing the OS to communicate with the system hardware. In addition to many other settings, the BIOS allows the user to control whether or not the computer will boot from the CD drive, if it has that capability.

the user does not press the key soon enough, the computer will boot from the hard drive and thus start the existing operating system. I, for one, won't laugh at Drew if this is the case. It's been known to happen to the best of us. My students thought it was quite funny when I missed the prompt twice in a row!

Installation Aborts

Today just doesn't seem to be Anna's day. The first two times she tried to install Windows Server 2003, the installation kept getting "hung up" and froze midway through at the same point. After a little research, she discovered that the network card she had installed was not listed as compatible on the HCL. Once she replaced the network card, the installation seemed to be going without a hitch. At least, it was until she knocked the plug out of the wall! After three tries, she's getting a little tired of repartitioning, reformatting, and reinstalling over and over again.

Resuming a Failed Installation

We've all had days like Anna's, and Microsoft knew that it was possible for an installation to freeze or a computer to be shut down in mid-install. That's why, in most cases, an installation can be restarted and picked up where you left off.

Once the install program reboots into the graphical interface, the operating system is essentially running off the hard drive and is configuring itself. In such cases, you can simply rectify the problem (put that plug back in the wall!) and reboot the machine; the installation will pick up where it left off. In those rare cases when an installation fails during the text mode portion, it might be necessary to repartition and reformat. However, those situations are thankfully rare.

Post-Installation Problems

Lauren can't quite pin down what's wrong with her computer, but something isn't quite right. She was able to upgrade her Windows 2000 system to Windows Server 2003 without a hitch and has been using it for several days. However, it seems she's experiencing far more crashes and errors than she should be with an operating system of this caliber. To date she's had problems every time she's tried to print and numerous problems transferring files over her network. She's really beginning to feel that her computer may be haunted!

Addressing Unexpected Performance Problems

Lauren just might be right. It's quite possible that her machine is "haunted" by outdated software and drivers. Some of her device drivers, such as the one for her printer, may not be fully compatible with her new operating system, and that could be causing some of her problems. Some of her other difficulties could be due to older applications that might have behaved okay under Windows 2000 but, for whatever reason, are not working correctly under Windows Server 2003. My first suggestion to Lauren would be to check for driver and application updates and see if that helps.

Lauren's machine could also be haunted by internal demons within the operating system itself. Perhaps her unique combination of hardware and software is triggering a flaw in Windows Server 2003. In that case, a visit to Windows Update might correct her problems by providing an upgrade to whatever in the operating system isn't working correctly.

If all else fails, Lauren might need a complete exorcism. Sometimes there are problems with a particular computer that are just about impossible to pin down. In such cases, it sometimes helps to start from scratch. We might suggest to Lauren as a final option that she back up all of her data and reinstall Windows Server 2003, this time as a clean installation. It's a bit of a hassle, but sometimes starting over really does give you a fresh start.

Chapter 2 Review

■ Chapter Summary

After reading this chapter and completing the Step-by-Step tutorials and Try This! exercises, you should understand the following facts about installing Windows Server 2003.

Check Hardware Compatibility

■ Microsoft's Windows Upgrade Advisor utility, which can be run from the installation CD, provides an easy method for checking hardware compatibility prior to installing the OS. However, this utility can only be run on computers with installed operating systems that are eligible for upgrade to Windows Server 2003.

■ The Windows Server Catalog is an online tool for checking hardware compatibility without using the Windows Upgrade Advisor. It is available at `http://www.microsoft.com/windows/catalog/server/`.

■ The Windows Server Catalog replaces the Hardware Compatibility List (HCL), which was the primary compatibility reference for Windows 2000.

Choose an Installation Method

■ An attended installation requires the user to be present throughout the process to respond to queries by the installation program. They require little preparation but can take 45 minutes or longer to complete.

■ Unattended installations make use of an answer file to respond to all installation program queries. They save time by allowing for multiple, similar installations to occur simultaneously without user monitoring.

■ Editing the answer file for unattended installations requires preparation and can be time consuming. Some errors can actually cause the process to run slower than an attended installation.

■ Installation files can also be hosted in a network shared folder, thus eliminating the need to use a CD.

■ In some cases, a completely installed and configured computer can be imaged and that image can be used to set up identical computers, saving a significant amount of time.

Make Pre-Installation Decisions

■ Windows Server 2003 can be installed as a clean installation or as an upgrade installation. There are some limits as to which operating systems can be upgraded.

■ The Windows Server 2003 installation program allows the user to manage hard drive partitions. It's a common practice to create a partition smaller than the entire drive's capacity, thus retaining capacity for later storage management.

■ Although Windows Server 2003 will format partitions as either FAT or NTFS, the NTFS file system is the preferred option. Use FAT only if it will be necessary to directly access the partition after booting from an earlier operating system that does not support NTFS.

■ Windows Server 2003 supports Per Server and Per Device or Per User licensing. Per Server licensing is based on the number of concurrent connections to the server, while Per Device or Per User licensing is based on the total number of potential connections within the network to any server on the network.

■ Although the server's name can be changed at a later time, it is wise to plan out the name so that a simple and yet unique name may be chosen from the beginning. Changing the name after the network has been set up can cause problems in sharing resources.

■ When creating the initial administrator password, weak, easy to guess passwords should be avoided. Strong passwords consist of six or more characters and include a mixture of upper- and lowercase letters, numbers, and symbols.

■ The administrator password must be vigorously protected, as the administrator account has complete control over the server and the network.

■ The typical networking settings configure the server to use the TCP/IP protocol and automatic addressing. If the user chooses the custom option, they need to manually configure the networking settings.

Install and Activate Windows Server 2003

- After installing Windows Server 2003, the user should check to see that they can log on to the computer using the administrator account.

- The first time Windows Server 2003 is booted, the Manage Your Server window will appear. This window allows for easy configuration of the operating system to handle certain server roles. The window can be redisplayed at any time by selecting Start | Administrative Tools | Manage Your Server.

- Microsoft Product Activation is meant to help prevent software piracy. Windows Server 2003 must be activated within 30 days either over the Internet or by phone.

Update Windows Server 2003

- Windows Update is a web-based service built into the newer Microsoft operating systems that allows for quick and easy checking for updates and installing of updates.

- Critical updates address security flaws or problems that could result in serious data loss or system failure.

- Service packs are collections of updates that are released periodically as major updates to the operating system.

- Windows Server 2003 family updates include minor refinements and additions to the operating system.

- Driver updates are improvements to the software programs that allow hardware components to communicate with the operating system.

- Windows Update can be configured in several different ways to download and install updates either with or without user intervention.

Troubleshoot Windows Server 2003 Installations

- If Windows Server 2003 will not install, the problem could be due to an unsupported upgrade path or problems booting from the CD drive.

- In many cases, simply restarting the computer and restarting the installation program can resume an installation that fails or is interrupted in midstream.

- Problems with the operating system after installation could be due to incompatibilities with either hardware or software.

- In some cases, running Windows Update might fix post-installation problems.

- If all else fails, it might be worth trying to reinstall the operating system.

■ Key Terms

answer file *(37)*
attended installation *(37)*
clean installation *(40)*
critical update *(62)*
disk image *(40)*
downgrades *(41)*
driver update *(63)*
formatted *(42)*

Hardware Compatibility
   List (HCL) *(32)*
Microsoft Product Activation
   (MPA) *(56)*
partition *(42)*
Per Device or Per User
   licensing *(44)*
Per Server licensing *(44)*
service pack *(62)*

software piracy *(56)*
strong password *(46)*
unattended installation *(37)*
upgrade installation *(40)*
weak password *(46)*
Windows Server Catalog *(32)*
Windows Update *(58)*
Windows Upgrade Advisor *(29)*

■ Key Terms Quiz

Use terms from the Key Terms List to complete the sentences that follow. Don't use the same term more than once. Not all terms will be used.

1. An improvement to the software that allows hardware components to communicate with the operating system is a _____.

2. An example of a _____ would be your birth date or your dog's name.

3. _____ is a web-based utility that scans the computer for potential upgrades and helps the user download and install those upgrades.

4. Microsoft recommends that Windows Server 2003 be installed as a _____ whenever possible. This limits the chances of conflicts with old drivers and applications.

5. _____ was instituted in an attempt to prevent people from illicitly copying and using Microsoft operating systems and office suites they did not legally own.

6. Illicitly copying and distributing computer programs is known as _____.

7. Since Windows Server 2003 does not support _____, you must do a clean install if you are running Windows 2000

Datacenter Server and you want to install Windows Server 2003 Standard Edition.

8. Periodically, during the life of an operating system, Microsoft releases a _____, which is a collection of tested upgrades and enhancements to the operating system.

9. A _____ is a physical area on a hard disk that forms the basis for the organizational structure on which files will be stored.

10. An unattended installation requires that you first edit a/an _____ that provides responses to the installation program's queries.

■ Multiple-Choice Quiz

1. The first window you see after logging on to Windows Server 2003 for the first time is the _____ window.
   a. Internet Explorer
   b. My Computer
   c. Manage Your Server
   d. Product Activation

2. Which of the following is *not* a recommendation for creating strong passwords?
   a. Mix upper- and lowercase letters.
   b. Use unusual animal names.
   c. Use six or more characters.
   d. Use symbols.

3. Per Device or Per User licensing used to be known as _____.
   a. Per Person
   b. Per Desk
   c. Per Seat
   d. Per Computer

4. Most attended installations take about _____ minutes.
   a. 30
   b. 45
   c. 60
   d. 90

5. Which of the following Windows 2000 versions could be upgraded to Windows Server 2003 Datacenter Edition?
   a. Windows 2000 Datacenter Server
   b. Windows 2000 Advanced Server
   c. Windows 2000 Server
   d. Windows 2000 Professional

6. What was the recommended partition size, in GB, mentioned in the chapter?
   a. 4GB
   b. 40GB
   c. 400GB
   d. 4000GB

7. Which of the following can be run from the command line to check the compatibility of a computer system before installing Window Server 2003?
   a. HCL
   b. Windows Update
   c. Windows Upgrade Advisor
   d. Windows Server Catalog

8. Commercial versions of Windows Server 2003 must be activated within _____ days.
   a. 14
   b. 30

c. 45

d. 60

9. When performing an attended installation, it is recommended that you select the _____ networking settings option.

   a. Typical

   b. Standard

   c. Normal

   d. Unmodified

10. Which option was not available when going through the process to Activate Windows?

    a. Activate by phone

    b. Activate by mail

    c. Activate by Internet

    d. Wait and activate later

11. Which of the following was replaced by the Windows Server Catalog?

    a. HCL

    b. Windows Update

    c. Windows Upgrade Advisor

    d. Windows Catalog

12. Which of the following would be an example of a weak password?

    a. 5$aV&wEw

b. A110n*B4

c. #2rT^

d. 5!d0MyD0g

13. Which of the following was *not* mentioned as one of the categories of updates provided on the Windows Update web site?

    a. Patches

    b. Service packs

    c. Critical updates

    d. Driver updates

14. If you choose Per Server licensing, you must also set the number of

    a. Servers

    b. Concurrent connections

    c. Installed clients

    d. Available seats

15. _____ allow/allows the creation of completely identical installations of the operating system and applications on identical computer systems.

    a. Shared folders

    b. Answer files

    c. Network shares

    d. Disk images

■ Essay Quiz

1. You have been asked to give a presentation to the employees in your company on the creation of strong passwords. Discuss some of the pointers for creating strong passwords and suggest some possible methods for creating passwords that are both strong and yet memorable to the user.

2. You've been hired to set up servers at several different companies. Under what circumstances would you consider performing an unattended installation? When would you perform attended installations?

3. A client has asked you to explain Microsoft Product Activation. Explain to them why it exists and how the process works.

4. One of your associates is having trouble installing Windows Server 2003 on a client's computer. Provide them with some possible reasons why they might be having trouble. Also explain some of the things they might do to solve the problem.

5. One of your associates always accepts the computer name suggested by the installation program. Explain why this isn't a good idea and what they should keep in mind when they choose computer names.

Lab Projects

• Lab Project 2.1

Take a survey of your classmates and others. Ask them to provide examples of actual passwords and password creation techniques they have used in the past. Also ask if anyone has ever had to deal with someone who was unauthorized either guessing or stealing their password. After collecting the data, which you should keep strictly confidential, perform the following analysis and report your findings:

1 How many of the passwords or password creation techniques resulted in strong passwords? What made these passwords strong?

2 How many of the passwords or password creation techniques resulted in weak passwords? What made these passwords weak?

3 If anyone had his or her password used by an unauthorized person, how did it happen? If the password was guessed, can you explain how that was done? If the password was stolen, can you explain how that happened?

• Lab Project 2.2

Now that you've worked through an attended installation of Windows Server 2003, you know that the process includes a lot of waiting around on your part for the setup program to prompt you for the next piece of information. In this lab, you are going to extract the Setup Manager utility from the Windows Server 2003 CD and use it to create an answer file that would duplicate your recently completed, attended, installation. Once the answer file is created, you can open it in Notepad and see how your configuration settings are represented in the file.

To complete this lab, you will need

- A working computer
- A Windows Server 2003 installation CD
- Your installation planning sheet from Step-by-Step 2.4

Then do the following:

1 To extract the Setup Manager file, setupmgr.exe, insert the Windows Server 2003 installation CD and wait for the Microsoft Windows Server 2003 family dialog box to appear. Click Perform additional tasks and then click Browse this CD to open a Windows Explorer window.

2 Double-click the SUPPORT folder, the TOOLS folder, and the DEPLOY.CAB file.

3 Locate the file setupmgr.exe and copy it. Close all open windows and paste the file on the desktop. When the file has been pasted to the

desktop, double-click it to begin the Setup Manager utility.

4 Click Next to move past the opening dialog box. Your first choice is whether to create a new answer file or modify an existing one. You would modify an existing file if you only needed to make a few minor changes to one you had previously created. For this lab you will be creating a new answer file. Make sure that the Create new option is selected and click Next.

5 The Setup Manager is capable of creating answer files for three different types of setup. The second two options, Sysprep setup and Remote Installation Services, are beyond the scope of the present discussion. Verify that the unattended setup option is selected and click Next.

6 Setup Manager is capable of creating answer files for Windows XP Home and Professional and Windows Server 2003 Standard, Enterprise, and Web Editions. Since you installed Enterprise Edition in Step-by-Step 2.5, select that operating system and click Next.

7 Setup Manager can configure the answer file to accommodate five levels of user interaction. Read over the descriptions of each. The Fully automated option allows for a true unattended installation. Select Fully automated and click Next.

8 Setup manager can copy the necessary installation files and the answer file to a network share for network-based unattended installations. It can also modify files that have already been placed on an available share. The last option, Set up from a CD, assumes that you will be creating a Windows Server 2003 CD that includes the installation files and the answer file. This option does not copy any files from the installation CD to your computer's hard drive or to the network. Choose Set up from a CD and click Next.

9 In order to perform an unattended installation, you need to accept the terms of the End User License Agreement (EULA) at this time. Although the EULAs for Setup Manager and for the product you are creating an answer file for are not accessible to you from this step, you really have no choice. If you do not accept the license agreement, you cannot continue creating an answer file. Check the box that signifies your acceptance and click Next.

10 Setup Manager will now walk you through 17 configuration steps to create your answer file. Please move through the steps one at a time and consult Table 2.2, and your installation planning sheet from Step-by-Step 2.4, for your settings. If you are told to skip a step, simply click Next to move to the next. If you miss a step, you may either click Back or click the step you missed on the right-hand side of the dialog box to return to it.

11 When prompted to save the unattend.txt file, click Browse and open your My Documents folder. Click OK to save the file. When the dialog box displays the message "Completing Setup Manager," click Cancel to exit the utility.

Now that you've finished the Setup Manager, you can open your answer file, unattend.txt, by opening My Documents and double-clicking the file. There are actually two files named unattend that the Setup Manager created. unattend.txt is the file we want to open. Its icon should look like a small notepad. The other file is unattend.bat. It is a batch file that can be used to start an installation using the answer file you created.

Table 2.2	Setup Manager Configuration Responses
Step	**Setting or Action**
Name and Organization	Enter your name and your school or workplace.
Display Settings	Skip. The default values are fine.
Time Zone	Choose your time zone from the list.
Product Key	Enter the product key from your installation planning sheet.
Licensing Mode	Enter the licensing mode from your installation planning sheet.
Computer Names	Enter the computer name from your planning sheet and click Add.
Administrator Password	Enter and confirm the administrator password from your planning sheet. Check the box labeled Encrypt the Administrator password in the answer file.
Networking Components	Verify that Typical settings are selected.
Workgroup or Domain	Enter the workgroup or domain information from your installation planning sheet. You do not need to create a computer account for this lab.
Telephony	Skip. These settings are used by modems.
Regional Settings	Skip. The default settings are usually fine.
Languages	Select the correct language. Western Europe and the United States is at the bottom of the list.
Browser and Shell Settings	Skip. The default settings are usually fine.
Installation Folder	Skip. A folder named Windows is usually fine.
Install Printers	Skip.
Run Once	Skip.
Additional Commands	Click Finish.

Open your unattend.txt file and answer the following questions:

1 Find the entry for your administrator password. What does it look like? Why does it look like that? What is the benefit of recording the password in this way?

2 What is your time zone according to the answer file? You may close your answer file after answering this question.

3 Imagine that you only had to be present for an attended installation just at the moments your input was needed. Consider only those interactions and ignore the time spent waiting for the next prompt. Did you spend more time answering questions during the attended install or during the preparation of the answer file?

4 Recall that an answer file can be configured to set up multiple computers. If your job were to set up new computers, at what point would you consider creating and using an answer file? Answer in terms of how many computers would justify, for you, doing unattended installations instead of attended installations and why? Are there any other factors you would take into consideration?

• Lab Project 2.3

Consider the following possible naming conventions and comment on their strengths and weaknesses. When you have commented on each, make a recommendation on which convention you would recommend. You may suggest a new alternative, of your own devising, if you wish.

1 Computers are named according to the name of their primary user.

2 Computers are named according to their physical location in the building.

3 Computers are named after animals and plants.

4 Computers are named according to their current function within the network.

A Net Improvement: Configuring Network Services and Protocols

"Addresses are given to us to conceal our whereabouts."

—HECTOR HUGH MUNRO

In this chapter, you will learn how to:

- **Describe basic TCP/IP concepts**
- **Configure TCP/IP**
- **Set up DHCP**
- **Set up DNS and WINS**

If you want to send someone a letter, you need to know his or her address. If you want to ask your neighbor if you can borrow their lawnmower, you dial their phone number and make your request. As you might have guessed, there also needs to be some sort of addressing system available on computer networks so that each computer can establish communications with the others. The physical location doesn't matter, when it comes to networking, so our addressing system really can "conceal our whereabouts." However, it has to be a system that unmistakably gets the right information to the right computer on the right network. Additionally, computers need to encode the information they exchange in such a way that the other computers on the network can understand it. After all, your neighbor would probably hang up on you if he or she answered the phone and heard you speaking a foreign language they didn't understand. At the very least, you'd be unlikely to get that lawnmower!

Although there are many possible ways of handling the problem of computer addresses and communication standards, Microsoft-based networks have narrowed the field down to just a few solutions that are implemented in most situations. In this chapter you will learn the basic concepts behind the primary method for handling network addresses and the encoding of data on Microsoft networks. You'll learn how to configure the server to use this addressing and communication standard and how to configure the server to handle the addressing needs of clients on the network to ensure that each receives a unique address. You'll also learn how to configure two different systems that allow the network to translate computer-friendly numeric addresses into more human-friendly names, and vice versa.

Understanding Basic TCP/IP Concepts

The most common **protocol**, or set of rules and standards, for handling network communications on Microsoft networks is known as **Transmission Control Protocol/Internet Protocol (TCP/IP)**. TCP/IP is actually two individual protocols, usually referred to as a protocol suite, that work together to handle the tasks of providing a network address scheme, encoding data for transport, and creating connections for the communication of data. TCP/IP became the preferred protocol for a number of reasons, but chief among them is the fact that it is the same protocol suite used by the largest of all networks: the Internet. Since, sooner or later, most networks will need to connect to the Internet, it only makes sense to start off using the same communication standard.

A truly comprehensive discussion of TCP/IP is worthy of a single text at least twice as lengthy as this book! However, for our purposes it will be sufficient to briefly discuss the three major areas of networking communications handled by TCP/IP so that we have a better understanding of what is going on below the surface.

Addressing

Like any addressing scheme, such as phone numbers or street addresses, computer networks require unique addresses for each connected device so that information sent from one device to another can reach the correct destination. The TCP/IP protocol suite meets this requirement by implementing IP addresses, which provide a unique identity for each properly configured device on the network.

Inside Information

Binary Basics

As you know, our decimal numbering system is based on the number 10. We use decimals because 10 is a natural number for human beings to use as a mathematical concept. You've got 10 fingers and, as we all remember, we first learn how to count to 10. It only makes sense that our numbering system is based on the number 10.

Computers are based on transistors, which are essentially tiny switches that can only be on or off. Basically, that leaves computers with the equivalent of two fingers. Thus, computers do all of their calculations using a number system that is based on the number 2.

In decimal, although it's based on the concept of 10, we don't actually have a single number that means 10. We have 0 through 9, and when we want to say 10, we put a 1 in the ten's place and a 0 in the one's place. In binary we have 0s and 1s, and when we want to express the value 2, we put a 1 in the two's place and a 0 in the one's place.

In both numbering systems, each place further to the left is x times the place to its right, with x being 10 in the decimal system and 2 in the binary system. Thus, the digits 1010 in the decimal system equal: 1*1,000 + 0*100 + 1*10 + 0*1, which is 1010. In binary 1010 is: 1*8 + 0*4 + 1*2 + 0*1, which, in decimal, is 10!

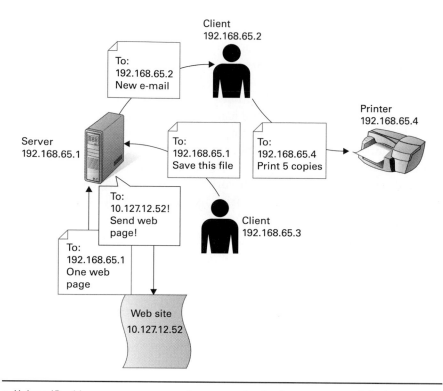

- Unique IP addresses are necessary for communication between network devices to occur.

IP addresses are normally expressed in a form known as **dotted decimal**, which is a sequence of four base-10 numbers, each ranging from 0 to 255, with each number separated by a period. Thus an IP address might be written as 192.168.127.63. Although a few addresses are reserved for special purposes and are not available for use by network devices, the IP addressing system provides for almost 4.3 billion unique addresses! That sure seems like plenty at first glance, but when you consider the fact that the largest network in the world uses this addressing scheme, and that every single networked device needs its own address, you've got a bit of a problem. If you find it hard to believe that 4.3 billion IP addresses isn't enough, consider the phone number situation in the United States for a moment. There are approximately 1.7 billion available telephone numbers under the current system in use in the U.S., and there's already a shortage! Chances are you or someone you know has experienced a change in area code as the telephone companies begin to use previously unused area codes to increase the number of available telephone numbers in a particular state or part of a state. In a similar fashion, there are moves to increase the number of available IP addresses. A new standard, known as **IPv6**, for Internet Protocol version 6, will provide over 4 million unique addresses for each square meter of the entire Earth's surface!

IP addresses have one other thing in common with telephone numbers. Telephone numbers begin with an area code and three-digit exchange that identify a particular geographical location from which the call originates. Within that exchange in that area code there are ten thousand possible phone numbers, from 0000 to 9999, that identify unique telephone lines. IP addresses also use part of the address information to identify the network the address belongs to. The remainder of the address is used to identify a unique device on that network. The key to this system is a little device known as the subnet mask.

The current implementation of IP addressing is technically known as IPv4. However, no one refers to it as that unless they need to differentiate it from the newer IPv6 standard.

Subnet Masks

A **subnet mask** is used to indicate what part of an IP address, or range of addresses, refers to the network and what part refers to the devices, referred to as hosts, on the network. In simple terms, masking off a smaller segment of the IP address gives you fewer networks with more possible hosts, while masking off more of the address gives you more networks with fewer possible hosts. This is just like our earlier telephone example. With the area code and exchange "masked off" as describing the area, or network, we have a maximum of 10,000 possible hosts, or telephone lines in the area. If we only "masked off" the area code, we'd have fewer possible areas, only 1000, but we'd be able to have up to ten million possible lines in each of those areas!

Subnet masks work in a way that is very similar to the operation of area codes and exchanges, but unlike the telephone system, subnet masks can be of variable sizes. Additionally, they work at the binary level of the address, which makes them a bit hard to grasp at first. In dotted decimal notation, a subnet mask might be expressed as 255.255.255.0. By converting this number to its binary form, you get the subnet mask 11111111.11111111.11111111.00000000. As you can see in Figure 3.1, everywhere you see a 1 in the subnet mask indicates the portion of the address that identifies the network. Everywhere you see a 0 indicates the portion of the address available for unique host addresses within that network. Since there are eight 0s left in this subnet mask for unique host addresses, we can have a maximum of 256 possible values from 00000000 to 11111111. Because of the way subnets use strings of ones and zeros, we cannot use the first or last of the 256 values, leaving us with 254 unique host IP addresses for this particular network. If we needed more than 254 unique addresses, we would use a shorter subnet mask that would make more bits available for host addresses. For instance, making just one more bit available for host addresses raises the available number to 510!

Just as using a shorter subnet mask makes more host addresses possible, using a longer subnet mask does the opposite. When a subnet mask is made shorter, the gain in host addresses comes at the expense of having fewer network addresses. However, when you lengthen the subnet mask, you gain more network addresses, albeit with fewer host addresses within each network. Through a process called subnetting, network administrators use custom subnet masks to further subdivide a single range of IP addresses into

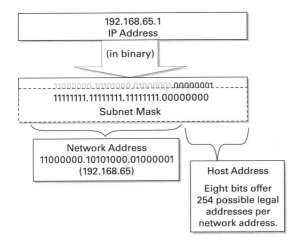

● **Figure 3.1**   A subnet mask "masks" off a portion of the IP address

Chapter 3: A Net Improvement: Configuring Network Services and Protocols two or more smaller ranges. This allows them to separate segments of the network, which can enhance security, ease management, and even enhance performance in some situations.

Subnet masks play a role in all TCP/IP networks, whether they are private networks isolated from the outside world or large corporate networks that connect each client machine directly to the Internet. In the case of the latter, subnet masks are an important tool in the struggle to conserve IPv4 addresses.

Public IP Addresses

Any network that is going to connect its clients directly to the Internet needs a way to ensure that each device has an IP address that is truly unique in the world. In addition, since organizations vary widely in size, from mom-and-pop operations to multinational corporations, we need a system that correctly allocates our dwindling supply of IPv4 addresses according to the organization's need.

The Internet service provider, or ISP, that actually provides Internet connectivity to organizations usually handles the actual assigning of IP addresses. ISPs get their allocation of IP addresses from either a Local (LIR), National (NIR), or Regional Internet Registry (RIR). For example, the **American Registry for Internet Numbers (ARIN)**, is the RIR responsible for allocating ranges of IP addresses within North America as well as a portion of both the Caribbean and Africa. ARIN, and the other RIRs—there are currently three others—receive their initial allocation of IP addresses from the **Internet Assigned Numbers Authority (IANA)** .

Up until about ten years ago, IP addresses for public networks were distributed using a system of three primary classes known as classes A, B, and C. As shown in Table 3.1, each of the three classes used a different subnet mask that determined the maximum number of networks within the class and the maximum number of host addresses available within each network. This system is no longer in use, because it was terribly inefficient. As you can see, there's a huge gap between any two of the three classes that led to a lot of wasted IP addresses. In some cases, organizations that needed only a thousand or so addresses ended up sitting on over 60 thousand unused addresses!

You may have noticed that the number of networks possible for each class is far fewer than you might expect given the subnet mask. This is because each class used a special addressing scheme that created a limited and unique range of addresses for each class. This was done so that network devices could automatically detect the class an IP address was from and thus automatically set the correct subnet mask for that class. In addition, certain ranges of addresses in each class were reserved by the IANA for special purposes. The actual address ranges for classes A, B, and C are listed in Table 3.2. Note that x represents the portion of the address available for use in creating host addresses within a network.

In 1993, the IANA introduced a new scheme for allocating IP addresses that allowed far greater flexibility. This scheme, which is

Table 3.1	The Obsolete Class-Based Scheme for Allocating IP Addresses		
	Subnet Mask	Number of Networks	Number of Hosts per Network
Class A	255.0.0.0	128	16,777,214
Class B	255.255.0.0	16,384	65,534
Class C	255.255.255.0	2,097,152	254

Table 3.2	Address Ranges for Class-Based IP Addresses
	Address Range
Class A	0.*x.x.x* to 127.*x.x.x*
Class B	128.0.*x.x* to 191.255.*x.x*
Class C	192.0.0.*x* to 223.225.255.*x*

referred to as **Classless Inter-Domain Routing (CIDR)**, makes use of variable-length subnet masks, rather than the three fixed masks used by the class-based system, to allow relatively fine control over the number of addresses available to any particular network. When combined with the advent of IPv6 addresses, this approach should ensure that we have plenty of IP addresses to go around for the foreseeable future.

Private IP Addresses

If a network never connects directly to any other network, there's really no need to be concerned about IP address duplication as long as the network's own devices have unique addresses. Because of this, many network administrators take the easy way out and arbitrarily assign IP addresses with no regard to the outside world. However, this can cause numerous problems later on if that network ever does connect to the Internet or any other network, upon which the same addresses are being used.

In order to avoid this problem, there are two possible solutions. On the one hand, since most networks do connect to the Internet or other networks eventually, it's not a bad idea to go through the process of obtaining a legitimate set of IP addresses from the appropriate agency. That way, the network is already prepared for future needs.

The other possible solution is to make use of special ranges of IP addresses that the IANA has reserved specifically for use within private networks. Such addresses are recognized as private addresses by both networking hardware and software and, as such, will never be mistaken for external addresses and thus cause no future conflicts. Table 3.3 lists the acceptable ranges for use as private IP addresses, their default subnet masks, and the number of networks and hosts each supports.

Try This!

Easy Decimal-to-Binary and Binary-to-Decimal Conversions

Don't be too concerned if you find the whole binary number system a bit hard to grasp. You didn't learn how to use the decimal numbering system overnight, so it's only natural that it would take a while to get used to binary. A handy tool for understanding how binary relates to decimal is right on your computer as we speak. The humble calculator accessory does a nice job of converting between the several numbering systems. To complete this task, you'll need access to a computer running Windows. Try this:

1. To open the calculator, click Start, select All Programs, Accessories, and click Calculator.

2. Calculator has two views: standard and scientific. The scientific view allows us to convert from one number system to another. To access this view, click the View menu and select Scientific.

3. Make sure that the option button labeled Dec is selected. Using either your keyboard or the onscreen keys, type the number **255**. To convert the decimal number 255 to binary, click the option button labeled Bin. What is the result?

4. Click the C button to clear the display but remain in Bin mode. Type the number **100**. To convert this binary number to decimal, click the option button labeled Dec. What is the result?

5. Try converting other decimal numbers, like your age, to binary. Try different binary numbers (remember you can only use zeros and ones) and see what decimal numbers they represent.

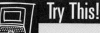

Try This!

Finding and Using IP Addresses Instead of Domain Names

Although we normally access web sites by typing domain names, each of those domain names merely represents one of the IP addresses we've been discussing. In fact, if you type the IP address for a domain name into your browser you'll arrive at the correct site with no problems. Let's take a look at an online tool for finding the IP address behind a domain name and try using the address to get to a few sites. To complete this task, you will need a computer with Internet access and a web browser. Try this:

1. Point your browser to network-tools.com. You do not need to type a www at the beginning of the domain name.

2. When the page loads, click the option button labeled Lookup. Enter **microsoft.com** in the text box above the Submit button and then click the Submit button.

3. An IP address should appear on the left side of your display. Type that IP address into the address bar of your browser and press the ENTER key. Did you end up at Microsoft's site?

4. Use the Back button on your browser to return to the Network-Tools site. Look up the IP address for google.com, a popular search engine. Use the IP address to go to the site.

5. Try some other sites you are familiar with. Can you classify the IP addresses you discovered according to the old class A, B, or C scheme?

Microsoft has also reserved another range of addresses for use in conjunction with a feature they call Automatic Private IP Addressing. For your reference, the range is from 169.254.0.1 through 169.254.255.254 and uses a subnet mask of 255.255.0.0. Automatic Private IP Addressing is employed to connect computers if IP addresses are not set manually or assigned by a server.

When such networks do need to communicate with external networks, they can do so through a device called a **router** that supports **Network Address Translation (NAT)**. A router is used to connect two or more different networks together. NAT allows the router, which has a legal public IP address, to "stand in" for the machines on the network using private IP addresses. It internally translates those private addresses and sends out any communication from them as if it were coming from the router's public IP. Messages coming in receive the reverse treatment. This technology allows even relatively large networks to require only a few public IP addresses, thus conserving our, currently, limited supply.

Table 3.3	Acceptable Ranges for Private IP Addresses		
Private IP Address Range	**Subnet Mask**	**Number of Networks**	**Number of Host Addresses**
10.0.0.0 through 10.255.255.255	255.0.0.0	1	16,777,214
172.16.0.0 through 172.31.255.255	255.240.0.0	16	1,048,574
192.168.0.0 through 192.168.255.255	255.255.0.0	255	65,534

Verifying TCP/IP Configuration

Before we begin reconfiguring our TCP/IP settings, it would be a good idea to take a look at how the server is currently configured. There are actually several ways of doing this, but one of the quickest makes use of the command line utility **ipconfig**. The ipconfig utility quickly reports the status of important network configuration settings without the need to click a half-a-dozen times here, there, and everywhere! We'll use the ipconfig report to analyze our current settings and record them before we begin making changes in the next section.

To complete this Step-by-Step, you will need

- A properly configured computer with Windows Server 2003 installed

- Access to an administrator-level account on the computer

Step 1

To run ipconfig, we need to open a command prompt window. By default, a shortcut to the command prompt is pinned to the Start menu, which means it appears at the top of the left column. Click the shortcut to open the command prompt window.

Tip: If the command prompt shortcut is not pinned to the Start menu, you can access it by clicking Start and selecting All Programs | Accessories | Command Prompt.

Step 2

Type the command **ipconfig** at the command prompt and press the ENTER key. Take a moment to record the information displayed. Keep this information for later reference.

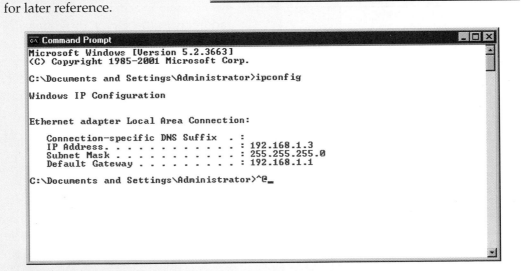

IP Addresses and Subnet Masks

IP addresses and subnet masks are both crucial elements in allowing networks to communicate and share resources. However, they tend to be difficult concepts to master because of the need to understand how the computer looks at addresses and how networks interpret them. Let's take a minute or two to summarize what we've learned. If you like, review the preceding sections and answer the following questions:

1. How does a subnet mask work?

2. What's the difference between a public and a private IP address range?

3. Who allocates public IP addresses?

■ Configuring TCP/IP

If you configured your server during the initial setup to use the Typical networking settings, TCP/IP is already installed as a networking protocol. Additionally, if your server was connected to an existing network that already had a DHCP server on it, your server was automatically assigned an IP address and can already access the network and its resources. However, for a server, getting an IP address from a DHCP server is not generally the best way to go. Before we get to configuring our TCP/IP settings manually, let's take a moment to discuss the difference between the two basic ways of assigning IP addresses on a network.

Dynamic Versus Static IP Addressing

As you might recall, DHCP stands for Dynamic Host Configuration Protocol. A DHCP server provides a **dynamic IP address** to each device as it connects to the network. A dynamic IP address is one that can change, sometimes each time a connection to the network is established. Although DHCP has many advantages, which we'll explore a bit later in this chapter, the fact that

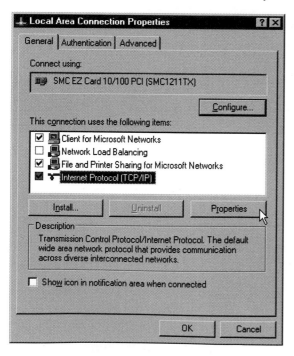

• **Figure 3.2** The Local Area Connection Properties dialog box

the IP addresses can and do change can present a bit of a problem. The biggest problem is that servers, and some other devices, won't work properly if their IP address keeps changing. In fact, the server that provides DHCP services to the network cannot function correctly if its own IP address is assigned dynamically. Since we will configure our machine as a DHCP server, we need an IP address that isn't dynamic, or changeable.

A **static IP address** is an IP address that does not change. In addition to the server providing DHCP to the network, other servers, printers, and other devices that provide network resources to users typically function best when their IP addresses do not change from time to time. Static IP addresses usually need to be set manually, which is what we're about to do for our server.

Changing Connection Properties

IP addresses, and related settings, are accessed through the Local Area Connection Properties dialog box. In the middle of the dialog box, as shown in Figure 3.2, is a list of the various protocols and services that are configured to work with the NIC listed at the top. By selecting Internet Protocol (TCP/IP) on this list and clicking the Properties button, you can configure the IP address and several related settings. Let's take a closer look at these settings and then configure them ourselves in the Step-by-Step that follows.

Internet Protocol (TCP/IP) Properties

The Internet Protocol (TCP/IP) Properties dialog box is relatively simple. As you can see in Figure 3.3, this is where we choose between obtaining our IP address automatically or entering the information manually. In addition, we can configure settings for a special service known as DNS, which helps match up IP addresses with Internet domain names so that we don't have to type all of those numbers. We'll be configuring DNS on this server a bit later, so we'll talk more about the DNS settings then.

Once you've chosen to enter the IP address manually, you need to also enter the subnet mask for that address. As discussed previously, the subnet mask is used to divide the address into a network address that identifies the network as a whole and a host, or client, address that identifies the individual device. If the server is going to have a public IP address, then your ISP will most likely provide both the address and the subnet mask to you. If the server is going to use a private IP addressing scheme, the subnet mask will depend on how many client machines, or hosts, need to connect to the network. The default subnet mask of 255.255.255.0 provides for 254 unique device addresses within the network.

The default gateway setting allows you to point the computer toward a router for access to other networks, such as the Internet. As mentioned before, a router is a device that allows information to be exchanged between two different networks. Like any other computer on the network, the router has an IP address, which should be static. When a computer on the network needs to reach an IP address outside of the network, it passes the data to the default gateway, which then communicates with the outside network. On a completely self-contained network with no access to the Internet or other networks, the default gateway setting may be blank.

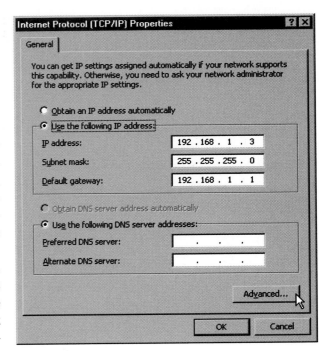

• **Figure 3.3**   The Internet Protocol (TCP/IP) Properties dialog box

> The Advanced button provides access to a few settings that rarely need to be changed, as well as an alternative way of configuring the IP address and the gateway. We'll get a chance to use it later in the chapter.

Step-by-Step 3.2

Configuring a Static IP Address

Before configuring a server with a static IP address, you should first plan out your IP addressing strategy. First of all, decide whether you will be using a private addressing scheme, or you will be requesting IP addresses from your ISP or directly from an organization like ARIN. Second, determine the subnet mask for your IP address. If you have been allocated a public IP address, this will have been provided to you. If you are using a private IP

address, you can normally use the default mask for the address you've chosen. Since the 192.168.x.x range used with a subnet mask of 255.255.0.0 provides over 65 thousand hosts, it will likely do nicely! Last, if your network will be connecting to the Internet or another network through a router, or gateway, you will also need the IP address of that device. Don't worry about the DNS settings for now. We'll come back and take care of them in a bit.

Please ask your instructor for the proper settings for your lab environment. The settings given in this example are only for illustrative purposes and should not be used unless you are instructed otherwise. However, don't worry about hurting anything if you do make a mistake. Incorrect IP settings do no harm other than temporarily disrupting network connectivity. They can easily be changed to the proper values.

To complete this Step-by-Step, you will need

- A properly configured computer with Windows Server 2003 installed

- Access to an administrator-level account on the computer

- Proper IP, subnet mask, and default gateway settings for your network

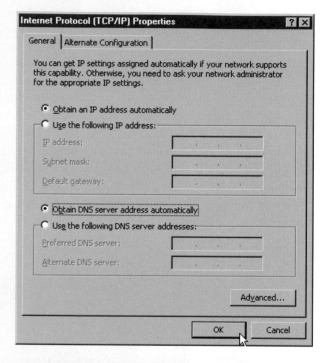

Step 1

To open the Internet Protocol (TCP/IP) Properties dialog box, click Start and then select Control Panel followed by Network Connections. When the Network Connections cascading menu appears, right-click your local area connection and choose Properties from the shortcut menu. When the Local Area Connection Properties dialog box opens, select Internet Protocol (TCP/IP) from the list and click the Properties button.

Step 2

If there is already information entered in the fields for IP address, subnet mask, and default gateway, you can easily erase it by clicking Obtain an IP address automatically and then clicking Use the following IP address. If the entry boxes are empty and "grayed out," simply click the Use the following IP address option button.

Step 3

Enter the IP address. Since the entry fields are segmented to hold the four parts of the IP address and other addresses, some people have trouble using the mouse to click the fields to begin entering the information. They tend to click the wrong part of the field. A good technique is to press the TAB key after clicking the Use the following IP address option button. This will take you to the beginning of the IP address field. Enter the IP address by keying both the numbers *and* the periods between them. The periods advance the cursor to the next portion of the address if you've entered only a one- or two-digit number. Even though the cursor advances automatically when you enter a three-digit number, it is still okay to key the period. Press the TAB key when you are finished.

Tip: If you make a mistake in entering the information, simply use the BACK-SPACE key to correct it.

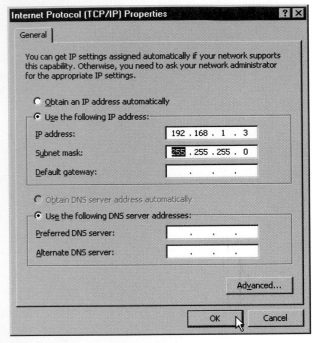

Step 4

You'll notice that a subnet mask was entered automatically for you when you pressed the TAB key at the end of the last step. Windows chooses this subnet by considering the first part, or first octet, of the IP address according to the subnet masks associated with the public IP address ranges for classes A, B, and C. Always check the subnet mask to be sure that it is correct, since this assumption by Windows could be wrong. For instance, in my example, I'm actually using an IP address from the range reserved for private use. This particular range, 192.168.0.0 through 192.168.255.255, actually has a default subnet mask of 255.255.0.0, which would give me 65,534 host addresses. Windows recommended a subnet of 255.255.255.0, which leaves me with 254 possible host addresses. Even 254 addresses are far more than I need in a lab situation, so Windows' suggestion will work just fine. However, if I needed a larger number of host addresses on my network, I would need to change this subnet mask.

If the subnet mask Windows filled in for you is acceptable, press the TAB key. Otherwise, change it and then move to the next field.

Step 5

If your network is connected to a gateway device, such as a router, enter the device's IP address in the Default gateway field. Additionally, if there are addresses entered in the DNS fields, you may leave them filled in for now. However, if the Default gateway and DNS fields are empty, you may leave them so, unless told otherwise by your instructor. Click OK to close the Internet Protocol (TCP/IP) Properties dialog box. Click Close to close the Local Area Connection Properties dialog box.

■ Setting Up DHCP

As we mentioned earlier, the Dynamic Host Configuration Protocol (DHCP) automatically configures the TCP/IP settings of client computers on the network. For that reason alone, you can see why having a DHCP server on the network would be beneficial. Let's face it; configuring TCP/IP

Cross Check

TCP/IP Configuration Settings

IP addresses can be configured in several ways, and there are several steps to the configuration process. Let's take a minute or two to summarize what we've learned. If you like, review the preceding sections and answer the following questions:

1. What is the difference between a static IP address and a dynamic one?

2. What are the potential disadvantages of using a dynamic IP address? What are the advantages?

3. What are the potential disadvantages of using a static IP address? What are the advantages?

on our server wasn't hard, but do you want to trudge around to 50 or 100 client computers and go through the same process? However, there are more than just time savings at stake here. Setting our server up to act as a DHCP server has other benefits as well.

DHCP Benefits

The first benefit arises from human nature. I don't know about you, but I occasionally type rather poorly. Windows will gladly accept a mistyped TCP/IP address or subnet mask. You'll not see a single error message as long as what you typed looks like the real thing. However, if the information you input isn't correct, that machine is not going to be able to connect to the network. I can just about guarantee that after 50 or so machines, you're bound to make a mistake or two.

I'm sorry to say that our second benefit also exists because of human failings. You'll recall that no two network devices can have the same IP address. It just won't work, as I know from personal experience! Trying to track even a relatively small number of IP addresses, especially as machines are added and removed from the network, is not an easy task. Fortunately, DHCP has absolutely no trouble at all ensuring that each address is used once and only once.

Our third, and final, major benefit doesn't have as much to do with human weaknesses as it does computer strengths! It simply helps address a little problem we've mentioned before: the scarcity of IP addresses. Imagine a company trying to run a network using one of those old class C IP address schemes. A class C address provided only enough host addresses for 254 devices on the network. Between servers, printers, routers, and client machines, even a relatively small company could find itself running out of addresses rather quickly. However, since DHCP assigns IP addresses dynamically, it is capable of reusing any currently not-in-use address as needed. In other words, as long as no more than 254 devices need to connect *at one time*, it is possible to use DHCP to support a larger number of total devices. For instance, if our small company had 500 devices that connected to the network but only half were ever connected at one time, perhaps due to shifts, DHCP would have no problem assigning IP addresses from a pool of 254.

In order to take advantage of DHCP, at least one server on the network must be configured as a DHCP server. We're going to set our servers up to fill this role, but first we have to take care of one little weakness that DHCP has. DHCP, like several other useful networking services, isn't installed with Windows Server 2003 as part of the typical networking settings! Let's take care of that right now.

Installing DHCP, DNS, and WINS

Before we can configure DHCP, we need to get it installed on our server. Since the procedure for installing DHCP also presents the opportunity to install other missing components, we'll go ahead and install two others that we'll be covering later in this chapter: Domain Name System (DNS) and Windows Internet Name Service (WINS).

To complete this Step-by-Step, you will need

- A properly configured computer with Windows Server 2003 installed
- Access to an administrator-level account on the computer
- Access to the Windows Server 2003 source files, either on CD or over the network

Step 1

Windows components like DHCP, DNS, and WINS are installed through the Add or Remove Programs applet on the Control Panel. Click Start, select Control Panel, and click Add or Remove Programs to start the applet. When the window appears, click the icon on the left side labeled Add/Remove Windows Components to start the Windows Components Wizard.

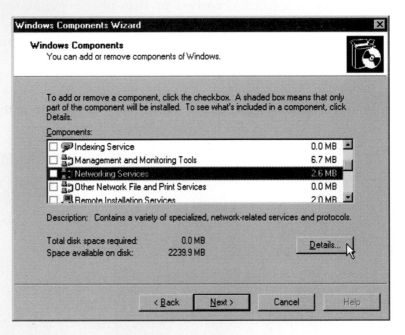

Step 2

Scroll down the list of components until you see Networking Services. Select this entry by clicking on the words, not the check box, and click the Details button to see the components in this category.

Step 3

When the Networking Services dialog box appears, place a check mark in the boxes for DNS, DHCP, and WINS. Click OK to close the dialog box.

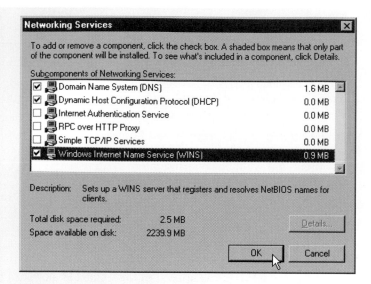

Step 4

When you return to the Windows Component Wizard, click Next to begin installing the new components. After a few moments, you'll be prompted to insert the Windows Server 2003 CD. If you have the CD, insert it; in most cases, the installation will continue without your having to click OK. If it does not, or if you need to get the files off of the network, click OK and Windows will either read the CD or prompt you for an alternate location.

Tip: If the Welcome to Windows window appears, simply close it to complete the installation.

Step 5

Click Finish to close the Windows Component Wizard window and then click Close to close the Add or Remove Programs window.

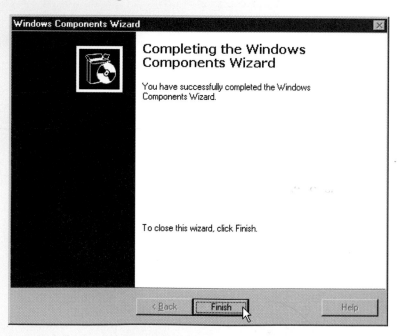

Configuring DHCP

DHCP manages IP addresses by issuing a **lease** to client computers for a particular address it draws from a pool of IP addresses called the **scope**. The scope consists of a range of IP addresses that are valid for the network the DHCP server is connected to, excluding any addresses that have already been assigned as static IP addresses. The lease that is issued to clients is good for a limited time for a particular IP address. When the lease begins to near its expiration date, the client can request a renewal and thus keep the same IP address for a longer time. Leases may expire if the client does not connect prior to the expiration date or cannot negotiate a renewal due to some other problem. When leases expire, clients go through a process of requesting a new IP address from the DHCP server and, if successful, are granted a new lease.

Adding a New DHCP Scope

The first step in configuring DHCP is to add a new scope. A New Scope Wizard makes the process quite painless and actually allows you to configure a good bit more than just the range of available IP addresses. Let's take a look at the settings the wizard walks us through.

Name and Description   On larger networks, it is possible to have more than one DHCP scope. In such cases it helps to have each scope clearly labeled with a name and, if desired, a longer description of the nature of the scope. Only the name is required by the wizard.

IP Address Range and Subnet Mask   The IP address range is defined by simply entering the first address in the range and the last address in the range along with the subnet mask. Keep in mind that client machines may not use certain addresses. Those addresses that, in binary, give a host address of all ones or all zeros cannot be part of the scope. In simple terms, this eliminates addresses where, in decimal, the host portion of the address is all zeros or all 255s. For example, if you were using the range from 192.168.1.0 to 192.168.1.255 with a subnet mask of 255.255.255.0, you would use from 192.168.1.1 to 192.169.1.254 as your scope range.

Excluded IP Addresses   Any IP addresses that are being assigned statically must be excluded from the DHCP scope. If they aren't, they may get leased to a client machine, creating a conflict. At the very least, the address of the DHCP server itself must be excluded. It is also possible to exclude an entire range of addresses.

Lease Duration   Lease duration is set in days, hours, and minutes. A general rule of thumb is that networks with relatively stable client bases benefit from longer leases. This is because there's less need to conserve addresses, assuming enough exist to begin with. Longer leases also may improve network performance slightly, since lease requests generate network traffic and longer leases reduce lease requests. Networks with a dynamic client base, perhaps from many portable computers, may benefit from shorter leases in order to conserve IP addresses. The default lease of eight days is ideal for the average small office, since most leases will never expire during the work week without renewal. Microsoft suggests that lease duration should be set to longer periods on larger, more stable networks if IP address availability is good.

When setting lease duration, don't forget to take a close look at the nature of the organization's total schedule. An eight-day lease works great until the organization, say a college, takes a three-week break! That first day back can be a real bear as every machine tries to request a new lease at the same time! I speak from experience.

Default Gateway DHCP also has the ability to automatically configure networking settings beyond IP addresses. If necessary, you can enter the address of a router that serves as the default gateway to an external network like the Internet. Several such addresses can be entered, and you can also set the order in which they should be accessed.

DNS and WINS Settings Both DNS and WINS are services that help match up cryptic IP addresses with more easily remembered computer names. If your network is running DNS and/or WINS, it is possible to have DHCP automatically configure client computers as to where to find the servers running these services.

Step-by-Step 3.4

Adding a New DHCP Scope

Now that DHCP is installed, we're ready to add our first scope and configure it. It's important to gather all the necessary information before you begin so that you don't have to stop in the middle of the process and go searching. Remember to obtain the addresses of any machines that are configured to use a static IP address so that you can exclude those addresses from the scope. Also consider in advance what lease length would be best for your network. Ask yourself: what would work best for your school? What about where you work?

To complete this Step-by-Step, you will need

- A properly configured computer with Windows Server 2003 installed

- Access to an administrator-level account on the computer

- All necessary information regarding static IP addresses, IP address range and subnet mask, and default gateway addresses

Step 1

DHCP is configured through the DHCP snap-in, which is a specialized management tool that works within Windows' Microsoft Management Console, or MMC. To open the DHCP snap-in, click Start, select Administrative Tools, and click DHCP. When the console opens, click the name of your server on the left to display the message about adding a scope in the right-hand pane.

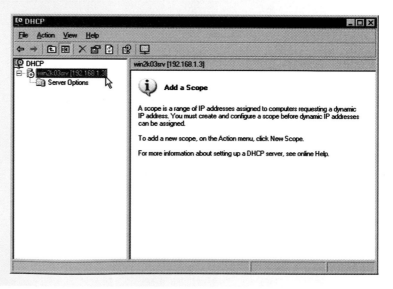

To begin the New Scope Wizard, open the Action menu and choose New Scope. When the wizard opens, click Next; name your scope **test scope** and enter **created by** *your name* as the description. Click Next to continue.

Enter the range of IP addresses for your scope. Get this information from your instructor. Windows will enter a subnet mask for you, as it did when you configured the server's TCP/IP settings. If the subnet mask is not correct, you may choose to either enter it as an IP address or by selecting the number of bits the subnet mask "masks" of the IP address range. Click Next to continue.

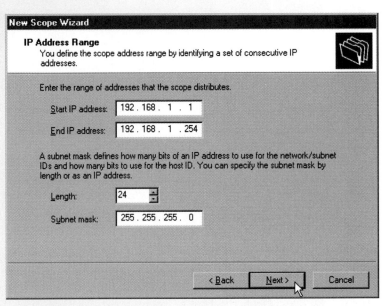

Add the IP address of your server to the exclusions list by typing its address in the Start field and clicking Add. If you need to exclude a range of addresses or any other individual addresses for your lab configuration, you may do that now. Click Next to continue.

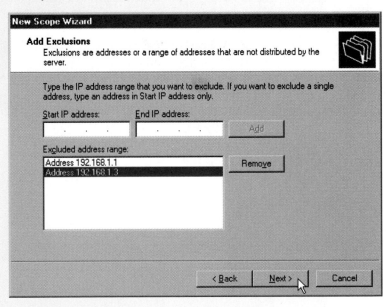

For this exercise, you may leave the lease duration at its default value of eight days. Read the description and click Next to continue.

Step 6

The next step of the wizard offers us the chance to configure a variety of other settings to be automatically configured by DHCP. Since we're not yet ready to work with our DNS and WINS settings, choose No, I will configure these options later. We'll see in a moment how these options can be configured after the scope is created. Click Next and then click Finish to complete the wizard.

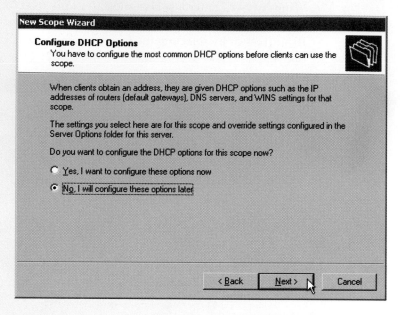

Step 7

You should see your new scope listed on the left side of the DHCP snap-in under the name of your server. Click it to select it. Newly created scopes are deactivated by default, as is indicated by a downward red arrow over the name of the scope. To activate the scope, right-click it and choose Activate from the shortcut menu. If you cannot see the full name of the scope, you can widen the left-hand pane by moving the vertical border with your mouse. Click the plus sign next to your new scope to open its components on both the left- and right-hand sides of the console. Let's briefly discuss what each of these components allows us to do.

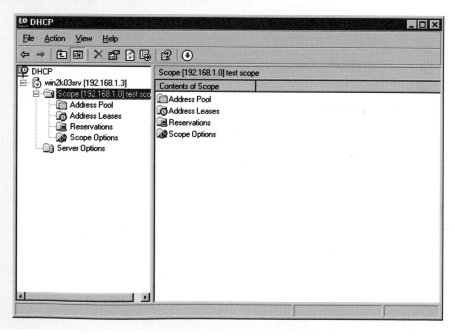

The Address Pool can be used to enter new exclusion ranges for the scope. This is useful if you later realize you missed one or more static IP addresses on the network. Address Leases merely displays information about current leases that have been allocated by DHCP. This can be helpful in monitoring the effectiveness of your lease duration. Reservations are used to permanently associate a particular IP address with a particular client. This is like setting a static IP address at the client but is administered through DHCP. Scope Options allows us to configure things like the default gateway, DNS, and WINS settings, among others.

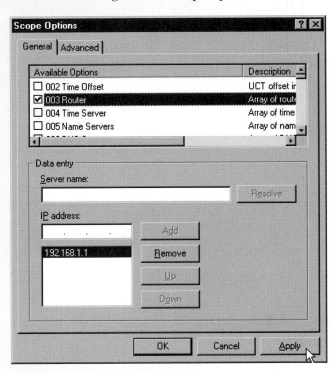

Click Scope Options on the left side of the console to select it. Then right-click it and choose Configure Options. Put a check mark beside Router to open the Router properties at the bottom of the dialog box. This is where you can configure the default gateway for your clients. If you have a gateway router on your network, enter and add its IP address now. You do not need to enter a server name. When you are done, click the OK button. If you do not wish to configure the gateway router at this time, click the Cancel button.

Step 8

Close all open windows and return to the desktop.

Tip: If you ever need to delete a scope, simply right-click it and choose Delete. If the scope is currently active, you will be asked to confirm the deletion. Be aware that deleting an active scope, which has issued leases, will create problems for the clients that hold those leases. However, it does allow us to create test scopes and remove them with relative ease. It is best to not activate such test scopes if you create them on a production network. That way, no leases will be issued to clients from the test scope.

 Cross Check

DHCP

DHCP is a powerful tool for network administration. It also requires the understanding of some new concepts. Let's take a minute or two to summarize what we've learned. If you like, review the preceding sections and answer the following questions:

1. What does DHCP do?

2. What is a DHCP scope? What is a lease?

3. Why might you need to exclude some IP addresses from the DHCP scope?

■ Setting Up DNS and WINS

As mentioned earlier, both the **Domain Name System (DNS)** and the **Windows Internet Name Service (WINS)** take more easily remembered computer names, such as Internet domain names, and translate them into the IP addresses the network needs to be able to establish communication. This translation process, known as **name resolution**, certainly makes computer networks much easier to use. Personally, I have trouble remembering phone numbers, including my own! I can't imagine what would happen if I had to memorize IP addresses for every network server, printer, and web site I need to use.

The Difference Between DNS and WINS

WINS is actually a bit of a dinosaur. Newer operating systems, such as Windows 2000 and Windows XP, understand the concept of domain names and make use of DNS to perform name resolution. DNS resolves the **IP host name**, which is typically the computer's name, to the IP address. However, operating systems like Windows NT and Windows 98 communicate over networks using **Network Basic Input/Output System (NetBIOS)** names. NetBIOS names need the services of WINS to be resolved into IP addresses. Thus, if your network will service clients running older operating systems, you should install WINS and configure DHCP to automatically configure clients to refer to the WINS server for name resolution. On the other hand, if you have only Windows 2000 and above clients on your network, you can safely skip installing and configuring WINS.

DNS should be installed on most Windows Server 2003 networks. The possible exception is very small networks where the internal resolution of names isn't a crucial need. In such cases the only DNS server may be an external server maintained by the ISP or another agency for resolving Internet domain names to IP addresses. However, it's never a bad idea to install DNS, and, in fact, it is necessary if you wish to establish a Windows Active Directory domain. An Active Directory domain–based network provides greatly enhanced security and manageability beyond that provided by a simple workgroup.

As you'll see in Chapter 4, DNS can be automatically installed as part of the Active Directory installation, which is the best way to handle things if you're installing both on a single server. However, there are many times when it's a good idea to run more than one DNS server on a network. For instance, if one DNS server goes down, clients can still resolve domain names if there are one or more backup DNS servers on the network. In this chapter, we'll install DNS manually, which would be a common approach if we were setting up such a backup DNS server. When we get to Chapter 4, we'll remove DNS from our server and allow Active Directory to reinstall and configure it, which is a common approach for the first DNS server in a domain.

The final difference between DNS and WINS concerns their configuration. In most cases, merely installing WINS is all the configuration that particular service requires. It is necessary to go back to DHCP and set it up to automatically configure WINS clients, but that's about it. In fact, Microsoft recommends sticking with the default settings wherever possible. DNS, on the other hand, requires a bit of configuration when it is installed manually before it's fully functional. After DNS is ready for action, the DHCP service should also be configured to communicate the DNS settings to the clients.

Configuring DNS

DNS configurations range from the relatively simple to the unbelievably complex, depending on the nature of the network DNS will be serving. On many small to medium-sized networks, the task is relatively easy. On huge networks, divided into many subnets, with heavier traffic, configuring DNS servers is a job in and of itself. Let's take a look at the basic settings we have to make and then try setting up a simple DNS server on our lab machines.

> Modern operating systems, in order to preserve compatibility with earlier operating systems that use WINS and recognize only NetBIOS names, will truncate computer names, if necessary, to create the NetBIOS name. This leaves the machine with two names that may be quite different.

Lookup Zones

At the very least, we need to create a **forward lookup zone** on our DNS server. A forward lookup zone sends name resolution requests for names that are outside of our domain to some external DNS server. The internal DNS server handles all requests for internal name resolution. As the DNS server receives each name resolution request, it determines whether or not it can resolve the name, and if it can't, it begins a process of querying known external DNS servers. By default, a forward lookup zone is configured to contact one of the Internet **root servers** to begin the process of resolving external names. These root servers direct the query to the DNS server responsible for the Internet domain (.com, .org, .edu, and so on), and from there the query works its way to a DNS server that knows the name and the address that goes with it.

In some cases, especially on large networks, it's a good idea to also set up a **reverse lookup zone**. A reverse lookup zone, as you probably guessed, allows the DNS server to do the reverse of what it usually does. With a reverse lookup zone, the DNS server can take an IP address and return the IP host name it corresponds to. Although reverse lookup zones can be useful for troubleshooting, they are not always necessary.

Zone Name

In order for the DNS server to understand which names are internal and which are not, it needs to know the **zone name** of the area it is responsible for. On a small network, this will simply be the domain name of the network. On a larger network, this could be some portion of the domain that this particular server is responsible for. Although we do not yet have a domain set up on our lab network, we can go ahead and give the DNS server the name of the domain we will be using. All we have to do is be sure that the eventual name we give our domain matches the name we've given for our zone. If, for some reason, our DNS server is incorrectly configured after we install Active Directory and create our domain, it will be relatively easy to remove the incorrect zone and create the correct one.

Cross Check

DNS and WINS

DNS and WINS have a common purpose, and yet they are distinctly different. Let's take a minute or two to summarize what we've learned. If you like, review the preceding sections and answer the following questions:

1. What is the purpose of both DNS and WINS?

2. How do DNS and WINS differ most?

3. What role does DHCP play in relation to DNS and WINS?

Configuring DNS and Activating DNS and WINS Options in the DHCP Server

In this Step-by-Step, we are going to make use of the New Zone Wizard to create our DNS zone. Once we have the zone created, we need to make a quick adjustment to our server's networking settings and add the DNS and WINS options to the DHCP server so that clients can be configured automatically. Consult with your instructor as to what zone name to use in the wizard. Ideally, the same name will be used later, when we create our Active Directory domain.

To complete this Step-by-Step, you will need

- A properly configured computer with Windows Server 2003 installed

- Access to an administrator-level account on the computer

Step 1

To open the DNS management snap-in, click Start, select Administrative Tools, and click DNS.

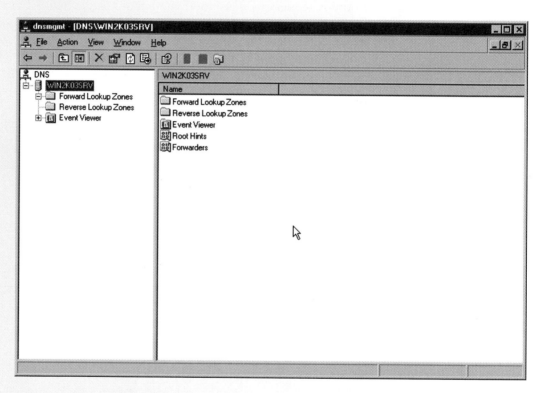

Step 2

Start the wizard by right-clicking the name of your server on the left of the window and choosing Configure a DNS Server. If you like, you can click the DNS Checklists button to review some guidelines from Microsoft on setting up DNS servers. When you are done, click Next to continue.

Step 3

You are now given the choice between creating just a forward lookup zone, creating both forward and reverse lookup zones, or not creating any zones. In the last case the wizard will configure the root servers that help with queries that go beyond the limits of the network. All other zones, both forward and reverse, would have to be configured manually. Leave the first option selected and click Next to continue.

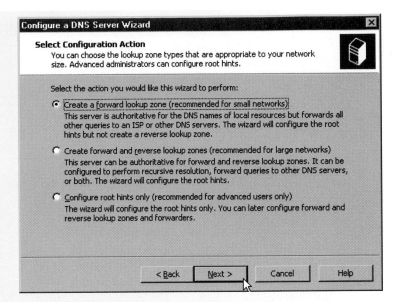

The wizard now needs to know who will actually maintain the records for the zone. In most cases, the local server will handle this, but in some instances an ISP may provide this service. Leave the first option selected and click Next to continue.

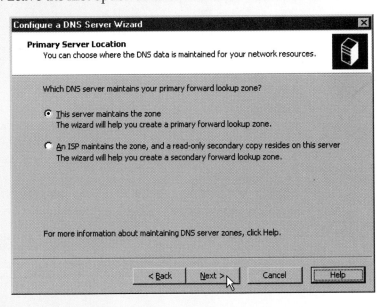

It's now time to name our zone. Remember that we are setting up DNS in advance of actually installing Active Directory and creating our domain-based network. However, if we use the same domain name here as we do when we set up our domain, then the DNS server should be properly configured. The name will normally be something like *xyzcorp.com*. However, some networks that do not have a registered Internet domain use single names or names like *xyzcorp.local* or *xyzcorp.localhost* to prevent any confusion with actual Internet domains. This isn't recommended in most cases, since the possibility always exists that the network will need to be connected live to the Internet. However, for the purposes of our current lab, and later for Active Directory, we should use a non-Internet domain. I'm going to use *ecktek.local* for my example. Once you've typed your name, click Next to continue. On the following screen, click Next again to accept the name of the database file.

Chapter 3: A Net Improvement: Configuring Network Services and Protocols

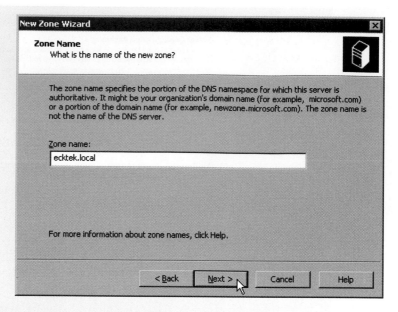

Tip: *Registering a domain is actually relatively inexpensive, averaging around $70 a year. It's wise for most networks to register a domain early on, even if they're not ready to connect their network directly to the Internet as of yet, so that they can go ahead and use the name for their Active Directory domain. Then, if they ever do need to go "live," there will be no conflict between their domain and others on the Internet.*

Step 6

DNS has the ability to dynamically update information in the zone database file as changes occur within the domain. This means that as clients undergo changes that affect their information in the file, known as resource records, the changes are written automatically. Although this can reduce some of the overhead involved in managing a DNS server, it can also expose the server to external threats. Without Active Directory, any client can make changes to its database records. In certain cases, this can expose the server to outside attack. However, once Active Directory is installed, we'll be able to tie it in to DNS so that dynamic updates are permitted only from authenticated, or genuine, clients. For now, leave the last option selected and click Next.

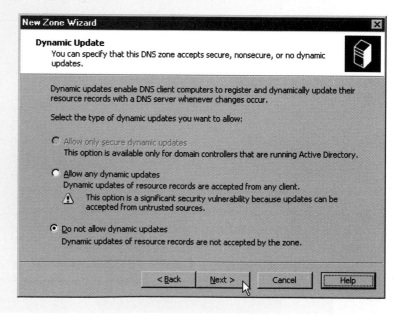

Although DNS automatically configures itself to forward queries it can't handle to the root servers, it is also possible to designate specific forwarders, or external DNS servers, to handle such queries. Such forwarders may provide faster response times, thus improving performance. However, they are not required, and for now we'll leave them blank. Choose No, it should not forward queries, and then click Next and then Finish to close the wizard. Close the DNS console when you are done.

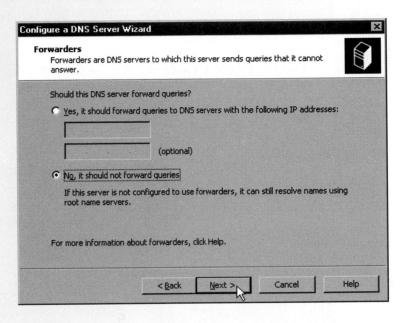

Step 8

Since our server is now both a DNS and a WINS server, we need to change its network settings so that it looks to itself for name resolution. To open the Internet Protocol (TCP/IP) Properties dialog box, click Start and then select Control Panel followed by Network Connections. When the Network Connections cascading menu appears, right-click your local area connection and choose Properties from the shortcut menu. When the Local Area Connection Properties dialog box opens, select Internet Protocol (TCP/IP) from the list and click the Properties button.

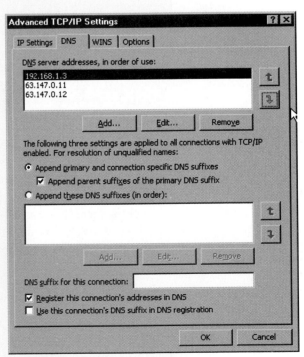

Step 9

Click the Advanced button and then click the DNS tab. Click the Add button and type the IP address of the server. Click the Add button and, if there are any other DNS addresses above the address of the server, use the green up arrow to move the server address to the top.

Note: There's no harm in directing a machine to more than one DNS server. It will use the alternate servers only if the first server is unable to respond. Having more than one DNS server available is actually good insurance.

Step 10

Click the WINS tab and add the server's IP address in the same way you did on the DNS tab. When finished, click OK to close the Advanced TCP/IP Settings dialog box, click OK to close the Internet Protocol (TCP/IP) Properties dialog box, and click Close to close the Local Area Connection Properties dialog box.

Step 11

Our last task is to configure DHCP to handle the DNS and WINS settings. To open the DHCP snap-in, click Start, select Administrative Tools, and click DHCP. If necessary, click the plus sign beside your server, and then the plus sign beside the scope to reveal the Scope Options container. Click the Scope Options container to select it, and then right-click it and choose Configure Options.

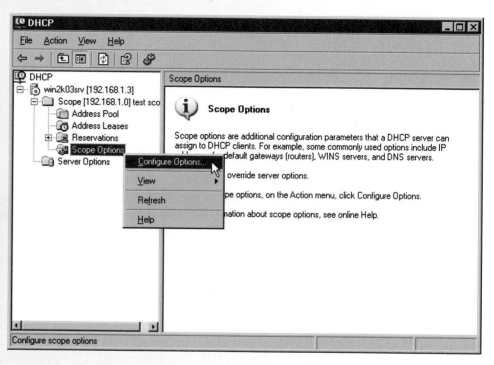

Step 12

Scroll down through the list until you find 006 DNS Servers. Put a check in the box and then enter the IP address of the server. Click the Add button to add the IP address to the list. Next scroll down until you find 015 DNS Domain Name. Put a check in the box and then enter the domain name you used when configuring DNS; for example, I used ecktek.local. Next scroll down until you find 044 WINS/NBNS Servers. Put a check in the box and then enter and add the IP address of the server. Finally, click OK to close the Scope Options dialog box and close all open windows.

Client Configuration

Don't forget that any clients connected to the network must also be properly configured to work with DHCP in order to benefit from all the work you've done. On operating systems such as Window XP and Windows 2000, this is usually just a matter of configuring the TCP/IP settings to obtain both the IP address and the DNS server address automatically. On older operating systems, it will usually be necessary to configure WINS to use DHCP for WINS resolution.

Try This!

Testing the DNS Server Configuration

Although it isn't foolproof, there is a quick test you can run to check the functioning of your DNS server. This test should work even though our server is not yet a member of the domain we used when naming our zone. Try this:

1. Open the DNS management snap-in using the procedure from Step 1 of Step-by-Step 3.5.

2. Right-click the name of your server and choose Properties from the shortcut menu.

3. In the Properties dialog box, click the Monitoring tab. Put a check in the box for A simple query against this DNS server. The recursive test would likely fail at this point, but you may try it if you like. It will do no harm.

4. Click the Test Now button and view the results of your test at the bottom of the dialog box. As long as the result of your simple query was a Pass, you have most likely configured your DNS server correctly.

Chapter 3 Review

■ Chapter Summary

After reading this chapter and completing the Step-by-Step tutorials and Try This! exercises, you should understand the following facts about configuring network services and protocols in Windows Server 2003.

Describe Basic TCP/IP Concepts

■ Transmission Control Protocol/Internet Protocol (TCP/IP) is a protocol suite that handles network addressing, data encoding, and the communication connections for networks. TCP/IP is the preferred protocol on most modern networks and is also the protocol suite used by the Internet.

■ IP addresses are normally expressed in a form known as dotted decimal, which is a sequence of four base-10 numbers each ranging from 0 to 255, with each number separated from the next by a period.

■ The IP addressing scheme provides almost 4.3 billion unique addresses, but the supply is running out. A new addressing scheme, known as IPv6, will provide over 4 million unique addresses for each square meter of the Earth's surface.

■ Subnet masks are used to divide IP addresses into one component that identifies the network and another that identifies the host, or client, on the network. This is similar in fashion to the way the area code and exchange of a telephone number work.

■ Subnet masks, in binary, consist of a string of 1s followed by a string of 0s. When matched up to the binary expression of an IP address, the portion of that address that coincides with the 1s of the subnet mask is read as the network ID. The portion corresponding to the 0s of the subnet mask is read as the host ID.

■ Public IP addresses are allocated by the Internet Assigned Numbers Authority (IANA) to organizations such as the American Registry for Internet Numbers (ARIN). ARIN allocates numbers to national or local Internet registries or directly to ISPs. ISPs typically assign IP addresses to the organizations that are their customers.

■ IP addresses used to be distributed using a three-class scheme, which was terribly inefficient. In 1993, the IANA started using Classless Inter-Domain Routing (CIDR), which uses variable-length subnet masks to allow greater control over the number of host addresses available in a particular network.

■ Private IP addresses for networks that will not connect directly to the Internet should be chosen from special ranges reserved by the IANA. Private networks can connect to the Internet through the use of routers that are capable of using Network Address Translation (NAT).

Configure TCP/IP

■ A dynamic IP address is assigned to a client by a Dynamic Host Configuration Protocol (DHCP) server. Dynamic IP addresses can and do change from time to time, which can be a problem for servers, and some other devices.

■ A static IP address does not change and is usually set manually at the client. Many servers need a static IP address.

■ Configuring TCP/IP requires entering an IP address and an appropriate subnet mask. You can also configure a gateway address that points to a router connecting the network to other networks or the Internet.

Set Up DHCP

■ DHCP prevents mistyped IP addresses, averts inadvertent duplication of addresses, and helps to conserve limited addresses by reusing addresses as necessary.

■ DHCP, DNS, and WINS are not installed as part of the typical networking settings.

■ DHCP manages a pool of IP addresses called the scope. These addresses are leased for a limited amount of time to clients on the network.

- Addresses that are assigned as static IP addresses must be excluded from the DHCP scope.

- Lease duration is set in days, hours, and minutes. Lease duration should be increased for larger, more stable networks if there are available IP addresses.

- DHCP can also configure client settings for default gateways, DNS, and WINS.

Set Up DNS and WINS

- Both DNS and WINS translate computer names and domain names into IP addresses in a process known as name resolution.

- WINS is used by older operating systems that use Network Basic Input/Output System (NetBIOS) names.

- DNS should be installed on most Windows Server 2003 networks to handle internal name resolution and forward queries it can't handle to external

DNS servers. DNS is required in an Active Directory domain–based network.

- DNS requires more configuration than WINS. DNS configuration includes the creation of a forward lookup zone, which forwards requests for external name resolution to external DNS servers while handling internal name resolution.

- DNS configures access to root servers on the Internet to aid in the process of resolving external domain names.

- A reverse lookup zone can be used to look up a domain name based on an IP address. This can be useful for troubleshooting.

- A DNS zone name, which is usually the domain name of the network, defines the internal network for the DNS server. The zone name could be a portion of the domain on larger networks.

- Client machines must be properly configured to work with DHCP.

■ Key Terms

American Registry for Internet Numbers (ARIN) *(78)*

Classless Inter-Domain Routing (CIDR) *(79)*

Domain Name System (DNS) *(94)*

dotted decimal *(76)*

dynamic IP address *(82)*

forward lookup zone *(95)*

fully qualified domain name (FQDN) *(94)*

Internet Assigned Numbers Authority (IANA) *(78)*

IP host name *(94)*

ipconfig *(81)*

IPv6 *(76)*

lease *(89)*

name resolution *(94)*

Network Address Translation (NAT) *(80)*

Network Basic Input/Output System (NetBIOS) *(94)*

protocol *(75)*

reverse lookup zone *(95)*

root servers *(95)*

router *(80)*

scope *(89)*

static IP address *(82)*

subnet mask *(77)*

Transmission Control Protocol/ Internet Protocol (TCP/IP) *(75)*

Windows Internet Name Service (WINS) *(94)*

zone name *(95)*

■ Key Terms Quiz

Use terms from the Key Terms list to complete the sentences that follow. Don't use the same term more than once. Not all terms will be used.

1. The _____ divides IP addresses into one portion that identifies the network and a second that identifies the host.

2. A set of rules and standards for communication is a _____.

3. Although IP addresses are actually handled by computers as binary numbers, they are usually written in a format known as _____.

4. The _____ command can be used at the command line to check the current IP address and subnet mask for a computer system.

5. Some routers make use of _____ to enable networks that use all private IP addresses to still communicate easily with the Internet.

6. The pool of IP addresses managed by DHCP is known as the DHCP _____.

7. _____ is the component of Windows Server 2003 that helps translate names to IP addresses for Windows 2000 and later client operating systems.

8. Since we are running short of IP addresses like 192.168.1.54, a new system, called _____, is being introduced.

9. The process of translating computer names into IP addresses is known as _____.

10. _____ is the most common communication protocol suite in use today both on LANs and on the Internet.

■ Multiple-Choice Quiz

1. Which of the following would most likely be an actual IP address?

   a. 10.269.15.5
   b. 172.64.1560.12
   c. 64.58.23.87
   d. 1.58.8.58.9

2. Which of the following is ultimately in charge of allocating IP addresses globally?

   a. ARIN
   b. IANA
   c. FQDN
   d. NAT

3. How many octets, or bytes, will an IPv6 address consist of?

   a. 6
   b. 16
   c. 32
   d. 128

4. Which of the following binary numbers represents the decimal value 255?

   a. 11011001
   b. 10101010
   c. 11110111
   d. 11111111

5. IANA has addressed the shortage of IPv4 addresses by replacing the class-based addressing scheme with a scheme known by the acronym?

   a. DNS
   b. CIDR
   c. RIR
   d. NAT

6. If the IP address is 85.172.19.5 and the subnet mask is 255.255.255.0, what is the host ID?

   a. 5
   b. 19.5
   c. 172.19.5
   d. 85.172.19.5

7. DNS automatically configures _____, which aid in the process of resolving external domain names.

   a. Reverse lookup zones
   b. WINS
   c. DHCP servers
   d. Root servers

8. There are approximately how many usable IPv4 addresses?

   a. 4.3 billion

   b. 4 million per square foot of the Earth's surface

   c. 4.3 million

   d. 16.7 million

9. Which organization is responsible for allocating IP addresses within the United States?

   a. IANA

   b. ISPs

   c. FQDN

   d. ARIN

10. For which of the following devices did the text say a static IP address was required?

    a. Windows 98 client computer

    b. Print server

    c. DHCP server

    d. Windows XP Professional client

11. Which of the following would *not* be a good reason to set a longer lease duration in DHCP?

    a. The network is large.

    b. Limited IP addresses are available.

    c. Most clients are desktop machines.

    d. Most clients remain connected to the same physical network at all times.

12. According to the text, IP addresses are most similar to

    a. Phone numbers

    b. Social security numbers

    c. Zip codes

    d. Names

13. Which of the following does TCP/IP *not* do?

    a. Run error checking on transmitted data

    b. Establish connections between communicating computers

    c. Handle the addressing of network clients

    d. Encode the data for transmission

14. Which of the following is *not* an acceptable IP address for a private network?

    a. 192.168.2.2

    b. 191.255.10.19

    c. 172.30.10.98

    d. 10.255.255.128

15. Which of the following does Windows fill in for you automatically when configuring a static IP address?

    a. The IP address

    b. The subnet mask

    c. The default gateway

    d. The WINS server IP address

■ Essay Quiz

1. Your supervisor wants to use an IP numbering scheme where all computers on your new network will belong to the network ID 1.1.1.*x*, with the first computer configured with the static IP of 1.1.1.1, and the second as 1.1.1.2, and so on. Comment on some of the problems that this plan has.

2. One of your newly hired assistants was poorly trained at her last job. She has trouble keeping IP addresses and subnet masks straight in her head. Give a brief explanation of the purpose and functioning of the two concepts that she will understand. Try to put things into your own words as much as possible.

3. You've put in a request to approve some overtime so that you can configure a DHCP server for your growing network. As you expected, the department manager wants you to justify why the company needs this "DHCP thingy," as he puts it. Put together an explanation that helps him see how a DHCP server will eventually save time and increase your efficiency as a network administrator.

4. Explain name resolution. Why is it necessary?

5. When deciding whether to use a static or dynamic IP address, what should you consider? When would you use each?

Lab Projects

• Lab Project 3.1

Earlier in the chapter, in one of the Try This! exercises, you were shown how you could use the calculator accessory to convert decimal numbers to binary and vice versa. You were also told how subnet masks, in their binary form, were matched up against binary IP addresses to "mask out" the network ID from the host ID. Recall that everywhere there is a 1 in the binary subnet mask indicates that the same binary digit in the IP address is part of the network ID. The 0s of the subnet mask correspond to the parts of the IP address that are the host ID. From the information in the first table, identify the decimal network ID and the decimal host ID for each binary IP address/subnet mask pair. You may record your answers in the table provided here.

Problem	IP Address (in Binary)	Subnet Mask (in Binary)
1	11010111.11101010.11111001.00110010	11111111.11111111.00000000.00000000
2	11110011.00010010.10101101.10000011	11111111.00000000.00000000.00000000
3	10101110.10000011.00111001.11001101	11111111.11111111.11111111.00000000

Problem	Network ID (in Decimal)	Host ID (in Decimal)
1		
2		
3		

• Lab Project 3.2

Do some Internet research and find out how one goes about requesting a block of IP addresses. In addition to ARIN, check other sources, such as ISPs. What is the procedure for applying for and being granted IP addresses? What types of costs are associated? Keep in mind that ARIN really isn't set up to assign addresses to smaller organizations. Their smallest allocation provides 4096 addresses!

• Lab Project 3.3

Research your network at school or work and find answers to the following questions. Estimate the number of devices on your network, including clients, servers, printers, and other devices that require an IP address. What is the block of IP addresses used on your network? What subnet mask is used? How many host addresses does that make available? Does your network make use of DHCP? If DHCP is in use, is it being used to automatically configure DNS and WINS?

Preparing to Serve: Understanding Microsoft Networking

"First comes thought; then organization of that thought, into ideas and plans; then transformation of those plans into reality. The beginning, as you will observe, is in your imagination."

—NAPOLEON HILL

In this chapter, you will learn how to:

- **Identify the logical structures of domain-based networks**
- **Explain the features of Active Directory in Windows Server 2003**
- **Create a domain by installing Active Directory**

Well, now that we've installed Windows Server 2003, we've got our client/server network, right? Not exactly, I'm afraid. We're missing a component that doesn't have anything to do with wires or hubs. In addition to the physical structure of computers and their connections, a network needs a logical structure. As you may remember from Chapter 1, Microsoft refers to client/server networks as domains. However, the word "domain" is more than just a name; a domain is actually the essence of what a network is and a tool for linking one related network to another.

We will begin this chapter by identifying domains, trees, and forests, which are the primary logical structures of Microsoft networking. We'll talk about what they are, what their purpose is, and how they work. Then we'll take a closer look at Active Directory, which is the service that makes this whole system possible and manageable, including some of the new features introduced in Windows Server 2003. Finally, we'll install Active Directory on our servers, thus creating our own domain.

Identifying the Logical Structures of Microsoft Networks

In order for a server running Windows Server 2003 (or Windows 2000 server) to act as the central point of administration for a client/server network, that network must have a system of logical structures that allow the server to clearly identify what does and does not belong to the network. Ideally, this system should also provide a way for the network to grow in size and complexity as the needs of the organization change. In Microsoft networking, this system consists of domains, trees, forests, organizational units, and sites. These structures organize the entire network: whether it is a simple local network or a global group of related networks. Each structure, and all of the information concerning the network objects they organize, is actually contained within and managed by a special directory service called **Active Directory** that runs on one or more servers within the network.

It is difficult to separate the discussion of domains, trees, forests, organizational units, and sites from the discussion of Active Directory, since they are so interrelated. After all, the only existence these structures really have is as information in the Active Directory data store. Although we'll discuss several key Active Directory concepts in this section, we will take the time in the next section to make a closer examination of its basic features and a few new features introduced in Windows Server 2003.

Domains

Imagine for a moment I'm a cattle rancher establishing a brand new ranch: the *EZ-E Ranch.* Among the first tasks I'd have to tackle would be to build a ranch house and fence in the property surrounding the ranch. The house would become the central point of administration for my ranch while the fence would define what was and was not ranch property. The fence would also act as a boundary between my ranch and the surrounding area and provide a certain measure of security. You can laugh if you like, but in some ways my imaginary ranch has a lot in common with a domain.

Every Microsoft client/server network begins with a domain, which is depicted in Figure 4.1. The domain becomes the container for everything in the network, much like the rancher's fence. It also forms a security boundary between the domain and the rest of the environment. The domain is formed when the first server on the network is **promoted** to become what is called a **domain controller (DC)**. DCs (there are usually more than one on a network) become the central point of administration for the network and everything within it, much like my ranch house. Installing Active Directory on the first network server makes the server a DC and actually forms the domain and the actual database of information, which is managed by Active Directory. When there is more than one DC, Active Directory maintains synchronized directories on each through a process known as **multimaster replication**. Because of multimaster replication, if any one DC

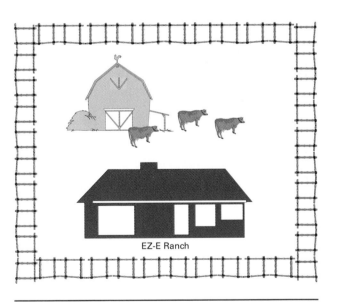

EZ-E Ranch

• The function of a domain is similar to that of the fence around this ranch.

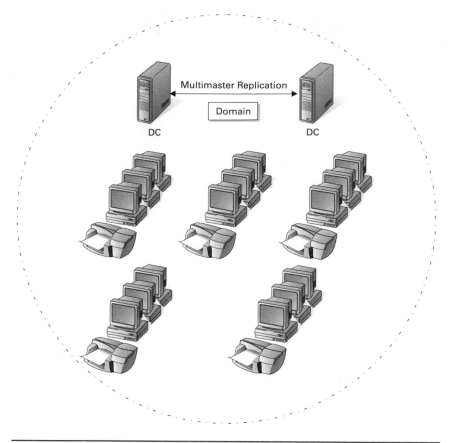

goes down for any reason, the other DCs still maintain the complete Active Directory store of information, which includes computer accounts, user accounts, and the like. This is important because the DCs are responsible for granting the proper access to the network and its resources by authenticating users as they log on. Without DCs, there simply isn't a network.

Each domain, much like my ranch, has to have a name. In the case of an Active Directory domain, this name is referred to as, you guessed it, the **domain name** and might take a form like ezeranch.com. That name becomes part of the identification of every object within the domain, including users, computers, and printers, which is an awful lot like me, as a rancher, branding the cattle and putting signs on the buildings with the name of my ranch. Although Active Directory domain names look like the Internet **Domain Name System (DNS)** names used by web sites, they are not necessarily the same thing. Companies can choose to use the same domain name as their existing DNS name in order to

• **Figure 4.1** The domain acts as a container for all network objects and as a security boundary.

> The names of objects in Active Directory actually take several different forms. We will discuss these forms in Chapter 5, when we use Active Directory to create various network objects.

provide seamless access to both internal and external network resources. However, that potentially exposes sensitive information to the outside world. Other companies use a different name that is purely for internal use, which has the disadvantage of requiring separate logons to access internal and external networks. In the latter case it is still wise to formally register the "internal" domain name with an Internet DNS registrar so that there will be no conflict with other organizations. Additionally, this provides the option of later allowing external Internet access to the internal Active Directory domain, if that's what is desired.

As you will see as we discuss the other logical network structures, the idea of domains and their names is an important part of how these structures are put together. Microsoft refers to Active Directory as being a **namespace**, which means it is a logical area in which names can be resolved, or understood, as identifying the objects they represent. This concept of namespace, which begins with the naming of our first domain, typically referred to as the **root domain** of the namespace, is part of what we must consider when we plan the structure of the overall network.

A single domain can range in size from just a few network objects up to a theoretical limit of ten million or so. In fact, Microsoft recommends that the ideal situation is to create networks of only a single domain. However, it is sometimes necessary to create new, but related, domains to deal with network growth. This might be done to allow for local management of geographically distant locations or to accommodate the need to support more than one language. In such situations, multiple related domains form what is called a tree.

Trees

Imagine that my ranching business has grown and I've established branch ranches (sorry!) in three other countries. For reasons of both language and distance, it isn't feasible for me to continue to manage each branch directly, so each is treated as a more-or-less independent operation. However, I should still be able to access all information at each ranch without any added hassles, since the branch locations are still part of my organization. This situation is similar to a tree of domains in Microsoft networking.

Try This!

Research a DNS Domain Name

Before you can register a domain name, you must first make sure no one else already has! There are many sites available for checking on the status of domain names. These sites make use of an Internet utility called whois, which can be used to display the registration information for a particular domain name. Try this:

1. Point your browser to `http://www.whois.net`.

2. Start by researching a domain you know is registered. Type the name of the domain (`yahoo.com`, for instance) in the WHOIS Lookup box. Look through the results, making note of the dates of creation and expiration and of the IP addresses of the domain servers.

3. Look up one or two more domain names you know to be registered.

4. Try looking for a name that has not been registered. Make up a name you'd like to use and enter it in the Get your own Domain Name box. You might have to try several times and be pretty creative to find one that hasn't been registered yet!

5. Take a look at the whois records for the names you try that are already registered.

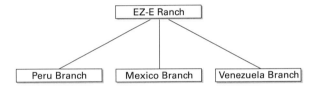

- The expansion of this ranch through the addition of new locations forms a tree-like structure.

A **tree** is made up of a hierarchy of related domains. The domains exist within what is called a **contiguous namespace**, which merely means they all bear the same root domain name. In the case of our earlier example, `ezeranch.com`, adding the domains `peru.ezeranch.com`, `venezuela.ezeranch.com`, and `mexico.ezeranch.com` would form a tree, like the one depicted in Figure 4.2. All of the domains in a tree possess a **two-way, transitive trust** between them. The trust is two-way in that each domain is trusted by and trusts each other domain. The trust is transitive in that if one domain trusts another, it also trusts all other domains trusted by the other. In simple terms, it means everybody trusts everybody, by default, in a tree! What this means from a practical standpoint is that it is possible for a user on one of the domains to easily access resources on any other in the tree. As soon as a resource is shared in one domain,

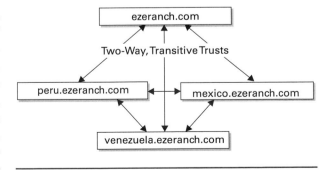

- **Figure 4.2** A tree consists of domains that share a contiguous namespace.

When resources in a domain are shared, certain permissions are granted to a group named "Everyone," which represents all authenticated domain users, including those from trusted domains. In the case of shared printers, the Everyone group is granted permission only to print, but not to manage print jobs or print devices. In the case of shared folders, the Everyone group is granted only the permission to read the contents of folders, but not the permission to add or change contents.

Inside Information

Understanding Trusts

Two-way, transitive trusts can be hard to understand. Think of them like this: if domain A and domain B trust each other, that's a two-way trust because A trusts B and B trusts A. If the trust between A and B is transitive, any domains that have a trust relationship with B will automatically have a trust relationship with A. That means that if B trusts and is trusted by domains C and D, then A also trusts and is trusted by C and D.

One-way trusts and nontransitive trusts do exist. There are also combinations of one- and two-way and transitive and nontransitive trusts. However, the default condition between domains in a tree (or a forest) is a two-way, transitive trust. The other forms are used only in special circumstances. Trust me, if you'll excuse the pun!

users of that domain, as well as users in any trusted domain, are instantly granted access, albeit limited, to that resource.

The domains that make up a tree also must share a common **schema**, which is the set of attributes, both required and optional, and the parent/child relationships that describe classes of network objects in Active Directory. As an example of this, consider user accounts. The schema defines that user accounts have certain required attributes, such as the user name, and other attributes that are optional, such as the phone number and title. Schema is one of those Active Directory terms that sound rather intimidating at first but are really rather simple. It only makes sense that if two domains in a tree are going to have the two-way, transitive trust we talked about a moment ago, the domains need to talk about network objects like users using the same schema. Otherwise, how could one domain know exactly what another domain was doing?

Since the domains in a tree are separate, they do not directly replicate each other's Active Directory data stores. Instead, at least one DC acts as the **global catalog (GC)**. The GC gets around the problem of dealing with multiple domains by keeping track of a few key pieces of information for every object in every domain in the tree. The domain controllers of the various domains in the tree replicate the most commonly searched fields for each of their network objects to the GC as part of normal replication. This is much quicker than trying to have the GC replicate each domain in its entirety! When a user of one domain needs to find a network object from another domain, the search is directed to the global catalog, which finds the object and returns the results to the user, including the "home" domain of the object they searched for.

Interestingly enough, a tree always exists, even when the network consists of only a single domain. The first, or root, domain simply creates a new tree that consists of only that single domain. From there it is possible to create new domains as children of the root domain, which are called **first-layer domains**. The domains in our example, `peru`, `venezuela`, and `mexico`, are all first-layer domains, as they are children of the root domain `ezeranch.com`.

First-layer domains, in turn, can have **second-layer domains** formed beneath them. Thus, the first-layer domain `mexico.ezeranch.com` might have as its child the second-layer domain `sonora`, which would have the full name `sonora.mexico.ezeranch.com`. Keep in mind that creating more than one domain should be done only if it is absolutely necessary, since a single domain is much easier to manage in many cases. However, it is necessary for many larger networks to split their networks into first- and even second-layer domains to make them more manageable or create stronger boundaries between parts of the organization. In fact, in some cases, it's necessary to go even further and create the largest logical structure of Microsoft networking: the forest.

Forests

What if I were so successful as a rancher (it could happen!) that I decided to expand my horizons and start a chain of steak houses? Even though the new organization would be run as a separate company under a different name, it is reasonable to assume that I, and other members of my management team, would need to be able to access resources of both the original company and the new operation. The Microsoft networking solution to such a situation is the creation of a forest. As you might have already guessed, a forest is made up of trees!

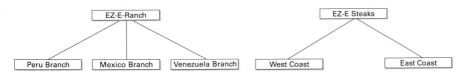

• Two tree-like organizational structures

Suppose we needed to expand the network from the previous examples with a network structure based on a different root domain. If the new proposed network structure consists of a tree of domains including `ezesteaks.com`, `east.ezesteaks.com`, and `west.ezesteaks.com`, it is possible to link them to the tree from our previous example and form a forest, as depicted in Figure 4.3. Forests are exactly like trees, with one key difference: there is a **disjointed namespace** between the domains of one tree and the domains of another. The namespace is disjointed because the domain names in two or more trees do not share a common root. However, there is still a two-way, transitive trust between the domains of the trees in the forest, and it is still possible for users in any domain in the forest to access resources on any other forest domain. Forests still share a common schema and common global catalogs. Additionally, as was the case with trees, a forest exists as soon as the first domain is created on a new network. Such new forests contain a single tree that contains the single, new domain.

Organizational Units and Sites

Whereas linking together domains creates both trees and forests, organizational units and sites exist within a domain. These optional structures can be used to improve the manageability of the domain and the replication of the Active Directory data store between domain controllers.

Organizational Units

Organizational units (OUs) are used to subdivide a single domain into more manageable parts without the need to create new domains. OUs, as depicted in Figure 4.4, allow administrators to group together user accounts, user

One of the differences between DNS domain names and Active Directory domain names is their use of the term "root domain." In DNS, the root domains are .com, .net, .org, and the like. A web site like `ezeranch.com` would be read as "ezeranch is a subdomain of the .com root domain." In Active Directory, the root domain is the entire name of the first domain in the tree. Thus, to Active Directory, `ezeranch.com` becomes the root domain.

There really aren't any hard and fast rules as to what the domain names of child domains in a tree can be, but they should be at least four characters long, at least at the first layer. This avoids any confusion with the DNS root domains and the two-letter codes used for identifying domains in other countries.

It's even possible to link two or more forests together. Unfortunately, there's no cool name to go with it; they're merely called "multiple forest" networks. They're also way beyond the scope of this text! That's not a big problem, since they're relatively rare.

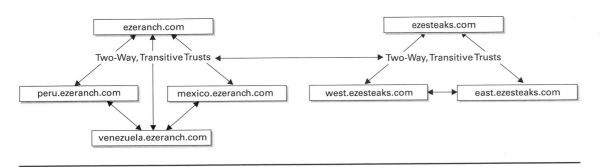

• **Figure 4.3**   A forest consists of domains in a disjointed namespace.

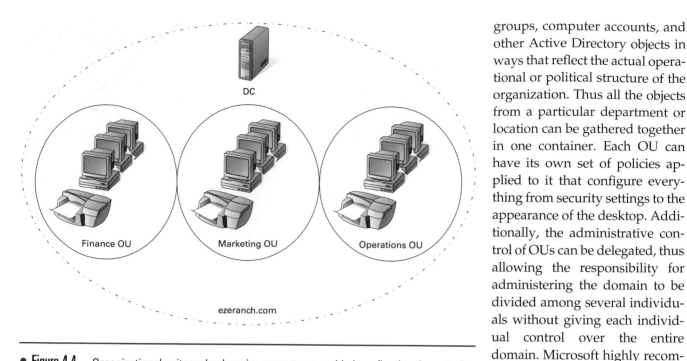

DC

Finance OU   Marketing OU   Operations OU

ezeranch.com

● **Figure 4.4** Organizational units make domains more manageable by reflecting the actual structure of the organization.

OUs can also be nested to create structures that accurately reflect organizational hierarchies.

One site is created during the installation of Active Directory. This site bears the appropriate name "Default-First-Site-Name" but can be renamed to something a bit more manageable!

groups, computer accounts, and other Active Directory objects in ways that reflect the actual operational or political structure of the organization. Thus all the objects from a particular department or location can be gathered together in one container. Each OU can have its own set of policies applied to it that configure everything from security settings to the appearance of the desktop. Additionally, the administrative control of OUs can be delegated, thus allowing the responsibility for administering the domain to be divided among several individuals without giving each individual control over the entire domain. Microsoft highly recommends making full use of OUs to ease management of large domains instead of adding additional domains. This is because OUs are much easier to create and administer than domains and are much more adaptable to organizational changes. Whereas deleting or reorganizing the hierarchy of OUs is relatively simple, accomplishing the same tasks with domains can be much more difficult!

Sites

Sites address the physical structure of a network; they really aren't logical structures like OUs and domains at all. Different sites can be created that group one or more domain controllers and client computers according to their IP addresses. Sites require that the network be divided into subnets, which are separate ranges of IP addresses within the overall network. By assigning computers and servers to subnets according to their physical closeness and the speed and convenience with which they connect, it becomes possible to create separate sites for the use of Active Directory.

By using sites, Active Directory can ensure that the closest domain controller processes client machine logons within the subnet, thus improving the responsiveness of the network. This can be important when the domain spans a relatively large area with widely separated domain controllers. Sites also allow for customization of the multimaster replication process between domain controllers so that controllers with slower, or more expensive, or less reliable connections replicate less frequently than those with faster, cheaper, more reliable connections. This might be desirable if one or more domain controllers required the use of an expensive connection, such as a satellite, in order to replicate. Replication policies can even be modified to schedule sites for replication when connection costs are lower.

If you find the concept of sites hard to understand, just remember that they basically tell Active Directory how domain controllers and other computers are connected. When the nature of the network connection

Introduction to Windows Server 2003

between domain controllers causes Active Directory replication to take too long or cost too much, creating separate sites allows you to control the timing and frequency of replication between the domain controllers at those sites. It's like telling Active Directory which domain controllers are "long distance" and which are "local" and then calling the "local" DCs more often than the "long distance" DCs!

 Cross Check

Logical Network Structures

Planning the logical structures of a network is an important first step in network development. Although not all networks make use of all of the structures at first, it's important to understand the different ways networks can grow and be better structured to improve manageability. Let's take a minute or two to summarize what we've learned. If you like, review the preceding sections and answer the following questions:

1. Explain, in your own words, the nature and function of a domain in Windows networking.

2. Explain the relationship between domains in a tree.

3. Explain the relationship between domains in a forest.

■ Active Directory Features in Windows Server 2003

You already know a good bit about what Active Directory does. For instance, you know that it contains information about every network object in the domain. You also know that it uses multimaster replication to keep multiple domain controllers and global catalogs synchronized. You even know that the logical structures of Microsoft networking are configured and managed through the Active Directory Service. However, we really haven't addressed what Active Directory does that makes it so beneficial. It's a tool with features that provide real benefits to both administrators and users. It has also been improved in some significant ways with the release of Windows Server 2003. Let's take some time to look at some of the basic benefits of Active Directory and some of the new features available in Windows Server 2003.

Basic Benefits of Active Directory

Once Active Directory is installed, it becomes the primary tool for managing the domain. From a basic standpoint, Active Directory tools are used to add network objects such as user accounts, computer accounts, and user groups to the domain. Active Directory is also used to organize the network through the creation of OUs and sites. However, the real key to understanding Active Directory is realizing what benefits it provides for those that administer the network and those that use it. We'll be working with many of the features that provide these benefits in later chapters, starting with the next. For now, let's take a look at the benefits to management, security, and interoperability in more general terms.

Active Directory Simplifies Management

Active Directory simplifies managing and otherwise working with the network in several ways for both users and administrators. For instance, administrators benefit from the central representation of all network objects and structures, which greatly decrease the amount of time they have to spend running from place to place creating accounts, controlling shared resources, and monitoring network performance. Administrators can even modify the layout of users' desktops throughout the domain with a couple of quick clicks. When a new application or utility needs to be installed on client machines, it's possible to use Active Directory to automatically roll out the program to all the clients that need it without ever leaving the server room!

Users, of course, also benefit from some of these capabilities, but they are even more directly affected by the way the directory service eases their access to shared resources. Active Directory is capable of publishing shared printers and folders in such a way that they can be easily searched for, and in the case of printers, installed, with little technical knowledge. Users can do sophisticated searches that allow them to find specific resources, such as printers capable of duplex printing, thus improving their effectiveness on the job.

Active Directory Strengthens Security

Active Directory allows administrators to be highly selective in determining which users have what type of access to particular resources. A variety of standard and special permissions provide for just about every type of access imaginable, from no access to full access and everywhere in between. Active Directory allows these permissions to be applied correctly to users or groups through a one-time authentication of the user at logon. Additionally, administrators have the ability to control the activities of users and client machines, thus reducing exposure to inadvertent or malicious damage to the network and its components.

Users benefit from the generally transparent nature of the security measures Active Directory makes possible. A single logon at any domain computer is all that is needed to allow the proper permissions and rights to be applied to the user's account. From that point the user is no longer troubled to constantly re-enter passwords or otherwise re-authenticate, thus avoiding work interruptions even as they access resources belonging to domain computers that might be thousands of feet, or even thousands of miles, away. And like administrators, users also have extensive flexibility in controlling how other users access their own personal shared resources, including local files, folders, and printers.

Active Directory Extends Interoperability

Interoperability is a fancy word that stands for a simple concept: Active Directory is able to cooperate and share its resources with other applications. Since Active Directory already contains all of that handy information that describes the domain, it's in a great position to make things easier for other programs by providing them access to that data. Thus, programmers can make use of security settings and access permissions to modify how users interact with software. For instance, an application could restrict its configuration options to only certain users. Active Directory can even be used to adjust the performance of hardware components, such as routers, to the needs of the organization. As an example of that, I've heard of situations where a router was configured to prevent certain types of network communications for certain user groups. Why do such a thing, you ask? Well, you wouldn't believe how much bandwidth gets eaten up when people start downloading those .mp3 music files! Not to mention the legal issues of allowing it to continue!

New Features of Active Directory

Remember from Chapter 1 that Active Directory was itself a new feature when Windows 2000 was released. As such, it's not surprising that Microsoft found a few areas that called out for some improvements and/or additions. Not all of the new or improved features are that earth shattering, but there are three that I think are pretty darned important.

Improved User Interface

You may find this hard to believe, but the ability to drag and drop items in Active Directory is a *new* feature! For whatever reason, the Windows 2000 version of Active Directory did not allow you to drag and drop objects, like user or computer accounts, from one location to another. This made reorganizing the structure, say by moving accounts into an OU, much more of a hassle than it needed to be. You can also now select multiple objects at one time and, in the case of user accounts, even do some editing of multiple objects. These and a few other more subtle enhancements make the Active Directory interface much more intuitive and should make basic management tasks much easier than they were previously. We'll be working with this improved interface in the next chapter, and from time to time throughout the text.

Group Policy Management Console

Group Policy allows administrators to control a variety of settings that affect user accounts and computers. These settings can modify the appearance of the desktop environment, security settings, where files are stored, which applications appear on the Start menu, and a myriad of other options. Group Policy can be applied to domains, sites, and organizational units, and more than one policy can have an effect on a computer or user account, depending on the domain, site, and/or organizational unit the account belongs to.

The problem with Windows 2000 Active Directory was that there was no centralized utility for managing Group Policy and the tools that did exist were clumsy and inconvenient to use. Since it was possible for several policies to affect one domain, site, or OU, it was difficult to know exactly what the final resultant policy was going to be. Microsoft has addressed this problem by including the **Group Policy Management Console (GPMC)** in the Windows Server 2003 version of Active Directory. This new utility allows administrators to more easily edit policies across multiple OUs, domains, or sites. It's even possible now to back up and restore policies, which comes in handy if you make a mistake! Considering how difficult Group Policy was to work with in the past, and how incredibly useful it can be, this is a valuable new feature. We'll be working extensively with Group Policy in Chapter 11.

The Ability to Rename Domains

I don't want to give you the wrong impression; you could certainly rename domains in Windows 2000 Server. All you had to do was take all of the domain controllers and **demote** them. When you demote a domain controller, it isn't a domain controller anymore. When you demote all of a domain's domain controllers, you don't have a domain anymore! Essentially, under Windows 2000, you had to destroy the domain to rename it. Doesn't sound like fun, does it?

 Although GPMC is considered a new feature for Active Directory in Windows Server 2003, it is not available on the installation CD. To download GPMC, go to http://www.microsoft.com/downloads.

The ability to rename a domain is available only if the domain is configured to use only Windows Server 2003 domain controllers. This is referred to as raising the domain functional level. Several other new features of Windows Server 2003 domains also share this requirement. A similar setting must also be configured for the forest to enable several new features at that level of the logical network structure. After installing Active Directory, we will discuss this setting and make the required change.

Windows Server 2003's implementation of Active Directory *does* provide for domain renaming. It's still not something you want to do on a whim, but it's now possible to undergo a domain renaming operation and still preserve the logical structures of the affected domain, tree, and forest. If you're wondering why someone would rename a domain, just watch the business news next time you have a moment. As companies go through mergers, acquisitions, and other structural changes, it is sometimes desirable to change the logical structure of the network to accommodate the new organizational structure. With Active Directory in Windows Server 2003, this is now possible.

■ Creating a Domain by Installing Active Directory

There are actually two situations in which you would install Active Directory on a Windows Server 2003 machine. One possibility is installing Active Directory on a server that currently belongs to a domain to create an additional domain controller on that domain. In that circumstance, the server would be referred to as a **member server** that we promote to a domain controller. The second possibility is the one we're going to address here. In our case we are going to install Active Directory on a server that is not a member of a domain. This will create the first domain controller on a new domain. In this case, the server we promote to a domain controller is referred to as a **stand-alone server**. Promoting a stand-alone server is actually the more involved of the two possibilities. This is because you have to properly configure the domain rather than simply joining an existing domain. Once you've been through the process of creating the first domain controller of a new domain, promoting a member server on an existing domain is a piece of cake!

Our final task, after installing Active Directory and creating the new domain, will be to configure both the new domain and the new forest to enable all of the features present in Windows Server 2003's Active Directory. This final step will also provide confirmation that the installation was successful.

Cross Check

Benefits and New Features of Active Directory

Since we're going to spend a lot of time working with Active Directory from here on out, it makes sense to start with a general idea of the benefits it provides. Additionally, since Active Directory underwent some major improvements since Windows 2000, it helps to be familiar with at least a few of the new features. Let's take a minute or two to summarize the benefits and new features we've discussed. If you like, review the preceding sections and answer the following questions:

1. Describe, in your own words, the benefits provided by Active Directory.

2. What key new features are present in Active Directory? Why are they important?

Planning the Active Directory Installation

Just as we preplanned our installation of Windows Server 2003, we should also take some time to prepare ourselves before beginning the installation of Active Directory. The good news is there are relatively few decisions we have to make. However, since we have to make sure we properly establish the domain, we'll take a few moments to talk about the choices we'll be presented with.

Domain Name

As we discussed in the previous section "Domains," we need to give our domain a name. Keep in mind that the name should take the form of Internet DNS names, even if you plan to keep the domain strictly internal. As we discussed in Chapter 3, you should seriously consider obtaining a registered DNS name to prevent future problems that could come from another organization using the same domain name. Registering a domain is cheap, sometimes as low as $35 a year, and doesn't take too long. Just be sure to renew the registration before it runs out each year!

You may also remember from Chapter 3 that you can choose a domain name that is strictly internal by basically using a name that looks like a DNS domain but really isn't. As an example, you could name the domain `mydomain.local` or `mydomain.localhost`. The advantage of using this type of naming is there is no danger of the internal domain ever coming into conflict with real DNS domains. Although it's really a better idea to register and use a real domain name, we'll be using a "local" name for our lab installation.

Regardless of whether the name you choose is a registered DNS domain name or not, there are some other guidelines you should follow. Ideally the name should be relatively short, since that makes it both easier to remember and easier to type. In order to prevent problems with older client operating systems, which don't understand domain names, it's best to keep the name to 15 characters or less. This is because the name older operating systems *do* understand, the NetBIOS name, is automatically taken from the first 15 characters of the domain name. Thus, if your domain name is already 15 characters or less, all operating systems still refer to the network using essentially the same name. That makes life easier for everybody!

Folder Locations

During installation, you will be asked to choose locations for two files and one folder. The two files, the Active Directory database and log file, are normally stored in the NTDS subfolder of the WINDOWS folder. Although you will be told they should ideally be on separate drives, this is really not necessary. The folder you will be asked about is the SYSVOL folder. This folder contains all of the information that gets replicated between domain controllers. It is also usually located in the WINDOWS folder, which is just fine, as long as the drive the folder will reside on has been formatted using the NTFS file system. If the drive is not formatted using NTFS, you *must* convert it prior to installing Active Directory. To do this, enter the command **convert C: /fs:ntfs** in a command prompt window, which you can access from Start | Command Prompt. This utility will convert the drive during the next reboot of the system.

DNS

One of the prerequisites for installing Active Directory is that the DNS service be installed and properly configured. Although it is possible to do this

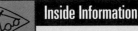

manually, as we did in Chapter 3 prior to installing Active Directory, that is not always the best option. The Active Directory installation program has the capability to install and configure DNS as part of the process. This is actually preferable to performing a manual DNS installation because it ensures that DNS is properly set up to accept dynamic updates from Active Directory. That means that Active Directory can update the DNS records to reflect the creation of new objects, such as computer accounts, as they are created. It is possible to modify an existing DNS installation to accept the same type of updates, but it does require some additional configuration. For this reason, we will begin our installation of Active Directory by first removing the DNS service from our server so that it may be reinstalled and configured to allow dynamic updates.

Support for Pre–Windows 2000 Server Operating Systems

At one point during the installation of Active Directory, you will be asked whether you want to enable support for older server operating systems like Windows NT. Prior to Windows 2000, anonymous users had access to information about users and groups that allowed certain older applications to work. If you are creating a new domain, there is little chance that you will be adding Windows NT servers, so you can safely choose to use only permissions compatible with Windows Server 2003. If you later find that there is a need to accommodate older operating systems and applications, the ability can be added after the fact, but you are much better off upgrading your software instead!

Restore Mode Administrator Password

The Directory Services Restore Mode administrator password is different from the administrator password you chose when you first installed Windows Server 2003. At least, it should be! If the Active Directory data store should become corrupt, Restore Mode can be used to try to fix the problem, and this password is necessary to use that mode. As always, choose a strong password and keep it secure.

Step-by-Step 4.1

Installing Active Directory on a Stand-Alone Server

Active Directory can be installed using one of two methods on a Windows Server 2003 computer. One method is to use the Manage Your Server utility and choose Add or remove a role. From there the Configure Your Server Wizard will start and, after scanning the computer for network connections, allow you to choose the Domain Controller (Active Directory) role from a list of all available server roles. However, a slightly faster approach is to simply run the dcpromo.exe utility, which is used both to promote member or stand-alone servers to domain controllers and to demote domain controllers. The

dcpromo.exe utility will start the Active Directory Installation Wizard, and from there it's a relatively simple process to complete the installation.

To complete this Step-by-Step, you will need

- A properly configured computer with Windows Server 2003 installed. This Step-by-Step assumes you are promoting a stand-alone server.

- Access to an administrator-level account on the computer.

- A domain name supplied by your instructor.

- The Windows Server 2003 installation CD.

Step 1

Log on to the server using the administrator account. Insert the Windows Server 2003 installation CD into the CD drive. The Active Directory Installation Wizard may need to access the CD during the re-installation of DNS. Close any open windows, including the Welcome to Microsoft Windows Server 2003 window, which should appear shortly after you insert the CD.

Step 2

Our first task is to remove the current DNS installation. Click Start | Administrative Tools | Manage Your Server. In the Manage Your Server window, click Add or Remove a Role and then click Next to allow the wizard to scan your system.

Step 3

Select DNS server from the list of server roles and click Next. Check the box to remove the DNS server role and click again to begin the removal. When the removal is complete, click Finish.

Step 4

Click Start | Run, and then type the command **dcpromo** in the Open text box and click OK. This will start the Active Directory Installation Wizard. Click Next to continue.

Step 5

The Operating System Compatibility dialog box informs you that client computers running Windows 95 and Windows NT 4.0, prior to the third Service Pack, will not be able to connect to a domain hosted on a Windows Server 2003 domain controller. This shouldn't be an issue for a new domain, although it could be a concern if you were upgrading an existing network. Click Next to continue.

Step 6

The Domain Controller Type dialog box allows you to choose between installing a domain controller for a new domain and adding a domain controller to an existing domain. Since we are promoting a stand-alone server and creating a new domain, make sure the Domain controller for a new domain option is selected and click Next to continue.

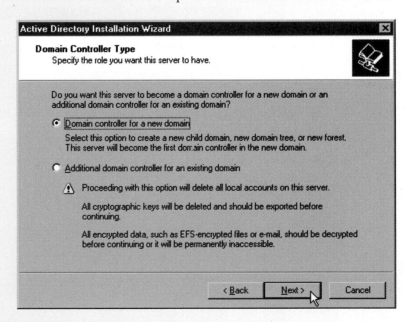

Step 7

The Create New Domain dialog box displays the three options available for this type of installation. Our new domain controller will actually be the start of an entirely new forest, which is the first option. However, we could also be installing a child domain under an existing domain tree, or we could be founding a new tree in an existing forest. Verify that the first option is selected and click Next to continue.

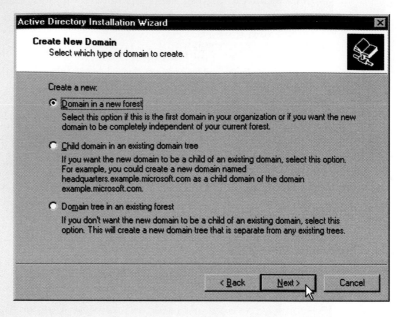

Step 8

The New Domain Name dialog box is used to enter the full name of the new domain. Since we are installing in a lab environment, I suggest using a domain name that ends in .local. The actual domain name should be obtained from your instructor so as to ensure no conflict in the lab or on the rest of the network. For this example, I'm using the domain name ecktek.local. After carefully entering the new domain name, click Next to continue.

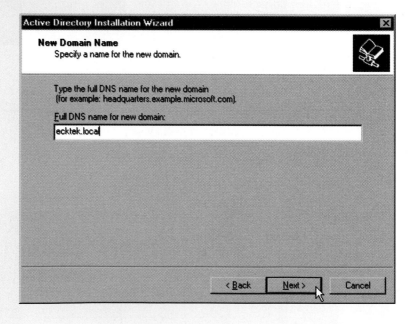

Step 9

The Active Directory Installation Wizard will use the first part of your new domain's name as the NetBIOS name. The NetBIOS name is used by older operating systems that do not understand domain names. This name should be accepted as is. Click Next to continue.

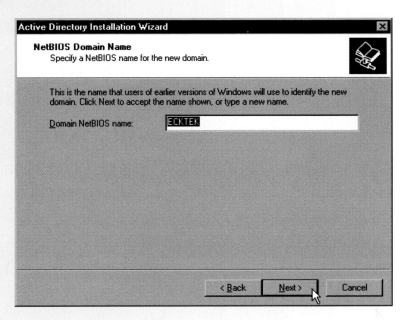

Step 10

The Database and Log Folders dialog box asks you to either confirm the location to be used for storing the actual Active Directory database and activity log or choose a new location for each. Despite the recommendation that these files be stored on separate hard disks, it is quite common to leave them in their default folders. Click Next to continue.

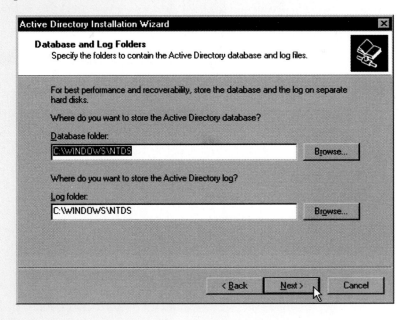

The Shared System Volume dialog box displays the default location for the SYSVOL folder, which is replicated between domain controllers. Do not change this location but do verify that the location is on a drive that has been formatted with the NTFS file system. This is required. Click Next to continue.

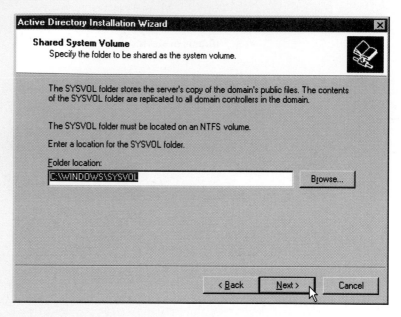

Since we've removed DNS, the DNS Registration Diagnostics dialog box will appear and inform you that there is a problem with the DNS configuration. Choose the second option, labeled Install and configure the DNS server on this computer, and set this computer to use this DNS server as its preferred DNS server. Click Next to continue. If you are prompted for the Windows Server 2003 CD, make sure you have it in the drive so that the necessary files may be copied.

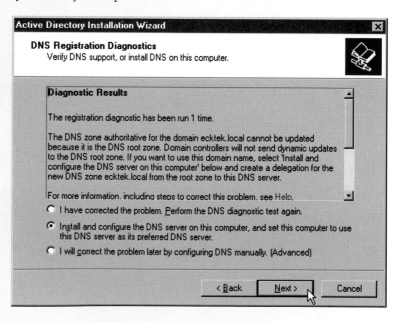

Step 13

When the Permissions dialog box appears, select Permissions compatible only with Windows 2000 or Windows Server 2003 operating systems. The other option is necessary only when running older applications intended for pre–Windows 2000 server operating systems. It is also a security risk, as it makes certain information openly viewable to anonymous users. Click Next to continue.

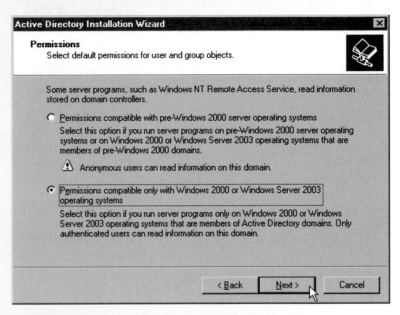

Step 14

Enter and confirm the Restore Mode administrator password. This password should be different from the normal administrator account password. Click Next to continue.

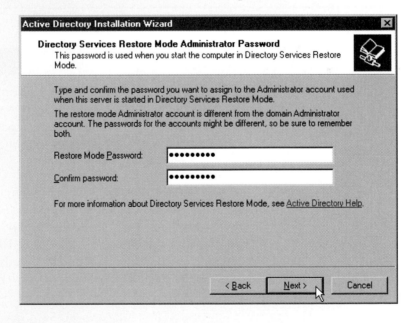

Step 15

When the Summary dialog box appears, review the information displayed. If everything is in order, click Next to begin the installation. The installation will take about five to ten minutes and will display a progress dialog box during the process. Wait for the installation to finish.

Step 16

When the process is complete, click Finish to close the wizard. You will then be prompted to restart the computer. Click Restart Now and wait for the computer to reboot. When the logon prompt appears, log on using the administrator account.

Step 17

As a quick check to see that Active Directory is installed, click Start | Administrative Tools. You should see three new entries. They are Active Directory Domains and Trusts, Active Directory Sites and Services, and Active Directory Users and Computers. You may certainly open each of these and take a look, but be careful not to change anything! We'll be working with Active Directory Users and Computers extensively in the next chapter. We'll use Active Directory Domains and Trusts in just a bit to complete our installation.

Try This!

Test Your Active Directory Installation from the Command Line

There are a few command line utilities that can be used to check your Active Directory installation. One of these, dsquery, can be used to obtain a wide variety of information about different objects, such as users, computers, servers, and OUs on the network. Try this:

1. On your server, click Start and then command prompt. From the command prompt, type the command **dsquery server**. The information returned by the command is your server's distinguished name, which fully describes where your server exists within the Active Directory hierarchy. The CN abbreviation stands for common name, while the DC stands for domain component. We will talk more about Active Directory naming conventions in the next chapter.

2. Try typing the command **dsquery computer** from the command line. This command identifies all computers on your network. As such, the result for your server will be a bit different when using this version of the dsquery command. However, either command can verify that the server exists as a domain controller and that Active Directory has been installed.

3. Close the command prompt window.

Raising the Domain and Forest Functional Level

As you might imagine, a company with an established network is not necessarily going to love the idea of upgrading all of their domain controllers to the latest server operating system every time a new version is released. In light of this, domain controllers running different Windows server operating systems are generally capable of coexisting on the same network. However, the downside is that mixed networks can't take advantage of all of the features of the latest OS.

When Windows 2000 was released, it offered two different modes of operation: mixed mode and native mode. If a domain consisted of a mix of both Windows 2000 domain controllers and Windows NT domain controllers, the network had to operate in mixed mode. If the domain controllers were all running Windows 2000, the full advantages of the newer operating system were available in native mode.

Window Server 2003 still offers the ability to coexist with Windows 2000 and Windows NT domain controllers but no longer uses the terms mixed mode and native mode. Under the new OS, modifying the **domain functional level** and the **forest functional level** controls the mode of operation.

The default domain functional level for a Windows Server 2003 domain controller is called Windows 2000 mixed. This mode supports servers running Windows Server 2003, Windows 2000, and even Windows NT 4.0. The highest level is simply called Windows Server 2003; as you surely guessed, it requires that all domain controllers be running Windows Server 2003. In between is Windows 2000 native, which supports Windows Server 2003 and Windows 2000, and Windows Server 2003 interim, which supports Windows Server 2003 and Windows NT 4.0. Raising the domain functional level to the Windows Server 2003 level is necessary if you want to take full advantage of several new domain features, such as the ability to rename domains. However, once the domain functionality level has been raised, it cannot then be lowered.

Forest functionality levels work much like domain functionality levels. The default setting, called Windows 2000 level, supports all three network operating systems. The highest level bears the same name as the highest domain functionality level: Windows Server 2003. Forests also offer a Windows Server 2003 interim level that supports Windows NT 4.0 and Windows Server 2003. The change to forest functionality level is irreversible, as it was for domains, but you do not have to raise the forest functionality level just because the domain functionality level changes. However, forest functionality levels cannot be raised until the domain functionality level has also been raised to a high enough level to support the change.

 The Windows Server 2003 interim levels for both domains and forests are intended for temporary use as a Windows NT network is upgraded.

Cross Check

Creating a Domain by Installing Active Directory

Although installing Active Directory isn't exactly rocket science, there are still a few key points to remember that can make the difference between a botched installation and a fully functional domain controller. Let's take a look at a couple of those key elements of the installation process. If you like, review the preceding sections and answer the following questions:

1. What factors should you consider prior to beginning the actual installation of Active Directory?

2. What should you do after the installation is complete if you want to take full advantage of all the Active Directory features available in Windows Server 2003?

Since we will want to experience as many of the new Windows Server 2003 features as we possibly can, we will go ahead and raise both the domain and forest functional levels of our new domain. However, check with your instructor before doing so, to verify that your domain will not later need to accommodate Windows 2000 or Windows NT servers.

Step-by-Step 4.2

Raising Domain and Forest Functionality Levels

Not only will raising the domain and forest functionality levels give us access to advanced features, it will also give us a chance to verify the success of the Active Directory installation process. It's easiest to change these levels using the Active Directory Domains and Trusts console, and that console exists only if Active Directory has been installed correctly.

To complete this Step-by-Step, you will need

- A properly configured Windows Server 2003 domain controller

- Access to an administrator-level account on the domain controller

- Permission from your instructor to raise the domain and forest functionality level

Step 1

While logged on to the domain controller as the administrator, click Start | Administrative Tools | Active Directory Domains and Trusts. Maximize the window when the console opens.

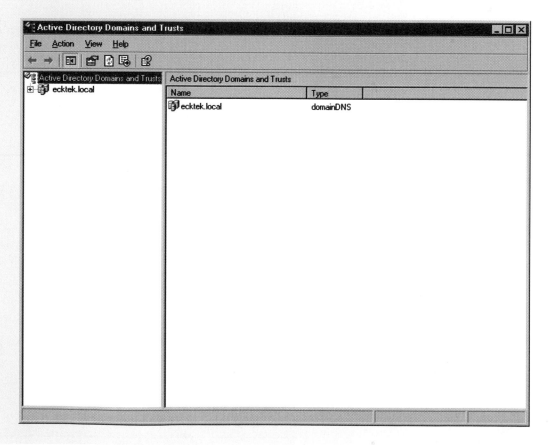

Step 2

Right-click the name of your domain on the left side of the console and choose Raise Domain Functional Level. When the dialog box opens, select the Windows Server 2003 level from the selection list and click the Raise button. When you are warned that this process is irreversible, click OK to continue. You will then be informed that the level was successfully raised and that it may take a short time for the change to replicate to any other domain controllers on the network. Click OK.

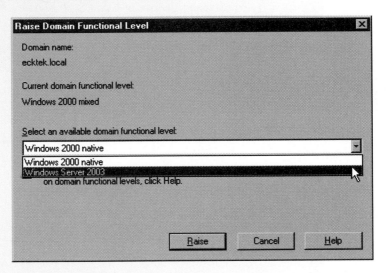

Step 3

To raise the forest functionality level, right-click the entry on the left side of the console that says Active Directory Domains and Trusts. This is the entry right above your domain's name. Choose Raise Forest Functional Level.

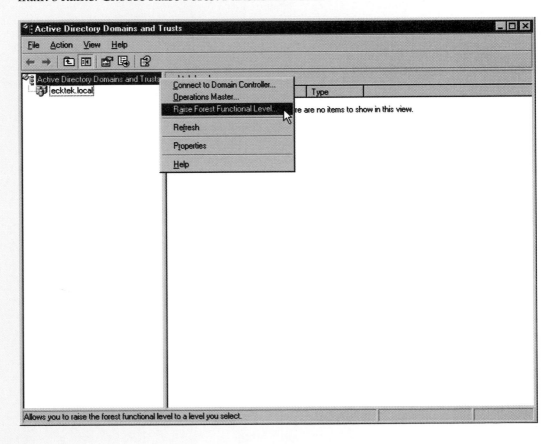

Step 4

Verify that the Windows Server 2003 level appears in the selection list. It should be the only option available. Click the Raise button, click OK when warned about the permanence of the change, and click OK when informed that the change was successful.

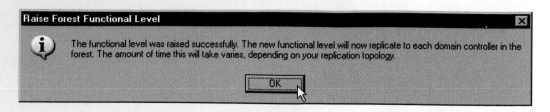

Step 5

Close the Active Directory Domains and Trusts console.

Chapter 4 Review

■ Chapter Summary

After reading this chapter and completing the Step-by-Step tutorials and Try This! exercises, you should understand the following facts about logical network structures and Active Directory.

Identify the Logical Structures of Domain-Based Networks

■ Every Microsoft client/server network begins with a domain, which becomes the container for everything in the network and forms a security boundary between the network and the rest of the environment.

■ Domains are formed when the first server on the network is promoted to become a domain controller (DC).

■ Servers are promoted to DCs through the installation of Active Directory, which maintains a database that manages all network objects.

■ Active Directory uses multimaster replication between multiple DCs to maintain synchronized versions of itself. This allows the network to continue to operate even if one DC goes down for some reason.

■ Each domain has a domain name, which is similar to an Internet DNS domain name. Although the domain name may not be used for Internet access to the network, it should still be registered.

■ Microsoft networks exist within a namespace, which is a logical area in which names can be resolved. The root domain forms the initial namespace for the network.

■ A tree is formed by a hierarchy of domains with a contiguous namespace. The domains in a tree share a common schema and a common global catalog. A two-way, transitive trust exists between them.

■ The global catalog tracks only key information for the objects in the domains of a tree, which saves time and allows the global catalog to help users in one domain find objects in another.

■ The child domains of the root domain are called first-layer domains, while their child domains are called second-layer domains.

■ The root domain also forms the first tree when it is created, but it is a tree of only a single domain.

■ A forest consists of two or more trees of domains with a disjointed namespace between the trees.

■ Forests share a common schema and a common global catalog and have a two-way, transitive trust between the domains.

■ Organizational units are used to subdivide a domain and make it more manageable. Administration of OUs can be delegated and can be created to reflect the actual operational or political structure of the organization.

■ Sites use subnets of the network to identify computers and servers by their physical proximity or the nature of their connection. Sites allow for modifications to the replication schedule between DCs.

Explain the Features of Active Directory in Windows Server 2003

■ Active Directory simplifies management for administrators by providing a centralized representation of all network objects and structures.

■ Administrators can use Active Directory to modify the layout of users' desktops and to roll out applications to clients remotely.

■ Users benefit from Active Directory's ability to publish shared printers and folders and allow them to be easily searched for. Printers can even be located by their features and installed with little technical knowledge.

■ Active Directory gives administrators extensive control over users' access to resources through the applications of standard and special permissions to authenticated users.

■ Administrators can control the activities of both users and client computers through Active Directory.

■ Users benefit from needing only a single authentication to have access to all appropriate resources. They also have the ability to control access to their own local resources.

- Active Directory can provide access to its data store to other applications, allowing them to make use of security settings or access permissions.

- Active Directory can interact with hardware components, allowing for changing configurations based on information stored in the directory.

- Active Directory in Windows Server 2003 provides an improved user interface with drag-and-drop capability, a new Group Policy Management Console, and the ability to rename domains.

Create a Domain by Installing Active Directory

- Both a member server, which already belongs to a domain, and a stand-alone server, which doesn't, may be promoted to become domain controllers.

- Planning for the installation of Active Directory requires choosing a domain name and folder locations, deciding whether to pre-install DNS or have the wizard install it, determining whether or not to support access from older operating systems, and choosing a Directory Services Restore Mode password.

- After installing Active Directory, it is necessary to raise both the domain functional level and the forest functional level if you wish to take advantage of all available new features.

■ Key Terms

Active Directory *(109)*
contiguous namespace *(111)*
demote *(117)*
disjointed namespace *(113)*
domain controller (DC) *(109)*
domain functional level *(127)*
domain name *(110)*
Domain Name System (DNS) *(110)*
first-layer domain *(112)*

forest functional level *(127)*
global catalog (GC) *(112)*
Group Policy Management Console (GPMC) *(117)*
member server *(118)*
multimaster replication *(109)*
namespace *(110)*
organizational unit (OU) *(113)*
promote *(109)*

root domain *(110)*
schema *(112)*
second-layer domain *(112)*
site *(114)*
stand-alone server *(118)*
tree *(111)*
two-way, transitive trust *(111)*

■ Key Terms Quiz

Use the Key Terms list to complete the sentences that follow. Not all terms will be used.

1. When you _____ a member server, it becomes a domain controller.

2. The process of _____ keeps multiple domain controllers synchronized.

3. The first domain created in a logical network structure is referred to as the _____.

4. If a server is not joined to a domain and does not have Active Directory installed, it is a

   _____.

5. The _____ includes required attributes, optional attributes, and parent/child relationships for network objects in Active Directory.

6. An _____ creates a subdivision within a domain. Several of these can be used to reflect the actual organizational structure within the domain.

7. One or more domain controllers within a tree or forest act as a _____ and maintain a record of the most frequently used attributes of network objects from all domains within the tree or forest.

8. A domain that is a child of the root domain is referred to as a _____.

9. A server on which Active Directory is installed becomes a _____.

10. A _____ allows the network to be separated, through the use of subnets, into segments that reflect physical proximity or the speed, expense, or reliability of connection.

Multiple-Choice Quiz

1. Which of the following network structures is most closely connected to the physical structure and connections of the network?

   a. Domain

   b. Tree

   c. Forest

   d. Site

2. Which of the following terms refers to removing Active Directory from a server?

   a. Promote

   b. Deconfigure

   c. Demote

   d. Partition

3. Which of the following allows domains in a tree or forest to find objects in other member domains and saves replication time by tracking only a limited amount of information about network objects?

   a. GPMC

   b. DNS

   c. GC

   d. OU

4. The effect of raising the domain and forest functional levels to the Windows Server 2003 level is

   a. Trees can be linked into forests.

   b. Features like domain rename are available.

   c. Member servers may be promoted.

   d. Windows NT may be used on domain controllers.

5. Which of the following does *not* need to be decided before or during installation?

   a. OU structures

   b. Directory Services Restore Mode password

   c. Whether to pre-install DNS or have the wizard install it

   d. Choosing a domain name

6. Which new feature is supported by the Active Directory user interface?

   a. Copy and paste

   b. The ability to rename a site

   c. Drag and drop

   d. The ability to create OUs

7. How many times would a user have to log on, assuming they had the appropriate permissions, to access resources in four different domains in a tree?

   a. Once

   b. Twice

   c. Three times

   d. Four times

8. Which of the following is not included in the schema?

   a. The number of objects that can be created

   b. The required attributes

   c. The parent/child relationship of the object

   d. The optional attributes

9. The two-way trust between domains in a tree or forest is also

   a. Transactional

   b. Transitional

   c. Transferitive

   d. Transitive

10. The logical area in which names can be resolved is the

    a. Schema

    b. Namespace

    c. OU

    d. Site

11. Which of the following can administrators *not* do using Active Directory?

    a. Track files stored on users' computers.

    b. Control the appearance of users' desktops.

    c. Centrally administer the entire domain from one utility.

    d. Automatically roll out software applications to users.

12. Which of the following is used to make a domain more manageable and can be used to delegate control of parts of the domain?

    a. Site

    b. Tree

    c. Domain

    d. OU

13. Which of the following can be automatically installed by the Active Directory Installation Wizard?

    a. GPMC

    b. DNS service

    c. DHCP service

    d. TCP/IP protocols

14. In the chapter, we used the _____ console to raise the domain and forest functional level.

    a. Active Directory Domains and Trusts

    b. Active Directory Sites and Services

    c. Active Directory Users and Computers

    d. Active Directory Domains and Forests

15. If you are positive that you don't want a registered Internet DNS domain name as your internal network's domain name, the chapter suggests you name it `mydomain.` _____.

    a. `.private`

    b. `.internal`

    c. `.org`

    d. `.local`

■ Essay Quiz

1. Your supervisor knows that the domains in a tree can work together and access each other's resources. He'd like you to configure the new network so that each of the seven different departments in the company has its own domain. There's really no need for strong security boundaries between the departments. Present your reasoning for why this isn't the best idea and explain how you would structure the network to ease management and yet reflect the actual structure of the organization.

2. The assistant you've been training is having a really hard time understanding the difference between a tree and a forest. They seem to understand the concept of trees pretty well, but they can't grasp the nature of a forest or why one would ever be necessary. Try to explain the concepts to them in the simplest possible terms.

3. A fellow network administrator from another company just called you with a problem. She really needs to rename a domain in her Window Server 2003 network, but she doesn't seem to have access to that new feature. Explain to her what the problem likely is and how to go about correcting it.

4. Explain, in your own words, what Active Directory's basic function is.

5. Explain the concept of two-way, transitive trust.

Lab Projects

• Lab Project 4.1

Take the following list of domains, which belong to a conglomerate that owns both a toy company and a party supplies company, and sketch out the logical structure of the network they belong to. Indicate parent/child relationships with lines. Surround the individual trees formed by domains with a circle around each tree. Surround any forests that are created with a rectangle. Here's a hint: start off by reorganizing the list (it's scrambled) so that first-layer and second-layer domains are listed with their root domain.

- `east.somefunparties.com`
- `retail.west.somefunparties.com`
- `happyfunco.com`
- `wholesale.east.somefunparties.com`
- `americas.happyfunco.com`

- `retail.east.somefunparties.com`
- `asia.happyfunco.com`
- `wholesale.west.somefunparties.com`
- `sales.americas.happyfunco.com`
- `west.somefunparties.com`

- `europe.happyfunco.com`
- `sales.europe.happyfunco.com`
- `somefunparties.com`
- `sales.asia.happyfunco.com`

• Lab Project 4.2

Analyze your school or place of employment. Consider the entire organization. What recommendations would you make as to a logical network structure? Your analysis should include recommendations on domains, trees, forests, OUs, and sites. Keep in mind the purpose of the various structures and recommend them where appropriate, but also strive for as simple a structure as is feasible.

• Lab Project 4.3

Choose any media, such as Microsoft PowerPoint, overheads, charts, or physical models, and create your own teaching tool for explaining domains, trees, forests, OUs, and sites. Prepare a presentation to use with your teaching tool and present it to the class. Feel free to develop original analogies, similar to the EZ-E Ranch analogy, to help in your explanation. After the presentations, discuss which models or concepts helped improve everyone's understanding of logical network structures.

Directory Assistance: Administration Using Active Directory Users and Computers

"A complex system that works is invariably found to have evolved from a simple system that works."

—JOHN GALL

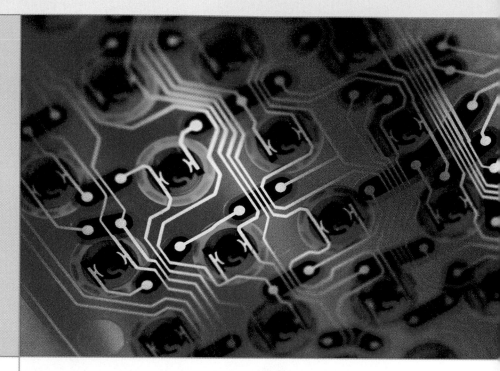

In this chapter, you will learn how to:

- **Identify Active Directory objects**
- **Create objects using Active Directory Users and Computers**
- **Manage objects using Active Directory Users and Computers**

Active Directory provides several powerful tools for the day-to-day management of a domain and the various objects in the domain, such as user and computer accounts. The most commonly used of these tools, Active Directory Users and Computers, allows network administrators to easily create computer and user accounts, organizational units (OUs), and groups, which are used to control access to resources on the network. Active Directory Users and Computers is also the primary tool for managing such objects after their creation, which means that most network administrators end up working with this powerful utility on a nearly daily basis.

In this chapter, we will begin by discussing the Active Directory objects that administrators need to create on a regular basis. We'll then move on to exploring the primary tool for creating these objects: the Active Directory Users and Computers console. Once we're familiar with the layout and general operation of this utility, we'll go ahead and create a few common objects for our network. Finally, we'll discuss and practice some of the more common object management tasks we can accomplish using Active Directory Users and Computers.

■ Identify Active Directory Objects

Once Active Directory is installed, a good next step is to start adding and organizing the objects, such as user accounts, which our network is going to need. However, before we start learning how to use the tools that allow us to do that, we should first take some time to discuss some of the more common Active Directory objects we'll be creating in this, and later, chapters.

You'll remember from Chapter 4 that Active Directory is just that: a directory of all the objects that make up the network. Some of these objects represent network resources, while others represent groups or collections of other objects. While some objects get created automatically as a result of some other action, most are created by the network administrator to suit the needs of the network. As in any other administrative task, a little bit of understanding and a little bit of planning go a long way toward creating a more effective network. Let's take a look at these Active Directory objects, their purpose, and the planning that precedes their creation.

Computer

Windows Server 2003 requires that computers running Windows NT, Windows 2000, Windows XP Professional, and Windows Server 2003 join a domain in order to access the domain's resources. One of the methods for joining a domain requires the user to enter the account name and password of a domain account that has authorization for joining computers to the domain. Doing so creates a **computer account** for that computer in Active Directory. However, that gets a little unwieldy when you're trying to connect multiple, scattered systems to the network. A better method is to create the computer account before trying to join the computer to the domain. Then you can configure the account to allow any domain user to perform the join.

A computer account uniquely identifies a client computer or member server. Not only does this account allow the computer to join the domain, it can also be used later to remotely manage the computer over the network. It's even possible to create computer accounts that allow you to install and configure an OS on a client computer from the server. Talk about saving some time! Most importantly, a computer account is one of the **security principals** in a domain. A security principal is a network object that can be given access to resources on the network. Active Directory uniquely identifies each security principal with a **security ID (SID)**. The SID created for each security principal is completely unique, which means that even if the account is deleted and then re-created with exactly the same information, the SIDs will be different and the re-created account will not automatically have access to the resources of the old account.

In order to create a computer account, there are a couple of things you need to know about the computer. First off, each account must have a unique name, which is also the name of the computer as it's entered in the client operating system. This presents two problems. On one hand, you need to make sure that every computer's name *is* unique, which can be challenging on a large network. On the other hand, to be of much use, the account should easily allow us to identify which physical computer we're working with. There are a number of different approaches to the first

Chapter 5: Directory Assistance: Administration Using Active Directory Users and Computers

problem, including the use of serial numbers or other coding schemes, but how can we, as humans, work with a name like "KRD043912LZH?" The answer is "pretty easily," with the help of Active Directory!

Once a computer account is created, Active Directory allows us to define for the account a description, a location, and even the person responsible for managing the computer. We can then easily access this information any time we need it. It's even possible, through Active Directory, to search for computers using this additional information. However, this doesn't mean we shouldn't try to develop a sensible naming system that people can understand. There are still plenty of times when it helps to be able to pick a computer from a list of names or when it's necessary to type out a computer's name. Just keep in mind that the name should be relatively short (15 characters or less) and consist of only letters and numbers, but not numbers only. Although periods and hyphens and some other characters are allowed, using them can cause compatibility problems in some areas. Longer names are also possible but should be avoided for the same reasons.

What's in a Name?

Before we move on, there are a few "names" we need to know that describe the different ways Active Directory objects are identified. For one thing, although we give objects names and Active Directory appears to refer to them by those names, for security principals the real behind-the-scenes identity of objects is the security ID, or SID. As mentioned already, this allows Active Directory to know that, just because a new account is created that bears the name of an old account, it isn't the same user and shouldn't have access to the same resources. An example of a SID would be S-1-5-21-397955417-626881126-188441444-501. And you thought remembering phone numbers was hard!

Obviously we, the users, need easier-to-remember names. The names we use to refer to objects tend to be *relatively* simple. I emphasized the word "relatively" because it may help you to remember the official term for names like *MYSERVER* and *HPPRINT01*. Those relatively simple names are known as **relative distinguished names (RDNs)**, which means they are distinguishable, or unique, relative to where they are and what they are. For example, imagine you name a computer *FIRST* and then name a printer *FIRST*. In Active Directory this would be possible, as long as the two objects were not in the same OU, because they belong to different object classes. They can be distinguished relative to their container and/or class. It's like knowing two people named Bob: one at work and one on your street. For the most part, if you say "Bob" at work, people don't need to ask "which one?" because they understand the name relative to the container, which is work.

Active Directory objects also have **distinguished names (DNs)**, which fully distinguish between objects. For example, if I refer to Bob as "Bob from the second floor, in the accounting department, in office 2B, at EZ-E Ranch," I would be giving his distinguished name. In Active Directory a distinguished name might look like *CN=WIN2K03SRV,CN=Servers,CN=Home, CN=Sites,CN=Configuration,DC=ezeranch,DC=com*, where CN stands for common name and identifies the names of various Active Directory containers while DC stands for domain component.

The last name type you should know about is the **user principal name (UPN)**, which is an easy way to identify both a user and their domain with one name. In fact, simple e-mail addresses, like *eecklund@ezeranch.com*, are actually UPNs.

Remember, all of these different "names" exist to make life easier. In most cases, we can simply use the relative distinguished name, which is short and sweet, and we're good to go. However, in those cases where we have to completely identify an object and its place in the network hierarchy, we have distinguished names to do the job. Finally, when we need to send information to a user in another domain, their e-mail address, or user principal name, compactly identifies both the who and the where! Of course, we could just use SIDs, like Active Directory does, but I don't feel like typing out S-1-5-21-397955417-626881126-188441444-501 every time I need to send an e-mail to my boss!

User

There's no getting around it; users have to have accounts if they want to log on to the network. A **user account** is also a security principal, so it not only allows users to log on to the network, it also becomes their network identity and is the basis for controlling nearly every aspect of their interaction with and use of the network as a whole. From an administrator's perspective, it's a rare day that doesn't require the creation of new accounts or management of existing ones. When you consider their importance and the percentage of time we're likely to spend working with them, it's a good thing that at least creating user accounts is pretty darned simple!

You really need to know only three things before you create a user account: the user's full name, the user's logon name, and the initial password for the account. The full name should consist of at least the first and last names, but you should certainly consider including the middle initial since it helps avoid duplication and Windows Server 2003 will not accept two accounts with the same full name. If necessary, it's even possible to enter up to six characters for the middle initial, which fixes problems like *Jim Bob Brown* and *Jim Beau Brown*. Of course, you could just call one *James*!

Logical Logon Names

Logon names need to be unique because Active Directory requires it. They need to make sense, and be created in a logical fashion, so that users can remember them easily and administrators can assign them easily. Ideally you'll want to develop a consistent convention for creating logon names for your network. However, as our preceding example shows, the obvious choices (like using the user's last name and first initial, or vice versa) are bound not to work for long. So, the question remains: what system should you use?

The short answer to this question is you should use whatever system works best for your network, but that isn't much help. However, let's take a look at two approaches that are very similar, with the exception that one worked while the other didn't.

One common approach is to combine some, or all, of the user's last name with a series of digits. In many cases, the digits are taken from the user's Social Security number, which makes them easy for the user to remember and relatively easy for the administrator to collect. I've seen this system work very well when it consisted of the first four letters of the last name followed by the last four digits of the Social Security number. However, with just a slight change, the system quickly breaks down.

Imagine you used the first three characters of the user's last name and the first three digits of their Social Security number. Do you see any problems with that? Well, neither did I, until I ran into the twins! The problem is that twins have a lot of things in common, even if they aren't identical. For instance, they're likely to have the same last name, unless one has changed due to marriage or other circumstance. But the name isn't the problem; it's the number. Of course they had different numbers, but they started with the same three digits! Why is that? It's because the first three digits reflect the area of the number holder's mailing address when they applied for the card. Since most numbers are now issued soon after birth, it's not surprising that a set of twins would share the same number!

It's worth mentioning that both of these approaches share another possible flaw. People are increasingly reluctant to publicly reveal even part of their Social Security number, and for good reason! Identity theft frequently begins with the illicit gathering of someone's Social Security number. Consider using a department number or employee number in combination with some or all of the user's name and you should be able to come up with a system that is both logical and easy to use.

Initial Password

The only other information you need when creating a user account is the initial password. This isn't too big a deal because by default the user will be forced to change this password immediately upon logging on for the first time. Thus they can pick a password they can remember and they don't have to worry about anyone having had access to the initial password. However, it is necessary that the initial choice meet the complexity requirements for passwords, which Windows Server 2003 enforces by default. This is a change from Windows 2000 that makes life a bit more difficult for administrators. To meet the complexity requirements, the password must be at least seven characters long and include at least one character from each of three of four possible groups: uppercase letters, lowercase letters, numbers, and special characters. The password must also not include any part of the user's name. This eliminates the old "easy password of the day" approach, which used a single, simple initial password for all accounts created on a particular day and depended on users to secure their accounts with a strong password. Although it is possible to change the complexity requirement, the best solution is to generate a list of random initial passwords that meet the requirements and work from that as you create accounts.

> The complexity requirements actually only require a password of at least six characters. However, the default domain security policy in Windows Server 2003 requires passwords of at least seven characters. In such situations, the more stringent requirement takes precedence.

Finally, it's also a good idea to collect additional user information, including addresses, telephone numbers, titles, and more when creating accounts. As was the case with computer accounts, this information can be entered for the account after it is created and comes in quite handy when users are searching for other users or when the administrator is trying to track down the physical location of a particular user.

Contact

A **contact** isn't really an object that represents a part of the network. Contacts are created to provide (you guessed it) contact information for people who are *not* members of the network. That's really their sole purpose, which means that collecting the complete contact information would be an important step in preparing to create a contact! However, to actually create the contact, all you need is the contact's full name. As before, this name must be unique, and by unique I mean it can't be the same as any other contact, or user name, or computer name, or anything else for that matter! That's not a new limitation; you also can't have a user name that duplicates a computer name or vice versa! However, it is more likely that the name of an external contact might match the name of an internal user, whereas user names and computer names should rarely conflict.

If you're having trouble imaging why you would need Active Directory to keep track of contacts from outside your organization, consider the following example. Remember my global ranching empire, the EZ-E Ranch, from Chapter 4? Well, by creating contacts for key customers, suppliers, and other business partners, I can make it easier for the users of my network to get in touch with those people when they need to. Hey, I didn't get to be that successful without effective communication, did I?

I've actually seen a situation where it was helpful to create a contact for people who *were* users on the network. In that situation, I wanted to provide an easy way for users to choose between sending e-mail to an internal address and an external address. Since choosing the user's account name directed the e-mail internally, I created a contact with the word *external* as part of the name and gave it the external e-mail address. This allowed the users to easily find the external address and use it if it was necessary.

Group

Groups are pretty darned important because they are the primary mechanism for managing network security. Since they're more of a security concept, we'll cover only the basics here and then come back to them in-depth when we get to Chapter 8. However, we do need to at least mention them now, since they are one of the Active Directory objects and we'll actually be encountering a few pre-existing groups in just a bit.

A group, or **group account**, is a security principal that can be used to collectively manage resource access for other security principals, such as user accounts and computer accounts. The basic concept is to make computers, users, and even other groups members of a group, which either has or is given access to resources. Each member of the group then inherits those security measures just as if they had been applied individually. This makes the job of a network administrator much more manageable, since they can work with just a handful of groups rather than with several hundred or thousand accounts! When groups are used in this way, they are referred to as **security groups,** which differentiates them from **distribution groups,** which are used only to send messages to multiple users through a single address.

There are actually three types of security groups, which differ in their **group scope**. What that means is that they provide access to resources at different levels within the overall logical network structure. For instance,

domain local groups can be given, and convey, permissions only for the domain in which they were created, whereas **global groups** have the same limitation but, unlike domain local groups, can become members of groups in other trusted domains, thus gaining permissions there. The third type, **universal groups**, can potentially be given permissions throughout all trusted domains, in a forest, for instance, without needing to join any other group. Each of the three types also differs in other ways, but we'll dig into that when we cover security in Chapter 8.

Groups are easy to create. All you need to choose is the name, whether the group is a security group or distribution group, and, for security groups, whether it's Domain, Global, or Universal. Even after creation, the only other task is to assign members to the group, which isn't too hard either. All in all, groups are deceptively simple since they are really the whole key to effective and efficient security management in even the largest of networks. We'll be working with groups extensively in Chapter 8 when we explore their role in controlling access to network resources.

Organizational Unit

You'll recall from Chapter 4 that organizational units (OUs) are used to subdivide a domain into more manageable segments. They allow administrators to easily group together Active Directory objects that share a relationship within the actual organization's structure. For example, I might group all the computers, printers, users, and other resources within the accounting department of the *ezeranch.com* domain into a single OU and do the same for other departments like marketing and operations. Of course, this provides the immediate benefit of helping us keep track of the relationships between our objects, but as we mentioned in the preceding chapter, OUs do much more than just that.

OUs provide two major benefits beyond simply organizing objects. The first benefit is that we can delegate administrative tasks for the OU to someone else, which is certainly a good thing from the point of view of an administrator! We can be very selective about how much responsibility we delegate, which allows us to retain certain administrative tasks while allowing someone else to handle relatively simple tasks like account creation and management. The second major benefit is that we can apply a **group policy** to an entire OU, which allows us to control everything from the appearance of client desktops to advanced security settings. As you might imagine, the *ezeranch.com* accounting OU might have more stringent security needs than the operations or marketing OUs.

Planning an OU is simplicity itself, since all you need to enter is the name! The first OUs are created as first-level containers under the domain itself. However, after that, you can also create OUs within other OUs if necessary. It's possible after creation to enter location and management information, as it is for computer accounts and user accounts. You can also choose to delegate management and set group policies after the OU is created. We'll be working with group policies in Chapter 11.

Printer and Shared Folder

The printer and shared folder Active Directory objects are pretty self-explanatory. The printer object represents a shared printer, while the shared folder object represents a shared folder. Believe it or not, that's really all there is to it! However, these objects do serve a purpose because not all shared printers or folders become Active Directory objects, and there are some reasons that they should be.

When an Active Directory object represents a shared printer or folder, users can easily perform searches to find the resource. When such resources are *not* represented within Active Directory, the process of finding them can be a bit more difficult, especially on a large and complex network. I don't know about you, but I'll take easy over difficult any day!

We use the term **publish** to refer to the act of creating an Active Directory object for a shared resource. You don't have to do a thing to publish a printer object if the shared printer is on a Windows Server 2003 computer. All shared printers in Windows 2000 and Windows Server 2003 are automatically published. However, to publish a shared folder, or a printer from Windows NT, you will need to know the network path to the shared resource. In the case of shared folders, you'll also be asked to give the folder a name.

> Printers that are automatically published in Active Directory do not appear as icons in Active Directory Users and Computers. Printers that are manually published do.

> Printers shared from Windows XP machines are not published automatically. However, they can be published by checking the appropriate option in the Sharing tab of the printer's properties dialog box.

■ Create Objects Using Active Directory Users and Computers

As you might recall from Chapter 1, the Microsoft Management Console (MMC) was introduced with Windows 2000 to provide a relatively consistent and customizable interface for a variety of management tools. Each tool is referred to as a **snap-in**, and you can configure the MMC with whatever selection of snap-ins you like and save the console for later use. Installing Active Directory actually creates some premade MMC consoles, each containing a single snap-in, and makes them accessible from the Administrative Tools menu. These consoles include Active Directory Users and Computers, Active Directory Sites and Services, and Active Directory Domains and Trusts. Of the three, Active Directory Users and Computers is the most commonly used during day-to-day management tasks. Through Active Directory Users and Computers, we can create accounts for computers and users on the network, OUs, groups, and other Active Directory objects and then manage them as needed.

Cross Check

Common Active Directory Objects

Understanding the nature of the objects in Active Directory is an important step toward creating efficient and effective networks. It's also important to understand what type of planning and preparation is necessary before beginning to create a new object. Let's take a minute or two to summarize what we've learned in this section about the nature and planning of objects in Active Directory. If you like, review the preceding sections and answer the following questions:

1. What is the function of a computer account? What information is necessary to create one?

2. What is the function of a user account? What information is necessary to create one?

3. What other types of information should you gather for computer accounts and user accounts, even though it is not required for creating them?

Active Directory Sites and Services is used only when creating sites or managing the replication settings for sites. Active Directory Domains and Trusts comes into play only when the network consists of more than one domain. In our simple lab setup, neither tool will really be necessary. Even on large networks, these two tools are used far less frequently than Active Directory Users and Computers.

Try This!

Run Active Directory Consoles from the Command Line

Although the Active Directory consoles have shortcuts already in the Administrative Tools menu, it is sometimes quicker to launch them from the command line. Try this:

1. To open Active Directory Users and Computers, click Start | Run and enter the command **dsa.msc**. Click OK.

2. To open Active Directory Sites and Services, click Start | Run and enter the command **dssite.msc**. Click OK.

3. To open Active Directory Domains and Trusts, click Start | Run and enter the command **domain.msc**. Click OK.

4. After viewing each of the three consoles, you may close them.

The Active Directory Users and Computers Interface

The consistent design of the MMC and its snap-ins was meant to make it easier to work with tools that are otherwise unfamiliar to the administrator. However, this helps only once you are already familiar with the console interface! Let's take some time in the following Step-by-Step to familiarize ourselves with the Active Directory Users and Computers snap-in and the information it contains.

Step-by-Step 5.1

Exploring Active Directory Users and Computers

The best way to get comfortable with the way the Active Directory Users and Computers interface works is to open it up and start working with it. In this Step-by-Step we'll focus our attentions on learning our way around and gaining a general familiarity with the type of information we'll be working with in this utility. After we're finished,

we'll move on to creating our own Active Directory objects in the next section.

To complete this Step-by-Step, you will need

-   A properly configured Windows Server 2003 Domain Controller

-   Access to an administrator-level account on the computer

Step 1

Although Active Directory Users and Computers can actually be started several different ways, the most common method is by clicking Start | Administrative Tools | Active Directory Users and Computers. Start the utility and maximize the window once it opens.

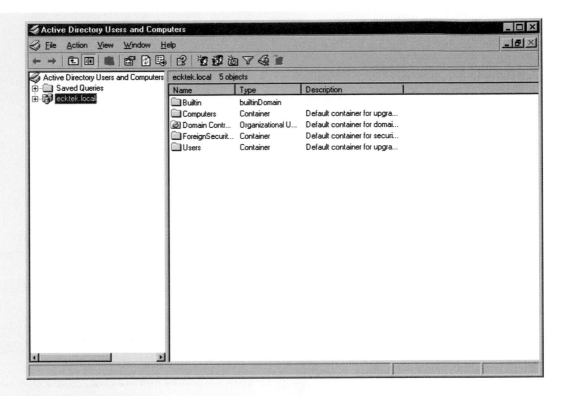

Step 2

The window is divided into two panes, much like Windows Explorer. In fact, the similarities between the two utilities don't end there. As in Windows Explorer, the left pane is used to display a hierarchy of locations while the right pane is used to display the contents of those locations. Unlike in Windows Explorer, the left-hand pane doesn't really display folders, although many of the icons appear to be folders, and the right pane does not display folders and files. In Active Directory Users and Computers, the left pane is used to display a hierarchy of **containers**, which contain other containers and the various Active Directory objects that get displayed in the right pane. To expand the hierarchy one level, double-click the name of your domain in the left pane. The icon beside it represents the server or servers that are your domain controllers. Double-clicking the name, or the icon, both opens the hierarchy by one level and displays that level in the right pane.

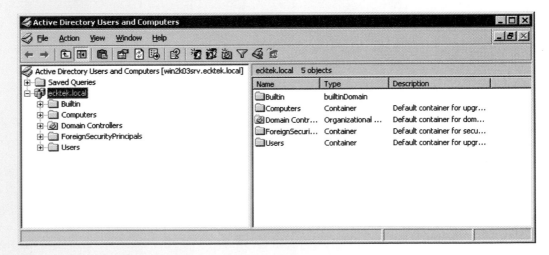

Tip: You can resize the panes by dragging the vertical border between them with your mouse.

Step 3

You should see at least five containers (Builtin, Computers, Domain Controllers, ForeignSecurityPrincipals, and Users) in the hierarchy under your domain in the left pane. You should also see two icons above your domain. The uppermost of these merely represents the Active Directory Users and Computers tool itself. The second, Saved Queries, is used for saving past object searches for re-use. If your screen looks significantly different from the illustrations, it may be because someone else has been working with the server. Another possibility is that the Advanced Features option has been turned on. Click View and look to see if Advanced Features has a check mark beside it. If it does, click it to deselect it and your screen should look more like the illustrations. You may also turn Advanced Features on to see what it looks like, but be sure to turn it off before you continue. The extra containers it adds are rarely needed during normal administrative tasks, and the simpler interface is easier to work with! However, the Advanced Features option also makes additional information available when working with object properties, so it is sometimes necessary to turn it on.

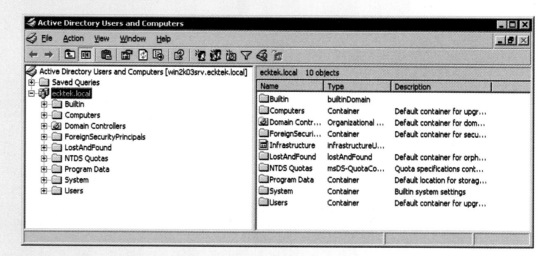

Step 4

The plus signs next to each of the containers work just as they do in Windows Explorer; they open up lower levels of the hierarchy *without* changing your current location. However, as is also the case in Explorer, they sometimes appear even when there aren't any lower-level containers. Click each of the plus signs beside the containers now and notice that they simply disappear, indicating that there are no further levels within those containers. The minus sign that currently appears beside your domain's name is used to collapse levels of the hierarchy. Click it once to hide the five containers and then click the plus sign to show them again. Notice that during this step the contents of the right pane have not changed at all.

Step 5

To open a container, you can either click once on either its name or icon in the left pane or double-click it in the right pane. Both methods will display the contents of the container in the right pane, but neither method will open lower levels of the hierarchy. If you want to both see the contents of a container *and* open the next level of the hierarchy, if it exists, you should double-click the name or icon in the left pane. Try using both the double-click method in the right pane and the single-click method in the left pane to open each of the five containers. Note that some containers, such as Computers, are probably empty, while the rest contain one or more objects. We'll be discussing the objects each container holds in much greater detail later. When you are done trying the different methods, leave the Users container open.

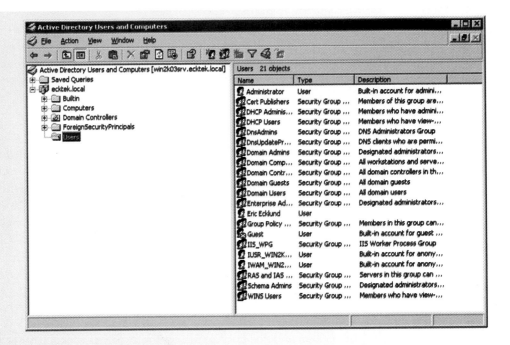

Step 6

The right pane is currently displaying the objects in the Users container in Detail view. This view displays (you guessed it!) details about the objects through the use of one or more columns that provide additional information beyond the object's name. Although other views are available either through the View menu or from the right-click shortcut menu, the Detail view is far and away the most useful view when working in Active Directory Users and Computers. The width of each column can be adjusted either by manually dragging the right border with the mouse to the desired width or by double-clicking the right border of the column to automatically size it to fit its longest entry. Try double-clicking the right border of the Type column to size it automatically. Try manually sizing the Description column by widening it a bit at a time. If any of the descriptions still ends with a "..."—the column still isn't wide enough! You can double-click the column border to size it automatically if you like, but depending on the size of your monitor, it may not help! The entries in the Description column are sometimes so long that they won't fit on a smaller screen. Also resize the Name column to fit its contents before moving on to the next step.

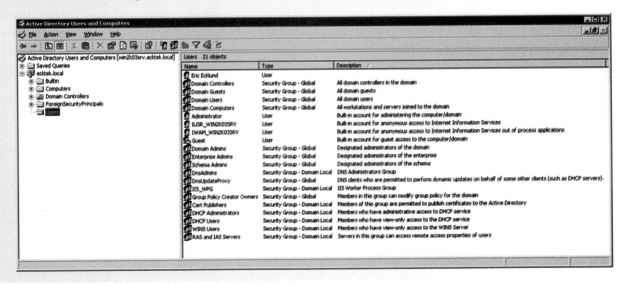

Chapter 5: Directory Assistance: Administration Using Active Directory Users and Computers

Tip: You can add additional columns and change their order through View | Add/Remove Columns. You can also sort the display in either ascending or descending order for any column by clicking the column header. Click once to sort in ascending order and click a second time to sort in descending order. The default display sorts in ascending order according to the information in the first column.

Step 7

Above the columns of the right pane you'll notice the description bar. This reports both your current location and the number of objects in the container. Above the description bar, and to the left, is a toolbar. Most of the functions represented by the toolbar buttons can also be executed through the right-click shortcut menu or from the menus on the menu bar. However, the first four buttons perform functions that are not available using either of those methods. The first three buttons (Back, Forward, and Up One Level) are used to navigate the hierarchy, while the last (Show/Hide Console Tree) can be used to hide or redisplay the left pane, which displays the hierarchy. Although you can certainly do without the navigation buttons, if you wish, it is sometimes helpful to hide the left pane to allow the viewing of multiple columns of information in the right pane.

Rest your mouse cursor over each button to see its name. Explore both the menus on the menu bar and the submenus on the shortcut menu (right-click) to see if you can find where each button's function is duplicated. When it comes time to perform these functions, you can use whichever method (menu bar, toolbar, or shortcut menu) you prefer.

Tip: Other buttons will also appear on the toolbar when certain objects are selected.

Step 8

Close the Active Directory Users and Computers console and immediately reopen it. Notice that the console saves your viewing preferences, including column widths and last location, when it closes, and reopens with those preferences in effect. This is great when you're the only one using the server but can be irritating whenever two, or more, people are using the console and have different ideas about how it should look! The good news is that these preferences are stored as part of the profile for the account you use to log in. If each person uses a different account to log on to the server when performing administrative tasks, their settings will apply only to them. You can close the console when you finish this step.

Caution: Multiple administrators should always have separate administrator-level accounts rather than using the same default administrator account created during installation. Not only does this help prevent conflicts over how things should look, which is certainly a minor problem, it also helps keep track of who did what! We'll be creating a new administrator-level account later in this chapter.

The Initial Active Directory Containers and Objects

The five default containers that appear under the domain in Active Directory Users and Computers form the initial, basic structure of the domain and provide a framework for creating new Active Directory objects. They also contain a number of objects that are created as part of the Active Directory installation process. We'll be adding our own containers and creating some common Active Directory objects in just a bit, but before we begin, we should understand the purpose of these original five containers and their contents.

The Builtin Container

The Builtin container gets its name from the fact that it contains many of the security groups that come "built in" with the installation of Active Directory. Each security group provides different levels of access and different privileges to the users or groups that become members. The group descriptions in Figure 5.1 give a pretty clear indication of how they are used. For instance, users who are made members of the Administrator group have the same level of access as the initial Administrator account does. These security groups allow you to easily assign predefined roles to network users by simply making them members of the appropriate group. Keep in mind, however, that each of these groups is a domain local group, so the permissions apply only to the local domain even if there are other domains in the tree or forest.

The Computers Container

The Computers container is the default location for upgraded computer accounts from earlier network operating systems such as Windows NT. This container is empty when it is first created as part of a new installation, but you might create computer accounts here that don't belong to a specific OU.

The Domain Controllers Container

The Domain Controllers container simply contains the DCs for the domain. Actually, this container is a bit different from the others in that it is actually an OU. The advantage to this is that security policies can be applied to OUs, but not to normal containers. Thus, a single Domain Controller security policy can be applied to this one container, which makes it easy to set a consistent set of policies across all DCs. If you look at this container in Active Directory Users and Computers, you will notice that the icon is even slightly different from the rest. This icon identifies a container as an OU.

The ForeignSecurityPrincipals Container

The ForeignSecurityPrincipals container is another container that is likely to be empty when the domain controller is first promoted. This container is

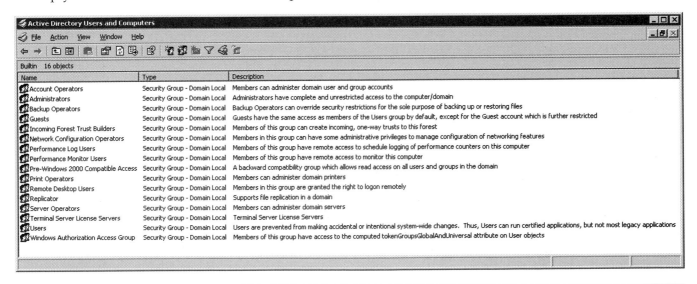

- **Figure 5.1**   The initial contents of the Builtin container

used to hold the security identifiers (SIDs) of security principals from external, trusted domains. Of course, if the network consists of only a single domain, it's unlikely you'll need to create any objects in this container.

The Users Container

The Users container is a bit of a mixed bag. It is the location for upgraded user accounts from Windows NT. It's also the location of the initial Administrator account, which we've been using since we installed Windows Server 2003. It can also be used to hold user accounts you create that don't belong to a particular OU. However, as you can see in Figure 5.2, its initial contents include some nonuser account objects as well, including domain local groups, global groups, and universal groups.

We'll come back and discuss these initial groups further when we reach Chapter 8, but there are a few special groups we should take just a moment to mention. Included in the Users container are global groups named Domain Computers, Domain Controllers, and Domain Users. The interesting thing about these group accounts is that every newly created computer account, DC, and user account automatically becomes a member of its corresponding group. The convenience of that, especially for user accounts, is that you can easily give every domain user access to a resource simply by giving that access to the Domain Users group.

> There is also a Guest account and a Domain Guests group created with the installation of Active Directory. However, the Guest account, which is the only member of the Domain Guests group, is disabled by default and should remain so for security reasons. Guest accounts are a frequent point of access for hacking attacks against networks.

Creating Common Active Directory Objects

As the opening quote of this chapter implied, if we want to build a complex network that works, we need to start with the little things and make sure

Active Directory Users and Computers

File   Action   View   Window   Help

Users   21 objects

Name	Type	Description
Eric Ecklund	User	
Domain Controllers	Security Group - Global	All domain controllers in the domain
Domain Guests	Security Group - Global	All domain guests
Domain Users	Security Group - Global	All domain users
Domain Computers	Security Group - Global	All workstations and servers joined to the domain
Administrator	User	Built-in account for administering the computer/domain
IUSR_WIN2K03SRV	User	Built-in account for anonymous access to Internet Information Services
IWAM_WIN2K03SRV	User	Built-in account for anonymous access to Internet Information Services out of process applications
Guest	User	Built-in account for guest access to the computer/domain
Domain Admins	Security Group - Global	Designated administrators of the domain
Enterprise Admins	Security Group - Global	Designated administrators of the enterprise
Schema Admins	Security Group - Global	Designated administrators of the schema
DnsAdmins	Security Group - Domain Local	DNS Administrators Group
DnsUpdateProxy	Security Group - Global	DNS clients who are permitted to perform dynamic updates on behalf of some other clients (such as DHCP servers).
IIS_WPG	Security Group - Domain Local	IIS Worker Process Group
Group Policy Creator Owners	Security Group - Global	Members in this group can modify group policy for the domain
Cert Publishers	Security Group - Domain Local	Members of this group are permitted to publish certificates to the Active Directory
DHCP Administrators	Security Group - Domain Local	Members who have administrative access to DHCP service
DHCP Users	Security Group - Domain Local	Members who have view-only access to the DHCP service
WINS Users	Security Group - Domain Local	Members who have view-only access to the WINS Server
RAS and IAS Servers	Security Group - Domain Local	Servers in this group can access remote access properties of users

• **Figure 5.2**   The initial contents of the Users container

they work first. When it comes to Active Directory, the objects we've been discussing are those simple building blocks that "flesh out" the network structure we created in Chapter 4. Now that we've had a chance to discuss the nature of these objects and get comfortable with Active Directory Users and Computers, let's create a few of the more common objects for our network.

Step-by-Step 5.2

Creating Computer Accounts, User Accounts, and Organizational Units

Of all the Active Directory objects we've discussed, computer and user accounts are by far the most numerous and the most commonly created. Organizational units, on the other hand, may not be created as frequently or in anywhere near the same quantity, but they should be planned out and created fairly early on. Although OUs aren't a necessity, they greatly assist in keeping the network organized, even if you don't initially need to delegate management or apply separate group policies.

In this Step-by-Step we will be creating a computer account, a user account, and an OU. In the next part of this chapter, we will use these objects to explore the typical object management tasks, which can be performed on existing objects.

To complete this Step-by-Step, you will need

- A properly configured Windows Server 2003 Domain Controller

- Access to an administrator-level account on the computer

Step 1

Open Active Directory Users and Computers by clicking Start | Administrative Tools | Active Directory Users and Computers. Maximize the window when it opens, if necessary.

Step 2

You'll recall that to create a computer account, you need, at minimum, the computer's name. However, no check is made to see if the computer actually exists, so unless your instructor gives you different directions, we'll make an account for an imaginary computer. To begin creating the computer account, right-click the name of your domain in the left pane and choose New | Computer.

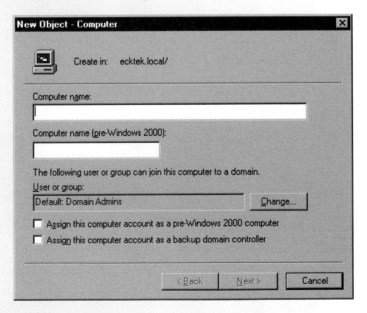

Step 3

The only information we have to enter at this point is the computer's name. For this exercise, enter the name **TestClient** in the Computer Name text box. Note that the pre–Windows 2000 name is entered automatically. Windows uses the first 15 characters of the computer name to create the name for older operating systems. This is one of the reasons you should keep computer names to 15 characters or fewer. The two check boxes at the bottom of the dialog box also apply only to older operating systems, so we can ignore them for now. However, there is one other change we may want to make. You'll notice that, by default, only members of the Domain Admins can join the computer to the domain. If we want to allow any domain user to join the computer to the domain, we need to change this. Click the Change button and enter **Domain Users** in the text box. Click OK to close the Select User or Group dialog box. Click Next to continue.

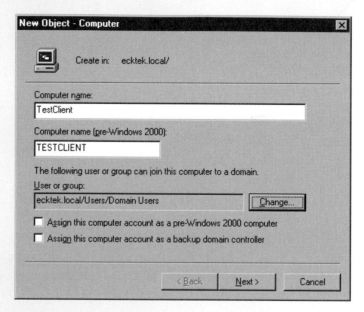

Step 4

In certain situations, which we'll be discussing in Chapter 10, it is necessary to enter a special identifier called the GUID in this dialog box. However, this isn't necessary for most computer accounts. For now, click Next and then Finish to create the account. Because we did not select a location for this account, and it was created manually, it appears inside the top-level domain container. We'll move it to the proper place in the next section.

Step 5

We're next going to create a personalized account for ourselves. With the domain selected in the left pane, begin creating the account by selecting the Action menu followed by New | User. You could also have used the shortcut menu or the new user button on the toolbar. Enter your first name, middle initial, and last name and note that Windows enters your full name for you. For your user logon name, enter your first initial followed by your last name with no spaces. Although this wouldn't be ideal for most networks, it will work fine for our lab. Windows automatically creates your pre–Windows 2000 logon name from the first 20 characters of your user logon name. Click Next to continue.

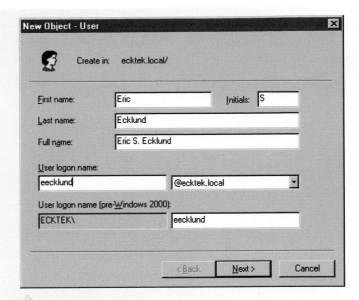

Step 6

We now need to enter, and confirm, our initial password. Remember that it needs to be at least seven characters long and cannot be any part of your user logon name. It also must contain three of the following four things: lowercase letters, uppercase letters, numbers, and symbols. I'm going to use the password one234! for mine. Enter your password and carefully re-enter it in the confirmation box. Notice that, by default, the user will have to change the password at the next logon. I suggest unchecking that option for now, since this is our account. We can also prevent the user from changing the password, which we might do if several people used one account. We can also override any preset password age limitations by checking Password never expires. However, that's not a good idea, as it makes it more likely someone will eventually be able to guess a user's password. The default password age in Windows Server 2003 is 42 days. The final option, Account is disabled, is sometimes used when creating a new account for an employee who hasn't started yet. The account would then be enabled when they actually began working. For now, uncheck all four check boxes and click Next and then Finish to create the account. Note that the account appears in the top-level domain container with the computer account we created.

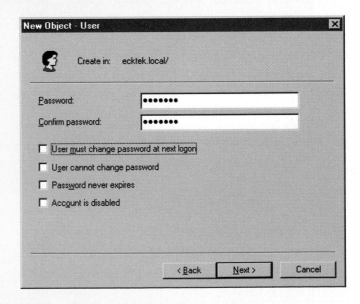

Our final task is to create an OU into which we can later move our computer account and user account. Right-click the domain in the left pane and choose New | Organizational Unit. Type the name **TestOU** and click OK to create it. Note that the OU now appears as part of the hierarchy in the left pane and bears the OU icon. Close Active Directory Users and Computers.

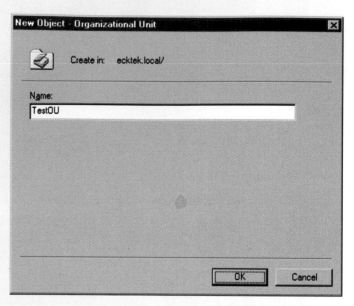

■ Managing Objects Using Active Directory Users and Computers

Object management in Active Directory Users and Computers typically consists of just a few basic tasks: moving objects, deleting objects, and editing object properties. No special knowledge is necessary for moving and deleting objects, although some caution is called for when deleting. Although these objects look like files and get deleted like files, there's no Recycle Bin to pull them back out of! However, when it comes to editing object properties, it helps to first know what your options are before you begin. Let's take a look at the available properties for computer accounts, user accounts, and OUs, and then we'll do some editing on the objects we created.

Object Properties

Every object has a properties dialog box that offers one or more

---

Try This!

Local Logon Limitations

You'd think that once a new account is created you should have no trouble logging on to the server. Unfortunately, if you really meant logging on to the server, and not just the domain, you'd be mistaken! Windows Server 2003's Default Domain Controller security policy allows local logons to the server only by members of one of five groups: Administrators, Backup Operators, Account Operators, Server Operators, and Print Operators. Since the personal account you created in Step-by-Step 5.2 does not belong to any of those groups, you will not be able to log on. Try this:

1. Log off as Administrator and attempt to log back on as your personal account.

2. Make note of the notification you see. Think about how this limitation helps increase network security.

3. Log back on as the Administrator. We'll address this problem in Step-by-Step 5.3.

tabs of information. Some of this information can be edited after the object is created, while some is filled in automatically. Each object has different available options, so we'll discuss them individually.

Computer Account Properties

As you can see in Figure 5.3, the properties dialog box for a computer account consists of the following seven tabs.

General The General tab primarily displays information you cannot edit directly. This information includes the computer's pre–Windows 2000 name, its DNS name (if it has logged on to the domain at least once), and the role it plays (workstation/server or domain controller.) The one piece of information that you can edit is the description of the computer.

Operating System Once the system has logged on to the domain, this tab will display information about the OS it's running. This information is not directly editable, but it does come in handy when you're checking to see if a particular Service Pack has been installed.

☑ Cross Check

Working with Active Directory Users and Computers

Make no mistake: there isn't another tool in Windows Server 2003 that you'll spend more time with than Active Directory Users and Computers. As such, it is absolutely essential that you be comfortable with the layout of the interface and how to accomplish essential tasks such as object creation. Let's take a moment to review some of the information we've covered concerning this very important tool. If you like, review the preceding sections and answer the following questions:

1. What common Windows utility is Active Directory Users and Computers most similar to? What are the similarities?

2. When creating user accounts, what are the default password complexity requirements?

3. What's the one container type that appears different from the rest? What's special about this type of container?

The properties dialog boxes depicted in the screen shots and discussed in the text are those that appear when Advanced Features is *not* turned on in the View menu of Active Directory Users and Computers. When that option is activated, two other tabs, Object and Security, will also appear. The Object tab presents information about when the object was created and modified. The Security tab is used to control which users and groups have access to or control over the object and what type of actions they can perform.

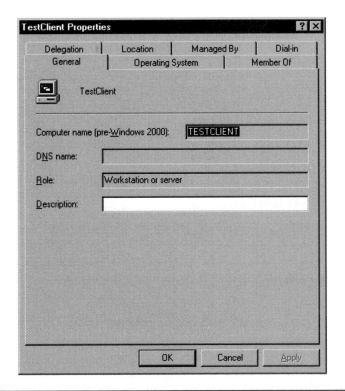

• **Figure 5.3** The computer account properties dialog box

Member Of   The Member Of tab displays the domain local, global, and universal groups the computer account belongs to. By default, as mentioned earlier, the computer will belong to the Domain Computers domain local group. You can use this tab to easily join or leave any other group within the domain.

Delegation   The Delegation tab is used to allow the computer account to delegate tasks to operating system services and allow those services to act on its behalf by impersonating the computer account. Make sense? I didn't think so. Delegation is a tricky subject that, in rare circumstances, can improve the functioning of certain network applications. However, it always introduces a significant security risk because it essentially allows parts of the OS and other services to act as if they were the actual account. In the worst-case scenario, a malicious service could end up with the ability to impersonate an account with administrative-level permissions and really wreak some major havoc. Unless you know without a doubt that you need to activate delegation, leave this tab the way it is, with delegation turned off.

Account delegation is completely different from delegating the management of an OU.

Location   What is it they say in real estate? Location, location, location! Let's be realistic, when you *do* need to leave the safety of the server room and work directly on a client computer, it sure helps to know where it is! This tab simply allows you to document where this computer is located.

Managed By   Although the Managed By tab is technically used to choose a user who is responsible for managing the computer, I find it useful on smaller networks for associating the current user of the computer with the account. This is especially helpful when dealing with laptop computers, since it'll probably be necessary to locate the user in order to find the computer! However, in larger networks, it's useful to be able to see which tech is responsible for the machine if it needs service. When you choose the user, all of their contact information from their account is automatically displayed for reference.

Dial-in   The Dial-in tab is used to control the ability of the computer to access the network remotely. Of course, this is usually not necessary for computer accounts for desktop machines, but it can be vitally important for laptops. The settings include a variety of options that increase security, including the use of caller ID to verify the phone number from which the connection is being made.

User Account Properties

As you can see in Figure 5.4, the properties dialog box for a user account consists of 13 tabs. Since the Member Of and Dial-in tabs serve the same purpose they did for computer accounts, we'll focus on the 11 tabs that are unique to user accounts.

General   The General tab already contains the first and last names of the user, the user's middle initial, and the user's display name. These values can be changed here without problem, since Windows actually identifies the account by its SID. This comes in handy as names change due to changes in marital status! You can also enter a longer description for the account, an office location, an e-mail address, and multiple telephone numbers and web page addresses. The telephone numbers are intended to be work numbers, since a separate tab exists for home contact information. For some strange reason, there is no provision for multiple e-mail addresses, which are probably more common than multiple web sites! Heck, at last count I had only one web site and somewhere around a dozen e-mail addresses. Go figure!

Address   By entering a user's address into the address tab's fields, you allow Active Directory to truly act as a directory within the network. Additionally, this information is accessed at other times, such as when you assign a user as the manager of a computer account. I highly recommend taking the time to collect and input this information for any user. It's also a good idea to create a system for users to report any address changes on a regular basis so that the directory will be accurate.

Account   The Account tab presents, and allows changes to, the user's logon name. You can also use this tab to limit when the user can log on and which computers the user can use to log on. You can also select certain account options, including the password options, and disable account options that were available when the account was created. Finally, you can also set an expiration date for the account. I particularly like the expiration date option, since, in the real world, I primarily create student accounts. I'll usually set the expiration date for their approximate graduation date, in case I should be slow to clean up inactive accounts. Of course, that sometimes presents a bit of a problem if they end up taking longer than expected to graduate! In those cases, I simply re-activate the account.

If my global ranching empire really existed, I could still find a use for expiration dates for user accounts. For instance, if I had a consultant come in to do some maintenance on my computers, I might create a short-lived account for them to use. That way, I don't have to worry about disabling the account when the job is done; it will happen automatically!

Profile   The Profile tab actually serves three purposes. First, it allows you to associate the account with a particular profile, which makes sense in light of the tab's name but doesn't exactly tell you a lot, does it? Profiles are used either to present a constant, unchangeable desktop to a user every time they log on, or to allow a user to move from computer to computer and always see their desktop, programs, favorites, and so on. The second purpose of the Profile tab is to associate a script with the user's logon, which can be used to map network shares to local drives or to run special utilities every time the user logs on to the network. The third purpose is to control the location of the user's home folder, which is usually located on the network and becomes the primary place for the user to store files on the network.

Telephones   The Telephones tab is used to enter a wide variety of different contact numbers for the user, including home, cellular, and fax. It also provides a notes section for recording any comments about the account. Some administrators use the notes to record maintenance tasks they've performed on the account.

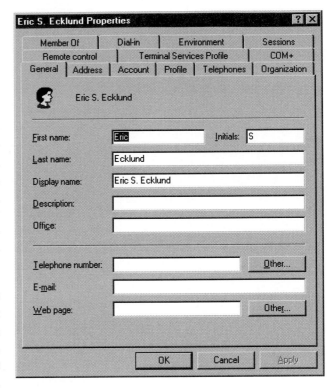

● **Figure 5.4**   The user account properties dialog box

Organization   The Organization tab allows you to describe the user in terms of their place within the company. Here you can even associate the account with their manager and their subordinates. It's not a bad idea to fill this information in, especially in larger organizations. Just imagine how useful it would be for me, as the head of the EZ-E Ranch empire, to be able to track the manager/subordinate relationships in my company directly through Active Directory. I've even heard rumors that this particular feature sees heavy use in a certain corporation based in Redmond, Washington, if you know what I mean!

Terminal Services Profile   **Terminal Services** allows users to connect to the server and run applications just as if they were running on their local machine. This can come in really handy when clients need to run high-powered applications from relatively underpowered client computers. Additionally, Terminal Services can be used to remotely administer the server from a client machine, which makes it nice for the administrator by freeing them from being locked in the server room all the time. The Terminal Services Profile tab works just like the Profile tab but applies only to these special connections.

Sessions   The Sessions tab is also used to control the nature of Terminal Services connections from the user. For the most part, these settings control what happens if the Terminal Services session gets interrupted or is left connected, but unused, or idle.

Environment   I'm sorry to disappoint you, but the Environment tab doesn't have anything to do with recycling paper or eating dolphin-safe tuna (not that those are bad ideas, mind you). The Environment tab affects what happens when the user account connects to the network using Terminal Services. This tab allows you to select a program to run when connecting with Terminal Services and to choose whether or not to connect client devices such as shared drives and printers.

Remote Control   It's possible to remotely control a user's Terminal Services session, if you have the right permissions. This tab allows you to set the options for whether or not remote control is possible and whether or not the user must first give permission. I know it sounds a little like Big Brother snooping over your shoulder, but this feature can be very helpful in troubleshooting problems for users.

COM+   This tab controls which COM+ partition sets the user account can access. COM+ stands for Component Object Model. It's a technology for developing specialized networked applications, which are then run on special servers called application servers. On an application server, these COM+ applications reside in logical partitions and these partitions can be grouped together into partition sets. This tab allows you to designate which partition sets, if any, this user should have access to. This allows you to control who can run these COM+ applications. COM+ application development and application servers are just a wee bit outside the scope of this text, so that's all we'll say about that!

Organizational Unit Properties

As you can see in Figure 5.5, the properties dialog box for OUs consists of the following four tabs.

We'll be working with the Sessions tab in Chapter 12 when we explore one of the ways that Terminal Services can be used to allow administrators to manage a server from remote locations.

General The General tab for an OU is essentially the Address tab for a user account with the addition of a Description text box. This tab allows you to further describe the nature of the OU and, if appropriate, define its physical location.

Managed By This tab *does not* delegate management of the OU; that's done by right-clicking the OU and choosing Delegate Control, which starts a wizard that takes you through the process. However, if you do delegate control of an OU, you should certainly use this tab to identify that person. This tab works the same way as the Managed By tab for computer accounts worked.

COM+ This tab serves the same purpose as the COM+ tab for user accounts, but it controls the partition set for an entire OU.

Group Policy For an OU, the Group Policy tab is frequently what it's all about. This is where you can define a custom set of policies for the members of the OU ranging from password policies to desktop appearance and just about anything else you can think of. This tab allows you to create new policies, edit existing policies, and control the order in which policies take precedence, if more than one is applied to the OU.

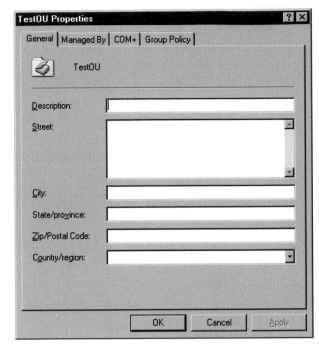

● **Figure 5.5** The organizational unit properties dialog box

Basic Active Directory Users and Computers Object Management

Because of the way objects are created, most need at least a little editing after the fact. It's also likely that, from time to time, you'll need to reorganize objects to reflect changes in the organization. In the following Step-by-Step we'll perform a few basic management tasks on the objects we created in Step-by-Step 5.2.

Step-by-Step 5.3

Moving and Editing Objects in Active Directory Users and Computers

When creating Active Directory objects, you can choose to create them in an existing OU. However, it's not unusual to need to move objects into a newly created OU or to sometimes accidentally create objects in the incorrect container. In this Step-by-Step we will begin by relocating our computer account and user account into the OU that we created. We'll

then go ahead and make some basic changes to the properties of those objects.

To complete this Step-by-Step, you will need

- A properly configured Windows Server 2003 Domain Controller
- Access to an administrator-level account on the computer

Step 1 Open Active Directory Users and Computers by clicking Start | Administrative Tools | Active Directory Users and Computers. Maximize the window when it opens, if necessary. Click the name of your domain in the left pane to display its contents in the right pane.

There are basically two ways to move objects within Active Directory Users and Computers. The first method, which was available in Windows 2000, is to use Move from either the shortcut menu or the Action menu. The second option, which is new to Windows Server 2003, is to simply drag and drop. To move your personal user account using the first method, simply right-click it in the right pane and select Move. Select TestOU from the Move dialog box and click OK. To move your TestClient computer account using drag and drop, simply drag it in the right pane until it is over the TestOU icon in either the left or right pane and then let go. Open the TestOU container to verify that both objects are now in it.

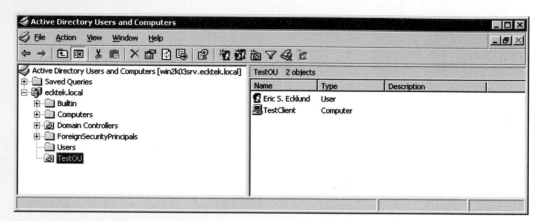

We'll edit the properties of the computer account first. Right-click the TestClient object and choose Properties. On the General tab, enter the description **This computer does not exist**. Use the Location tab to enter the descriptive information for the lab you are in. For instance, you might enter **Lab A, Building 4** or something of that nature. Click OK to close the dialog box.

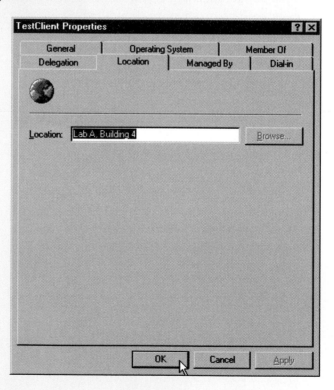

Step 4

You should see the description for your computer listed in the right pane, if you are in Detail view. Change to Detail view if necessary. Verify that the information appears and then reopen the properties dialog box by double-clicking the computer account. Please note that the double-click method of accessing properties does not work on OUs because they are containers. Double-clicking a container opens it.

Step 5

Click the Managed By tab. We're going to make your personal account the management contact for this computer. Click the Change button to open the Select User or Contact dialog box. Type either your full name, with initial, or your logon name in the white text area and then click the Check Names button. When your full name, followed by your logon name and the domain, appears underlined, you know that Active Directory understood who you were trying to identify. Click OK to return to the properties dialog box for the computer account and leave it open.

Step 6

Notice that the Properties button on the Managed By tab is no longer grayed out. Click it and the properties dialog box for your user account will open. This is the same properties dialog box you could have opened by right-clicking your user account and choosing Properties. On the General tab, fill in your phone number, and then select the Address tab and fill in your information. Finally, use the Telephones tab to fill in at least a fax number (you may certainly make one up!). Click OK when you are done to close the properties dialog box for your user account. Note that your address information, telephone number, and fax number now appear in the Managed By tab of the computer account's properties dialog box. Close the dialog box after you verify this.

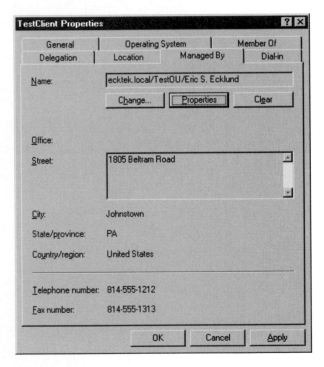

Reopen the properties dialog box for your user account using whatever method you prefer. If you attempted to log on to your account in the Try This! a few pages back, you know that it didn't work. If we want to be able to log on and use this account as an administrator-level account, we have to join the account to the correct groups. Select the Member Of tab and then click the Add button to begin adding groups. Since we actually have to join several groups, it will be easier to pick them from a list than it will be to type out each name. To begin this process, click the Advanced button.

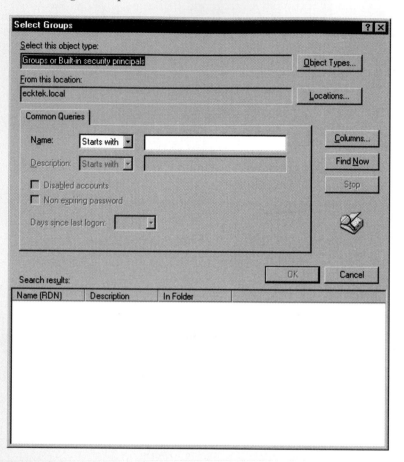

The advanced form of the Select Groups dialog box allows us to search for a group by name. However, it's also a great way to see a list of all possible groups. To do this, click the Find Now button without entering any search criteria. When the list of groups appears, double-click the right border of the Name (RDN) column header to automatically size the column to match its longest entry. Note that the names of the various groups are listed alphabetically by default.

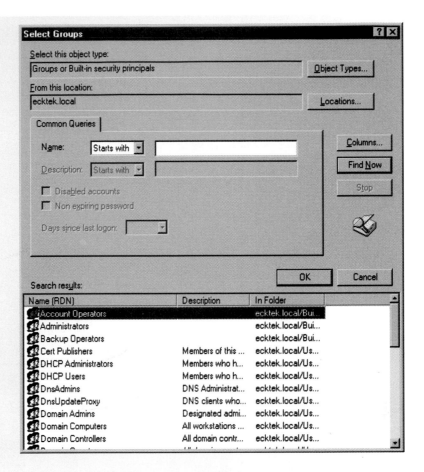

Step 9

We need to select five different groups simultaneously. To do this, we will need to select the first group and then hold down the CTRL key on the keyboard as we click each of the other four. We don't want the first group, Account Operators, so do not hold the CTRL key as you click the first group we do want, which is Administrators. Then hold CTRL down on the keyboard and click the following four groups, using the scrollbar as necessary to move through the list: Domain Admins, Enterprise Admins, Group Policy Creator Owners, and Schema Admins. Verify that all five are selected simultaneously by carefully scrolling through the list without clicking any other group name. If necessary, give it a second try. When you have all five selected, click OK twice to close both Select Groups dialog boxes. Your Member Of tab of the user account's properties dialog box should now display the five groups you just selected along with the original Domain Users group. Click OK to close the properties dialog box and close Active Directory Users and Computers.

Tip: In most cases it would have been sufficient to merely make the user account a member of the Administrators group to enable server administration. The other groups would be added only if the account really needed the level of access they provide. However, we've exactly replicated the membership of the original Administrator account in case multiple people need to work on the same server in your lab. This should prevent the need to use the original Administrator account for the remainder of the text.

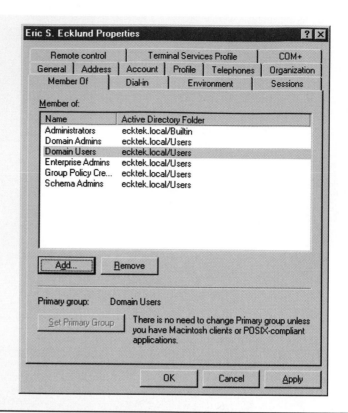

Object Management in Active Directory Users and Computers

The nature of the process for creating objects in Active Directory just about requires us to revisit what we've created and either do a little organizing or add additional information. In some cases the additional information can ease the job of the administrator or improve the experience of the user on the network. Let's take a moment to talk about some of the changes we make to Active Directory objects after their creation. If you like, review the preceding sections and answer the following questions:

1. When you choose a user to manage a computer in the Managed By tab of the computer account properties dialog box, what other information may appear?

2. Why did we need to add groups in the Member Of tab of our personal user account?

Chapter 5 Review

■ Chapter Summary

After reading this chapter and completing the Step-by-Step tutorials and Try This! exercises, you should understand the following facts about working with Active Directory objects in Active Directory Users and Computers.

Identify Active Directory Objects

■ When a computer running Windows NT or higher joins a domain, it creates a computer account. This account can be precreated, which is typically more efficient.

■ A computer account identifies a network computer. It can be used to manage the computer and to remotely install an OS. Most importantly, a computer account is a security principal in the domain, which is uniquely identified by an SID for the purpose of accessing resources.

■ Each computer account must have a unique name. It can also include other information such as description and location.

■ A user account is a security principal that represents users in the domain.

■ Creating user accounts requires a unique full name, a unique logon name, and an initial password that meets the complexity requirements.

■ Additional information, including addresses, telephone numbers, titles, and more can be added to the user account after it is created.

■ A contact is typically used to store contact information for someone from outside the network.

■ A group account is a security principal that allows the collective application of permissions to users and other groups. Distribution groups also exist that are used strictly to send messages.

■ There are three types of security groups, which are domain local groups, global groups, and universal groups. The different groups vary in their group scope, which is the level of network structure at which they may provide access to resources.

■ Creating group accounts requires only a unique name and the type of group. Other information, including the members of the group, can be added later.

■ An organizational unit (OU) is used to group together user accounts, computer accounts, and shared resources within a domain to subdivide the domain and make it more manageable.

■ OUs allow for delegation of management and the application of group policies.

■ Creating an OU requires only a unique name. After an OU is created, additional information can be added.

■ Printer and shared folder objects are generally created automatically, unless they exist on a pre–Windows 2000 system.

Create Objects Using Active Directory Users and Computers

■ Active Directory Users and Computers is actually an MMC snap-in. Like most snap-ins, it closely follows the familiar user interface of Windows Explorer.

■ Active Directory Users and Computers initially has five containers under the domain.

■ The Builtin container holds most of the initial domain local security groups.

■ The Computers container holds upgraded computer accounts.

■ The Domain Controllers container holds the DCs for the domain. It is actually an OU.

■ The ForeignSecurityPrincipals container holds the SIDs of security principals from external, trusted domains.

■ The Users container holds upgraded user accounts, the initial Administrator account, and an assortment of domain local, global, and universal groups.

Manage Objects Using Active Directory Users and Computers

■ Object management consists of tasks such as moving objects, deleting objects, and editing object properties.

■ The properties dialog box for the computer account object includes tabs labeled General, Operating

System, Member Of, Delegation, Location, Managed By, and Dial-in.

■ The properties dialog box for the user account object includes tabs labeled General, Address, Account, Profile, Telephones, Organization,

Terminal Services Profile, Sessions, Environment, Remote Control, COM+, Member Of, and Dial-in.

■ The properties dialog box for the OU object includes tabs labeled General, Managed By, COM+, and Group Policy.

■ Key Terms

computer account *(137)*
contact *(141)*
container *(145)*
distinguished name (DN) *(138)*
distribution group *(141)*
domain local group *(142)*
global group *(142)*

group account *(141)*
group policy *(142)*
group scope *(141)*
publish *(143)*
relative distinguished name (RDN) *(138)*
security group *(141)*

security ID (SID) *(137)*
security principal *(137)*
snap-in *(143)*
Terminal Services *(158)*
universal group *(142)*
user account *(139)*
user principal name (UPN) *(138)*

■ Key Terms Quiz

Use terms from the Key Terms list to complete the sentences that follow. Don't use the same term more than once. Not all terms will be used.

1. A _____ is primarily used to provide information about people outside the network.

2. Each of the initial five objects under the domain in Active Directory Users and Computers is known as a _____.

3. Each of the security group types differs in its _____.

4. A _____ uniquely identifies a client computer or member server.

5. An e-mail address is an example of a _____.

6. A computer account is one example of a _____.

7. A _____ is a security principal that allows the collective application of permissions to users and other groups.

8. The computer name SERVER01 is an example of a _____.

9. Each security principal is identified by Active Directory by its _____.

10. A _____ can be given permissions only within the domain in which it was created.

■ Multiple-Choice Quiz

1. Which of the following Active Directory objects has a Group Policy tab in its properties dialog box?

    a. Computer account

    b. User account

    c. OU

    d. Contact

2. A name that begins *CN=WIN2K03SRV,CN= Servers,CN=Home,CN=Sites* is a

    a. UPN

    b. RDN

    c. DN

    d. GUID

3. Which container in Active Directory Users and Computers holds SIDs of accounts from external, trusted domains?

   a. Builtin

   b. Computers

   c. ForeignSecurityPrincipals

   d. Domain Controllers

4. Which of the following Active Directory objects requires only a name during its creation?

   a. OU

   b. Group account

   c. User account

   d. All of the above

5. Which network object is generally created automatically?

   a. User account

   b. OU

   c. Printer

   d. Group account

6. Which type of group is found initially in the Builtin container?

   a. Domain local

   b. Global

   c. Universal

   d. The Builtin container contains all three group types.

7. Which type of group is found initially in the Users container?

   a. Domain local

   b. Global

   c. Universal

   d. All of the above

8. Which container displays an icon different from the others?

   a. Builtin

   b. Users

   c. ForeignSecurityPrincipals

   d. Domain Controllers

9. Which network object appears in the left pane of Active Directory Users and Computers during normal viewing?

   a. Computer accounts

   b. User accounts

   c. Group accounts

   d. OUs

10. Which option is on by default when creating a new user account?

    a. Disable account

    b. User must change password at next logon

    c. Password never expires

    d. Delegate

11. Which of the following can you do in the Active Directory Users and Computers interface?

    a. Hide the left pane

    b. Resize the panes

    c. Re-order the Detail view

    d. All of the above

12. Which of the following passwords would *not* meet the requirements for password complexity?

    a. 2#fourLBS

    b. LpKmNvbb

    c. Count1234

    d. !@#$Vzz

13. Which OS would not require a computer account or create a computer account on joining a domain?

    a. Windows 98

    b. Windows 2000

    c. Windows XP Professional

    d. Windows Server 2003

14. Try to keep computer account names to no more than

    a. 10 characters

    b. 15 characters

    c. 20 characters

    d. 63 characters

15. Which network object has the most tabs in its properties dialog box?

    a. Contact

    b. Computer account

    c. User account

    d. OU

■ Essay Quiz

1. Your supervisor doesn't understand why you want to stay late and create computer accounts for the 50 new machines being brought online tomorrow. He figures it's easier to just join them to the domain using his administrator account. Justify your reasons for wanting to precreate the computer accounts.

2. Explain the concept of security principal. Which Active Directory objects are security principals?

3. Your boss, the senior network administrator, never creates OUs. She says she's too busy to take the time. Explain how OUs could benefit her personally.

4. Your users want to know why their user logon names aren't simply their first and last names. Explain to them the problems with that naming convention.

5. Explain why the Domain Controllers container is an OU. What is the benefit?

Lab Projects

• Lab Project 5.1

Collect the necessary information from your classmates to create user accounts for them on your server. Record the information, including information to be entered after creation. Record a unique password that meets complexity requirements for each account. Create these accounts in Active Directory Users and Computers. Be certain to use a logical naming system for the user logon names that will minimize the chance of duplicate names even if the number of users were to grow significantly. Do *not* use any part of the user's Social Security number in your user logon names. Create an OU named LabUsers and place the user accounts into that OU.

Tip: Feel free to substitute made-up information for any contact data that students wish to keep private, such as addresses, telephone numbers, and the like!

• Lab Project 5.2

Collect the necessary information from your classmates to create computer accounts for the other servers in your lab (assume for the sake of the project that they are client machines). Create computer accounts for each of the lab computers. After creating the accounts, make each user account you created in Lab Project 5.1 responsible for the correct computer account using the Managed By tab of the computer accounts properties dialog box. Be sure that all of the user's information appears in the dialog box. Finally, create an OU named LabComputers and place the computer accounts into that OU.

• Lab Project 5.3

Computer naming conventions are at least as important and probably more challenging to develop than user logon naming conventions. Begin this project by researching the naming convention used on the network at your school or work. Write up a description of it and analyze its strengths and weaknesses. Follow this by researching the topic online. Write up a description of at least one system you encounter and analyze its strengths and weaknesses. Finally, write up a suggestion for a naming system you would use if you were setting up a new network. Make sure your system addresses the weaknesses you found in the other systems you've researched.

A Place for Everything: Storage Management

In this chapter, you will learn how to:

- **Define the difference between basic and dynamic disks**
- **Manage disk volumes on dynamic disks**
- **Use the Windows Backup Utility**
- **Troubleshoot storage problems**

Storage management is pretty easy on nonnetworked computers. Typically, you have one hard disk represented by a single drive letter, and all you have to do is keep your files organized into folders and subfolders. Things are just a tad more complicated when you're managing a network server.

The complexity of storage management on a server arises from two basic factors. The first factor is that many different users may use the server for storage and those users have different needs in several areas. The second factor is that we usually expect better performance and reliability from server storage than we do from storage on client-level machines.

In this chapter, we'll take a look at some of the tools and techniques available in Windows Server 2003 for effectively managing hard disk storage. We will begin by examining the difference between basic disks, which are used by all Microsoft operating systems, and dynamic disks, which were introduced with Windows 2000. We'll then look at some of the special storage configurations that are made possible by dynamic disks and how to configure them. We'll also explore the much improved Windows backup utility, which allows us to protect our data from catastrophic drive failures. Finally, we'll take a look at some techniques for addressing common problems with hard disk storage.

■ Basic Disks Versus Dynamic Disks

Prior to the introduction of Windows 2000, this section wouldn't even have existed. Back then, all disks were basic disks, but because there was no other type, no one called them that. However, with the introduction of Windows 2000, Microsoft introduced dynamic disks, which provide some advantages not available when using basic disks. Since dynamic disks cannot be used in all situations, we'll take a look at both options and the differences between them.

Capabilities and Limitations of Basic Disks

Basic disks are, well, basic! Since hard drives first made their appearance in personal computers, they've been handled in the same basic way. Each physical disk can be divided into from one to four partitions, which become the underlying structure for the storage of data on the disk. In truth, there are actually two types of partitions: primary partitions and extended partitions. **Primary partitions** are the partitions upon which most operating systems are installed. Each primary partition gets treated as a separate drive identified by a drive letter, such as C. On most home computers and many client-level computers, the hard disk is configured with only one partition that uses the entire available space and gets treated as the C: drive. In some cases where the drive is particularly large or if the user wants to run different operating systems on the same computer, the disk might be divided into two, three, or even four primary partitions.

What about **extended partitions**? Well, as you can see in Figure 6.1, if you use only primary partitions you can divide a basic disk into only four discrete drives. Unlike primary partitions, which each get treated as a single drive, extended partitions can be divided into multiple **logical drives**. If you use one extended partition to take the place of a primary partition, you have much greater flexibility in creating separate storage areas. By using an extended partition and primary partitions, you can subdivide the hard disk into as many as 24 different drives, each with its own drive letter. I know it might seem a bit excessive to have so many drives, but in some cases it helps organize your storage just as folders do. On some older operating systems, extended partitions were actually a necessity, due to limitations on the maximum size of a partition. If the operating system supported only 2GB partitions and you had a 10GB drive, you would have wasted 2GB of storage if you used only the four primary partitions.

Basic disks are still a viable form of storage for many computers, including servers running Windows Server 2003. In fact, when you installed the operating system in Chapter 2, you installed it on a basic disk. For computers that have only a single physical hard disk, basic disk storage will work just fine. However, for servers that make use of multiple hard disks, there are some significant advantages to be had by converting those disks to dynamic disks.

Although a computer hard disk may have up to four primary partitions, each bearing different operating systems, only one partition can be marked as active at any one time. The computer boots from the active partition, thus booting from the operating system on that partition. Special programs called boot loaders or boot managers allow the user to select which partition, and thus which operating system, to boot from during the boot process.

● **Figure 6.1** You can increase the number of discrete drives by using one extended partition in place of one of the four possible primary partitions.

Advantages of Dynamic Disks

Dynamic disks were first introduced as a storage option with Windows 2000. The primary difference between basic disks and dynamic disks is that the latter do not depend on partitions for dividing the physical disk into storage areas. Instead, dynamic disks make use of **volumes**, which are actually a lot like partitions in that they become basic storage areas for data on the hard disk. However, unlike partitions, volumes can be expanded if they later need to be larger than their initial capacity. In fact, this expansion can even take place over multiple physical drives! In addition to the ability to grow in size, volumes also make several options available for improving performance, reliability, and flexibility that were not available with partitions.

Because of the heavy user loads some servers must withstand, any improvements to the reading and writing of data can be very beneficial. Dynamic disks have the ability, in certain configurations, to increase the speed with which data is read and written, thus speeding access to the data for users. This is done by allowing the computer to read and write to more than one disk simultaneously, thus increasing overall performance. Depending on the uses to which a server is put, this can be a significant advantage of using dynamic storage.

One disadvantage of using a server-based network is that users tend to store their important data on the server. This can lead to a real vulnerability if anything should happen to the hard disk the server uses to store data on. Dynamic disks allow some volumes to address this problem by either creating live backup copies of the data or tracking special error correcting data that allows for corrupted or lost data to be recovered. This greatly enhances the reliability of our data storage system by allowing data to survive problems that would normally cause it to be lost. This ability to withstand normally catastrophic events is referred to as **fault tolerance**.

Remember our earlier discussion about extended partitions? The advantage of extended partitions on basic disks was that they allowed for the creation of logical drives so that a computer could have up to 24 different drives, identified by drive letters (remember that A and B are normally taken by the system). Well, Windows can't do much about the number of letters in the alphabet, but it can give us another way to identify discrete storage areas. It does this through **mounted volumes**.

When you create a new volume on a dynamic disk, you are prompted to assign it one of the available drive letters *or* mount it to an empty folder on an existing volume that has been formatted using NTFS. Mounting the volume to a folder merely makes that volume accessible as a folder to users on the local system or on the network. By mounting volumes, you can easily have as many different discrete storage areas as you want without worrying about running out of letters!

When to Use Dynamic Disks

Before we start playing with dynamic disk volumes in the next section, we should talk about when dynamic disks should and should not be used. A simple rule of thumb to remember is that machines with only one hard drive really won't see much benefit from dynamic disks. This is because both the volumes that improve performance and the volumes that increase fault tolerance do so by using multiple physical drives. Without multiple drives, dynamic disks only convey to the user the ability to grow volumes beyond their original size by allocating unused space on the existing disk. Although this might be useful, it may not be enough to counter the one great weakness of dynamic disks.

Because dynamic disks are a relatively new storage technology, they are not usable by earlier operating systems. Although older operating systems can access files from a dynamic disk volume, you cannot boot an old version of Windows from such a volume. If you feel you might ever have the need to boot your server into an older OS, you should not convert from basic to dynamic disks.

Converting basic disks to dynamic disks is a simple and nondestructive process, as you'll see in the next Step-by-Step. However, the simplicity of the process can be deceiving. Although you can convert from basic to dynamic at any time with no data loss, the same is not true of converting back from dynamic to basic. Oh, it can be done, all right. You'll just lose all of your data if you don't back it up first and restore it properly afterward. Because of this little inconvenience, it is wise to hold off on converting your disks until you are absolutely sure you will never have to boot into an older operating system. Consider the conversion process to be a one-way street. Even though you can theoretically reverse your choice later, it's a hassle you don't want to deal with if you don't have to.

Cross Check

Basic Versus Dynamic Disks

Now that you've had a chance to learn about the differences between basic disks and dynamic disks, let's take a minute to summarize what you've learned. If you like, review the preceding sections and answer the following questions:

1. In your own words, summarize the essential differences between basic disks and dynamic disks.

2. Describe a situation in which it would be wise to use dynamic disks. When would you be just as well off sticking with basic disks?

 The conversion of basic disks to dynamic disks is handled on a disk-by-disk basis. This means that, if you want, you can convert some of the hard disks in a server to dynamic while leaving others as basic disks. In this way, you can, with enough hard disks, enjoy the benefits of dynamic disks while still retaining a basic disk on which older operating systems can still boot.

Step-by-Step 6.1

Converting Basic Disks to Dynamic Disks

In order to take full advantage of all the features dynamic disks make possible, it is necessary to convert at least <u>three</u> physical hard disks. If you do not have three different hard disks in the computer, converting two disks will at least make some of the volume options available. However, you can always add other hard disks at a later time; upon converting those disks, you will be able to access the remaining volume types. Keep in mind that this process is difficult to reverse if data exists on the disks and should not be used on computers that need to boot into older operating systems.

Please consult with your instructor for specific instructions appropriate to your lab computer setup before proceeding with this Step-by-Step. Although ideally you should have three drives to convert (for

the next Step-by-Step), two drives will suffice for most exercises. If your lab computer has only a single drive, you can still convert it to a dynamic disk, with your instructor's permission, but you will be unable to perform some of the steps in later Step-by-Step exercises.

To complete this Step-by-Step, you will need

- A properly configured computer with Windows Server 2003 installed.

- Two to three installed hard disks. Each hard drive should have at least 1GB of available space that has not been allocated. This space will be set up as volumes in the next section.

- Access to an administrator-level account on the computer.

Caution: *Although converting from basic to dynamic disks is usually a very safe procedure, it is always wise to back up your data before undertaking major configuration changes of any type.*

Step 1

To convert basic disks to dynamic disks, we need to access the Computer Management tool. To do this, click Start | All Programs | Administrative Tools | Computer Management. When the Computer Management console opens, maximize the window, if necessary. Using the left pane, click Disk Management. (You may have to first click the plus sign to the left of Storage, if Disk Management is not visible.)

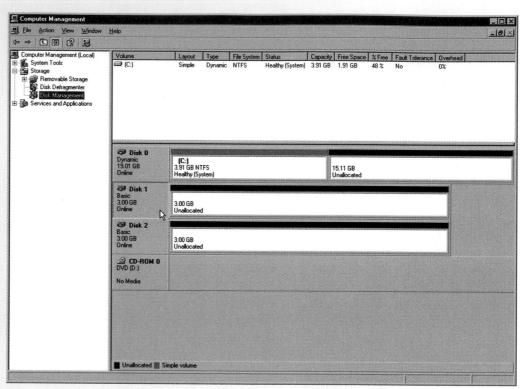

Note: *You must be logged in as an administrator-level account to convert disks.*

Step 2

After a few seconds, the right pane will display information about the disks currently installed in your system. If you look at the bottom half of the screen, you should note that one or more of your disks (Disk 0, Disk 1, and so on) bear the label "Basic." Right-click one of these basic disks (it doesn't matter which one) in the gray area where the label appears. Select Convert to Dynamic Disk from the shortcut menu.

Step 3

The Convert to Dynamic Disk dialog box will appear, displaying all of the basic disks installed in your system with a check box for each. Check each disk you wish to convert (follow your instructor's directions) and click OK.

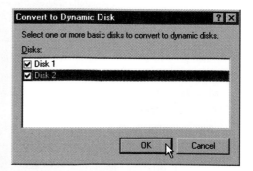

Step 4

If this is the first time these disks have been converted, you will be prompted to allow the computer to restart in order to complete the process. After the computer has restarted and you have logged back on, you will normally be prompted that your system settings have changed and yet another reboot is necessary. After rebooting the second time, log back on and re-open the Computer Management tool. You should now see that your disks are labeled as Dynamic.

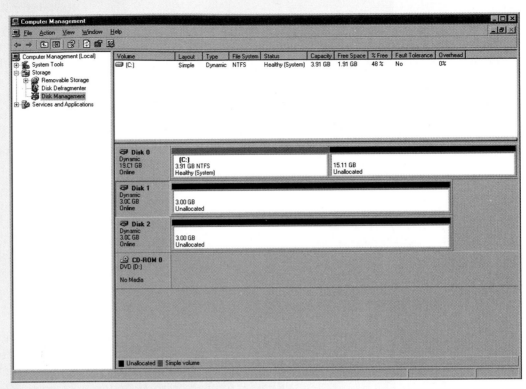

■ Using Volumes to Manage Storage

Now that we've converted our disks, we can take advantage of the various volume types made possible by dynamic storage. As I mentioned earlier, volumes provide benefits in several areas that partitions on basic disks did not. Some volumes are just simple storage areas but can grow in size, while some provide improved performance and some increase the fault tolerance of our storage system. The ability to mount volumes to empty NTFS folders is shared by all volumes. Let's take a look at the actual volumes in terms of the unique benefits they offer.

Volumes That Grow

The category of volumes that hold data much like a partition does, but offer the ability to increase in size, includes three different volumes: simple volumes, extended volumes, and spanned volumes.

Simple Volumes

Simple volumes, as depicted in Figure 6.2, exist on a single hard disk and offer no improvement to performance or the fault tolerance of the data storage system. In this way, they are the closest things to partitions. However, a simple

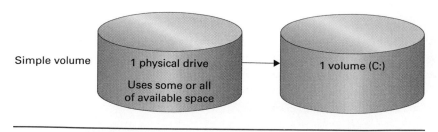

Simple volume — 1 physical drive, Uses some or all of available space → 1 volume (C:)

● **Figure 6.2**   A simple volume

volume can be expanded, if necessary, which allows them to grow to meet changing user needs.

Extended Volumes

An **extended volume** isn't really a separate type of volume at all, but rather a way of expanding, or extending, an existing simple volume. For instance, a simple volume can be extended to include unallocated space on the same disk, which merely increases the capacity of the simple volume. However, when viewed through the Disk Management tool, the extended portions do appear as separate segments of the drive, albeit with the same drive letter and name as the original simple volume, which is why they are sometimes referred to as "extended volumes."

Of course, sometimes there isn't any space left on the original disk, which makes it necessary to extend a simple volume to other disks. In such cases, extending a simple volume actually creates a new volume type, which is where spanned volumes come into play.

Spanned Volumes

As you can see in Figure 6.3, **spanned volumes** allow for storage areas to be spread across up to 32 different hard disks. Spanned volumes can be created from scratch or by extending an existing simple volume over multiple disks. Windows writes to spanned volumes by writing to the allocated area on the first disk until no more space remains before moving on to the next disk. Like extended simple volumes, spanned volumes merely allow flexibility in allocating storage capacity. They do not offer performance or fault tolerance improvements. In fact, if even one disk that is part of a spanned volume fails, the entire volume will be lost! That means fault tolerance is actually *decreased* when using spanned volumes. It's a good idea to consider whether or not the ability to offer up a larger storage space as a single volume is worth the increased risk of losing everything because of a single bad drive.

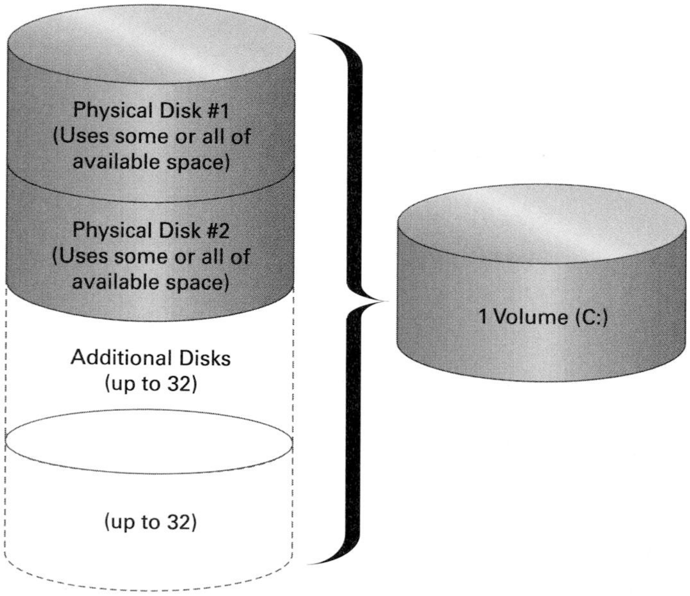

Volumes That Improve Performance

Writing to and reading from hard disks is fairly time-intensive. In some situations, the ability to shave a few milliseconds off of those processes can significantly improve the performance of the server. For those times when a little more speed means a lot, we have a volume to do the job.

Physical Disk #1 (Uses some or all of available space)

Physical Disk #2 (Uses some or all of available space)

Additional Disks (up to 32)

(up to 32)

1 Volume (C:)

● **Figure 6.3**   A spanned volume

Striped Volumes

A **striped volume** at first seems to be identical to a spanned volume. Like a spanned volume, a striped volume consists of segments of up to 32 different hard disks. However, when Windows writes to a striped volume, it simultaneously writes some of the data to each of the individual disks that make up the whole volume. The result of this is a much faster writing process and a slightly faster reading process. Unfortunately, striped volumes are like spanned volumes in another way: striped volumes will also lose all data if even a single involved hard disk should fail.

Since Windows writes simultaneously to all segments of a striped volume, each segment on each drive must be the same size.

Volumes That Improve Reliability

With all of these dire warnings about losing all of your data from the failure of a single drive, you might start to think dynamic storage isn't all that great. You'd be nearly right if it weren't for our last category of volumes: the volumes that increase the reliability of our data storage systems by increasing their fault tolerance. There are two specimens that fit the bill for this category.

Mirrored Volumes

Mirrored volumes are actually a pretty simple concept. As you can see in Figure 6.4, you take one volume of a particular size on one hard disk and mirror it, or copy it, in real time to a duplicate of the volume on another disk. That way, if anything happens to one disk, you have an up-to-the-minute copy ready to go! As you might expect, there's a bit of a catch. While mirrored volumes don't decrease performance as they increase our fault tolerance, they do "waste" storage space. It really isn't a waste, since you are protecting what is presumably pretty important data, but it does take twice as much storage space as what you are actually storing. For example: to mirror a 1GB volume, you need another disk with 1GB available for the mirror. That means that 2GB of storage space is being used to store only 1GB maximum of data. Trust me, there are times when this level of safety is well worth the cost!

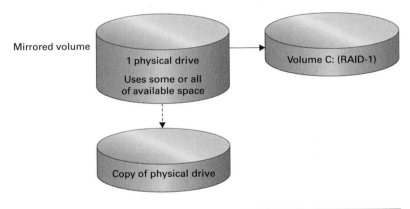

Mirrored volume

• **Figure 6.4** A mirrored volume

RAID-5 Volumes

RAID-5 volumes are sort of the "new and improved" version of our old friend the striped volume. In fact, striped volumes are also known as RAID-0 volumes (see the upcoming Inside Information on RAID levels). But what exactly is RAID?

RAID stands for Redundant Array of Inexpensive (or Independent) Disks. What it describes is a system that makes use of smaller, cheaper, individual disks to provide the capacity of larger, more expensive disks while also providing redundancy, which basically translates into fault tolerance. A RAID-5 volume, as depicted in Figure 6.5, is at its heart a striped volume that adds fault tolerance. The way that it does that is actually pretty neat.

The reliability of mirrored volumes can be enhanced through the technique of duplexing, which requires that both disks in the mirror set use different disk controllers, rather than sharing the same controller. The advantage is that if there is a problem with one controller, the other will likely still work, thus preserving the data on at least one disk.

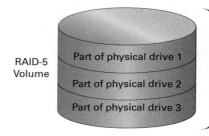

RAID-5
Volume

Part of physical drive 1

Part of physical drive 2

Part of physical drive 3

Volume C:
Combines segment spaces
(Some lost—redundancy)

● **Figure 6.5** A RAID-5 volume

As Windows writes data to the multiple disks that make up a RAID-5 volume, it also periodically writes blocks of additional information, called a **parity-information stripe**, that can be used to re-create any data that gets lost from a hard disk failure. RAID-5 volumes do not lose all of their information if one disk fails, as striped volumes do. Instead, they refer back to that parity-information stripe that's been spread across all of the involved disks, and they can re-create the missing data (within limits). Plus, since RAID-5 volumes are essentially striped volumes, you also get faster performance and more potential storage than you could get from a single disk.

RAID-5 volumes and all of the goodies they offer do come at a price. First of all, you can only create them with a minimum of three disks. Two just won't cut it. Second, that parity-information stripe takes up some space. To be specific, you lose the equivalent of one divided by the number of disks you're using worth of space on any RAID-5 volume. Sound confusing? It really isn't. Say you use the minimum of three disks and you allocate 100MB from each of those disks. Normally that would give you a 300MB storage area. However, to accommodate the parity-information stripe, you lose 1/3 (3 being the number of disks) of that 300MB. Since you lose 100MB (1/3 of 300), your 300MB of storage space really holds only 200MB of actual data. Still, it's a small price to pay compared with what you get in return.

☑ Cross Check

Volume Types

Now that you've had a chance to learn about the different types of volumes made available by dynamic disks, let's take a minute to summarize what you've learned. If you like, review the preceding sections and answer the following questions:

1. In you own words, summarize the features and benefits of the five different volume types. (Remember that an extended volume isn't really a volume type.)

2. Which two volumes offer fault tolerance? What is different between them?

Try This!

Best Practices for Using Dynamic Disks

Microsoft offers a lot of guidance on how to best use various features of its operating systems. Microsoft frequently refers to "Best Practices" and offers documentation through both help files and online files that explain these concepts in detail. Dynamic disks are no exception. Take a moment to read over Microsoft's documentation on dynamic disks to learn some of the more technical details behind this technology. To complete this task, you will need a computer with Internet access and a browser. Try this:

1. Point your browser to www.microsoft.com.

2. In the search box, type the number **816307** and press ENTER. This is the number of the Knowledge Base article that discusses dynamic disk best practices. The Knowledge Base is Microsoft's store of technical articles for their products.

3. Click the link for the article titled "Best Practices for Using Dynamic Disks on Windows Server 2003–Based Computers" and read the article.

4. When finished reading the article, close your browser.

Step-by-Step 6.2

Creating Volumes on Dynamic Disks

Creating the various volumes we've been discussing is actually very easy. Windows provides a wizard that takes you through the process, which is nearly the same for each volume type. In this Step-by-Step, you'll get a chance to create a few volumes of your own.

Most of the procedures in this Step-by-Step require the use of one or two hard disks. In order to work with RAID-5 volumes, the computer must have three hard disks installed. If your lab machine has only two disks installed, you will not be able to create RAID-5 volumes but you can read over the steps to see how it is done. If your computer has only one hard drive, you will only be able to create simple volumes and extended volumes. You may read over the steps for the remaining volume types to see how they are created.

To complete this Step-by-Step, you will need

- A properly configured computer with Windows Server 2003 installed.

- Two to three installed hard disks. Each hard drive should have at least 1GB of available space that has not been allocated. These drives should have already been converted to dynamic disks in the preceding Step-by-Step.

- Access to an administrator-level account on the computer.

Step 1
Open the Computer Management tool by choosing Start | All Programs | Administrative Tools | Computer Management. When the Computer Management console opens, maximize the window, if necessary. Using the left pane, click Storage Management. (You may have to first click the plus sign to the left of Storage, if Disk Management is not visible.)

Step 2

The first volume we will create will be a simple volume. To create a simple volume, right-click the unallocated space of one of your drives and choose New Volume. When the New Volume Wizard dialog box appears, click Next.

Step 3

As you can see, a simple volume is the default choice when running the New Volume Wizard. Read the description of a simple volume

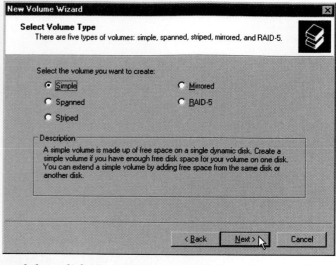

at the bottom of the dialog box and then click Next. The next dialog box shows the drive you right-clicked as the selected drive on the right-hand side and any other dynamic drives you have installed on the left-hand side. The unallocated space on each drive is listed, and by default, the entire unallocated space of the selected drive is set as the size of the new simple volume. If you had right-clicked the incorrect drive, you could have used the Remove button to remove it and then chosen a different drive using the Add button. Since this is a simple volume, which exists only on a single physical drive, you cannot add more than one drive at a time to the Selected area.

Since we are creating this volume only to illustrate the process and we will need some unallocated space in later steps, set the size of this drive to 100MB. You can do this by using the arrows to the right of the text box labeled Select the amount of space in MB, but it is easier to just delete the current value and type **100**. When you've set the size of the volume, click Next.

Step 4

The next step of the New Volume Wizard asks you to either assign the new volume an unused drive letter or mount it to an empty folder on an existing NTFS volume. You also have the option of choosing to do neither at this point, since you can assign, and even reassign, drive letters and mounting volumes later. For now, accept the default drive letter and click Next.

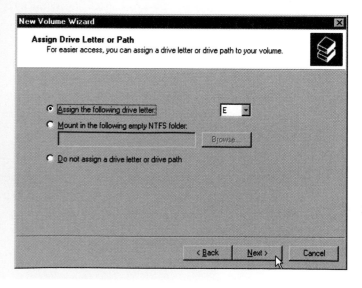

Just like partitions on basic disks, new volumes need to be formatted. On this step of the New Volume Wizard, you choose the file systems, determine the size of the allocation units, and enter a label for the new volume. Although you are given a choice of file system and allocation units, in most cases you are better off going with NTFS and the default value for allocation units. If you wished to format the volume later, you could choose not to format at this time and continue to the next step of the wizard. You can also choose to do a quick format and to enable file and folder compression. Quick formats do not adequately examine the surface of the disk for errors and so are not recommended. File and folder compression can be turned on at a later time and so does not have to be selected at this point.

It's a good idea to give new volumes a descriptive volume label. For this volume, type the label **Simple Volume** (just to help us pick it out from the other volumes we're going to create) and click Next.

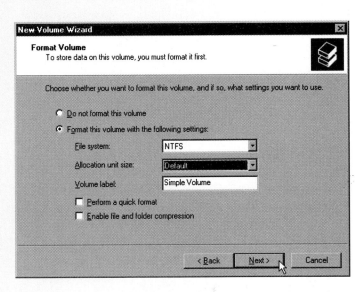

The last step of the New Volume Wizard summarizes the settings you chose. Click the Finish button and Windows will set up the volume and begin to format it. For such a small volume, this will take a minute or less. During formatting, the newly created volume will appear in the lower-right pane of the Computer Management console with a progress indicator. When formatting is complete, the capacity, file system, and current status of the volume will appear beneath its label and drive letter in the lower-right pane and further details about the volume will appear in the upper-right pane.

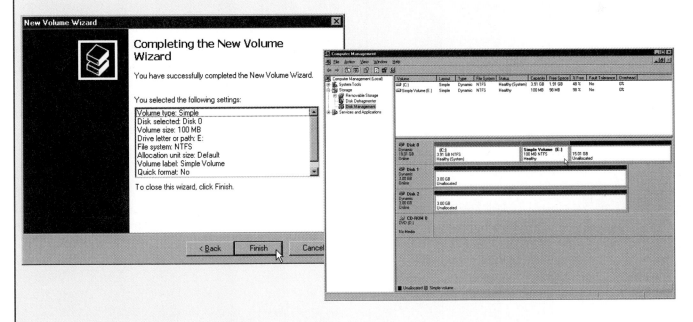

Step 7

Now that we have created a simple volume, it is only natural to try our hand at creating an extended volume for it. Recall that extended volumes are used to "grow" existing simple volumes. To begin the process, right-click the newly created simple volume and choose Extend Volume from the shortcut menu. When the Extend Volume Wizard starts, click the Next button.

Step 8

The second step of the Extend Volume Wizard allows you to choose the disk or disks to which you wish to extend the volume and set the amount of space you would like to allocate to the extended volume. The disk the existing volume is on is currently selected, and once again, the entire remaining capacity is set by default. Change the space value to 100MB and you will see that the Total volume size changes to read 200MB. This reflects the original 100MB volume with the 100MB extended volume added. Click Next and then click Finish. You should now see the extended volume appear in the lower-right pane of the screen as a discrete area but labeled with the same volume label and drive letter as our simple volume. Note that both simple volumes and their extensions use the same color-coding.

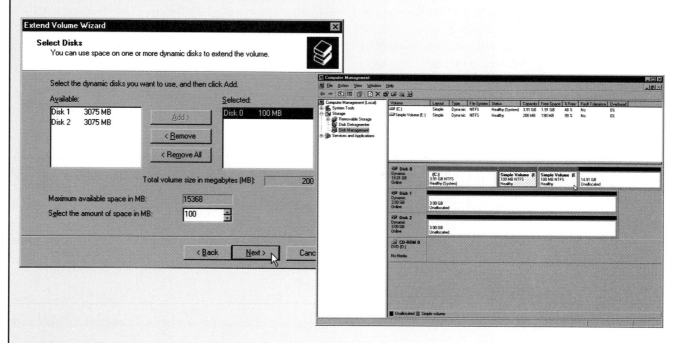

Step 9

To begin creating a spanned volume, right-click the unallocated space on one of your drives and choose New Volume from the shortcut menu. When the New Volume Wizard starts, click Next and then select Spanned Volume. When you have read the description of a spanned volume, click Next.

Step 10

As you know, spanned volumes use space on more than one physical disk to create a single volume. On the third step of the New Volume Wizard, we can select the disks we wish to use and set the amount of space to allocate to our spanned volume. By default the entire capacity of our current disk will be selected. Change the space to 100MB for the current disk. Then choose another disk from the Available disks list and click the Add button. Select the newly added disk on the right side of the dialog box and change the amount of space to be used on this disk to 100MB also. You can add up to a maximum of 32 disks, with varying amounts of space on each, to create a spanned volume. Click Next.

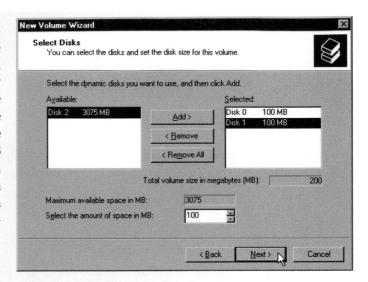

The remainder of the New Volume Wizard continues as it did for the simple volume we created. Choose a drive letter for the volume and click Next. Accept the default formatting settings but change the volume label to Spanned Volume and click Next and then Finish. You should now see the new volume, spanned across two drives, appear and begin to format.

Tip: The process for creating striped volumes is completely identical to that for creating spanned volumes with the exception that the allocated space on each drive must be identical. To save time and space, we'll skip creating a striped volume for now.

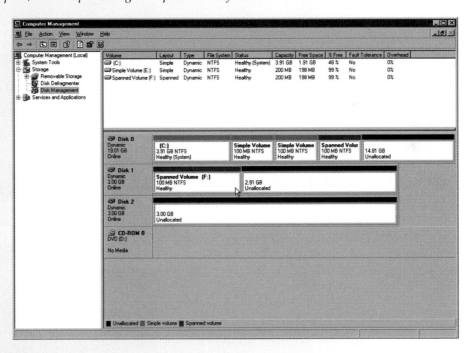

Mirrored volumes can be created from scratch, creating both a simple volume and its mirror at the same time, or else an existing simple volume can have a mirror added to it after it has been created. We're going to add a mirror to our original simple volume. To begin the process, right-click the simple volume we created earlier and choose Add Mirror. When the Add Mirror dialog box appears, select a disk to host the mirrored volume and click Add Mirror. When the new volume appears in the lower-right pane of the Computer Management screen, you will see both the original simple volume and its extended volume go through a resynching process. During this process, Windows is making an exact duplicate of the simple volume, including its volume extension, on the mirrored volume. From here on out, the two volumes will be kept in perfect synch.

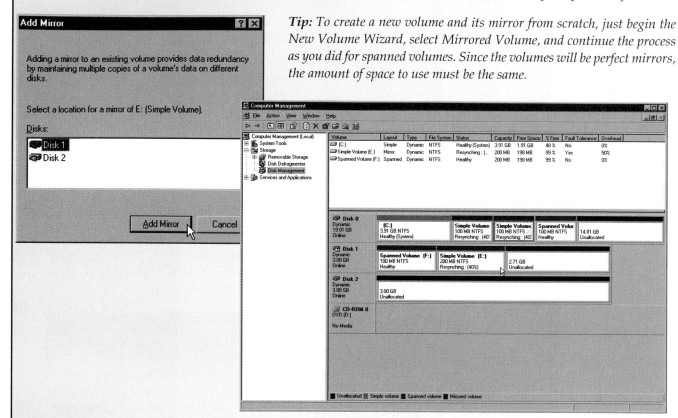

Tip: To create a new volume and its mirror from scratch, just begin the New Volume Wizard, select Mirrored Volume, and continue the process as you did for spanned volumes. Since the volumes will be perfect mirrors, the amount of space to use must be the same.

Step 13

Creating RAID-5 volumes follows essentially the same steps that we used to create a spanned volume. Start the New Volume Wizard and click Next, then choose RAID-5 and click Next again. Since a RAID-5 volume requires a minimum of three disks, you must now select two other disks in addition to the one currently selected. Once you have three disks selected, set the capacity to 100MB. Note that although you've allocated 300MB of total space, the total volume size is only 200MB. This is because of the space required for the parity-information stripe. Click Next.

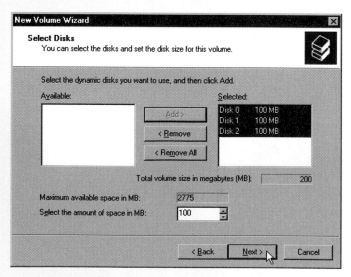

Finish out the wizard as before using RAID-5 as the volume label. When the wizard is finished, your RAID-5 volume should appear and begin formatting. You may close the Computer Management console when you are finished

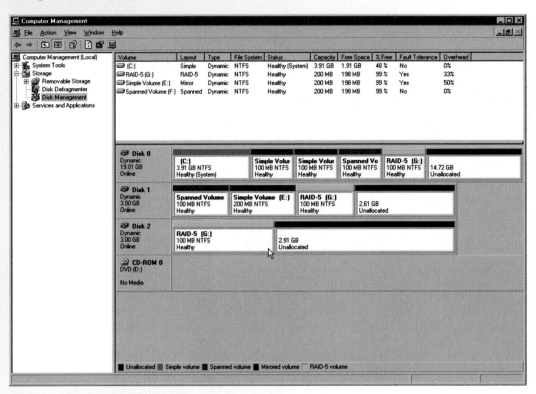

Using Windows Backup

Even though mirrored volumes and RAID-5 volumes do a lot to help improve the fault tolerance of our data storage systems, they still don't offer complete protection against the loss of data. As part of storage management, we have to plan for the catastrophic failure of one or more drives and/or the entire server. Whether the damage comes from simple mechanical failure or something more destructive like flood or fire, we need to do what we can as administrators to try to ensure that as little data as possible is lost. That's where backing up comes in.

Backup Options

Many products, both hardware and software, exist to help us in backing up our data. On the hardware side, there's a dizzying array of tape drives and other devices that can store the large amounts of data found on most server hard drives. On the software side, there are nearly as many products meant to ease the making of backups and the restoring of lost files. Make no mistake about it, there are many fine options available above and beyond

On smaller systems, or in a pinch, writable optical drives (CD-Rs, CD-RWs, and DVD-Rs, and the like) can be quite useful. However, working with optical devices and Windows Backup, which we're covering in this section, takes some doing, as you'll see.

Researching Backup Hardware

If you administer networks, sooner or later you are going to have to choose some sort of backup system to use with your server. Take a moment to browse some of the options available and get some ideas about the range of features and costs. To complete this task, you will need a computer with Internet access and a browser. Try this:

1. Point your browser to a shopping site such as `shopper.cnet.com` or `www.mysimon.com`. Search for **tape backup drive**.

2. Get an idea of the range of prices offered by tape backup drives. Make sure you are comparing only drives, as media (blank tapes) frequently will appear in the search results.

3. Check out a few of the tape drives and compare their features. What features do you find that would be especially useful to a network administrator? Do the higher-priced devices really offer more features?

4. Choose one device to research in depth, and share your findings with your classmates.

what's already in your system and part of Windows Server 2003. But what about what you've already got? I don't know about you, but I'm cheap! I hate to spend money if I really don't have to.

Backup Hardware

On the hardware side of things, we're probably going to have to make some purchases. Backing up to the hard disk drives is out for the obvious reasons. If something destroys the server, it will probably destroy the drives. That's why we can't depend on RAID-5 or mirrored volumes. Backing up to optical media such as writable or rewritable CDs or DVDs might be an option. Most computers now include some sort of writable optical device. However, the storage capacity, even on a writable DVD, is limited compared to the size of today's drives, and writing to optical media tends to be pretty slow. In the end, we'd probably need to buy some sort of tape drive or other backup device that enabled us to copy large amounts of data onto some type of removable media with as little inconvenience as possible. But since this isn't a hardware course, we'll work with what we have for now.

Backup Software

On the software side, things are looking a bit better. Windows Server 2003 comes with a quite capable backup utility called (wait for it!) **Windows Backup**! As it turns out, this little utility is actually pretty darn powerful and, in many cases, all you need. It's also much improved when compared to previous backup utilities included with Windows! Other backup utilities are available, of course, and some of them are very good. In fact, most backup drives come with some sort of backup utility that is often custom made to accommodate that device's special features. But since we're being budget-minded, let's take a closer look at what Windows Backup offers.

Features and Shortcomings of Windows Backup

Many people tend to overlook Windows Backup as an option or simply assume that any free (well, maybe "included" is a better word) backup utility can't be very good. In some cases, this is due to bad experiences with earlier versions of the utility that were, shall we say, not quite up to snuff. However, Microsoft has heard the cries of the masses and put some real work into making Windows Backup a seriously useful program. Although

Windows Backup still has a few shortcomings, it's now surprisingly capable and full-featured. Let's take a look at both its features and where it falls short before we try it out.

Features

One really nice feature of Windows Backup is the Backup or Restore Wizard, which has been greatly improved since Windows 2000. This handy little wizard is now the default mode for Windows Backup and leads you through the process step by step. If you want more control, you can always access Advanced Mode, which for the experienced user allows detailed configuration of all backup settings. You can also choose to disable the wizard from its first dialog box, shown in Figure 6.6, and then access it any time you want from within the utility. New users typically find the wizard helps them create backups and restore files with little trouble.

Window Backup has some great new features. One that is particularly useful is its ability to create an **Automated System Restore (ASR) backup set**. An ASR set allows for relatively painless recovery from complete system failures by backing up all of the essential system files and settings. The "automated" part of an ASR set is the creation of a floppy disk that carries out the restoration, well, automatically!

Another new feature is one we mentioned way back in the first chapter. Windows Server 2003 now offers Volume Shadow Copy, which allows Windows Backup to back up even files that are currently opened by users or the system itself. What that means is you can do a backup essentially anytime and be sure that you've got a current copy of all files, without first disconnecting all users. The end result is that backups can be taken whenever it's convenient for the person doing the backups, not just when it's not inconvenient for the users. This new feature is enabled by default, so you don't have to do a single thing differently to experience the benefits!

Of course, Windows Backup offers lots of other features in addition to these, such as the ability to keep a backup log that tracks each backup

An ASR set created in Advanced Mode does not include a backup of all of the data on your system unless you intentionally choose to also back up that data. However, choosing to back up all of your data and create a restore disk through the Backup and Restore Wizard does both tasks at once.

• **Figure 6.6**   The Backup or Restore Wizard for Windows Backup

Backups can also be scheduled in advance to occur at whatever time the administrator chooses. This can be done by clicking the Schedule Jobs tab in Advanced Mode and clicking the Add Job button. The Backup Wizard walks you through creating and scheduling the backup operation.

 Keep an eye on the Windows Update web site for a patch for Windows Backup that addresses the incompatibility with older operating systems.

 If you have a writable optical drive and no other backup device, simply back up to a hard disk volume and then copy the file to the optical device as a separate step. Although Windows Backup cannot use these devices for writing backup files, it can read files stored on optical media during a restore operation.

operation and the ability to schedule backups automatically. All in all, it's pretty feature-rich. However, there are two areas where, at least for now, Windows Backup might leave you a bit stranded.

Shortcomings

The first shortcoming of Windows Server 2003 may very well be fixed by the time you read this. It's not a bug, a mistake in the programming, or anything like that. It's actually an improvement that has an unfortunate consequence.

In coding the Windows Backup utility for Windows Server 2003, Microsoft made a small change in how the data is recorded in the backup file. This change actually allows for faster backups, which is, of course, a good thing. However, it also means that backups created in Windows Server 2003 cannot be restored on any other operating system. Thus, if you had a complete server crash and needed to restore your data temporarily to an older Windows 2000 server, you'd be out of luck. In all likelihood, Microsoft will eventually come up with a workaround for this problem, but in the meantime it's worth knowing about.

The other small problem with Windows Backup is that it does not support the use of writable optical drives as backup devices. I call this a small problem because such devices really aren't the best choice for backing up anyway. As I mentioned before, they have relatively little capacity and tend to be fairly slow. However, it is a constant surprise to people who aren't familiar with this limitation that you can back up to hard disks or even floppy disks (don't try it!) but not to a CD-R, CD-RW, or DVD-R. Later in the chapter, we'll take a look at a workaround for this issue. Check out the Tip in the margin for a workaround for the issue.

Performing a Backup and Restore with Windows Backup

Although Windows Backup provides an easy-to-follow wizard, there's nothing like running through a process at least once to make sure you understand it. As you work through the following Step-by-Step, keep in mind how our simple test backup differs from the real thing and how those differences might change the process when you actually perform a backup on a working server.

✓ Cross Check

Windows Backup Pros and Cons

Now that you've had a chance to learn about Windows Backup, let's take a minute to summarize what you've learned. If you like, review the preceding sections and answer the following questions:

1. In you own words, summarize the advantages of using Windows Backup. What features does it offer?

2. Describe the current shortcomings of Windows Backup. How can they be dealt with?

Backing Up and Restoring a Volume with Windows Backup

One of the reasons for chopping a hard disk up into different volumes is it can ease the process of backing up certain data as needed. Depending on the nature of the data being stored on a volume, one volume may need to be backed up on a daily basis, while another may require only monthly backups. Since backups are time consuming, we're better off backing up only what really needs it at the time we're performing the backup operation.

Caution: It's always a good idea to occasionally back up all data in case of a catastrophic server failure.

In this Step-by-Step, you will create a backup of the simple volume you created earlier this chapter. The fact that the simple volume is empty and quite small will work in our favor by allowing us to complete the process in a very short time. Since we cannot know for sure what backup hardware your

lab computer may have installed, we will save the backup file directly to a folder on one of our existing volumes. After we've backed up the volume, we'll go through the process of restoring it to see how easy Windows Backup makes it!

To complete this Step-by-Step, you will need

- A properly configured computer with Windows Server 2003 installed.

- One installed hard disk with at least the simple volume that was created in Step-by-Step 6.2. (If the simple volume no longer exists or was never created, consult with your instructor on how to proceed.)

- Access to an administrator-level account on the computer.

Step 1

To start the Backup or Restore Wizard, click Start | All Programs | Accessories | System Tools | Backup. When the wizard starts, click Next.

Tip: Backup can also be started from the Tools tab of the Properties dialog box for any volume. Right-click the volume in My Computer, Windows Explorer, or Computer Management, select Properties, click the Tools tab, and click Backup Now.

Step 2

The Backup or Restore Wizard, as the name suggests, is used for both creating backup files and restoring from them. Since we need to create a backup file, confirm that the Back up files and settings option is selected and click Next.

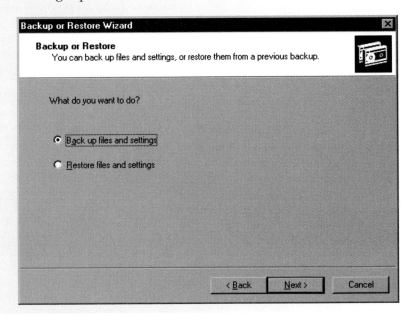

The next step lets you choose between backing up everything on the machine, which includes creating an ASR backup set, or backing up only selected data. To save time, we'll be backing up only one empty volume. Select Let me choose what to back up, and click Next.

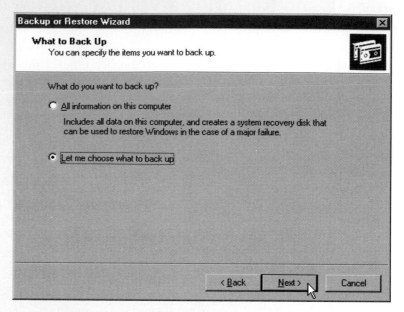

On the next screen, you will see an area on the left that lists various items on your computer and an area on the right that lists the contents of those items. Double-click My Computer on the left and you should see the various volumes on your server appear on the right. You will also see entries for various removable disks, including floppy drives and CD drives. At the bottom is a check box labeled System State. If you wished to make a backup of essential system files and configuration settings, you would check that box. For our purposes, just check the box for the simple volume we created earlier. Click Next.

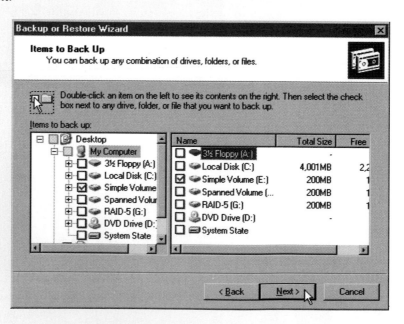

You will next be prompted to select a location in which to save your backup file and give it a name. If your lab computer has backup devices available for use, you should be able to select it using the pull-down list. Otherwise, you will have to browse for a location on an existing volume. Change the name of the backup to Test Backup and then click the Browse button. The default location for backups is in the My Documents folder. Although this is normally not a good place to store backups, it will work for our example. Click the Save button and then click Next.

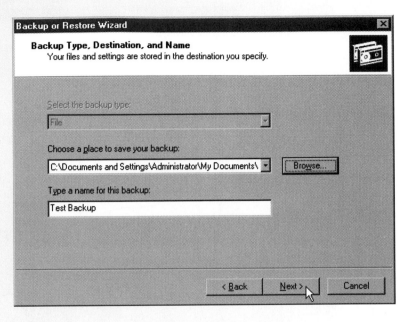

The Advanced button can be used to change the default behavior of the backup operation. For instance, it can be used to change the type of backup and even to schedule the backup for later. The default behavior is to do an immediate, normal backup. Click the Finish button and wait a few moments until the backup file is created and the Backup Progress dialog box reports that the backup is complete. Click Close.

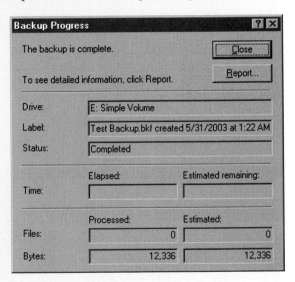

Step 7

To restore the data we just backed up, restart the Windows Backup utility and click Next. Choose Restore files and settings, and click Next again.

Step 8

Click the + beside File on the left side of the dialog box. Click the + beside the name of your backup file and then place a check mark in the box beside the name of the volume you just backed up. Click Next to continue.

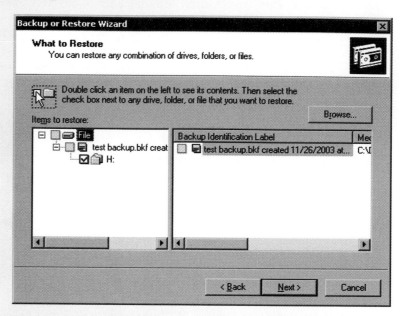

Step 9

Note that this restore operation will restore the files to their original location and will not overwrite existing files. If you wanted to change these settings, you would click the Advanced button. For this exercise, simply click Finish. Since our files have not changed since we did the backup, and still exist, no files will actually be restored. You should see confirmation of this in just a moment at the bottom of the Restore Progress dialog box, where it shows that 0 files were processed. Click Close when you are finished.

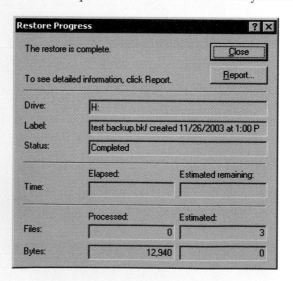

Backup Methods

Backup programs like Windows Backup depend heavily on the condition of a file's archive bit in determining which files to back up. The archive bit is part of the header information for a file that, when turned on, indicates that the file is either new or changed since the last time a backup was run and, thus, should be backed up again. Windows Backup actually offers five backup methods that differ in their handling of files and their archive bits.

In a normal backup, all selected files are backed up regardless of the condition of their archive bit and each has its archive bit turned off, indicating that the files have been backed up.

In a copy backup, all selected files are backed up regardless of the condition of their archive bit and the archive bits are left alone, thus indicating that the files have *not* been backed up. This is done because copy backups are not normally done to protect data integrity, but rather to transfer files from machine to machine.

In an incremental backup, only files with the archive bit on are backed up, after which the archive bit is turned off. This type of backup is frequently used in between normal backups to quickly back up only the files newly created or changed since the last normal backup.

A differential backup also backs up only those files with the archive bit on, but it does not turn the archive bit off after the backup is complete. Because of this, subsequent differential backups continue to back up the same files backed up by earlier operations in addition to any new or changed files. As you can imagine, this causes differential backups to grow quite large!

Finally, a daily backup backs up only files newly created or changed on the day the backup is taken and turns the archive bit off. This method is also useful between normal backups, which are often taken weekly, to ensure that at worst only a single day's worth of data is lost.

When using the Windows Backup Wizard, the default backup type is a normal backup. If you wish to change this, and other options, you can click the Advanced button, rather than Finished, when the wizard displays the summary of chosen options. Clicking the Advanced button also gives you access to additional advanced options that control other aspects of the backup operation, including data verification, scheduling, and whether or not to append successive backups to the same data file or create a new file.

■ Troubleshooting Storage

Like anything else, storage devices occasionally experience problems that require a little troubleshooting on the part of a network administrator. Let's take a look at some problem situations and some potential solutions for those problems.

Disk Errors

Bill has noticed that some programs that used to run perfectly well have started to crash on a regular basis. He's carefully checked to make sure he's

 If the disk you are trying to run error checking on is currently in use, you will be prompted to schedule the process for the next time the system restarts. This is because the error-checking utility cannot proceed while the disk is being accessed by either system- or user-initiated processes.

got the latest upgrades for both the OS and the programs, and he knows that nothing has been added to the machine recently in terms of either hardware or software. The problem seems to be getting worse, but it's affecting only programs installed on one volume of his hard disk. Other programs on other volumes seem to be running just fine. Unfortunately, the programs that are crashing are essential to the work the users of the network are doing, and they need this problem fixed soon.

Hard disk drives take more wear and tear than almost any other component in a computer. It's not too surprising that sometimes things will go wrong and a physical segment of the disk will go bad. In addition, even the best operating system occasionally miswrites a file or otherwise gets confused about where files are located. Windows offers an error-checking tool that will look for and try to fix both physical errors and file system errors.

To access the error-checking tool, you need to open the properties dialog box for the affected volume. This can be done by right-clicking the volume from My Computer, Windows Explorer, or Computer Management and choosing Properties. From the Properties dialog box, click the Tools tab and click the Check Now button.

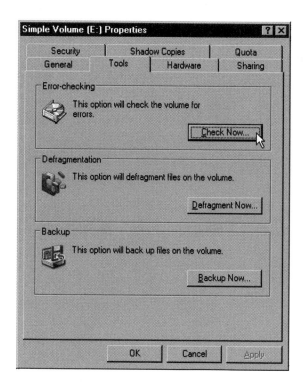

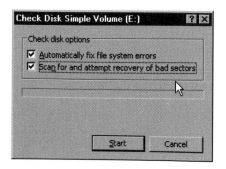

You can choose to check either file system errors or bad sectors which are literally bad areas on the physical disk, or you can check them both at once. Keep in mind that scanning for bad sectors can take quite some time on larger drives. Error checking a volume that's been having problems frequently turns up one or more errors that may have at least contributed to those problems. It's a cheap and easy first step at trying to set things right.

Failing Disks with Mirrored Volumes

Bill ran the error-checking tool on his problem volume, and the news isn't good. Judging by the number of errors he found, he's beginning to suspect that the disk the volume is on may be about to fail. Replacing the disk isn't that big of a deal; he's got a replacement handy and he has a recent backup. However, he currently has one of the volumes on another disk mirrored on this disk and he wants to stop that mirroring process as soon as possible so that errors from the volume on the bad disk won't end up on the volume on the good disk.

Bill actually has two options in this situation. His first option is to break the mirror. By right-clicking either of the volumes being mirrored and choosing Break the Mirrored Volume, he can stop the mirroring process. Breaking the mirror leaves you with two volumes that are identical up to the moment of the breaking but afterward have no connection. Creating and then breaking a mirror is sometimes used as a quick and dirty way of duplicating an entire volume.

Bill's second option is to remove the mirror. To do this, he would right-click the volume on the bad disk and choose Remove Mirror. Removing the mirror breaks the mirror relationship between two volumes but also removes the volume you perform the operation on. The end result is that only one volume remains. Since Bill is going to replace the drive that is going bad, either of these options would work for him. However, if he merely didn't want to mirror anymore and he wanted to reclaim the disk space being used by a mirrored volume, he would want to remove the mirror rather than just breaking it.

> The volume that you right-click when breaking a mirror will retain the original drive letter. The other volume will take on a new drive letter. You can always adjust drive letters after the fact if you need to.

Poor Performance

Dawn hasn't been experiencing the types of problems Bill has, but she has noticed that some of her volumes seem to have gotten much slower in accessing files. After some research, she's determined that the problem isn't related to a network slowdown or disk errors. However, the problem is slowly getting worse, and to top it all off, it seems to affect only the volumes that get the heaviest use from the network's users.

Fragmentation

Hard disks, and the volumes on them, use a technique for writing data that ensures most efficient use of the space available. However, the system does eventually lead to a slowdown when it comes to reading the data that was written. The following example (which is unfortunately true) will help you understand the problem.

When I put away my clean socks, which my wife says isn't too often, I tend to start at the top of my dresser and start shoving them in until there's no more room. When one drawer is full, I move on to the next. When I'm finished, I've put my socks away quickly and with an absolute minimum of wasted space. My wife, on the other hand, has (can you believe it?) a *sock drawer*! When she puts her socks away she goes directly to that special drawer and puts the socks in. It sometimes takes some rearranging to get everything in if the drawer is near full, but she works at it until it's nicely organized. Meanwhile, other drawers with plenty of space are never opened because, well, they aren't sock drawers! Even though it takes her longer to put her socks away and she wastes a lot of space, who do you think finds their socks faster when they need to? Yep, you're right. She's a sock-finding fiend!

Hard drives store data much they way I put away socks. They write pieces of files wherever they happen to see some empty space as the disk spins and the read/write heads scan the surface. When a drive is new, like when my drawers are all empty, most files get written in their entirety in one contiguous space. That means that all of the parts of the file are adjacent to each other. However, as files get deleted and new files get written, gaps begin to open that are free, but too small for a whole file. What happens next is that pieces of files get scattered hither thither and yon across the surface of the hard disk as the drive tries to make best use of the open spaces—like what happens when I squeeze in extra socks in the wrong drawers. When it comes time to find these files, it takes longer than it did when files were written in contiguous spaces. Disks that have many files spread all over their surfaces are said to be **fragmented** and begin to slow down significantly.

Defragmenting Volumes

Since fragmentation is a natural side effect of the way data is written to disks, Windows includes a tool that can be used to **defragment** volumes. The defragmentation tool actually rearranges the data on the segment of the hard disk used by the volume so that all of the pieces of individual files are as close to adjacent to each other as possible. This rearrangement sometimes leads to significant improvement in the performance of the defragmented volume, especially if the volume is one that is used heavily. To access the defragmentation tool, right-click the volume, choose Properties, click the Tools tab, click the Defragment Now button, and then click Defragment. Keep in mind that defragmenting a large volume can take a very long time.

Before defragmenting a drive, it is typically a good idea to turn off any disk-intensive programs or applications that are sensitive to disk reads and writes, such as antivirus programs. Of course, make sure you turn your antivirus back on when the defragmentation is complete!

Chapter 6 Review

■ Chapter Summary

After reading this chapter and completing the Step-by-Step tutorials and Try This! exercises, you should understand the following facts about storage management in Windows Server 2003.

Basic Disks Versus Dynamic Disks

- Basic disks make use of partitions to divide the disk into discrete storage areas. A basic disk can have up to four primary partitions or up to three primary partitions and one extended partition.

- Primary partitions are each identified with a single drive letter. Extended partitions are further subdivided into logical drives, which are identified by drive letters. By using both primary and extended partitions, a basic disk can be subdivided into as many as 24 discrete storage areas identified by drive letters.

- Basic disks are still a common form of storage on client-level computers and servers that use only a single hard disk.

- Dynamic disks make use of volumes rather than partitions to subdivide the hard disk into discrete storage areas.

- Dynamic disk volumes can grow in size on either the original disk or over other disks. Dynamic disk volumes can also improve performance, reliability, and flexibility beyond what was offered by basic disks and partitions.

- Dynamic disk volumes improve performance by allowing for an increase in the speed with which data may be written to or read from the hard disk.

- Dynamic disk volumes improve data reliability by improving fault tolerance. This is done either by maintaining a live backup of a volume's data or by tracking error-correcting information with the data.

- Dynamic disk volumes improve flexibility by allowing more than the 24 volumes made possible by primary and extended partitions. Dynamic disk volumes can be mounted to empty folders so that users may access them as if they were simply folders.

- Dynamic disks may not be used if the computer needs to boot into earlier operating systems, and they convey little advantage if the computer has only a single hard disk drive.

- Basic disks may easily be converted to dynamic disks with no data loss. Converting a dynamic disk to a basic disk results in a loss of all data.

Using Volumes to Manage Storage

- Simple volumes exist on a single hard disk and offer no improvement to performance or fault tolerance.

- Simple volumes may be extended to include unallocated disk space on the same disk as the simple volume. Although the volume is still a simple volume, the added segments appear separately and are sometimes referred to as extended volumes. Extending a simple volume does not increase performance or fault tolerance.

- Spanned volumes allow for storage areas to be spread across up to 32 different hard disks. Windows writes to spanned volumes by writing to the allocated area on the first disk until no more space remains before moving on to the next disk. Spanned volumes do not increase performance and actually decrease fault tolerance, since the loss of a single disk destroys the entire volume. Spanned volumes may be created from scratch or by extending simple volumes over multiple disks.

- A striped volume consists of segments of up to 32 different hard disks. When Windows writes to a striped volume, it simultaneously writes some of the data to each of the individual disks that make up the whole volume. The result of this is a much faster writing process and a slightly faster reading process. Striped volumes also decrease fault tolerance because the loss of a single disk can destroy the volume.

- Mirrored volumes take one volume of a particular size on one hard disk and mirror it, or copy it, in real time to a duplicate of the volume on another disk. Mirrored volumes do not increase performance but do increase fault tolerance. Mirrored volumes take up twice as much space as the data actually being stored due to the mirroring process.

- RAID-5 volumes increase fault tolerance because as Windows writes data to the multiple disks that make up a RAID-5 volume, it also periodically writes a parity-information stripe that can be used to re-create any data that gets lost from a hard disk failure. RAID-5 volumes also increase performance much like a striped volume. RAID-5 volumes use some space to store the parity-information stripe and so do suffer from some overhead. RAID-5 volumes require a minimum of three hard disks.

Using Windows Backup

- Windows Backup is a backup utility included with Windows Server 2003.

- Windows Backup offers a Backup and Restore Wizard that guides the user through the backup process.

- Windows Backup will create Automated System Restore backup sets that can automatically restore important system files and settings in the event of a catastrophic server crash.

- Windows Backup can back up even files currently in use because of Windows Server 2003's Volume Shadow Copy feature. This allows backups to be done whenever necessary.

- Windows Backup's shortcomings include a current inability to restore to older operating systems and a lack of support for writable optical drives.

Troubleshooting Storage

- Disk errors can frequently be found and fixed by running the error-checking tool found in a volume's properties dialog box. The error-checking tool will check for and try to repair both file system errors and physical errors on the surface of the hard disk.

- If a hard disk bearing a mirrored volume is failing, either the mirrored volume can be removed or the mirror can be broken. Removing the mirror breaks the mirror and deletes the affected volume, leaving only one volume behind. Breaking the mirror results in two independent volumes that are exact duplicates up to the moment of breaking.

- Poor performance in accessing files is frequently due to fragmentation on the surface of the hard disk. Defragmenting the hard disk volume will usually improve performance.

■ Key Terms List

Automated System Restore (ASR) backup set *(187)*	**fault tolerance** *(172)*	**RAID** *(177)*
basic disk *(171)*	**fragmented** *(196)*	**RAID-5 volume** *(177)*
defragment *(196)*	**logical drive** *(171)*	**simple volume** *(175)*
dynamic disk *(172)*	**mirrored volume** *(177)*	**spanned volume** *(176)*
extended partition *(171)*	**mounted volume** *(172)*	**striped volume** *(177)*
extended volume *(176)*	**parity-information stripe** *(178)*	**volume** *(172)*
	primary partition *(171)*	**Windows Backup** *(186)*

■ Key Terms Quiz

Use terms from the Key Terms list to complete the sentences that follow. Don't use the same term more than once. Not all terms will be used.

1. On a basic disk, each _____ is identified by a single drive letter and each disk can have a maximum of four.

2. If a volume on a dynamic disk is accessed as if it were a folder rather than through a drive letter, we say it is a _____.

3. Both mirrored volumes and RAID-5 volumes increase _____.

4. RAID-5 volumes record information to be used to re-create corrupted or lost data in the _____.

5. When a file is spread in pieces over the surface of the hard disk rather than having all of the pieces located adjacent to one another, we say it is _____.

6. A/an _____ can be created by Windows Backup to aid in restoring a server after a catastrophic crash.

7. An extended partition can be divided into many discrete storage areas. Each of these is referred to as a _____.

8. You can grow a simple volume by adding an _____.

9. A _____ is much like a spanned volume but actually offers a performance increase, since Windows writes simultaneously to the individual segments on different disks.

10. A _____ uses volumes, rather than partitions, to segment the available space on the hard disk.

■ Multiple-Choice Quiz

1. By using a combination of primary and extended partitions on a basic disk, you can have a maximum of _____ hard disk storage areas designated by drive letters.

   a. 5

   b. 24

   c. 26

   d. essentially unlimited

2. Which of the following is a reason *not* to use dynamic disks?

   a. A need may arise to boot into an earlier operating system.

   b. The system has only two hard disks.

   c. The system needs many discrete storage areas.

   d. The system has a lot of unallocated space available.

3. A striped volume may consist of segments of up to _____ disks.

   a. 3

   b. 4

   c. 32

   d. 128

4. Which of the following volumes actually *decreases* fault tolerance?

   a. Simple volume

   b. Spanned volume

   c. Mirrored volume

   d. RAID-5 volume

5. Windows Backup cannot write backup files to a

   a. Floppy disk

   b. Hard disk

   c. CD-R

   d. Tape

6. Rearranging files on the surface of the hard disk so that all parts of each file are adjacent is called

   a. Defragmenting

   b. Disfragmenting

   c. Departitioning

   d. Delimiting

7. If you create a RAID-5 volume from four disks of 400MB each, how much will the actual volume hold?

   a. 400MB

   b. 800MB

   c. 1200MB

   d. 1600MB

8. Which of the following requires the same amount of space to be used on each disk in the volume?

   a. Simple volume

   b. Extended volume

   c. Spanned volume

   d. Striped volume

9. Which of the following is *not* an advantage of dynamic disk volumes over basic disk partitions?

   a. Dynamic disks volumes are not limited in number like partitions.

   b. Dynamic disk volumes can be larger than partitions.

   c. Dynamic disk volumes can include space on several disks unlike partitions.

   d. Dynamic disk volumes, unlike partitions, can offer fault tolerance.

10. Which of the following volumes increases performance?

    a. Simple volume

    b. Extended volume

c. Spanned volume

d. Striped volume

11. Which of the following processes will cause a mirrored volume to no longer be mirrored and will recover the space that was used in mirroring?

a. Breaking the mirror

b. Extending the mirror

c. Removing the mirror

d. Converting the mirror

12. Which of the following is most similar to a primary partition?

a. Simple volume

b. Spanned volume

c. Striped volume

d. RAID-5 volume

13. Both the error-checking tool and the defragmenting tool can be found in which dialog box?

a. Details

b. Information

c. Status

d. Properties

14. If you had two hard disks, one of which was nearly full, what type of volume would you use to increase the size of the current storage area?

a. Simple volume

b. Spanned volume

c. Mirrored volume

d. RAID-5 volume

15. Why would you convert a dynamic disk back to a basic disk?

a. A mirrored volume became corrupted.

b. The disk ran out of space.

c. You needed to boot into an earlier operating system.

d. You needed to perform an emergency backup.

■ Essay Quiz

1. Your boss has heard about mirrored volumes from a fellow manager. She's convinced that all data on the company's servers should exist on mirrored volumes, including archived information that never changes. Explain why this isn't a good idea and when mirrored volumes should be used.

2. Larger hard drives are introduced on a nearly weekly basis. Explain the advantages of sometimes using multiple smaller hard drives instead of single large hard drives.

3. Although it's mildly irritating that Windows Backup will not write directly to CD and DVD media, it's really not that big a deal. Explain why optical media aren't really the ideal backup media and what makes tape such a good choice for backups.

4. Explain the difference between striped and spanned volumes.

5. Explain the difference between mirrored and RAID-5 volumes.

Lab Projects

• Lab Project 6.1

When to do backups is nearly as important a consideration as doing them in the first place. You also have to think about how many tapes (or other media) need to be used and how to rotate them. Using the Internet (and any other available source), research one of the most common methods: the

Grandfather, Father, Son scheme. Answer the following questions:

❶ Why is this method called Grandfather, Father, Son? How does it work?

② How many tapes (or other media) are needed using this scheme if you assume that each backup job uses one?

③ What are the strengths of this method? Can you see any weaknesses?

④ What backup plan (other than Grandfather, Father, Son) would you use? Be sure to detail

how your scheme would work and how many tapes (or other media) would be needed. What advantages does your plan offer?

• Lab Project 6.2

With so many different volume options, it's sometimes difficult to choose which option is best suited to a particular situation. For each of the volumes listed here, imagine and describe a realistic situation where each should be used. Please provide as much detail as you can in terms of the type of data being stored, the need for capacity, the need for increased performance, and the need for fault tolerance.

① Simple volume with extended volumes

② Spanned volume

③ Striped volume

④ Mirrored volume

⑤ RAID-5 volume

• Lab Project 6.3

Error-checking and defragmenting hard drives are two tasks that frequently get overlooked by computer users, until a problem arises! Get at least three computer users to agree to do the following on their personal computers and report the information back to you. This can be done in groups with your classmates. When you have collected the data, share it with your classmates and analyze your findings. How often do you think users should check for errors and defrag their drives? Why?

① Run the error-checking tool for their operating system, checking for both file system errors and physical errors. Were any errors detected, and if so, of what type? How long did it take to run the complete test, and what size was the drive that was tested? When had they last checked for errors?

Note: On some versions of Windows, the error checking tool is called Scandisk and is accessed through the System Tools submenu of the Accessories menu.

② Perform a defragmentation of their main hard disk partition/volume. How fragmented was the partition/volume? How long did the process take, and what size was the drive? Did the user note any performance improvement after defragging the drive? When had they last defragged?

Note: The defragmenting tool can be accessed through the System Tools submenu of the Accessories menu on versions of Windows that do not have a Tools tab in the Properties dialog box.

Preparing for Output: Printer Configuration and Management

"A paperless office has about as much chance as a paperless bathroom."
—Anonymous

In this chapter, you will learn how to:

- **Install a printer**
- **Configure and share a printer**
- **Manage printers and print jobs**
- **Troubleshoot common printing problems**

For many years, people have discussed the possibility that computers might allow us to completely do away with paper documents. The idea of a paperless office is certainly intriguing but, as the opening quote implies, not very practical! Whether you are working on a stand-alone home PC or a networked office PC, there are times when there's no substitute for printed output.

Computer networks, and the servers that run them, go a long way toward improving the printing process. From the point of view of the company, network printing offers savings of both money and time, as it decreases the number of printers that need to be purchased and administered. From the point of view of the user, network printing allows easier access to a variety of print devices and improved performance compared to what is available when using a locally connected print device.

In this chapter, we'll take a look at what is involved in network printing using Windows Server 2003. We will begin by looking at the different connection options that are available and how to go about installing a printer. We'll also take a look at how to configure and share installed printers and how to manage the print jobs users send to them. Finally, we'll take a look at some common printing problems and some strategies for addressing them.

▪ Installing a Printer

In Windows Server 2003 terminology, the term **logical printer** describes the software interface between the operating system and the actual device that does the printing. The familiar printer icon you see on the screen represents the logical printer. A **printer** is the actual piece of hardware that does the printing. In some cases, a printer is formally described as a **physical printer** or **print device** to help differentiate it from the logical printer. Although most users think about printers as either ink jet or laser, system administrators need to know that there are two different types of print devices, categorized by how they are connected to the computer that is doing the printing. There are also two different ways of describing the way data gets sent to the physical printer. As you'll see, each of these variations offers its own pros and cons when it comes to printing over a network.

> Print devices can actually connect to a number of other local ports or other interfaces, such as serial ports, SCSI interfaces, and even infrared connections, but parallel and USB are by far the most common connections.

Connection Options

Printers connect to computers in two basic ways: as local print devices or as network print devices. Since each method has several variations, let's take a closer look at each.

Local Print Devices

Local print devices are printers that are physically connected to one of the ports on the computer as depicted in Figure 7.1. Several different ports might be used, but the most common are the **parallel port** or a **USB port**.

For many years, most printers connected to computers through the parallel ports, usually designated as LPT1, LPT2, and so on. In fact, LPT stands for Local Printer Terminal, thus illustrating that parallel ports were originally designed for use with printers. Since most computers have only one parallel port, the most common connection was to the LPT1 port. Parallel ports like the one in Figure 7.2 are still perfectly suited to connecting printers but are quickly being replaced by USB ports due to the increased convenience they offer.

USB, or Universal Serial Bus, ports' primary advantage over parallel ports, when it comes to printing, is the ability to support more than one device on a single port. Although this capability is rarely used to support multiple printers, it does allow for other devices to connect to the computer at the same time as a print device, thus allowing for more flexibility. In fact, most modern computers offer at least two USB ports, as shown in Figure 7.3, each of which can handle up to 127 devices! USB ports are also much faster than parallel ports, but as I'm sure you know, printing is a relatively slow process to begin with. The added speed of a USB port rarely gives any advantages when one is being used to connect a printer.

Local print devices are very easy to connect and install, but they suffer from some disadvantages that limit their usefulness on networks of any size. The first major weakness is that local print devices have to be located relatively close to the computer due to cable length limitations that are inherent to each connection method. For instance, a single USB cable has a maximum length of about 16 feet. Even when you purchase additional cables and equipment to connect them together, the ultimate maximum is a

● Figure 7.1   A local print device

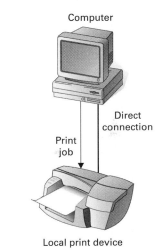

● Figure 7.2   A typical parallel port

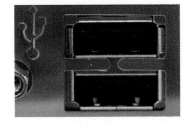

● Figure 7.3   Two USB ports

Multifunction printers, which offer scanning, faxing, and copying functions in addition to printing, do benefit from being connected to a USB port. This is because the built-in scanner can send data to the computer much faster over USB than it can over a parallel connection.

Local print devices are still used in most networks when it makes sense to directly connect a printer to a nearby system. These local print devices can also be shared out to the rest of the network, as we'll see.

We'll be installing a local print device in Step-by-Step 7.1, but we'll also take a look at the procedure for installing a network print device at the same time.

The external devices that allow printers normally used as local print devices to act as network print devices are sometimes called print servers. Unfortunately, this is also the name given to an actual server computer that primarily plays the role of providing access to the printers on a network. This confusing situation makes a little more sense when you consider that these external devices actually function as computers that the local print devices are connected to and so are, in a way, acting as print servers to the network.

measly 100 or so feet. Parallel cables rarely work well over distances much greater than 25 feet. In addition to the length problem, local print device connectors, such as parallel and USB, just weren't designed to support large numbers of printers simultaneously. In the case of parallel, there just aren't enough ports, while USB was designed to support multiple *different* devices, rather than a dozen or so printers for a network! This becomes a problem when we want to connect many printers to a single server, called a **print server**, to ease administration and improve the performance of network printing. We'll be talking more about print servers in just a bit.

Network Print Devices

Network print devices, as depicted in Figure 7.4, also connect to the computer doing the printing, but do so (you guessed it!) over the network rather than through physical ports on the system. This can actually be accomplished a number of different ways.

Some network print devices are designed to work as such from the get go. Some printers have their own network interface cards and connect to the network much as any computer would. In other cases, network interfaces can be added as options to printers that normally connect as local print devices. There are also external devices that can be used to connect non–network–capable printers to the network. Regardless of the method that is used, the printer becomes associated with a network IP address as its port that can be accessed by other computers on the network.

Although network print devices take a bit more setup than local print devices, they offer a great deal in the way of benefits that makes them more suitable for network printing demands. Since network print devices are connected like any other device on the network, they can also be located pretty much wherever needed within the physical network. It's easy to have 20 or more network print devices all connected to the network but spread throughout a building, or even several buildings. This arrangement allows users to easily use a printer that is convenient to their current location. Additionally, the multiple network print devices can all be associated with a single

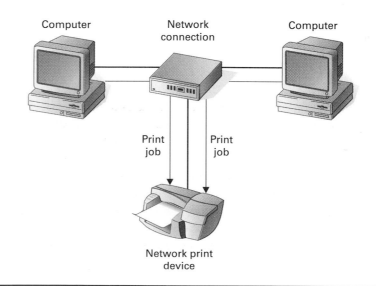

• Figure 7.4   A network print device

server that is dedicated to the task of handling all print jobs, even though this server is not located close to any of the printers. This is what allows print servers to centrally administer the printing process and improve performance for the client computers that need to print.

Data Handling Options

As mentioned earlier, two options are available for handling the actual data that is being sent to the printer. One option is to have the computer that needs to print communicate the data directly to the printer, either through a local connection or through a network connection. Microsoft refers to the print device in this situation as being "nonremote." The other option is to send the data to a print server and then let the print server send the data to a printer, again through either a local or a network connection. Microsoft's term for print devices in this situation is "remote." As with anything, each option has advantages and disadvantages.

Nonremote Print Devices

A **nonremote print device** is one that the printing computer communicates with directly, without the intervention of a server. When a home user sends a document to their personal printer, they are using a nonremote print device. The data goes directly from their computer to the printer. That printer is most likely also a local print device in that it is probably connected to the computer using either the parallel or USB port. However, it doesn't have to be.

Remember the network print devices we talked about earlier? Those devices can be installed at a client machine just like a printer that is connected through the parallel port. It's quite possible, and sometimes done, to have a computer directly communicate data to the network print device. In such cases, the network print device would also be a nonremote print device.

The advantage of nonremote print devices is that they require no specialized print server to act as an intermediary and they allow the individual computer great control over the printer being used. However, since each computer handles its own print jobs, there is a significant hit to performance as the computer takes the time to work with the printer. Additionally, if several different computers are connected to the same printer as a nonremote device, which is possible, they will each have to wait their turn to print if they try to print at the same time. During this wait, there can be a significant impact to performance as the computer keeps trying to submit its print job to the busy printer.

Remote Print Devices

A **remote print device** is connected to a print server, and all network computers that print to that device first send their print jobs to the server, which then communicates with the device. Although the client machines still print to a "printer," what they are actually doing is preparing the data for the printer in question and then sending that prepared data to the server. From that point on, the client computer can forget about the print job as the server takes over communicating with the printer itself. Most network print devices end up being connected as remote print devices, especially on larger networks.

Local print devices can also be connected to as remote print devices. I know that sounds confusing, but bear with me. Imagine that you are on a network but you have a printer physically connected to your computer, which makes it a local print device. It's possible for you to share that printer with other users on the network, which is something we'll set up later in this chapter. If you do share your printer, other computers that wish to print to it must first send the data to your computer, which then handles the actual communication with the printer. In such a case, your local print device is a remote print device to other users, and your computer acts as a print server for that printer.

You might imagine, in the example we just discussed, that if a lot of people tried to print to your printer, it might bog your machine down a bit. Printing is actually a pretty labor-intensive process for a computer. One of the chief benefits of using remote print devices is that we can pass the process off to a print server that is configured to handle the load and doesn't do much else. Thus our client computer can continue to work at peak efficiency while the print server handles the drudgery of printing. We can also use the print server to centrally administer the printers it connects to. By doing that, we can have better control over who can use the printers and how they are configured. All in all, the use of remote print devices, whether they be locally connected or connected through the network, is typically the most efficient way to handle printing on a network.

Print servers aren't always dedicated to just printing. Frequently, especially on smaller networks, the print server might serve double duty as a file server, which gives access to centrally stored data, or an application server, which allows clients to run centrally installed programs. However, since printing is labor intensive, it is usually a good idea to set up a dedicated print server once printing demands reach a high enough level that they start impacting the ability of the server to perform other tasks.

Installing a Locally Connected, Nonremote Printer

Since we are working on the server, most any printer we would install would be a nonremote printer from our perspective. To the clients, of course, the same printer would be a remote printer. To simplify matters, we'll go through the process of installing a printer that is connected locally, that is, through one of the physical ports on the server. We're doing this for a couple of reasons. First, it's quite possible that you don't have a network print device handy in your lab environment. Local print devices can be installed even if they are not connected, whereas network print devices will fail to install if the system cannot establish communication with the network address. Second, the process is actually similar regardless of whether the device is a local print device or a network print device. We'll take the time during this Step-by-Step to show you how you would go about handling a network print device.

Installing a Locally Connected Printer

Although the process of installing a locally connected, nonremote print device on a server isn't all that different from installing a printer on a typical home computer, it is still worth stepping through the process. On the one hand, the wizard has undergone some very slight changes from previous Windows versions, and this is as good a time as any to get a look at those. On the other hand, there are certain options that are important when installing printers on servers, such as the creation of network ports for network print devices, which are not normally used on client-level machines.

It is not necessary to have an actual printer connected to the computer for this exercise. In fact, for many printers, it is better to follow the manufacturer's directions for installation, which sometimes call for the use of a manufacturer-supplied installation program. However, the Add Printer Wizard is still a standard method for installing network print devices.

To complete this Step-by-Step, you will need

- A properly configured computer with Windows Server 2003 installed

- Access to an administrator-level account on the computer

Step 1

To start the Add Printer Wizard, click Start and then Printers and Faxes. When the Printers and Faxes window opens, double-click the Add Printer icon.

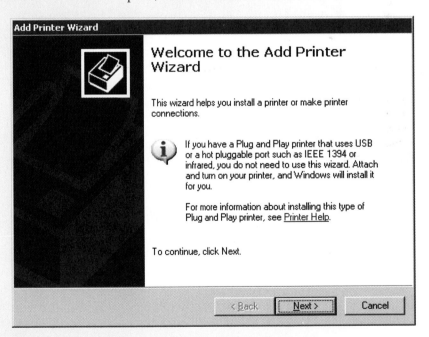

Tip: As mentioned at the beginning of the wizard, certain printers connected to "hot pluggable" ports do not require the wizard and will be installed automatically when plugged into their ports. A hot-pluggable port is a port that will accept the adding and removal of devices without first shutting down the computer.

Step 2

When the first step of the wizard appears, click Next to continue. The second step of the wizard actually introduces some confusion to this process. You're given the choice between installing a local printer or a network printer. However, as you'll note in the tip at the bottom of the dialog box, a network printer that is not attached to a print server is installed by using the local printer option. Local printer actually refers to nonremote printers, which you'll recall are printers that are directly accessed by the computer, rather than accessed through some other system, such as a print server. The network printer option is actually referring to remote print devices that are already connected to existing computers and are shared with the network. For our purposes, you should make sure that the local printer option is selected and you should uncheck the option for automatically detecting and installing Plug and Play printers, since we do not actually have a printer connected to the computer. Click Next to continue.

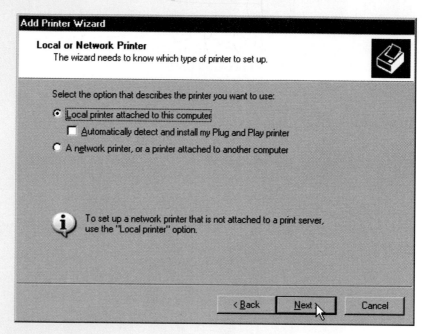

Note: If you feel confused after reading Step 2, I don't blame you. The multitude of different terms used to describe printers is confusing to many people. Just remember that, when using the Add Printer Wizard, if the printer you want to install is not connected to some other computer or print/server/device, then you will install it as a local printer regardless of whether you connect to it by physical port or by network address.

Step 3

The third step of the wizard is where our choices will differ, depending on whether we are installing a printer connected to a physical port or an actual network printer that has its own network address. If the printer we are installing is directly connected to the computer locally, we will select the correct port from the upper drop-down list. If we are actually installing a network printer, we need to create a TCP/IP port first. We'll come back to the local port in a moment, but for now choose the Create a new port option and select Standard TCP/IP Port from the drop-down list. Click Next. When the Add Standard TCP/IP Printer Port Wizard launches, click Next in that dialog box to continue.

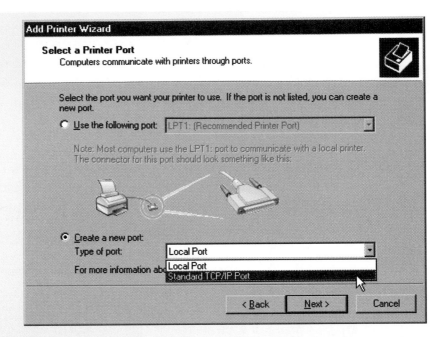

Step 4

If we were actually installing a network printer that had an established IP network address, we would type that address now. If you type an address, such as 192.168.124.15, in the Printer Name or IP Address box, you will see the wizard automatically fill in the name of the port as IP_192.168.124.15. You may type in an address to see this happen, but do not click Next, since there is no printer at that address. If there were a printer at the entered address, the remainder of the printer installation process would continue in much the same way as it does for a local print device. Since that's not the case, click Back and then click Cancel to return to the port selection dialog box of the Add Printer Wizard.

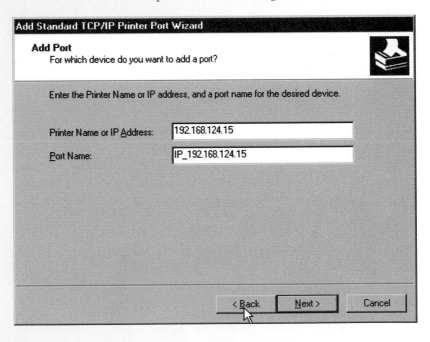

Step 5

Change your choice on the Select a Printer Port dialog box to Use the following port and make sure the upper drop-down box displays LPT1: (Recommended Printer Port). As you recall, LPT1 is the name given to the first parallel port in the computer system. Click Next to continue.

Step 6

The Install Printer Software dialog of the wizard allows us to choose the manufacturer and model of the printer we want to install. If the manufacturer or printer we are installing is not listed, we can either click Windows Update to get an updated list from Microsoft's web site or we can click the Have Disk button and insert a manufacturer-provided driver disk. The driver is the software that allows the printer to communicate with the operating system and vice versa. Choose HP as the manufacturer and scroll down the list to find the HP LaserJet 1100 (MS) driver. Click this driver to select it and then click Next to continue.

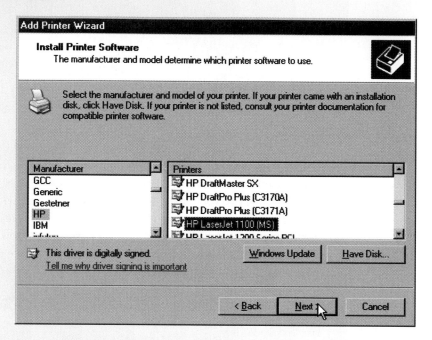

Tip: *You will notice that the driver you've selected displays an icon with a green check mark to the left of its name. As the dialog box explains, this indicates that Microsoft has digitally signed the driver. A digitally signed driver has been tested and certified as compatible with the operating system by Microsoft.*

Step 7

Our next task in installing a printer is to give it a name. As the wizard suggests, the name of the printer should be relatively short to ensure compatibility with some programs. However, the name should also describe the print device in some meaningful way. In many businesses, the name will indicate the location of the printer and its manufacturer and model. For our purposes, name the printer **Test HP 1100**. Be sure to answer No to the question about whether or not this printer should be the default printer. Since the printer doesn't actually exist, it wouldn't do us much good as our default! Click Next when you've named the printer and chosen No.

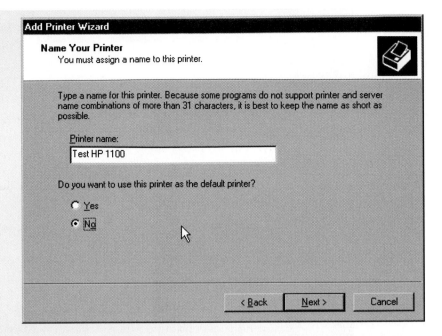

Since we are installing this printer on a computer running Windows Server 2003, it would be only natural to share it with other users on the network. As you can see, this is the default option for the Printer Sharing dialog of the Add Printer Wizard. For now, choose Do not share this printer, since we will set it up for sharing later in the chapter. When you click Next, you will be asked if you wish to print a test page to make sure the printer works properly. Choose not to, since there isn't any printer to print the test page, and click Next to see the summary of our choices. Once you've read over the summary, click the Finish button and you're done!

The Device Settings tab, which appears for many printers, is different for each printer, as it allows the user to control features and settings unique to that printer.

■ Configuring and Sharing Print Devices

There's a very good reason why you might not want to take advantage of the option to share a newly installed printer while working through the Add Printer Wizard. Although the printer is installed, you haven't yet finished configuring its settings to suit your preferences and there's no sense in making it available on the network until you've had a chance to take care of that task. Although each printer has different configuration options depending on its feature set, we can take a look at some of the more universal settings using our freshly installed test printer.

Configuring Print Device Properties

The properties for any installed printer can be accessed by right-clicking the printer's icon in the Printers and Faxes window and choosing Properties. The properties dialog box is divided into several tabs, labeled General, Sharing, Ports, Advanced, Security, and for some printers, Device Settings and other miscellaneous tabs. Since the first four tabs appear for all printers, let's take a look at the options available on each of those.

The General Tab

The General tab, shown in Figure 7.5, is more informational than anything else. Here you will find the printer's name, which you can change, as well as text boxes that can be used to describe the printer's location and any comments. The comments section can be used to record any other information users might find helpful. The General tab also displays information about the features of the printer, including the type of paper that is loaded and the speed and resolution of the printer.

The General tab also offers buttons that lead to the printing preferences and allow for the printing of a test page to check the printer's functioning. The printing preferences allow you to set the paper orientation, paper quality, and other basic options that will then be used for each print job handled by the printer unless changed by the user. These options vary widely from printer to printer and are frequently more involved then those shown in Figure 7.5. Adjusting your printing preferences can actually be quite useful. I, for instance, use the printer preferences for my home ink jet printer to force it into a low-quality, black ink only mode to save on ink consumption. I do have to remember to change those preferences, which can be done from the print dialog of most programs, when I want to print a photograph, but I save a lot of money by not using high-resolution color when I print web pages and other day-to-day documents.

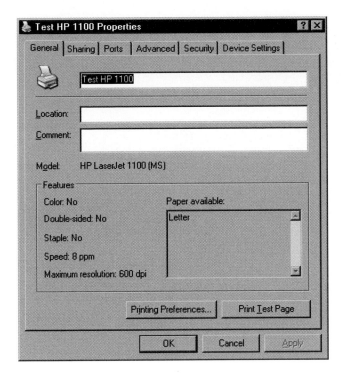

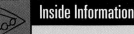

• **Figure 7.5**   The General tab

The Sharing Tab

The Sharing tab simply allows you to choose whether or not to share the printer and, if you are going to share it, to give the share a name. Although we haven't talked much about shares as of yet, since it's a topic for a later chapter, the concept for printers is simple. A shared printer is one that is made available to other users on the network. Each shared printer needs to have a name so that the network's users can choose the correct printer when they go through the network printer installation process. Like the printer name, the name should be relatively short but still descriptive of the device. Unlike the actual printer name, share names should not use spaces. As you can see in Figure 7.6, Windows creates a share name from the printer name automatically, but you can change it if you wish.

The Sharing tab also allows you to install printer drivers for operating systems other than Windows Server 2003. Installing a driver for, say, Windows 98 allows a client on a Windows 98 computer to install that shared printer on their machine without having the driver available. As indicated in Figure 7.7, the driver will be automatically transferred to their computer when they install the printer. However, in order to install additional drivers at the server, you do have to have access to the drivers for those other operating systems. Earlier drivers are not included as part of the Windows Server 2003 installation, but you can usually track them down with relative ease through the manufacturer's web site.

I Don't Want to Share! Why Can't I Have My Own Printer?

Most people print only a couple of documents throughout the average day. Meanwhile, that expensive hunk of metal and plastic spends most of the day sitting around humming to itself with nothing to do. Even if you assume a user who prints 100 pages a day, 5 days a week, for 50 weeks, at a low speed of 5 ppm, the printer would have been actually working for only a little over 80 hours for the whole year! That means that $500 laser printer sat idle for 48 weeks, or 96 percent of the year! I don't know about you, but that seems awfully inefficient to me.

Since most businesses have people working in relatively close proximity, it makes perfect sense to centrally locate a printer or two and share it among the employees. In most cases, people will have to walk only a few feet further and wait a moment or two longer than they would if the printer was sitting right at their desk. Meanwhile, the business gets a much more efficient use of its monetary resources.

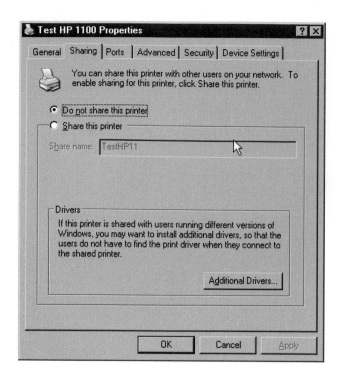

● Figure 7.6   The Sharing tab

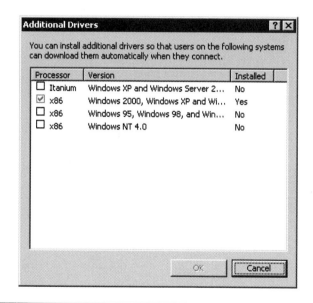

● Figure 7.7   Installing additional drivers

Step-by-Step 7.2

Sharing a Printer

Although printers can be shared during their initial installation process, it isn't uncommon to wait until later, after all configuration tasks are complete, to actually make the printer available to network users. Since we've just opened up the printer's properties dialog box and taken a look at the Sharing tab, this seems like a good time to go ahead and share the printer. Keep in mind that our printer doesn't actually exist, so if any users are actually logged on to the network you use for lab exercises, make sure no one tries to print to it! Nothing bad will happen if they do, but they certainly will have a hard time finding their output!

To complete this Step-by-Step, you will need

- A properly configured computer with Windows Server 2003 installed

- Access to an administrator-level account on the computer

Note: If you have not done Step-by-Step 7.1, do so before doing this exercise.

Step 1

You can access the Sharing tab of the printer properties dialog box one of two ways: you can right-click the printer's icon, select Properties, and then click the Sharing tab, or you can right-click the icon and select Sharing directly. Either way, you end up at the same place. For this exercise, you may use either method.

Step 2

Actually sharing the printer is usually a matter of a couple of clicks. Click the option button beside Share this printer and you'll notice Windows has already filled in a name for the newly shared printer. You'll probably notice that the name is different from the actual name of the printer. This is to ensure compatibility with older operating systems like MS-DOS and Windows 3.*x*. Those older operating systems can access only printer shares that are named according to the same rules that used to apply to filenames. Names should consist of no more than eight characters with, optionally, a period and an up-to-three-character extension. Even if you're fairly sure you won't need to support access by older operating systems, it is still common practice to use relatively short share names.

Step 3

Click OK to close the dialog box, and you've got a shared printer! You can always tell a shared printer by the appearance of the printer icon. A shared printer appears to be held in someone's hand. If you ever need to unshare the printer, simply repeat the preceding steps but choose the Do not share this printer option.

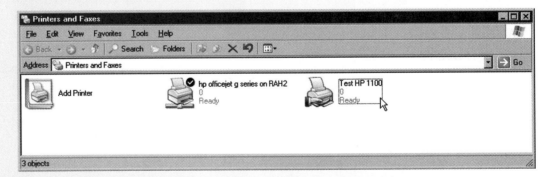

Note: Printer icons that appear to have a wire underneath them connected to the printer indicate network printers. Printer icons with a check mark indicate the default printer for that computer.

The Ports Tab

The Ports tab isn't usually a hotbed of activity. For the most part, it's a place to see which ports are being used by which printers, with a check mark indicating, as you can see in Figure 7.8, the port used by the current printer. However, as we'll see later in this chapter, the Ports tab can be useful in improving printing performance and solving printing problems in certain special situations. Since those processes are a little involved, they deserve their own section. For now, we'll move on to the next tab.

The Advanced Tab

The Advanced tab, shown in Figure 7.9, is where we really start to manage the print device for our network users. Whereas most of the settings here would have no meaning on an independent, client-level machine, they do allow us a great deal of control over how the printer behaves for those who access it from the network. Since this tab offers so many settings, we'll address them each individually.

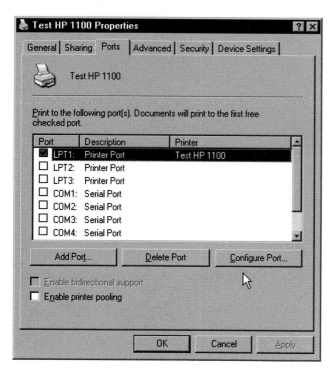

• **Figure 7.8** The Ports tab

In a later chapter, we will show how permission to use a particular printer can be granted to some users and withheld from others. This ability allows for better enforcement of printer availability.

Printer Availability By default, all printers are available at all times. However, it is possible to restrict the hours during which a printer can be used. This scheduling feature can be used to better control when certain print jobs, for instance those that are lengthy, take place. To do this, you create two logical printers that each refer to the same physical print device. Name the printers in such a way that users can tell which one should be used for time-consuming print jobs and make that printer available only during off-hours when such print jobs will not be disruptive. The other printer is left always available for normal, shorter print jobs. Print jobs sent to the "after hours" printer can be sent at any time and will be held by the print spooler until the printer is available for printing as indicated by its schedule. I know from personal experience that my co-workers would rather I not print out 60-page chapter printouts while they're trying to get last-minute work done in the mornings! This particular option can help eliminate such conflicts!

Printer Priority If you create two or more logical printers, as we did in the preceding example, you can use the printer **priority** setting to ensure that one logical printer will always print its print jobs before another. The printer priority setting is set to 1 by default, which is the lowest setting, and it can be set as high as 99. Whichever logical printer has the higher priority setting will print first if more than one printer is currently trying to process a print job.

Driver If a new driver becomes available for a print device, you can use this option to install the updated version.

Spool Print Documents/Print Directly   Normal printing behavior under Windows Server 2003 takes all submitted print jobs and sends them to the print spooler on the server. The **print spooler** is software that accepts the documents that are to be printed and stores them until the printer is ready for them. The collection of waiting documents is called the **print queue**. By sending documents to a print spooler, the client machines are able to continue on with other tasks without needing to wait for the printer to become available. The server does the waiting for them. Normally the printer begins to print as soon as the first page of the document reaches the spooler. However, in certain situations, usually as a troubleshooting measure, it is necessary to change this setting so that printing begins only after the spooler has processed the complete document. In very rare situations, it might be necessary to bypass the spooler altogether and print to the print device directly. In most cases, it is best to leave these settings alone unless you are experiencing some difficulty.

Hold Mismatched Documents   This option will prevent documents that are incorrectly sized or otherwise incorrectly formatted for the print device from being printed. This feature is not turned on by default, which is fine, since this isn't a common problem.

Print Spooled Documents First   This option, which is on by default, prevents documents that have not yet completely spooled from printing before those that have. In effect, this tends to allow shorter documents to print before longer documents that were submitted at about the same time. That makes a lot of sense, if you ask me!

Keep Printed Documents   This rarely used option keeps a copy of documents that have been printed already so that they may be printed again without being resubmitted. This is a very disk-hungry feature that should not be enabled on a regular basis.

Enable Advanced Printing Features   If the print device supports certain advanced features, such as printing multiple pages on a single sheet or printing book-like facing pages, this option allows those features to be used. In certain situations this option must be disabled if problems occur when trying to use the advanced features.

Printing Defaults, Print Processor, and Separator Page   The Printing Defaults button is one way to access the basic printer settings for a particular print device. From this button, you can set the paper size, orientation, print quality and quantity, and other basic defaults that will affect all users of the printer. The Print Processor button allows you to change the data type of printed documents and how they are processed. However, it is very rarely necessary to change from the default settings, so this button is best left alone. The final button allows you to choose a separator page to appear between print jobs. A simple separator page might include the user's name, a job identification number, and the date and time the print job was submitted. This can be

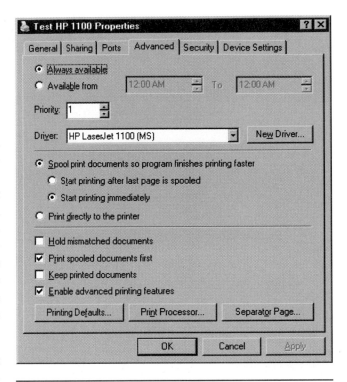

• **Figure 7.9**   The Advanced tab

The word "queue" is just a fancy word for line. Thus, documents waiting to be printed in the print queue are waiting in line to print. The word "spool" is actually an acronym that stands for *simultaneous print operations on line*.

The verb "spooled" simply indicates that a document has been placed in the print queue.

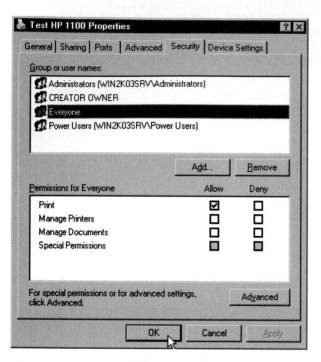

The Printing Defaults button of the Advanced tab gives access to the same options as the Printing Preferences button on the General tab.

● **Figure 7.10** The Security tab

Users do have the right to manage their own print jobs they have submitted to a network printer. However, they have no control over the jobs of others. Users can also make basic configuration changes to the printer for their jobs but cannot change the default settings of the device for other users.

advantageous if a large number of people will be using a print device because it can be used to identify the owner of each document that prints.

The Security Tab

Although we will be discussing security at great length in a later chapter, it's not a bad idea to take a look at what security settings are available for a shared print device. As you can see in Figure 7.10, several different groups have been given permission to use this printer, and their overall permission is taken from the basic permissions Print, Manage Printers, and Manage Documents. Special Permissions are also listed, but we can safely ignore those for now. Without going too far afield, let's talk about the implications of these groups and their basic permissions that are assigned by default for a shared printer.

One thing you should notice is that the group Everyone has been given only the Print permission for this print device. By default, any shared printer is immediately accessible to everyone on the network. However, this access is limited to printing. The Everyone group does not have permission to manage either the printer or its documents. Although you cannot see it in Figure 7.10, the only two groups that do have full permissions for the printer are the Administrators group and the Power Users group. The Creator Owner group, which represents whoever installed the printer, has the ability to manage documents in addition to having the ability to print that is given to the Everyone group.

When we discuss security later in the book, we will come back and take a closer look at printer permissions, including what's hidden behind those "special permissions." However, for now it is sufficient to know that by default everyone is able to print to a shared printer and that only the Administrators and Power Users have a complete set of permissions for managing both the printer and its print jobs.

■ Managing Printers and Print Jobs

As system administrators of a dedicated print server or other server that is providing print services, our job must include some management of the print devices and of the jobs our users send to them. While printer management and print job management is not difficult, it does include some "tips and tricks" that can improve the printing experience for network users. Let's begin by taking a look at how we can manage printers before we discuss managing the print jobs themselves.

Managing Printers

In addition to modifying the properties of printers as we discussed in the preceding section, there are some other management options that are occasionally necessary. In some cases, these options are useful for allowing us to temporarily remove a printer from operation without unduly disturbing the work of our users, while in other cases, we can improve printing performance if the load of print jobs becomes too great.

Controlling Printer Status

Let's face it, sometimes things go wrong and we have to fix them. As network administrators, we need to find ways to fix problems while causing the least amount of problems for our users. If a printer has a problem, it is usually unrealistic for us to be able to notify all of our users that they need to stop using the printer so that we can fix the problem. If we're not careful, the problem could be compounded as users continue to try to print to a device that has run out of paper, has jammed, or needs to be taken out of service temporarily for other reasons. Fortunately, we have some ability to modify the printer's status so that we can address such problems with minimal disruptions to the network users.

Have you ever tried to refill the paper supply of a printer while it was printing? The way most of today's printers load paper makes this difficult to do without creating a paper jam. Since we can't easily run around and tell everyone to stop printing so that we can throw in more paper, the secret is to pause the printer. Printers may be paused by right-clicking the printer icon in the Printers and Faxes window and choosing Pause Printing. This will cause the printer to, you guessed it, pause after it completes the current job. With the printer paused, you can add or change paper, replace ink or toner cartridges, or do whatever else needs to be done, and any remaining or new print jobs will simply sit in the print queue and wait. When you're ready, simply right-click the printer icon again and choose Resume Printing, and well, you can guess the rest!

The ability to use a printer offline is similar to pausing printing but is available only on local printers. If you right-click a local printer's icon and choose Use Printer Offline, any documents sent to the printer will be held in the print queue until you repeat the process and choose Use printer online. From a practical standpoint, taking a printer offline does about the same thing as pausing printing. The only real difference is that taking the printer offline is really a hardware change, while pausing the printing process is more of a change to the print spooler and how it processes the print queue. There is a very good reason, however, for knowing about the offline option, as you'll see later in our discussion of troubleshooting techniques.

Pooling Printers

Imagine for a moment a room of 40 students all printing to a single printer. As you might imagine, there's likely to be a bit of a line if everyone is printing at once! Even the fastest printer can be overwhelmed by too great a number of users. Of course, we can add more printers, but then you have to work out who is going to use which printers, and as users change, you may have

Cross Check

Configuring Printers

Now that you've had a chance to learn about the many different configuration options for printers, let's take a moment to summarize what you've learned. If you like, review the preceding sections and answer the following questions:

1. What configuration options exist on the General tab of the printer's properties dialog box?

2. What configuration options exist on the Advanced tab of the printer's properties dialog box?

to continuously readjust who uses what and when! Fortunately we have a less confusing option that can help in this situation.

Printer pooling refers to treating several identical printers as a single logical printer. What that really means is that from the user's perspective, they print to one printer but the actual print job may be printed from any one of several devices that are sharing the load. You're still adding more printers to increase performance, but you're treating them all as a single logical printer, so no one has to think about which printer they should use. Thus, you can get several printers running and print the same number of jobs in a fraction of the time it would have taken a single printer to do the job.

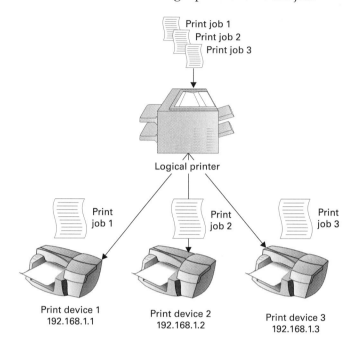

> Keep in mind, when pooling printers, that the printers in the pool should be located in the same place. Otherwise, users would be running all over the place trying to find their print-outs. In the printer pools I work with, printers are placed together in banks of two or more, and users simply grab their output from whichever printer handled the job.

In reality, the printers do not always have to be completely identical. It helps if they are, but printer pooling will sometimes work as long as each of the pooled devices will work with the same print driver. To set up printer pooling, you simply connect multiple printers in the same physical location, typically using IP-addressed network print devices. Then you install your logical printer using one of the networked print devices and configure it to pool the multiple printers at different ports into one logical printer. When a user prints to the pooled printers, the print spooler will look to see which port is currently available, or not busy, and send the document to that print device. As more print jobs arrive, they get distributed more or less equally, depending on their size, among the printers that make up the pool.

Step-by-Step 7.3

Creating a Printer Pool

Printer pooling is a relatively easy and inexpensive way of improving printer throughput, or printing speed, for multiple users without having to manually allocate different users to different devices. Since printer pooling requires multiple, identical printers, which are typically nonremote network print devices, this exercise may not be doable in a lab environment. However, you can read through the steps to get an idea of what is involved in creating printer pools.

To complete this Step-by-Step, you will need

■ A properly configured computer with Windows Server 2003 installed

■ Two identical network print devices

■ Access to an administrator-level account on the computer

■ IP address information for the network print devices from your instructor

Step 1

We begin the process of creating a printer pool by installing the first printer. Click Start | Printers and Faxes to open the Printers and Faxes window and double-click the Add Printer icon.

Step 2

Click Next to go to the second step of the Add Printer Wizard. Select Local printer attached to this computer and uncheck Automatically detect and install my Plug and Play printer. Click Next.

Step 3

Choose Create a new port and select Standard TCP/IP Port from the Type of port drop-down box. Click Next. Click Next on the first step of the Add Standard TCP/IP Printer Port Wizard that opens to advance to the next step.

Step 4

In the Printer Name or IP Address text box, type the IP address of one of the two identical printers that will make up the pool. Be sure to type this information correctly. When the information is entered, click Next. If the wizard requests more information about your device, enter it. Otherwise, the wizard should display a summary of the port information and you can click Finish to return to the Add Printer Wizard.

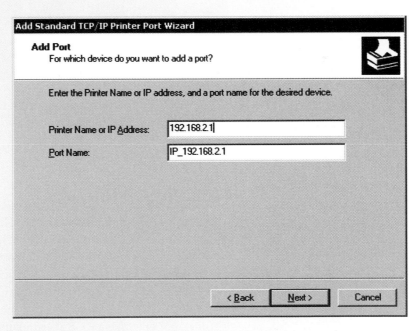

Step 5

Complete the Add Printer Wizard by selecting the correct printer driver, naming the printer, and sharing the printer. Do not set this printer as your default printer and do not print a test page. When the wizard is complete, click the Finish button to return to the Printers and Faxes window.

Step 6

Right-click the printer icon for the newly installed printer and select Properties. Click the Ports tab. Place a check in the check box for Enable printer pooling.

Step 7

Click the Add Port button, select Standard TCP/IP Port, and click the New Port button to begin the Add Standard TCP/IP Printer Port a second time. This time through, enter the correct port information for the second of the two identical printers that will make up the pool. When the wizard is complete, click Finish to return to the properties dialog box for the first printer. Check to make sure that both ports are checked and click OK.

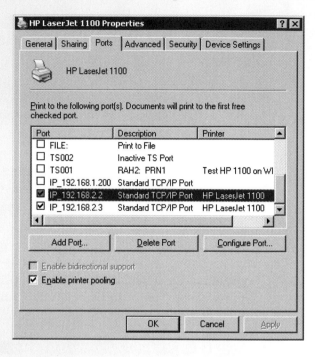

Step 8

To test the pooled printers, have several users install the first printer you configured. Ask the users to simultaneously send at least two or three print jobs each to that printer. Complex documents like graphics-heavy web pages work best, since simple documents may be processed so quickly that the print spooler never needs to balance the load between the printers in the pool. Ideally, you should note that each printer handles a share of the print jobs.

Managing Print Jobs

From time to time, it is necessary for administrators to manage groups of print jobs or even individual print jobs. In some cases, a particular print job may be "stuck," or not printing, due to some error, and thus keep other jobs from printing. In other cases, it might be necessary to redirect already-submitted print jobs from one printer to another or print an important document right away even though many other documents are already queued for printing. Let's take a look at some of the options we have for managing submitted print jobs.

Redirecting Print Jobs

As we said earlier, sometimes things just go wrong. Imagine a situation where a printer with 20 or more very important documents queued suddenly decides to go up in a puff of smoke. You can get a new printer in tomorrow, but those users want their documents today and they aren't too crazy about reopening all of their documents and reprinting them to another printer. The good news is they won't have to, because you can probably redirect those print jobs as long as another printer of the same type is available elsewhere on the network.

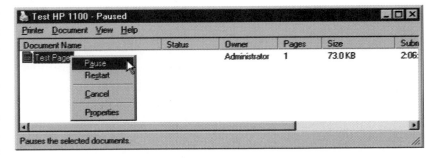

To **redirect print jobs**, simply open the properties dialog box and click our old friend the Ports tab. Redirecting works a lot like pooling, only instead of printing to more than one port, you're going to change ports. Once you've identified the port to which the other printer is connected, either click the check box or, if it isn't already listed, use the Add Port button to add it. As long as the other printer uses the same print driver, the queued print jobs should start printing out there instead of waiting on you to connect a working print device to the original port. The only fly in the ointment is that any document that was in "mid-print" when the original printer blew up is basically lost. That document will have to be reprinted by the user, but they can print to the same printer they used before and it will go to the redirected port and its printer. When the broken printer is back in service, simply change the printer's port back to the original.

Pausing, Canceling, and Restarting Print Jobs

When we looked at pausing the printing process earlier, we said that we were essentially pausing the print spooler and its queue. In addition to being able to pause the entire queue, we can also pause individual print jobs. To do this, simply double-click the printer icon in the Printers and Faxes window, right-click the print job you wish to pause, and choose Pause as shown in Figure 7.11. While that particular print job is paused, others will continue to print. If you wish to pause more than one print job, simply select multiple print jobs by holding down the CTRL key as you click each and then either right-click one of the selected jobs and choose Pause, or choose Pause Printing from the Printer menu. When you're ready to print the paused print jobs, just right-click them and choose Resume.

Print jobs can also be cancelled individually, or else you can cancel all waiting documents. To cancel a single print job, simply right-click it and choose Cancel from the shortcut menu. To remove all spooled print jobs, choose Cancel All Documents from the Printer menu. Keep in mind that canceled print jobs are just that: canceled. Users will need to reprint their documents if they still need them. Avoid canceling print jobs without notifying the users that you've done so, as it can be a bit frustrating waiting for a document that's been canceled without your knowledge!

The most misunderstood option on the print job shortcut menu is Restart. Many people confuse restarting a document with resuming a paused document, but the two are quite different. Whereas resuming a paused document continues a document where you left off, say with

• **Figure 7.11**   The shortcut menu for a print job

page 7 if the first six had printed when you paused the job, restarting a document reprints the entire document from page 1. You might use restart if for some reason the first few pages of a document didn't come out correctly due to low ink or toner or bad paper. In such a case, you might first pause the document, fix the problem, and then restart the document, since the original pages were flawed.

Changing Print Job Priorities

Earlier in the chapter, we discussed the ability to change the priority of a printer. Whereas this is useful if you take the time to create two logical printers and give access to the higher-priority printer to only those who need it, it isn't a good solution when you need to quickly get a particular document to the head of an already-long print queue. We've also discussed how pausing print jobs could be used to allow other documents to move ahead in the queue, but that method can be a little clumsy, especially if there are a lot of documents waiting to print. The best solution is to directly modify the priority of the important document, thus sending it to the head of the line!

To change the priority of a print job, double-click the printer in the Printers and Faxes window to open it and right-click the document in the print queue. Choose Properties from the shortcut menu and drag the priority slider as far to the right as you see fit. If all other print jobs have a priority of 1, changing a document to a priority of 2 should be enough to move it ahead. However, since this is the type of thing you normally do only occasionally, and only for really important documents, I tend to go overboard and shoot the priority the whole way up to 99. There's no use taking any chances, right?

Changes made to the priority of a particular document are good for only that document and have no effect on the priority of the printer or other documents. If you find yourself frequently changing the priority of individual documents for certain users, consider creating a separate logical printer for them with a preset higher priority. They'll love you for it!

If another, lower-priority print job has already spooled and Print spooled documents first is turned on in the Advanced tab of printer properties, the higher-priority job will not print until the spooled job is finished. To stop this from happening, you can disable the Print spooled documents first option.

In addition to changing the priority of a print job, you can also use the print job properties dialog box to set a schedule for an individual job. This can be useful if a large job is sent to the printer at a time when it would be inconvenient to allow it to print.

Cross Check

Managing Printers and Print Jobs

Now that you've had a chance to learn about the different ways you can manage printers and print jobs, let's take a moment to summarize what you've learned. If you like, review the preceding sections and answer the following questions:

1. What is printer pooling? What are its benefits?

2. What does it mean to redirect print jobs? Why would you do this?

3. How do you change the priority of a print job? Why would you do this?

■ Troubleshooting Common Printer Problems

We've already discussed a number of troubleshooting techniques, such as printer redirection and printer pooling, that can help us out when things either go wrong or we need a performance boost. However, there are a couple of other situations you might run into that are worth taking a look at.

Problem: Users Cannot Print to a Network Printer

Nate has two problems he keeps running into when using his networked Windows 98 computer. His first problem is that he frequently loses his network connection due to a loose network card. He usually notices this has happened when he starts to print and gets an error message that tells him the network printer cannot be found. His other problem is that he never seems to be able to print to the network printers even after he reconnects to the network. He keeps getting a message in his print dialog boxes that says something about user intervention being required. What's really got him steamed is that he finally got his network card fixed this morning and yet he still can't print.

Solution: Offline Printers Require User Intervention

Nate's two problems are certainly related. However, his bad network card wasn't really stopping him from printing; it was his attempts to print while not connected to the network that were the cause of the problem.

When you try to print to a network printer from a client machine while not connected to the network, the client operating system will change the status of the printer to offline. In many cases, especially while using Windows 98 on the client machine, the printer does not get reset to online when the network connection is reestablished. As a result, the user can send document after document to the printer and they just stack up in the client computer's print queue waiting for the printer to come back online.

If a user is having difficulty printing to a network printer while connected to the network and while other users are not having problems, look at the printer icon and see if it appears to be grayed out. If it is, then it is set to offline status and you should right-click it and change the status to Use Printer Online.

Problem: Pages of Nonsense Characters Print Instead of Document

Karli sent her first print job to the new network printer just a few minutes ago. She was proud of herself for installing the printer on her client machine all on her own, but now she's a little worried. Instead of the document she expected, the printer is spewing out page after page with only a few nonsense characters on each page. To make matters worse, the printer shows no signs of stopping any time soon.

Solution: Incorrect Printer Driver Results in Corrupted Output

It's quite easy to install the wrong printer driver for a printer, and in most cases, Windows, regardless of version, won't make a peep about it. However, printing with the wrong printer driver can cause everything from the problem Karli's having to no printing at all. In fact, there are even cases where the printer will work just fine but perhaps lack some features it should have.

In Karli's case, her document has been incorrectly processed for the printer she is trying to use. The result is that the printer is gamely printing what it is being sent, but since it's in a "language" it doesn't understand, the document doesn't look anything like it should. The immediate solution is to install the correct printer driver on Karli's machine. However, as an administrator, you would also want to make sure the correct drivers for all client machines are installed on the server so that they may be automatically sent to the client machines when they install the printer. You may also want to educate your users about the correct procedures for installing printers, since it is still possible to force the installation of the wrong driver in spite of your best efforts at the server.

■ Chapter Summary

After reading this chapter and completing the Step-by-Step tutorials and Try This! exercises, you should understand the following facts about printer configuration and management in Windows Server 2003.

Installing a Printer

■ A logical printer is the software interface between the operating system and the actual device that does the printing. The familiar printer icon you see on the screen represents the logical printer.

■ A printer is the actual piece of hardware that does the printing. In some cases, a printer is formally described as a physical printer or print device to help differentiate it from the logical printer.

■ Local print devices are printers that are physically connected to one of the ports on the computer.

■ Local print devices are easy to install but must be located close to the computer they connect to. The connections for local printers are not designed to support large numbers of printers simultaneously.

■ Network print devices connect to the computer doing the printing over the network rather than through physical ports on the computer.

■ Some network print devices connect directly to the network, while others can accept optional network cards. Local print devices can become network print devices by connecting to external devices called print servers that connect them to the network. Regardless of the method, the printer becomes associated with a network IP address as its port.

■ Network print devices can be located wherever needed on the network and can be centrally administered by a print server, which also handles all print jobs, thus improving client computer performance.

■ If a computer communicates directly with a printer, Microsoft refers to the device as nonremote. A nonremote print device requires no specialized print server and conveys greater control to the computer using the printer. However, computer performance may suffer and there may be delays if several computers connect to the same nonremote device.

■ If a computer communicates with a printer through another computer, Microsoft refers to the device as remote. A remote device requires some type of server that handles the task of communicating with the printer, thus relieving client computers of the load.

Configuring and Sharing Print Devices

■ The General tab of a printer's properties dialog box displays the printer's name, location, and any comments. Features of the printer are also listed here, such as the paper loaded, its speed, and its resolution.

■ The General tab also offers buttons that lead to the printing preferences and allow for the printing of a test page to check the printer's functioning.

■ The Sharing tab simply allows you to choose whether or not to share the printer and, if you are going to share it, to give the share a name. Printer drivers for other operating systems can also be installed from the Sharing tab so that they may be automatically downloaded to client computers that install the shared printer.

■ The Ports tab shows which port is being used by the printer and can be used to create printer pools.

■ The Advanced tab allows the configuration of printer availability, priority, printer driver, spooling behavior, and several other features.

■ The Security tab displays and allows the configuration of permissions concerning who can use a printer and what they can do with it. All printers may be printed to by all users by default. Only Administrators and Power Users have permission to print, manage printers, and manage documents.

Managing Printers and Print Jobs

■ Printers may be taken offline and the print spooler may be paused to allow a printer to be worked on while print jobs still enter the queue.

- Pooling printers allows multiple identical physical print devices to act as a single logical printer, thus improving printing performance.
- Print jobs may be redirected to another printer using the same print driver if something prevents the original printer from working properly.
- Print jobs may be paused, resumed, canceled, and restarted. The priority of a print job can also be changed.

Troubleshooting Common Printer Problems

- If a client computer cannot print to a network printer, the printer may be set to offline on the client computer. This can happen if the user tried to print without being connected to the network. The solution is to change the status of the printer to online.
- An incorrect printer driver can cause a host of problems, including the printing of nonsense characters. The solution is to install the correct printer driver.

■ Key Terms List

dots per inch (dpi) *(213)*
local print devices *(203)*
logical printer *(203)*
network print devices *(204)*
nonremote print device *(205)*
pages per minute (ppm) *(213)*

parallel port *(203)*
physical printer *(203)*
print device *(203)*
print queue *(217)*
print server *(204)*
print spooler *(217)*

printer *(203)*
printer pooling *(220)*
priority *(216)*
redirect print jobs *(223)*
remote print device *(206)*
USB port *(203)*

■ Key Terms Quiz

Use terms from the Key Terms List to complete the sentences that follow. Don't use the same term more than once. Not all terms will be used.

1. You can change the _____ of both printers and individual print jobs to change the order in which print jobs are handled.

2. Unlike a parallel port, a single _____ can handle up to 127 simultaneous devices.

3. The speed of a printer is measured in _____.

4. A nonremote printer connected to a parallel port is a _____.

5. If a computer communicates with a printer through some other computer that is connected to the printer, the clients would consider that printer to be a _____.

6. The documents that have been accepted by the print spooler are held in the _____.

7. Treating multiple physical print devices as a single logical print device for the purposes of improving printing performance is _____.

8. LPT1 is the name of a _____.

9. A higher _____ value means a higher-resolution printer.

10. The printer icon in the Printers and Faxes window represents the _____.

■ Multiple-Choice Quiz

1. When managing print jobs, you can do all of the following except
   a. Resend
   b. Resume
   c. Restart
   d. Cancel

2. Members of the Administrator's group have which permissions by default when a new printer is installed?
   a. Print
   b. Manage Printers
   c. Manage Documents
   d. All of the above

3. If a computer sends data to a printer through another computer, that printer may best be described as a

 a. Logical print device

 b. Remote print device

 c. Default printer

 d. Nonremote print device

4. Which of the following is quickly becoming the preferred port for connecting local print devices?

 a. Parallel

 b. USB

 c. PS/2

 d. Serial

5. The icon for a shared printer includes a

 a. Green check mark

 b. Black check mark

 c. Connected wire

 d. Outstretched hand

6. Network print devices become associated with a/an _____ as their port.

 a. Network IP address

 b. Printer priority

 c. Share name

 d. Print server

7. What is the primary advantage of a nonremote printer connected to an individual user's computer?

 a. No print server is required.

 b. Print jobs are finished faster.

 c. They are easily used by multiple users.

 d. They are usually less expensive.

8. _____ can be useful when many users print to the same printer.

 a. Printer comments

 b. A test page

 c. A separator page

 d. Offline printing

9. If a printed document is garbled or contains only nonsense characters, the problem may be because

 a. The printer is paused.

 b. The print driver is incorrect.

 c. The printer is on the wrong port.

 d. The printer is shared.

10. From the server's perspective, even a network print device is a

 a. Remote print device

 b. Logical printer

 c. Nonremote print device

 d. None of the above

11. The term dpi stands for

 a. Density printer imaging

 b. Diagonal printer index

 c. Dots per inch

 d. Drops per image

12. Which group is given *only* the print permission?

 a. Administrators

 b. Creator Owner

 c. Everyone

 d. Power Users

13. Which term does not mean "the physical device that outputs documents"?

 a. Logical printer

 b. Printer

 c. Print Device

 d. Physical printer

14. Pausing the print spooler has about the same effect as

 a. Canceling all print jobs

 b. Taking the printer offline

 c. Restarting a print job

 d. Changing print job priority

15. If you want to take advantage of the ability to assign a priority to a printer, you must

 a. Purchase two or more identical physical printers

 b. Connect the printers locally

 c. Create a printer pool that includes multiple physical printers

 d. Create multiple logical printers that refer to the same physical printer

■ Essay Quiz

1. Your boss wants to buy ten printers so that each of the ten employees in the marketing department can have their own. Explain the benefits of purchasing fewer printers, connecting them to the server, and sharing them over the network to all ten users.

2. The CEO finds it very frustrating when she has to wait for her print jobs when many other people are using the shared printer. How can you make sure that all of her print jobs get moved to the head of the print queue?

3. Explain the difference between resuming a print job and restarting a print job. When would you do each?

4. Explain printer pooling. Why would you pool printers?

5. Explain redirecting print jobs. When would you do this?

Lab Projects

• Lab Project 7.1

Earlier in the chapter, you were asked in a Try This! exercise to research the prices and features of print servers that allow local print devices to be used as network print devices. Continue your research by investigating print devices that are network capable out-of-the-box and comparing their pricing and features to the alternative. Answer the following questions:

1. What is the price range of print devices that have the built-in ability to be networked? How does that price compare to that of similarly capable local print devices? Avoid comparing apples to oranges by looking at printers with similar resolution, speed, and other features.

2. Do network-capable printers offer any advantages over local print devices with print servers in terms of features?

3. Do network-capable printers offer any cost savings over using local print devices with print servers?

• Lab Project 7.2

You've been asked to create a printing plan for a small business college that recently installed a campus-wide network. Consider the following facts and criteria and propose a complete plan for meeting the college's printing needs. Be sure to discuss the numbers and types of equipment to be used as well as any techniques we've discussed in this chapter that should be implemented.

1. The college is in a single two-story building with five classrooms on each floor. Each classroom can host up to 40 students and may be used for a wide variety of subjects from English to computer classes.

2. Five offices are occupied by individuals in administration. These individuals do almost all of their work from their offices.

3. There is one central business office with three employees on the first floor. These three employees work in this office most of the day. One of the employees is in charge of financial aid and prints a large number of documents daily. The other two employees only print occasionally.

4. There is a faculty room on both floors. Five faculty members who are in and out of the room all day occupy each.

5 The administration wants to minimize students' time waiting for output from printers so as to make better use of class time. However, due to the small size of the college, it is critical that this plan be as cost effective as possible.

• Lab Project 7.3

Do a survey of the printing arrangements at your school or place of business. Prepare a report that details the arrangements and comments on the following questions:

1 Are there any situations where shared printers might replace individual local printers, resulting in potential cost savings and increased efficiency?

2 Are there any situations where individual local printers should be installed rather than depending on currently installed shared printers?

3 Are there any situations in which printer pooling is being used? Are there any situations in which printer pooling could/should be used?

4 What is particularly effective about the printing arrangements? Are there any areas, other than those already discussed, where you can see potential weaknesses?

Crowd Control: Controlling Access to Resources Using Groups

"It takes tremendous discipline to control the influence, the power you have over other people's lives."

—CLINT EASTWOOD

In this chapter, you will learn how to:

- **Define Windows Server 2003 group accounts**
- **Manage folder, file, and printer access**
- **Troubleshoot share and access control problems**

Networks are created primarily for one purpose: to share organizational resources. However, shared resources such as folders, files, and printers, are rarely shared indiscriminately to anyone on the network. We need to selectively control who has access to shared resources on the network, and what can be done with them, just as we control the access and use of paper files and equipment in the physical workplace.

Imagine how difficult the job of a network administrator would be if they had to set individual permissions for each user for every resource shared over the network. Even on a small network of only a few hundred users with only a handful of shared folders, files, and printers, setting permissions for each user would quickly become overwhelming! In Windows Server 2003, we use group accounts to assign permissions to groups of users, which gives us a much more manageable approach to access control.

In this chapter, we will begin by defining the different group accounts that can be created in Windows Server 2003. We'll then learn how to manage users access and use files, folders, and printers through permissions. We'll also take a moment to talk about troubleshooting access problems.

Windows Server 2003 Group Accounts

Although we briefly discussed group accounts in Chapter 5, we need to know a bit more about them before we can effectively use them to help control users' access to resources. You'll recall that Windows Server 2003 offers **domain local groups**, **global groups**, and **universal groups**. Let's take a look at each of these to get a better understanding of how they differ and how they are best used.

Group Scope and Membership Rules

The essential difference between domain local, global, and universal groups is their **group scope**. In fact, the names we use for the different groups really are the names of their scope! As we explained in Chapter 5, the scope of a group determines its ability to access resources within the logical structure of the network. The scope of a group also determines what accounts can join a group as a member, and whether or not each group can join other groups. Once we understand the nature of each group's scope and membership capabilities, we'll be able to better understand how the three different groups combine to give us a great deal of control over how users access resources on the network.

Domain Local Groups

The domain local group scope allows for access to resources only within the domain in which the domain local group account was created. This means you cannot grant access to resources from other domains in the forest to any domain local group. Although this may seem rather limiting, it's merely a reflection of the actual intended purpose of domain local groups, which is to provide access to resources within a single domain.

The membership rules for domain local groups dictate that they can contain user and computer accounts and other domain local groups from their domain. Additionally, although domain local groups can be granted access to resources only within their own domain, they can also have as members global groups, universal groups, computer accounts, and user accounts from any other trusted domain. As you'll see, this makes domain local groups an effective tool for allowing users, computers, and groups from outside a domain to access a domain's resources. See Table 8.1 for a summary of the group scope and membership for domain local groups.

Table 8.1	Domain Local Groups Scope and Membership Rules
Domain Local Groups	
Group Scope	Domain local groups can be given access only to resources within their own domain.
Membership	Domain local groups may contain other domain local groups from the same domain and computer accounts, user accounts, global groups, and universal groups from any trusted domain.

As mentioned in Chapter 5, each of the three groups can be created as either a distribution group, for the sending of messages, or a security group, for controlling access to resources. Our focus in this chapter is security groups, but with the exception of setting permissions, distribution groups share the same characteristics as security groups of the same scope.

In this chapter, our discussion of groups assumes you raised the domain functional level of your domain controller as described in Chapter 4. If your DC is running at a functional level other than Windows Server 2003 or Windows 2000 native mode, there are some limitations on group membership and group creation beyond those mentioned here. For further information, use the Windows Server 2003 Help and Support Center to search for "group scope" and click the link labeled Group Scope: Active Directory. A table in the resulting article summarizes the limitations.

Although each group scope has the ability to contain other groups of the same scope, the practice, known as **nesting**, should be kept to a minimum. Unnecessarily nesting groups can make it very difficult to track down problems with access to resources. However, feel free to nest groups when it makes good sense to, as when you are trying to reflect the actual organizational structure through the network's groups.

Global Groups

The scope of global groups allows you to assign access to resources in any trusted domain. This can be done directly, without first making the global group a member of any other group. This means that any global group of any domain within a forest can easily be given permission to access files, folders, and printers in any other forest domain. However, as you'll soon see, global groups are not normally granted such permissions directly.

As you surely noticed, the scope of a global group is exactly the opposite of that of a domain local group. Well, it turns out that the same holds true of the membership rules for global groups. Whereas domain local groups could contain members from any trusted domain but grant access only to resources in their own domain, global groups, which have the ability to access resources anywhere, can contain global groups, computer, and user accounts only from their own domain! Strange as it may seem, this inverse relationship between domain local and global groups fits well with their intended use. See Table 8.2 for a summary of the group scope and membership for global groups.

Universal Groups

At first glance, universal groups seem to be quite similar to global groups. As with global groups, their scope allows you to assign permissions to access resources located in any trusted domain. However, the key difference between universal and global groups lies in the membership rules.

Universal groups are much like domain local groups in that they can contain user accounts, computer accounts, global groups, and universal groups from any domain in the forest. Like global groups, universal groups cannot contain domain local groups, since the scope of domain local groups allows them to access resources only from their own domain. See Table 8.3 for a summary of the group scope and membership for universal groups.

> Keep in mind that universal groups are available only if the domain functional level has been set to either Windows 2000 native or Windows Server 2003.

Best Practices for Using Group Accounts

Although the benefit of grouping together accounts when controlling access to resources is pretty easy to see, the proper use of the three different group scopes is not quite as obvious. Because the system isn't very intuitive, it's tempting, especially in small, single-domain networks, to just use domain local groups for everything and just forget about global and universal groups. Such a system will even work just fine, as long as that small network never grows any larger, and Windows Server 2003 won't raise a single objection. However, like death and taxes, the growth in size and complexity of networks is pretty much a sure thing. By understanding, and following, the best practices for using groups, you can increase the chances that future growth can occur with relative ease.

Even though you can join user accounts directly to domain local groups, ideally you should not. The best way to employ domain local groups is to use them to represent the resources being shared on the

Table 8.2	Global Groups Scope and Membership Rules
Global Groups	
Group Scope	Global groups can be given access to resources within any domain in the forest.
Membership	Global groups may contain other global groups, computer accounts, and user accounts only from their own domain.

network. For instance, imagine a
school network with ten folders
and a dozen printers that every student should have access to. In such
a situation, I would create one domain local group account, say,
named "Student Folders," to represent the folders and another, named
"Student Printers," to represent the
printers. I would then give each
group the appropriate permissions for their respective resources,
as shown in Figure 8.1. Of course, since no one, as of yet, belongs to these domain local groups, we need to do something
else to actually give the proper users access to the resources.
That's where global groups come in.

Global groups should be used primarily to hold the accounts of users and/or computers that are similar in function
and/or their need to access certain resources. Continuing our
preceding example, I would create a global group called "Students," as shown in Figure 8.2, to hold the actual user accounts of the students of the school. As illustrated by Figure
8.3, by making the Students global group a member of Student Folders and Student Printers, each of the members of
Students receives the permissions of the domain local groups
through the process of **inheritance**. One advantage to this system is that it is incredibly easy to give new users access to the
proper resources, or remove a user's access to resources, once
you've created the appropriate global and domain local
groups. In our example, I can give a new student access to all
the resources they need by simply making them a member of
the Student global group. I can just as easily remove an account from the global group and I've removed all the access
they inherited from that group with one operation. Additionally, if I later need to give the members of the Students global group access to resources in another domain in the forest, I can simply join their
global group to the proper domain local group in the other domain. If I had
put the user accounts into a domain local group in the first place I wouldn't
be able to do that, since a domain local group can be given access only to resources within its own domain!

Universal groups provide a sort of "shortcut" for giving users
in one domain access to resources in any other domain in the forest. Imagine trying to give the CEO of a large multinational corporation access to resources in domains spread around the world. If
you had only global and domain local groups, you'd need to make
the CEO's user account a member of a global group and then individually join that global group to every domain local group in every domain. Let's face it; the CEO should probably have access to
everything, right? Unfortunately, that would take a lot of work!

Instead of using domain local and global groups to provide access for our CEO, it would be better to create a universal group,
which can be given direct access to resources in any domain

Table 8.3	Universal Groups Scope and Membership Rules
Universal Groups	
Group Scope	Universal groups can be given access to resources within any domain in the forest.
Membership	Universal groups may contain other universal groups, global groups, computer accounts, and user accounts from any domain in the forest.

First Step:

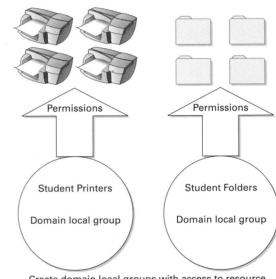

Create domain local groups with access to resource.

• **Figure 8.1** To set up global and domain local groups,
the first step is to create domain local
groups with access to resources.

Second Step:

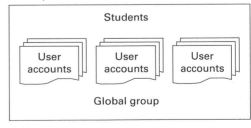

Create global groups to hold user accounts.

• **Figure 8.2** The second step: create global groups
to hold user accounts.

Third Step:

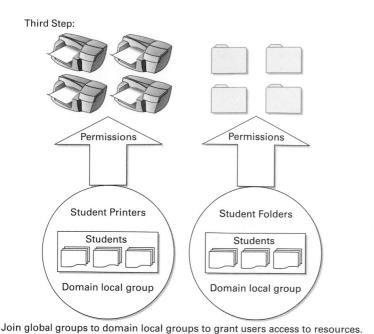

Join global groups to domain local groups to grant users access to resources.

• **Figure 8.3**   Finally, join global groups to domain local groups to grant users access to resources.

without the need to join domain local groups. Then it's a simple matter of making the CEO, and any other senior executives who need this level of access, members of the universal group. Although we could join user accounts directly to the universal group to accomplish this, it's still better to keep the user accounts in global groups and then join the global group to the universal group as we did before with domain local groups. The reason for this is that Active Directory replicates universal groups throughout the entire forest. That means that adding or removing members from the universal group forces all the domain controllers to send extra information, which can have an impact on the overall performance of the forest network. However, changing the membership of a global group that is a member of the universal group creates replication traffic only within the domain of the global group, thus reducing the traffic significantly.

I know it seems like there's a ton of things you have to remember about groups, but you really only have to keep the basics in mind. Group user accounts together, according to their similar needs for resource access, and place them in global groups. Figure out which resources should be accessible as a group and represent them with domain local groups with the proper permissions. Finally, give your users access to resources by making their global group a member of the appropriate domain local group. As for universal groups, unless you're working within a large multidomain network, you really won't need to use them. Even on such complex networks, the lion's share of access control is done through assigning permissions to domain local groups and then giving global groups membership in the domain local group. When you do use universal groups, you can assign access permissions to them directly and then give access to users by making their global group a member of the universal group.

Why Do I Have to Use Groups?

I frequently hear the question from students, "Why can't I just assign permissions directly to user accounts? Isn't that easier than creating and managing all of these groups?" To be honest, I understand where they're coming from. If you need to give Lynda access to a printer, why not just give Lynda's account the permission to use the printer? Is it really necessary to go through the process of representing the printer with a domain local group, making Lynda's account the member of a global group and making the global group a member

Cross Check

Group Accounts

Windows Server 2003 provides a system of several different groups to better manage how users access resources. Take a moment to review what we've covered and answer the following questions:

1. What are the two group types? What are the three group scopes?

2. Describe the best practices for using groups to administer how users access resources.

of the domain local group? I mean, when you write it out like that, it sure sounds like more work than is necessary!

It's true that it is possible to give Lynda access to the printer directly, without using groups. In fact, I can even think of at least one circumstance where that's what I'd do. However, before you nod smugly to yourself and say "I thought so!," take the moment to consider a few questions.

What do we know about the printer? Are there other printers that Lynda will need to use? If so, it is probably worthwhile to create a domain local group to at least represent those printers all at once, rather than deal with their permissions individually. What about Lynda? Does she need to use this printer because of a particular position she holds or role she plays within the organization, or is this just her personal printer, perhaps a network printer located in her office. If she needs access to the printer by virtue of her position or role, it might be a good idea to create a global group that represents that role and make Lynda's account a member. That way, if someone else later takes on that position or role, we don't have to hunt down all of the resources that should be accessible to the employee in that position. If we assign all permissions to Lynda directly, that's exactly what we'll have to do!

When would I, possibly, forgo the creation of groups? Well, I mentioned the situation in the preceding paragraph. If this is Lynda's own printer in her office, I might just directly assign her the appropriate permissions, rather than first creating groups. I might still need to change permissions later, but it would always be one user for one resource and thus not too difficult.

Situations where directly applying permissions to user accounts makes better sense than using groups are pretty rare. For the most part, it's better to start off as we've already described, with domain local groups representing resources and global groups containing user accounts. Even if the groups are initially very small and seem to be more hassle to set up than they're worth, they can really pay off in the long run when the network starts to grow by leaps and bounds.

Step-by-Step 8.1

Creating and Managing Group Accounts

Group accounts are created just like user accounts and computer accounts: in Active Directory. The process is relatively simple and only requires us to input the name, scope, and type (distribution or security) for the group to be created. After groups are created, the most common management task is to add members to the group or make the group a member of some other group. In this Step-by-Step, we will create a few sample groups on our server that we can use in the following sections when we discuss setting permissions.

This Step-by-Step assumes you created a personal user account and an OU named TestOU in Chapter 4. If you did not, please create them before beginning this exercise. Your instructor may also modify the assignment to suit your lab setup, if necessary.

To complete this Step-by-Step, you will need

- A properly configured Windows Server 2003 Domain Controller

- Access to an administrator-level account on the computer

Step 1

Open Active Directory Users and Computers by clicking Start | Administrative Tools | Active Directory Users and Computers. Maximize the window when it opens, if necessary.

Step 2

We will begin by creating a domain local account to represent a shared folder we will create later in this chapter. To begin the process, right-click the TestOU container in the left pane and choose New | Group from the shortcut menu.

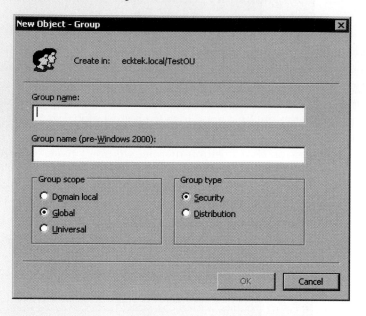

Step 3

Note that the default selection when creating a new group is to create a global security group. Since our first group will be a domain local group, begin by changing that option. Next enter the name **Share Test** in the Group name box and click OK to create the group.

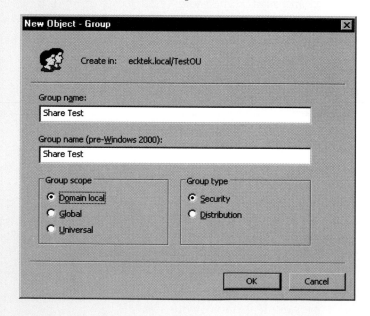

Step 4	Using the same basic procedure as in Steps 2 and 3, create a global security group named "Test Users."

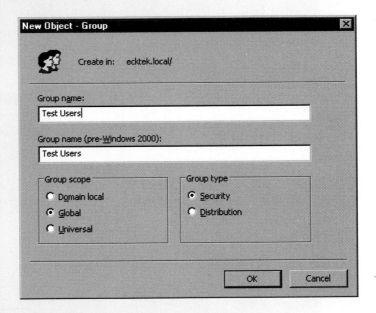

Step 5	Click the TestOU container in the left pane to display its contents in the right pane. Check to see that the two groups you just created are present before moving on to the next step.

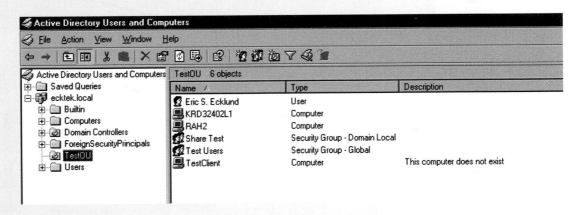

Step 6	Most group management tasks are performed from the group's properties dialog box. Open the properties dialog box for the Test Users global group by right-clicking the group and choosing Properties. Note that the dialog box consists of four tabs, which are General, Members, Member Of, and Managed By. As you might guess, the Members and Member Of tabs are used to manage group membership. The Managed By tab allows you to designate a particular user to be responsible for the group and will display information from their user account. The General tab can be used to rename the group, enter a description and/or e-mail, and change the group's scope and/or type.

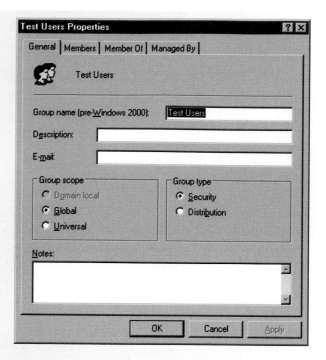

Tip: Group scope can be changed only under either the Windows 2000 Native or Windows Server 2003 domain functional level. Under those modes, you can make either domain local or global groups into universal groups as long as they contain no other groups of their same current scope.

Step 7

Using the Members and Member Of tabs, we can completely control the membership status of a group without the need to open the properties dialog boxes of either the members we wish to add or the groups we wish to join. Click the Members tab to begin the process of adding your personal user account as a member of the Test Users global group.

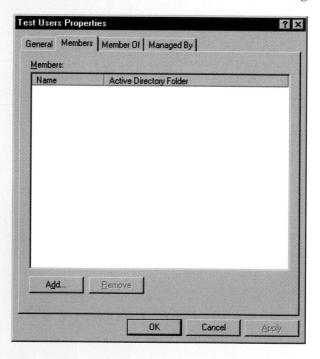

Step 8

Click the Add button to open the Select Users, Contacts, Computers, or Groups dialog box. You can directly enter the names of the objects you wish to make members of the group, or you can use the Advanced button to search for and display a list of objects from which you can choose. In this case, type your personal account's logon name or full name in the text area labeled Enter the object names to select. You can even enter just a partial name and Windows will still try to find the correct object for you and prompt you to choose if it can't decide between two or more objects. For instance, in my case, I was able to type simply the letter **e**, click OK, and Windows was able to identify my account! After entering your information, click OK to redisplay the properties dialog box.

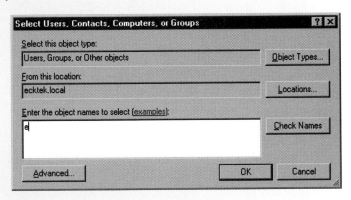

Step 9

Our last task is to make the Test Users global group a member of the Share Test domain local group. Click the Member Of tab and click Add to open the Select Groups dialog box. Click Advanced and then Find Now to display a list of the available groups. Select the Share Test group from the list and then click OK twice to return to the properties dialog box. Once you've confirmed that Test Users is now a member of Share Test, you may click OK to close the properties dialog box and exit Active Directory Users and Computers.

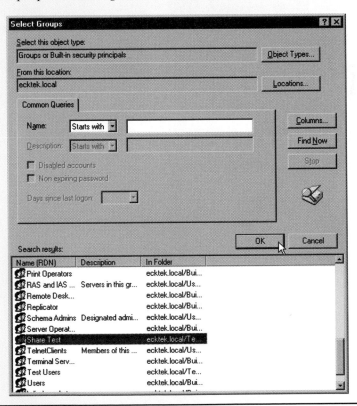

Manage Folder, File, and Printer Access

Folder and file access in Windows Server 2003 is managed through two separate systems. The first system uses **share permissions**, which control the ability of users to access shared folders over the network. The second system uses **NTFS permissions**, which determine what users can do with the files and folders stored on an NTFS-formatted hard drive. Both sets of permissions must be properly configured for file and folder resources to be usable.

Share Permissions

Share permissions, as the name indicates, are applied to folders that are shared over the network. Share permissions act as sort of a "first line of defense" in providing security for data stored on the server, with the NTFS permissions providing primary security. However, if shared folders are stored on a drive that has not been formatted with NTFS, share permissions become the sole security control. Let's take a look at the three share permissions displayed in Figure 8.4 and how they work.

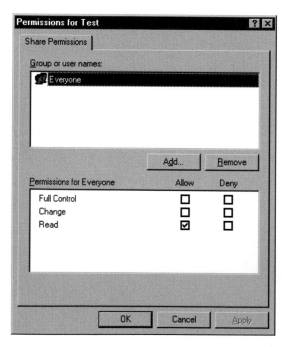

Read Permission

The Read permission allows users to run programs, open and view data files, and view the names of all files and folders within the shared folder. This is the lowest level of access for a shared folder, and it is granted, by default, to the Everyone group whenever a new folder share is created. You can see that there is already an **access control entry (ACE)** for the Everyone group listed in the **access control list (ACL)** at the top of the dialog box in Figure 8.4.

Since the Read permission allows users only to view information and run programs, it's frequently used on folders that hold either prepared documents or, of course, applications. However, if a shared folder contains documents or programs that should be accessible only to a select group of people, it is necessary to remove the Read permission from the Everyone group and apply it to the appropriate group or groups.

• **Figure 8.4** Permissions dialog box for a shared folder

Change Permission

The Change permission includes all the capabilities granted by the Read permission with the additional abilities to change data files and add and remove files and subfolders within the shared folder. Unlike with the Read permission, no group is automatically granted the Change permission.

Obviously the Change permission should be granted to only those users who need to be able to make changes to data in a shared folder. For instance, it would be necessary to grant the Change permission to users who were expected to save files to a shared network folder. Although the Change permission also would allow those users to delete files and subfolders from the shared folder, the NTFS permissions we will discuss later allow us to limit that behavior, if we need to.

Full Control

As was the case with the Change permission, the Full Control permission includes all the abilities of the lower-level permissions. In addition, the Full Control permission conveys the ability to change permissions on the shared folder. This would allow a user with the Full Control permission not only to change the permissions of users who currently have access but also to add new users and set their access level.

Although it is not listed in the permissions dialog box, the Administrator's group has full permission over all shared folders on the server by default. The reason this isn't listed within the permissions dialog box is that it really isn't a share permission at all but rather a function of the NTFS access control we'll be discussing in just a bit. It's typically not necessary, or even a good idea, to grant anyone the Full Control share permission. In fact, one of the changes in Windows Server 2003 from Windows 2000 is that in the older OS, new shares granted Full Control to the Everyone group by default. That's sort of like building a new house that, by default, uses a lock everyone has a key to and hoping the owner will remember to have it changed when they move in!

Additional Considerations

Keep in mind, as you work with share permissions, that users may belong to more than one group, each of which can have different share permissions. When combining share permissions granted by membership in different groups, the highest-level, or least restrictive, permission takes precedence. That means that if a user belongs to two groups, one of which is granted Read permission and one of which is granted Change permission for the same share, the user will have Change permission for that share. The one exception to this is if the permission is explicitly denied. As you can see in Figure 8.4, each share permission can be marked either Allow or Deny. If a user belongs to a group that has been explicitly denied a permission by placing a check in the Deny box, then access of that type will be denied regardless of the permission level of other groups the user may belong to.

Also remember that share permissions apply to folders only when they are accessed as network shares. For controlling access to the folder locally, at the server, we need to use the permissions of NTFS access control.

Creating and Sharing a Folder and Setting Share Permissions

The task of creating network shares and configuring the share permissions is a common one for most network administrators. I guess it's a good thing it's not too hard to do! In this exercise, we'll create a simple folder containing a single file. We'll then share the folder and assign share permissions to the domain local group we created earlier.

To complete this Step-by-Step, you will need

- A properly configured Windows Server 2003 Domain Controller

- Access to an administrator-level account on the computer

- The domain local and global groups created in Step-by-Step 8.1

Open Windows Explorer. On the left pane, under My Computer, find and click the C: drive. Click the File menu and choose New | Folder. Name this folder **Test**. Open the folder by either left-clicking it in the left pane or double-clicking it in the right pane. Click the File menu and choose New | Text Document. Don't bother renaming the file, just accept the default name New Text Document.txt.

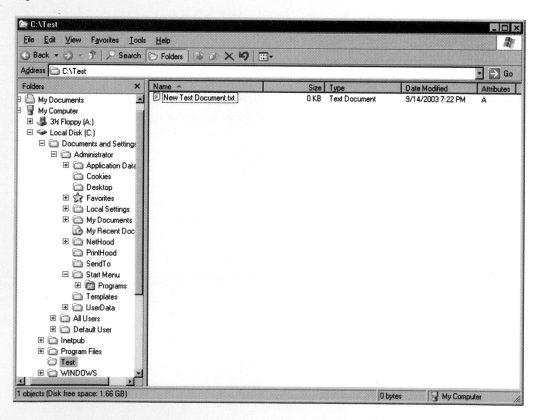

In the left pane, right-click the folder Test and choose Properties. When the properties dialog box opens, click the Sharing tab and click the option button labeled Share this folder. Note that Windows automatically fills in the Share name text box. You can change the share name, provide a description, set a maximum number of users, set permissions, and allow the folder to be cached for offline use. In this exercise, we'll be working with strictly the Permissions button, so go ahead and click it now.

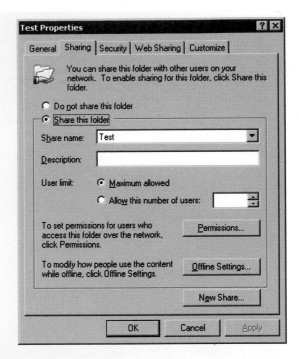

Step 3

Note that the Everyone group has automatically been granted the Read permission. We want to grant the Change permission to our Share Test group. To do this, click the Add button and type **Share Test** in the text area labeled Enter the object names to select. Click OK and verify that the Share Test group ACE now appears on the ACL for the Test folder. Make sure the group is selected and click the Allow check box for the Change permission. Both Change and Read should now be Allowed for this group.

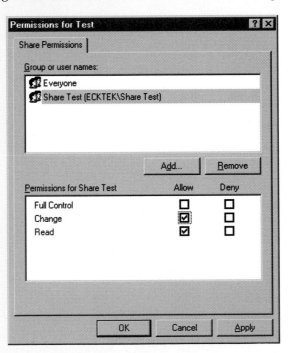

Step 4

Click OK twice to close the open dialog boxes and verify that the folder icon for the Test folder now displays the underlying hand that indicates a shared folder. You may then close Windows Explorer.

In addition to user accounts, computer accounts, group accounts, and the like, it is also possible to add shared folders to Active Directory so that they may be more easily managed. In this exercise, we will add the shared folder we just created in the chapter to Active Directory Users and Computers. Try this:

1. Open Active Directory Users and Computers and right-click the TestOU container. Choose New | Shared Folder.

2. Enter the name of the folder, **Test**, in the Name text box.

3. Enter the network path to the shared folder in the Network path text box. As the dialog box indicates, this will take the form of *servername***test**. Be sure to substitute the name of your server, not your domain, in place of *servername*. Click OK.

4. Open the TestOU container and verify that the shared folder object has been created. From here the share can be opened, explored, or mapped to a drive letter.

NTFS permissions are, as the name implies, available only on an NTFS-formatted volume. This is one of the reasons why the use of NTFS is so highly recommended for servers.

NTFS Permissions

NTFS uses a much larger set of permissions than those applied to shares to give greater control over what users can do with both folders and files. These permissions apply whether the files or folders are accessed over the network or locally. As was the case with share permissions, when a user is subject to different sets of NTFS permissions due to membership in different groups, the least restrictive permissions apply. However, when a user is subject to conflicting share permissions and NTFS permissions, the most restrictive of the two applies. That means that a user with the Change share permission for a folder who is not granted any NTFS permissions will be unable to make any changes. That's why I said at the beginning of this section that we had to configure both sets of permissions properly in order to provide access to resources!

Standard Permissions

Files and folders stored on NTFS volumes offer a variety of standard permissions that can be either allowed or denied to users and/or groups. As you can see in Figure 8.5, these permissions are listed under the Security tab of the properties dialog box under the ACL. Four of the permissions are slightly different in effect when applied to files and folders. Of the other two, one is essentially the same for both files and folders, while one applies to folders only. These permissions, and their effects on both files and folders, are summarized in Table 8.4. Since higher-level permissions usually include the abilities of lower-level permissions, they are listed in reverse order.

As you can see, the NTFS permissions give much greater control over what users can do with files and folders than that provided by share permissions. However, what's not immediately apparent is that each of the standard permissions actually represents a collection of even more detailed NTFS permissions, called the **special permissions**.

Special Permissions

Clicking the Advanced button on the Security tab of a file or folder's properties dialog box opens the Advanced Security Settings dialog box shown in Figure 8.6. Selecting an entry and clicking the Edit button opens the Permission Entry dialog box shown in Figure 8.7, which displays the special permissions for the file or

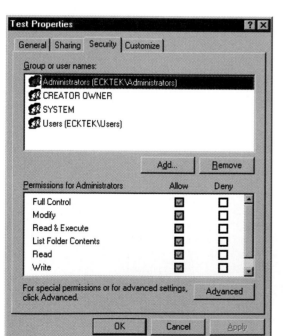

● **Figure 8.5**   NTFS permissions for a folder

Table 8.4	NTFS Standard Permissions As They Apply to Folders and Files	
Standard NTFS Permission	When Applied to Folders	When Applied to Files
Write	A user granted this permission may create new subfolders and files within the folder.	A user granted this permission may alter the file and its attributes.
Read	A user granted this permission may open the folder and see the contents. Files in the folder can also be opened. The user cannot execute program files.	A user granted this permission may open and see the contents of the file. The user cannot execute program files
List Folder Contents	A user granted this permission essentially has Read permission for folders only. They may view the contents of the folder but may not open and view files in the folder.	N/A
Read & Execute	A user granted this permission has both the Read and List Folder Contents permissions and may also execute files.	A user granted this permission has Read permission and may also execute files.
Modify	A user granted this permission has all of the preceding permissions and may also delete files in the folder.	A user granted this permission has all of the preceding permissions and may also delete the file.
Full Control	A user granted this permission has complete control over the folder and its contents.	A user granted this permission has complete control over the file.

folder. In the example depicted in these two figures, you can see that the standard permission Write is actually made up of four special permissions: Create Files/Write Data, Create Folders/Append Data, Write Attributes, and Write Extended Attributes. The implication of this is that you could customize the Write permission by removing one or more of its component special permissions. Of course, you could also add other special permissions to the set represented by any standard permission, again creating your own customized special permission. With the exception of the Full Control special permission, which automatically selects the other 13, each of the selections can be allowed or denied individually in any combination. Needless to say, you don't need this level of control very often, but when you do, it's nice to know that it's there!

Inheritance

Just as members of a group inherit permissions, permissions on folders are inherited by their contents. By default, all permissions applied to a parent folder are inherited by all of the files and subfolders it contains. However, this process can be refined in several ways.

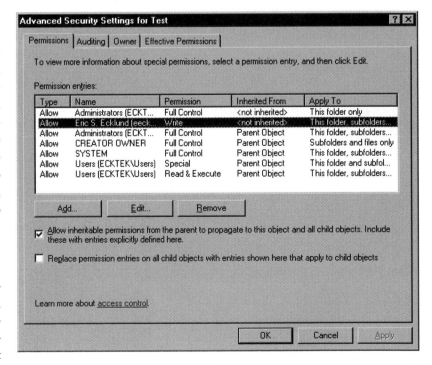

• Figure 8.6   Advanced Security Settings dialog box for a folder

A Strategy for Using Share Permissions with NTFS Permissions

As I mentioned when discussing share permissions, in Windows 2000 Server the Everyone group was automatically given Full permission on newly created shares. Although that has changed with Windows Server 2003, it's still the beginning of a relatively effective technique for integrating share permissions and NTFS permissions.

Microsoft suggests a system using solely NTFS permissions. Under this system, all share permissions are set to Full Control and security is handled through the application of the NTFS permissions. Assuming the NTFS permissions are set properly, this will work, since the most restrictive of the combined NTFS and share permissions will take precedence.

What about using only share permissions and setting the NTFS permissions to Full Control? Unlike the system we just described, this is a bad idea for several reasons. The most obvious is that the limited share permissions don't give the level of control possible with NTFS permissions. However, the most important reason not to use such a system is that the files on the server would be completely exposed to access that wasn't over the network. This means that, in addition to those who might gain physical access to the server, you'd also be exposing your files and folders to those who access the server remotely using tools like remote desktop and terminal services.

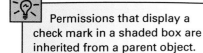

Permissions that display a check mark in a shaded box are inherited from a parent object.

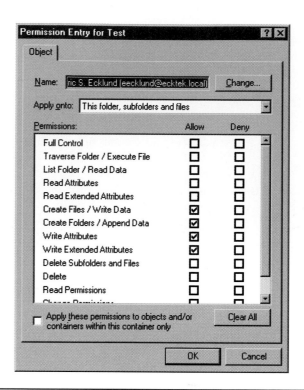

• **Figure 8.7**   Permission Entry dialog box for a folder

In the Permission Entry dialog box depicted in Figure 8.7, a drop-down list box labeled Apply onto allows you to choose the level at which you want to apply the special permissions. By default this is set, for folders, to "This folder, subfolders and files," which means that permissions will be inherited as normal. Other options include "This folder only," "Subfolders only," "Files only," and others. However, you can also limit inheritance by placing a check in the check box in the lower left-hand corner to limit it to only the current container and its first-level contents.

Inheritance can also be modified in the Advanced Security Settings dialog box depicted in earlier Figure 8.6. A check box at the bottom is checked by default to allow the inheritance of permissions. By clearing it, it is possible to break the connection between this folder (or file) and its parent container. You can also cause child objects to "re-inherit" the permissions of their parent container, assuming they've been manually edited already, by checking the box labeled "Replace permission entries." As was the case with the special permissions, the number of options is mind-boggling! Don't feel too overwhelmed, though. As with special permissions, in most cases you don't need to alter permission inheritance. The option exists for those rare times when you do need to.

Ownership

After the Permissions tab, the Advanced Security Settings dialog box displays an Auditing tab, an Owner tab, and an Effective Permissions tab. The Owner tab allows you to change the owner of the file or folder if necessary. By default, **ownership** of a file or folder belongs to the account that created it. The owner of a file or folder has Full Control over it, including the ability to give another account the permission to take ownership. This is typically done by giving the other account the Full Control permission, but there actually is a special permission called Take Ownership that can also be used. Changes in ownership are typically done to transfer files and folders from an account that no longer exists to another account. Once a user has been granted either the Full Control or Take Ownership permission for a file or folder, they can go to the Owner tab and simply select their account as the new owner. From there they can do whatever they please!

The Auditing tab can be used to monitor the success or failure of certain actions by users, such as reading a file or changing permissions on a folder. Unfortunately, a full discussion of auditing is beyond the scope of this text.

Effective Permissions

The Effective Permissions tab is a new feature of Windows Server 2003. It allows you to do a quick analysis of the **effective permission** for a user or group account, which is the overall effect of all combined permissions inherited from group membership. In other words, if a user or group account belongs

The Effective Permissions tab does *not* analyze the impact of share permissions.

to number of groups, some of which may belong to other groups, its actual permissions for a particular file or folder can be hard to determine. This tab provides an approximate estimate of what the final combined effects of all applicable permissions are for a single account. Of course, by approximate, we mean "sometimes wrong"! However, it does try to summarize the effective permissions, and this can be very helpful when you're trying to figure out why a particular account is having trouble accessing a resource!

Cross Check

Share Permissions and NTFS Permissions

Both share permissions and NTFS permissions are used to control which users can access resources and what they can do with those resources. Although these two sets of permissions work together, they are different in some very significant ways. Take a moment to review what you've learned and then answer the following questions:

1. What are some of the primary differences between share permissions and NTFS permissions?

2. Describe how share permissions and NTFS permissions from multiple sources are combined to result in the final effective permissions.

Step-by-Step 8.3

Setting NTFS Permissions and Demonstrating Inheritance

As we've discussed, users who need to access shared folders also need the proper NTFS access control permissions to work with the contents of those shares. The same is true for files and folders that will be accessed locally instead of through the network. In this exercise, we will assign appropriate NTFS permissions to the folder we shared in Step-by-Step 8.2. We will then check the inheritance of the permissions by the file in the shared folder.

To complete this Step-by-Step, you will need

- A properly configured Windows Server 2003 Domain Controller

- Access to an administrator-level account on the computer

- The domain local and global groups created in Step-by-Step 8.1

- The shared folder created in Step-by-Step 8.2

Step 1

Open Windows Explorer and locate the Test folder you created in Step-by-Step 8.2. Right-click the folder and choose Properties. Click the Security tab.

We'll begin by creating an ACE (access control entry) for our domain local group, which you'll recall is the preferred way of assigning permissions. Because our user account is a member of a global group, which is a member of the domain local group, our user account will inherit the permissions. Click Add and type **Share Test** in the text area and click OK. A new ACE should appear, with the default permissions of Read & Execute, List Folder Contents, and Read already applied. In addition, click the Deny check box for the Write permission and click OK to close the properties dialog box. You will be warned that your Deny permission will override any Allow permissions. Click Yes to continue.

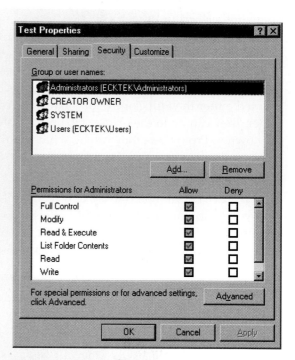

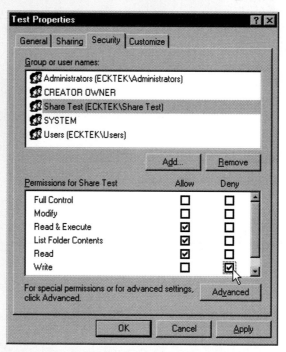

Verify that the NTFS permissions you just assigned were inherited by the New Text Document.txt file in the Test folder. Right-click the file, choose Properties, and click the Security tab. Select the ACE for Share Test and note that it displays the Allow Read & Execute and Read permissions and the Deny Write permission as inherited, shaded check boxes. The List Folder Contents permission is not displayed because this is a file. Close all dialog boxes and windows when you are finished.

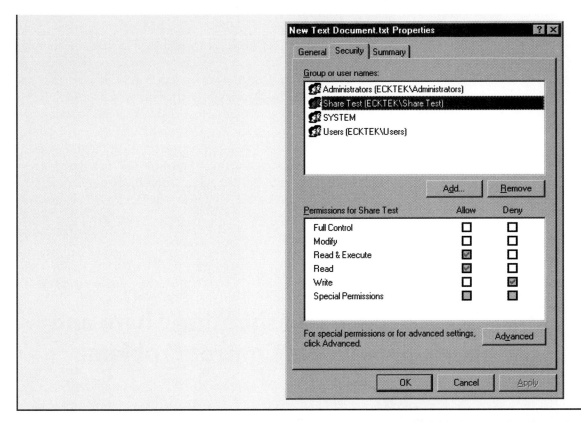

Printer Permissions

The **printer permissions** we discussed briefly in Chapter 7 are sort of hybrid creatures. In appearance and number, as seen in Figure 8.8, they appear similar to share permissions. However, like NTFS permissions, they appear on the Security, rather than the Sharing tab. Of course, they can't be NTFS permissions, since those apply only to NTFS volumes and printers aren't stored on the hard drive, even though their drivers are! The truth of the matter is that printer permissions aren't either share or NTFS permissions. They do, however, perform the same role, which is to control how users access and use resources. Let's quickly review what they offer.

Standard Printer Permissions

You'll recall that the standard printer permissions consist of Print, Manage Printers, and Manage Documents. As we noted in the last chapter, the Print permission, which is given to the Everyone group by default when a printer is installed, simply allows you to print documents at the printer. The Manage Printers and Manage Documents permissions do just what they say: they allow the user to manage the properties of the print device and the print jobs users send to it, respectively. As was the case with NTFS permissions, these standard permissions actually represent a slightly larger set of special permissions, which give even greater control over how users access and use the print device.

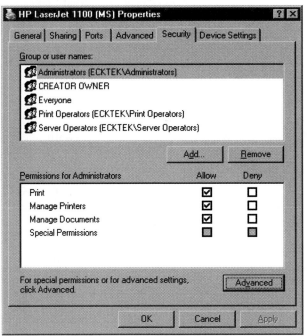

• **Figure 8.8**   Printer permissions are found on the Security tab of the printer's properties dialog box.

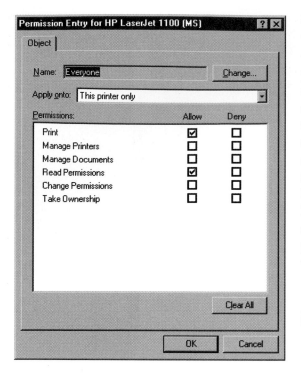

Special Printer Permissions

The special printer permissions are accessed in the same manner we used to access the special NTFS permissions. However, as you can see in Figure 8.9, the list is a good deal shorter! Another difference is that the three standard permissions are displayed along with three new permissions, which are Read Permissions, Change Permissions, and Take Ownership. In fact, you cannot select one of the three standard permissions on the list without also automatically selecting one or more of the three special permissions. For example, if you select Print, the Read Permissions box will also be checked. If you try to deselect Read Permissions, Print will be deselected as well! To tell you the truth, I've never seen a situation in which it was really necessary to edit the special permissions for a printer. However, if one ever comes up, at least we know where to go and what we'll find!

■ Troubleshooting Share and Access Control Problems

Whether you're talking about accessing files and folders or printers, sooner or later you'll run into a situation where someone can't access or properly work with a resource they seem to have the proper permissions for. The simple solution to such problems is that somewhere, somehow, the user does not have the permissions you think they do! However, tracking down the problem can take a little time, and there are some basic things you should keep in mind. Let's take a look at a scenario that illustrates a couple of permission problems and some possible solutions.

Imagine you arrive at work Monday morning just to find voice mails from three frustrated users who are having trouble accessing and working with the new shares you created for the product development team. Lindsay from Finance says she can't even find the share. Evan, who works in marketing, says he can find the share but he can't read the meeting minutes you placed there for everyone's reference. Meanwhile, the team head, Dylan, can find the share and read the minutes but has been trying since seven to save a progress report and is getting a little miffed at being told "Access Denied!" It's beginning to look like an aspirin and antacid day for sure. Oh well, things aren't going to fix themselves, right?

Check Both Share and NTFS Permissions

As we said at the beginning of this section, problems like those Lindsay, Evan, and Dylan are experiencing are simply a matter of the users not having the correct permissions. What often happens in such cases, especially when new shares are created for new folders, is that there is a lack of coordination between the share permissions and the NTFS access control permissions. In Lindsay's case, she might very well have all of the proper NTFS permissions that she needs, but she may not have the Read permission for the network share. Evan, on the other hand, apparently has at least Read permission on the share but, for some reason, does not have the NTFS Read permission for the meeting minutes file. Finally, Dylan seems to lack permission to write to the share, which could be a problem with the share permissions or with the NTFS permissions or even with both!

When troubleshooting resource access problems, always remember that share permissions from multiple sources, say groups, of the same type, share or NTFS, combine so that the least restrictive permission takes precedence. However, remember that when both share permissions and NTFS permissions apply to a resource, the two different types of permissions combine so that the most restrictive permission is enforced. Also keep in mind that a permission that is explicitly denied will override an allowed permission, regardless of the source. Of course, you still need to find the problem permission!

Use the Effective Permissions Utility

Although the Effective Permissions tab of the Advanced Security Settings dialog box only approximates effective permissions and does not consider share permissions, it's still a great place to start looking for potential permission conflicts. Imagine a folder permission entry for a user that shows full control, with the check box for each special permission checked, and yet the user cannot write to the folder. Using the Effective Permissions utility might reveal that, for some reason, the user doesn't actually have that permission. Unfortunately, Effective Permissions won't tell you why they don't have the permission they appear to have, but at least it might confirm whether or not Windows perceives their account as having the correct permissions. From there, you can start to search for the source of the problem.

Check Group Membership

Always keep in mind that the members of groups inherit permissions under normal circumstances. This applies even if the group member is a group that contains groups that contains groups that contains groups that contains users! As you might imagine, nesting that many levels of groups can make troubleshooting permission conflicts a bit on the difficult side, which is one of the reasons Microsoft recommends minimizing group nesting wherever possible. However, even when groups are not nested, a user account can belong to more than one global group, which may belong to more than one domain local group, and at some point along the way, one of those groups may have been denied the very permission the user needs. Because of this, it's a good troubleshooting step to check out the Member of tab in the user account's properties dialog box and then check the permissions of each group for the resource in question. Of course, if the groups contain nested groups, you'll want to check those out as well.

Check Special Permissions

As we mentioned when discussing special permissions, each standard permission actually represents one or more special permissions. In some cases, a user or group's account may have had the special permissions edited in such a way that, although the standard permission remains checked, one of the component special permissions has been denied for some reason. If all else fails, be sure to check the special permissions for the user account experiencing the problem and, if necessary, the special permissions for each involved group.

Chapter 8 Review

■ Chapter Summary

After reading this chapter and completing the Step-by-Step tutorials and Try This! exercises, you should understand the following facts about controlling access to resources in Windows Server 2003.

Windows Server 2003 Group Accounts

■ Windows Server 2003 offers security groups of three different scopes. They are domain local groups, global groups, and universal groups. Each may also be created as a distribution group.

■ Domain local groups allow access only to resources within the domain in which they were created. They may contain user and computer accounts and other domain local groups from their domain. Global groups, universal groups, computer accounts, and user accounts from other trusted domains may also be members.

■ Global groups may access resources in any trusted domain. Global groups can contain other global groups, computer accounts, and user accounts from only their own domain.

■ Universal groups may access resources in any trusted domain. Universal groups may have as members user accounts, computer accounts, global groups, and universal groups from any trusted domain.

■ Domain local groups should be used to represent resources within a domain. Global groups should be used to hold user accounts and should convey permissions to those accounts by joining domain local groups. Universal groups are used in large, multidomain networks to provide easy access to resources across the domains.

Managing Folder, File, and Printer Access

■ Share permissions are applied to folders that are shared over the network. They consist of the Read permission, the Change permission, and the Full Control permission.

■ The Read permission is granted, by default, to the Everyone group when a new share is created.

■ Multiple share permissions are combined so that the least restrictive permission prevails unless a permission is explicitly denied.

■ NTFS access control permissions control what users can do with files and folders, whether they are accessed locally or over the network. When combining different sets of NTFS permissions, the least restrictive permissions apply. When combining share and NTFS permissions, the most restrictive set of permissions applies.

■ NTFS standard permissions include Write, Read, List Folder Contents, Read & Execute, Modify, and Full Control.

■ NTFS standard permissions represent a more extensive set of special permissions, which can be modified through the Advanced Security Settings dialog box.

■ NTFS permissions on a folder are inherited by the contents of that folder. This inheritance can be modified in several ways.

■ The original creator of a file or folder is said to have ownership of that file or folder. Ownership allows the owner to give other accounts permission to take ownership and may be used to track disk usage.

■ The Effective Permissions tab of the Advanced Security Settings dialog box can be used to analyze the combination of NTFS permissions from various sources. The results are only approximate and do not include the effect of share permissions.

■ Printer permissions are neither share permissions nor NTFS permissions but rather almost a hybrid of both. Like NTFS permissions, the standard printer permissions represent a slightly larger set of special permissions.

Troubleshooting Share and Access Control Problems

■ When access problems occur, first check both the share and NTFS permissions for possible conflicts.

■ Try using the Effective Permissions tab to evaluate whether or not the account has the permissions it should have.

- Check group membership to see if one or more groups may be denying the permission to the affected account.

- Check special permissions in case they have been manually altered from their normal settings for the selected standard permissions.

■ Key Terms List

access control entry (ACE) *(242)*
access control list (ACL) *(242)*
domain local group *(233)*
effective permissions *(249)*
global group *(233)*

group scope *(233)*
inheritance *(235)*
nesting *(233)*
NTFS permissions *(242)*
ownership *(248)*

printer permissions *(251)*
share permissions *(242)*
special permissions *(246)*
universal group *(233)*

■ Key Terms Quiz

Use terms from the Key Terms list to complete the sentences that follow. Don't use the same term more than once. Not all terms will be used.

1. A _____ can be used to access resources only from within its own domain.

2. Subfolders end up with the same NTFS permissions as their parent folders because of _____.

3. The names of the group accounts in Windows Server 2003 also describe the _____ of the groups.

4. The original creator of a file or folder is said to have _____ of that object.

5. _____ seem to be almost a hybrid of share permissions and NTFS permissions.

6. Each NTFS standard permission actually represents one or more _____.

7. User accounts should be members of a _____.

8. When you consider all of the NTFS and share permissions that may apply to a particular account accessing a resource, you end up with the _____.

9. The group accounts and user accounts that have been granted permissions for a particular resource appear on the Security tab of the resource's properties dialog box in the _____.

10. A _____ is typically employed only on large, multidomain networks.

■ Multiple-Choice Quiz

1. Which of the following can contain a domain local group as a member?
   a. Domain local group
   b. Global group
   c. Universal group
   d. All of the above

2. Which of the following is a special NTFS permission?
   a. List Folder Contents
   b. Read & Execute
   c. Take Ownership
   d. Write

3. Manage Documents is a(n):
   a. Special permission
   b. NTFS permission
   c. Share permission
   d. Printer permission

4. Which of the following is granted to the Everyone group when a new share is created?
   a. Read
   b. Change
   c. Full Control
   d. None of the above

5. Which of the following is the default group scope?

   a. Domain local group

   b. Distribution group

   c. Global group

   d. Universal group

6. Which of the following cannot contain user accounts from outside its own domain?

   a. Domain local group

   b. Global group

   c. Universal group

   d. None of the above

7. A user is having trouble accessing a resource. What could potentially be the problem?

   a. The permission is denied to a group the user is a member of.

   b. The user has insufficient share permissions.

   c. The user has insufficient NTFS permissions.

   d. All of the above.

8. Why would you *not* be able to change the scope of an existing group?

   a. The domain functional level is Windows Server 2003.

   b. The domain functional level is Windows 2000 Native.

   c. The group is empty.

   d. The group contains other groups of the same type.

9. Each user or group account that appears on the ACL is considered to be a(n):

   a. ACE

   b. ICE

   c. NSF

   d. EOS

10. If a user account is granted the Read share permission from membership in one group, the Change share permissions from membership in another group, and the Full Control share permission from membership in a third group, what is the effective share permission for the user account?

   a. Read

   b. Change

   c. Full Control

   d. None of the above

11. Which of the following NTFS standard permissions grants the Take Ownership special permission?

   a. Full Control

   b. Modify

   c. Change

   d. Write

12. If a user account is granted the Full Control NTFS permission by membership in one group, the Modify NTFS permission by membership in another group, and the Read share permission as a member of the Everyone group, what is the effective permission?

   a. Full Control

   b. Modify

   c. Read

   d. None of the above

13. The Effective Permissions utility does not take into consideration

   a. Share permissions

   b. NTFS permissions

   c. Inherited permissions

   d. Special permissions

14. How many NTFS standard permissions apply to folders only?

   a. 1

   b. 2

   c. 3

   d. 4

15. When one global group is a member of another global group, we say they are

   a. Related

   b. Nested

   c. Connected

   d. Enclosed

■ Essay Quiz

1. Your assistant has asked you why you never create universal groups. Explain, in detail, when you would use a universal group, and why.

2. A user keeps saving confidential information in a public folder and has been embarrassed several times when other users were able to access the files. Explain to the user the mechanism that is causing this problem.

3. You've proposed to your boss that, from now on, you simply assign the Everyone group Full Control over network shares and perform all access control through NTFS permissions. Your boss thinks you're nuts and that users will be

able to delete all of the files on the server. Explain why your system would work.

4. Your assistant wasted an entire weekend assigning Read permissions to access a new network share to each of your 300 employees individually. Explain to her what she should have done instead.

5. Explain what you would look for if a user was experiencing difficulty saving to a network share but has no trouble opening files from the same share.

Lab Projects

• Lab Project 8.1

Create a structure of domain local and global groups for your school or place of business. It isn't necessary to comment on the actual permission levels that you would assign for this project. However, explain why you created the groups you did and what each would represent.

• Lab Project 8.2

Drawing on your answer to the preceding lab project, choose at least three specific groups of resources and the groups who would need to access them. Answer the following questions for each:

1 What share permissions would you grant and why?

2 What NTFS permissions would you grant and why?

• Lab Project 8.3

Using the following table, document which NTFS special permissions are associated with each NTFS standard permission. This table can be used as a reference when troubleshooting access problems that may be due to special permissions.

To complete this lab, add your personal account as a new entry to the ACL for the Test folder we created in the chapter. Apply the standard permissions one at a time and then use the Advanced Security Settings to edit your ACE and record which special permissions were applied for each individual standard permission. Some standard permissions also activate other standard

permissions, which is fine. Please completely record all associated special permissions.

Standard NTFS Permission	Associated Special Permissions
Write	
Read	
List Folder Contents	
Read & Execute	
Modify	
Full Control	

Traffic Control: Monitoring and Managing Server Performance

"The art of life lies in a constant readjustment to our surroundings."
—OKAKURA KAKUZO

In this chapter, you will learn how to:

- **Monitor the server using Task Manager**
- **Use the Performance Console for server monitoring and alerts**
- **Monitor event logs**

Even the most carefully configured server will eventually develop problems or other performance issues that need to be addressed. Change is something we cannot escape, and as our opening quote for this chapter implies, it's how we deal with that change that is the true test of our abilities. Fortunately, Microsoft Windows Server 2003 provides a variety of tools for monitoring the performance of our server so that we can detect and address any problems that may crop up as our network grows and changes.

In this chapter, we will be exploring the more commonly used tools for monitoring server performance. We will begin by learning to use Task Manager, a relatively simple tool that provides a quick method for checking on the server's current status. We'll then move on to the much more comprehensive System Monitor tool, which has the ability to monitor an incredible number of performance factors, and even allows for the creation of special log files and automated alerts. Finally, we'll learn how to use the various event logs Windows Server 2003 maintains to monitor the server for problems that may need to be addressed.

■ Server Monitoring Using Task Manager

As we mentioned way back in Chapter 1, Windows Server 2003 is an evolutionary product. As such, it shouldn't be too surprising to find that many of the monitoring tools we have at our disposal are either the same as, or closely related to, tools we're familiar with from Windows XP, Windows 2000, Windows 98, and Windows 95. **Task Manager** is one of those tools that have been around for quite some time, and so it should be relatively familiar to most users. However, it's even more useful in a server environment and certainly makes a good place for us to start our look at monitoring tools.

Opening and Exploring Task Manager

The traditional method for opening Task Manager in older Windows versions has always been through the old "three-fingered salute," which means by simultaneously pressing CTRL-ALT-DELETE. This method can still be used in Windows Server 2003, but it does not directly open the utility as it did in Windows 95 and Windows 98. Instead, this keyboard shortcut brings up the Windows Security dialog box depicted in Figure 9.1. As you can see, it's a simple matter of clicking the Task Manager button to open the utility. A better keyboard shortcut is the CTRL-SHIFT-ESC combination, which opens Task Manager directly. Of course, if you've got something against keyboard shortcuts, Microsoft hasn't neglected you! You can also right-click an empty area on the taskbar and simply select Task Manager from the shortcut menu. You can even use the command **taskmgr** to start Task Manager from the command line! Isn't it great to have options?

> When the Welcome to Windows dialog box is displayed, CTRL-ALT-DELETE brings up the logon dialog box instead of the Task Manager.

Each of the five tabs of the Task Manager utility, as shown in Figure 9.2, give the system administrator access to different monitoring and managing functions. Let's take a look at each in turn.

Applications

As you can see in Figure 9.2, the Applications tab presents information on the currently running tasks and their status. From here it is possible, either from the shortcut menu or the Task Manager menus, to switch between tasks, control their windows, or even end them, if necessary. It's this last option, the ending of unresponsive tasks, where Task Manager sees the most use for the average user of the desktop Windows operating systems. When all else fails and a misbehaving program just simply won't close, you can usually end it from here. You can also start new tasks from here, although it's rarely necessary, by clicking the New Task button, which opens what is essentially a Run dialog box.

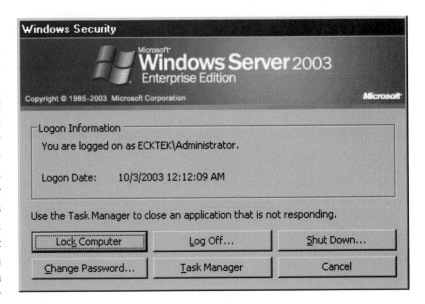

● **Figure 9.1**   The Windows Security dialog box

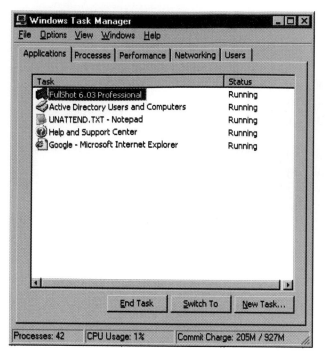

• **Figure 9.2**   The Task Manager dialog box

The status bar of the Task Manager dialog box also displays the current number of running processes, which is the number of actual executable programs, the current CPU usage, and the commit charge, which is a comparison of how much virtual memory is being used by the operating system and running programs compared to how much is available.

Processes

A **process** is simply an executable program that is running on the server. The Processes tab displays which files are currently being executed. As you can see in Figure 9.3, the actual filename of each process is listed in the Image Name column followed by information about the user who is running the program and the amount of CPU time and RAM the process is using. The list displays the files associated with the applications listed on the Applications tab, as well as files being used by the operating system. By default, only a few of these system files and files associated with the currently logged on user are listed. To see a more comprehensive list, simply check the box labeled "Show processes from all users".

As was the case with the Applications tab, a common use of the Processes tab is to end processes that are not working properly. By right-clicking a particular file entry, you can choose to end either that particular process or its **process tree**. A process tree consists of the process you select and any other related processes. You can also end processes by selecting them and clicking the End Process button at the bottom of the dialog box. If you want to know which processes are associated with a particular application, simply right-click the application on the Applications tab and choose Go To Process. This can be a good way to track down an application whose processes are "hogging" server resources.

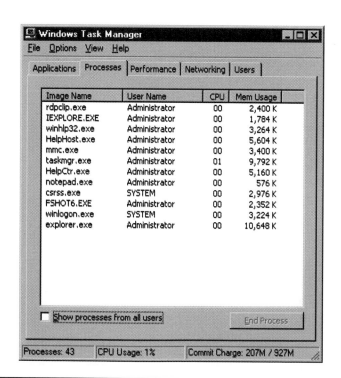

• **Figure 9.3**   The Processes tab of the Task Manager dialog box

The Processes tab also offers another neat, yet rarely used and slightly dangerous feature. Each running process has an assigned **priority**, which is used to determine which process gets "first dibs" on the server's resources. It's possible to change this priority by right-clicking a process and choosing Set Priority. A cascading menu, like that in Figure 9.4, lets you choose a priority from Low to Realtime. The reason this feature is rarely used is that there can be unpredictable results when you start manually allocating more processor time and memory to a process by raising its priority. Obviously, the raised process will run faster, but that may cause significant slowdowns for other running processes. It's also not feasible to have an administrator adjusting priorities on a regular basis. The danger I mentioned comes from improper use of the Realtime priority, which essentially gives the process the ability to demand CPU and memory resources to the exclusion of other processes. If it is assigned incorrectly, it's possible to lock up a server pretty darned tight as one demanding process completely consumes the available resources. Nevertheless, the option can be useful if several different application processes are running and one or more need to be completed as quickly as possible.

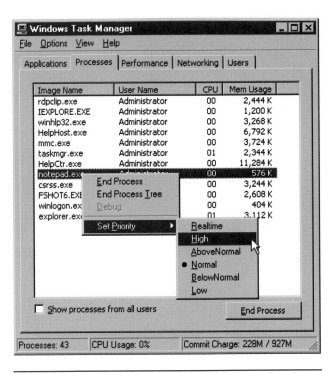

● **Figure 9.4**   Modifying the priority of a process

Most people find the idea of process priorities a little difficult to understand. After all, from a user's perspective, a multitasking operating system like Windows Server 2003 running on a sufficiently powerful computer seems to execute all programs and processes simultaneously. However, the real nature of the situation is a bit different from what it appears to be. Let's take a moment to consider an analogy that might make the whole concept a bit clearer and help you understand why changing priorities can be a tricky business.

Recall the best service you've ever had in a restaurant. You know, the type of meal where the server (the person bringing the food and drinks, not a computer!) seemed to use ESP to know exactly when your drink needed to be refilled or when you were ready for the dessert tray. In that situation, it's likely that the server had other diners that they were also waiting on. And yet, from your perspective, you seemed to have their undivided attention. This is because they were very skilled in dividing their time among all of their tables so that no one ever felt like they had to wait.

Window Server 2003 does much the same thing with multiple running processes. It allocates its time in what are called time slices and it assigns these slices to running processes according to their priority. If all processes have equal priority, they would each receive their assigned time slices and then be dealt with on an equal basis. However, all processes are not equal. Some processes have a higher priority than others. Higher-priority processes get their time slices before lower-priority processes, which do not get any time allocated until there are no higher-priority processes, or at least none that are ready to be run.

To help you visualize this, imagine that same restaurant meal, but with one small difference: at one of your server's other tables is a VIP, such as the President, or a movie star, or so on. Who do you think would get first shot at the server's attentions? You'd certainly still be taken care of, but not if the VIP was signaling the server! If you further imagine that this VIP demands constant attention from the server and won't release them to wait on their other tables, you can imagine the problems inherent in assigning a too-high priority to a process that is similarly demanding of the operating system's time!

Performance

The Performance tab provides several informative displays detailing the current and recent demands made on the server's CPU and memory resources. As you can see in Figure 9.5, the upper half of the dialog box consists of two column graphs and two line graphs while the bottom displays four different sets of numerical statistics. Since this tab presents so much data, let's take a look at what each of these graphical and numerical displays mean.

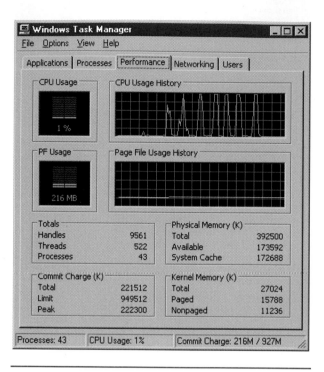

CPU Usage The CPU Usage column chart displays the current percentage of the overall CPU capacity in use. The information is identical to that provided in the Task Manager status bar.

CPU Usage History The CPU Usage History line chart displays the recent trends for CPU usage. By default, the display updates every two seconds. To adjust the update speed, choose View | Update Speed and choose from High (twice a second), Normal, Low (once every four seconds), or Paused (static display with no automatic updates). You can also force an update at any time by choosing View | Refresh Now. If more than one CPU exists, by default they will be displayed on separate charts. However, you can combine them into a single display by choosing View | CPU History. Additionally, you can display an additional line that represents the amount of CPU time being used by the operating system's kernel by choosing View | Show Kernel Times. The kernel time information will display in both the CPU Usage and CPU Usage History graphs in red.

- **Figure 9.5** The Performance tab of the Task Manager dialog box

PF Usage The PF Usage column chart displays how much of the server's virtual memory, or page file, is currently in use. This information is also displayed in the Task Manager status bar. However, the values are not always identical, although they are usually very close.

PF Usage History The PF Usage History line chart displays the recent trends for virtual memory usage. When changing the refresh rate for the CPU Usage History, you are also changing the refresh rate for this chart.

Totals The Totals section lists the number of **handles**, **threads**, and processes. As you already know, processes are simply executable program files. Threads are the actual subcomponents of a process that are performing calculations in the CPU. Each process can, and does, execute more than one simultaneous thread. Handles represent all the resources, such as open files or entries in the Registry, that are currently being used by the CPU. The CPU uses handles to keep track of such resources much the way CB radio users use handles, or nicknames, to keep track of the people they're talking to, which makes me wonder if one of the Windows programmers used to be a trucker!

Physical Memory (K)   The Physical Memory section details the status of the installed RAM. The (K) reflects that all of the numbers are in kilobytes. This section lists the total amount of installed RAM, the amount still available, and the amount being used by the **system cache**, which is memory used to hold the contents of files that are currently open by the operating system.

Commit Charge (K)   The Commit Charge section details the server's virtual memory status. In this section, the **commit charge total** is not the amount of available virtual memory, but rather the amount in use at the moment. The available value is actually used to reflect the maximum size of the page file, which is used by the OS to create the virtual memory. The most important figure here is the **commit charge peak**, which indicates the maximum amount of demand placed on the page file since Task Manager was run. On the other hand, the **commit charge limit** displays the total amount of memory available by combining both the page file and the physical memory. The idea behind monitoring the commit charge is that if you consistently use a large amount of virtual memory, the performance of your server will suffer. In such cases, you may need to change the size of the page file. However, an even better solution is to add more physical RAM.

Kernel Memory (K)   The Kernel Memory section displays information concerning the operating system kernel's memory usage. The total figure is simply the total amount of memory being used. The other two figures, paged and nonpaged, detail how much of the memory in use by the kernel is from the paging file and how much is from the physical memory, respectively.

Networking

When a network interface card is present in the server, the Task Manager's fourth tab is the Networking tab. Though the initial appearance of this tab, as displayed in Figure 9.6, is quite simple, this part of the Task Manager utility actually provides easy access to a great deal of information.

The initial display of the Networking tab consists simply of a line chart showing historical network utilization and a series of columns at the bottom detailing the adapter name, network utilization, link speed, and state. However, more information is available than meets the eye! For example, the initial chart tracks only the total number of bytes sent and received by the network. It is also possible, by selecting View | Network Adapter History, to display the bytes sent and the bytes received, either alone, or in combination with each other and the total bytes. This can be useful in determining both the incoming and outgoing load on the network.

The lower half of the display can also be highly modified. Selecting View | Select Columns displays the dialog box you see in Figure 9.7. From here it is possible to display as many as 26 unique columns of information concerning the functioning of the network adapter. Although Task Manager is

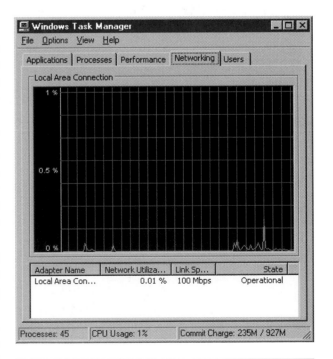

• **Figure 9.6**   The Networking tab of the Task Manager dialog box

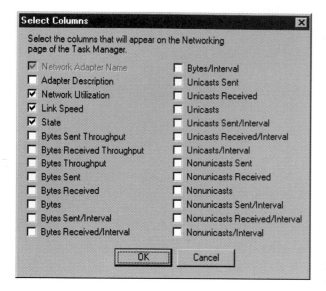

• **Figure 9.7**   The Select Columns dialog box

The System Monitor utility in the Performance Console, which we will be exploring later in this chapter, is a much better tool for extensively monitoring the performance of the network adapter. However, Task Manager can be much faster to both launch and use for simple monitoring tasks.

The Users tab displays only users logged on locally or through Terminal Services or Remote Desktop connections. Users who are merely logged on to the domain, on other computers, will not be displayed.

not the best utility for viewing this quantity of information, there are certainly times when it can come in handy.

Users

The Users tab of the Task Manager dialog box does a bit more than merely display who is currently logged on to the server. As you can see in Figure 9.8, in addition to displaying the user's name, a simple ID number, their status, and the name of the client machine they are using to reach the server, this tab also allows you to send messages to users and to either log them off the server or simply disconnect them directly! Although it probably isn't a great idea to go around logging off or disconnecting users without good reason, it is sometimes very necessary to send a particular user a message. For instance, you might need to tell them that you are about to disconnect their session, which is certainly more polite than simply doing it! Although other methods exist for sending messages to logged-on users, few are as fast or accessible as that provided by Task Manager.

Monitoring and Managing with Task Manager

Now that we're more familiar with the layout and features of Task Manager, it only makes sense to talk about some situations in which this particular tool can be useful in monitoring and managing the server's performance. Once we've taken a look at a few common scenarios, you'll get a chance to try your hand at using Task Manager on your own server.

• **Figure 9.8**   The Users tab of the Task Manager dialog box

Frozen or Improperly Running Programs

When you consider just how complex the actual code that makes up computer programs is, it's no real surprise that from time to time they misbehave. While this is a problem for both desktop and server computers, the nature of a network server is such that the simple expedient of a quick reboot isn't always feasible. Additionally, although Windows Server 2003 is specially designed to isolate applications from each other so that problems with one will not necessarily impact the rest, it's still important to be able to recover the resources being used by a program that is no longer usable.

As we indicated when discussing the Applications and Processes tabs, both can be used to terminate processes. In the case of the Applications tab, terminating an application should, ideally, terminate any of its processes. However, terminating a single process from the Processes tab may well leave other unneeded processes still running. For this reason, it is best to try to terminate improperly functioning programs from the Applications tab. However, from time to time, a malfunctioning program will still leave "orphan" processes running even after it has been terminated. In such cases, if the process can be identified, it might be necessary to make use of the Processes tab as well.

In order to detect situations like the one we've just mentioned, you can make use of the Performance tab. Once you've identified a program that tends to misbehave, you can make note of the resource usage prior to running it and the resource usage after terminating it. If you notice that not all of the used resources are released, specifically memory in most cases, you may have some of those orphan processes that need to be taken care of. Of course, the best solution is to fix the problem software, but in some cases that cannot be done as soon as you'd like.

Slow Server Performance

I can pretty much guarantee that you will not need any special monitoring software to tell you when the server begins to slow down. Network users tend to be much more sensitive detectors than any software made, and they're typically not shy about registering complaints with the network administrator! However, even a relatively simple utility like Task Manager can help you begin your search for the reasons behind significant server slowdowns.

One potential reason for a server slowdown is that the CPU is simply too busy. By monitoring the CPU Usage in the Performance tab, you should be able to see this occur. Momentary spikes of high usage aren't a problem, but continuous periods of high usage may indicate either a problem application

---

Try This!

Using Task Manager to Analyze the Impact of Common Tasks

Task Manager can be a real eye-opener in showing you which programs you run on a regular basis have the greatest impact on the system's CPU and RAM. Try this:

1. Launch Task Manager.

2. Watch the impact in the Performance tab of Task Manager as you launch several of the programs you use on a regular basis. Consider programs like Internet Explorer, Outlook Express, and, if you have access to them, various productivity packages. Wait a few seconds after launching each program before launching the next.

3. Right-click each application's listing in the Applications tab and choose Go To Process. Make note of the amount of CPU time and memory being used by each application's process.

4. Which everyday application made the greatest demands on your computer's CPU and memory?

or a need for more or faster processors. If you suspect a problem application, simply check the Processes tab for any processes using an inordinately large amount of processor time. You can even sort the list by CPU usage by clicking the CPU column heading. In the same manner, you can check for the second potential problem, which is a lack of sufficient memory. Again, if the Performance tab indicates a shortage of memory, you can look for the offending process in the Processes tab.

The third potential cause for an apparent server slowdown is a network communication problem. To rule this out, check the Networking tab and look for overly high usage rates. If you do find that the network utilization statistics are elevated, add both the bytes sent and bytes received data to the chart so that you can determine whether the problem is outgoing or incoming data. If it is outgoing, then there may be one or more users who are taking up more than their fair share of the bandwidth. If the problem is incoming, the network may be under attack from an outside source. Once you know the nature of the problem, you can consider your next steps in resolving it.

Step-by-Step 9.1

Working with Task Manager

Whether you're talking about power tools or software utilities, you're more likely to use a tool with which you are both comfortable and familiar. Because of that, it's worth taking a few minutes to open up Task Manager and play around with some of the features we've discussed up to this point. Although we won't be able to simulate the type of server load you'd be likely to see on a busy network, we can at least try some of the techniques most commonly used when working with Task Manager.

To complete this Step-by-Step, you will need

- A properly configured Windows Server 2003 Domain Controller
- Access to an administrator-level account on the computer

Step 1

Open Task Manager using whichever method you prefer. Remember that you can use CTRL-SHIFT-ESC or the command line command **taskmgr** to open it directly. You can also right-click the taskbar and choose Task Manager or use CTRL-ALT-DELETE and click the Task Manager button in the Windows Security dialog box. If you like, try each of the methods and see what you like best!

Step 2

Task Manager's default behavior is to always remain on top of any other open windows. This makes it easy to keep in sight as you work with other applications and monitor their impact. While Task Manager is open, go ahead and open a Notepad window by clicking Start | All Programs | Accessories | Notepad. Also open up a Search window by clicking Start | Search. We'll use Search in a few steps to put a brief load on the server that you can see in the Performance tab. Finally, open up Help and Support by clicking Start | Help and Support. We'll use it to demonstrate terminating a misbehaving program.

Step 3

In Task Manager's Applications tab, locate and right-click the entry for Help and Support Center. Although we will terminate this application in just a minute, let's first choose Go To Process to see which process is associated with this task. Task Manager will take you to the Processes tab and you should see the HelpCtr.exe process highlighted.

Find the Help and Support Center window and minimize it while you watch the HelpCtr.exe process entry. Now reopen the window by clicking the Help and Support Center button on the taskbar, again watching the process entry. Did you notice a change in both the CPU and Mem Usage columns? If not, continue to manipulate the window (minimize, restore, maximize) and watch the entry. Your numbers will vary, and they will sometimes change even when you are not manipulating the window, but you should notice that both CPU time and Mem Usage are much lower when the window is minimized. That's because the operating system does not dedicate as many resources to a minimized window, which makes sense because you aren't using it! Return to the Applications tab when you are done.

Step 4

On the Applications tab, right-click the entry for the Help and Support Center and choose End Task. As soon as the entry disappears, return to the Processes tab to verify that the HelpCtr.exe entry is also gone. Always try to terminate programs from the Applications tab, rather than from the Processes tab. If you do try to end a process, you will receive a warning that it could lead to system instability. To demonstrate this, go to the Processes tab, right-click the entry for notepad.exe, and choose End Process. Read the warning message that appears. Since we are only closing Notepad, and we had done no work in it, it's okay to click the Yes button. However, as you can see, ending a task from the Applications tab is much safer.

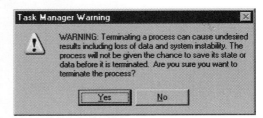

Step 5

Go to the Performance tab and watch the various charts and numbers for a minute. Unless you have active programs running, you'll see relatively little activity. What little you do see is due to the operating system performing its own tasks in the background. To see a bit more action, bring up the Search window you opened earlier. Enter **to** in the text box labeled "A word or phrase in the file" and click the Search button as you monitor the Performance tab of the Task Manager dialog box. Notice that there is a significant spike in CPU usage but relatively little change in PF usage. This is because searching is not an exceptionally memory-intensive task, but it does place demands on the CPU. Feel free to repeat the search, or perform other searches, to observe the impact on the various statistics.

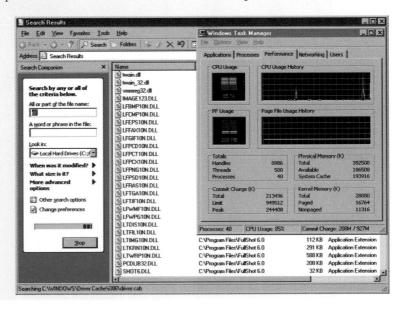

<table>
<tr><td>Step 6</td><td>Since this is a lab situation, you are unlikely to observe much activity on the Networking tab. However, if you are connected to the Internet, you can launch Internet Explorer and observe the changes as you visit different web sites. You can also verify your link's speed and its current status. When you are done, you may exit Task Manager and close any remaining windows you opened earlier.</td></tr>
</table>

■ Server Monitoring and Alerts Using the Performance Console

The Windows Server 2003 **Performance Console**, which is opened by choosing Start | Administrative Tools | Performance, is a perfect example of how the Microsoft Management Console (MMC) can be used to combine several useful, related, tools in one unified interface. In fact, Performance Console becomes a sort of "one-stop shopping" center for most of your monitoring needs by giving you easy access to both a powerful monitoring tool and the ability to create customized logs of performance statistics. It even allows you to create automated alerts that will notify you when certain situations occur, which saves you from having to sit in front of the server at all times!

Using System Monitor to Monitor Server Performance

As you can see in Figure 9.9, when Performance Console first opens, the **System Monitor** entry is already highlighted in the left pane and a few basic server statistics are already being monitored in the right pane as a sort of "demonstration." Before we can start monitoring our own statistics, we should first explore the interface and discuss the procedure for choosing what we want to observe.

The System Monitor Interface

The basic System Monitor interface consists of a single toolbar, a large display area for the actual data being monitored, a values area that displays summary information for the data being collected, and a legend pane at the bottom, which is used to identify the data being collected when it is displayed in the form of a graph. Since the functions of the toolbar buttons aren't really obvious from their appearance, you may want to refer to Figure 9.10 for their names and Table 9.1 for an explanation of their functions.

Each statistic tracked by System Monitor is referred to as a **counter**. Each counter is a specific measurement of the performance of some piece of hardware, software, or operating system component, each of which is called a

Cross Check

Task Manager

Task Manager is a quick and easy-to-use monitoring tool that has quite a lot to offer. Take a moment to review what we've covered and answer the following questions:

1. Describe the major features of the first three tabs in the Task Manager dialog box.

2. Describe common uses for Task Manager.

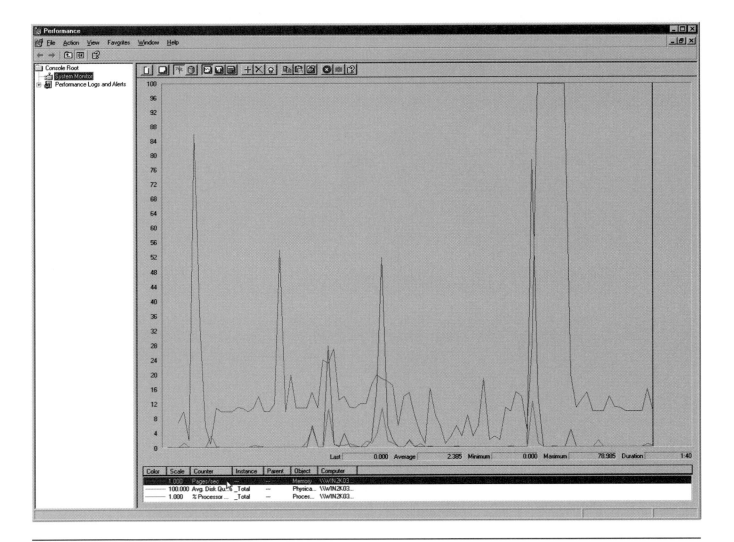

- **Figure 9.9** The System Monitor

performance object. The number of performance objects varies with the configuration of the server and its installed applications, and each performance object can have one or many counters associated with it. Additionally, some

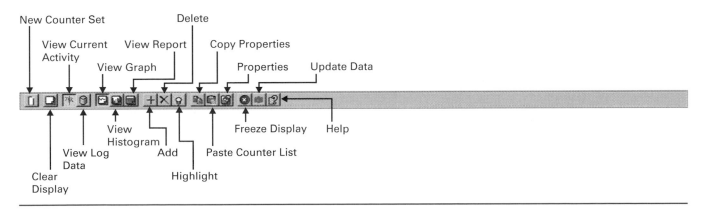

- **Figure 9.10** The System Monitor toolbar buttons

Chapter 9: Traffic Control: Monitoring and Managing Server Performance

Table 9.1	System Monitor Toolbar Button Names, Keyboard Shortcuts, and Functions	
Button Name	**Keyboard Shortcut**	**Function**
New Counter Set	CTRL-E	Stop current monitoring and remove existing counters in preparation for a new monitoring session
Clear Display	CTRL-D	Clear the current monitoring data but do not remove the existing counters
View Current Activity	CTRL-T	View data that is currently being collected
View Log Data	CTRL-L	View data that was collected previously and saved as a log file
View Graph	CTRL-G	View collected data in the form of a line chart
View Histogram	CTRL-B	View collected data in the form of a column chart, or histogram
View Report	CTRL-R	View collected data in the form of a text report
Add	CTRL-I	Add a new counter to monitor
Delete	DELETE	Delete the selected counter
Highlight	CTRL-H	Highlight the selected counter (only available in Chart or Histogram displays)
Copy Properties	CTRL-C	Copy the complete properties of the current System Monitor session
Paste Counter List	CTRL-V	Paste the properties of a copied System Monitor session into another System Monitor session
Properties	CTRL-Q	Display the Properties dialog box for the current System Monitor session
Freeze Display	CTRL-F	Stop the capturing of data samples
Update Data	CTRL-U	Capture one sample of data for the current counters with each click of the button
Help	F1	Display the System Monitor Help dialog box

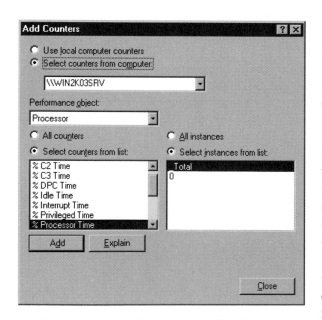

• **Figure 9.11**   The Add Counters dialog box

counters for a single performance object can apply to more than one "thing," which we call an **instance**. For instance (if you'll excuse the pun!), the %Processor Time counter, one of the default counters when System Monitor opens, is associated with the Processor performance object and measures CPU usage just as the Performance tab did in Task Manager. If the server had more than one CPU, there would be a separate %Processor Time counter for each processor as well as one for the total usage of all processors. Each of these measures would be considered an instance of the %Processor Time counter. What it *really* means is that there are potentially hundreds upon hundreds of different aspects of a server's performance that we can monitor and measure! I told you System Monitor was powerful, didn't I?

Adding counters to System Monitor is accomplished through the Add Counters dialog box, which can be opened either by using the Add button on the toolbar or by right-clicking the display area and selecting Add Counters. As you can see in Figure 9.11, you can select which computer to monitor, which means you can also use System Monitor to monitor the performance of other computers on the network. You then select the performance object and the counter to monitor. Although you can choose to monitor all of the counters for a performance object, I don't recommend it in most cases. It's pretty tough to interpret a chart with 15 different lines jumping all over the place at once! Finally, if the counter in question has more than one instance, you can either choose to monitor the total or choose a particular instance. However, the most important feature of this dialog box is that little button in Figure 9.11 labeled Explain. Once you've selected a counter to monitor, simply click the Explain button and a dialog box like that in Figure 9.12 will pop up with a full description of what the counter is actually monitoring. Once the dialog box is open, you can also click any other counter and see its description as well, which means you don't need to memorize the hundred or more counters System Monitor can measure! Isn't that a relief?

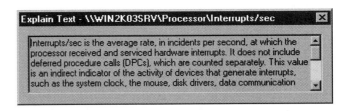

● **Figure 9.12**   The Explain Text dialog box for the Interrupts/Sec counter

Using System Monitor

System Monitor is one of those tools for which you seem to find new uses every day. It can monitor so many different aspects of server performance that the possibilities are practically limitless. In this Step-by-Step, you'll have the chance to monitor a few simple counters and work with some of the more common System Monitor options.

To complete this Step-by-Step, you will need

- A properly configured Windows Server 2003 Domain Controller

- Access to an administrator-level account on the computer

Step 1

Open the Performance Console by clicking Start | Administrative Tools | Performance. If System Monitor is not already highlighted in the left pane and monitoring in the right-pane, click its entry in the console hierarchy. You can immediately see the dynamic nature of the monitoring process if you do a Search for a common word like **to** within a file as we did back in Step-by-Step 9.1. After you've tried that, go ahead and click the New Counter Set button on the toolbar to begin setting up a new monitoring session.

*Tip: When doing Searches in this Step-by-Step, remember to search using simple, common words like **to**, **and**, and **the** in the text box labeled "A word or phrase in the file". Use a different word for each search.*

Step 2

Right-click the empty display area and select Add Counters. In the Add Counters dialog box, choose the Use local computer counters option button. Then select the PhysicalDisk performance object from the selection list. Scroll through the list of counters. There should be about 21 different counters for this one performance object. Note that, if your computer has more than one physical disk, there are also instances listed for each counter. Click the Explain button and read the description of a few of the counters.

Step 3

Select the first counter in the list, %Disk Read Time, and verify that _Total is selected in the Instances list. Click the Add button. Note that System Monitor immediately begins tracking this new counter. In the same manner, add the %Disk Write Time counter. Note that each counter is color-coded and tracked simultaneously. If you don't see any activity, do file search for another common word as you did in Step 1, which should produce a few peaks for both counters.

Tip: *You can adjust the widths of the columns in the legend pane at the bottom of the console so that you can better view their information.*

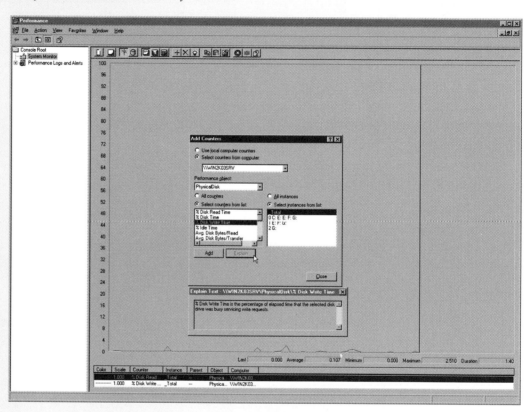

Step 4

System Monitor can accommodate counters from different performance objects at the same time. With the Add Counters dialog box still open, change to the Memory performance object and scroll to the top of the list of counters. You should see three entries for Available memory: one in bytes, one in kilobytes, and one in megabytes. Add the Available Bytes counter and look closely at the graph in the background. You should be able to detect a new colored line, corresponding to the legend entry for this new counter, being drawn at the very top of the graph. This is an example of a common pitfall when monitoring multiple counters. The first two counters we added measured disk activity as a %. The Available Bytes counter for the memory performance object is attempting to report the actual number of available bytes, rather than a percentage. Because the scale of the graph currently runs from zero to 100, and your server certainly has more than 100 bytes of memory available, we can't read the actual amount for this counter in this view. Close the Add Counters dialog box and we'll see what we can do to address this problem.

One potential solution to our problem is to change our view. Click the View Histogram button and observe the results. Do another file search or two. You should now notice that one colored column fills the screen from top to bottom while two other columns only rarely rise above the floor of the graph. As was the case in the graph view, these three counters just don't work well together graphically. Instead, click the View Report button and again do a few file searches. At least in this view it is possible to get an actual reading on the values for the counters you are tracking.

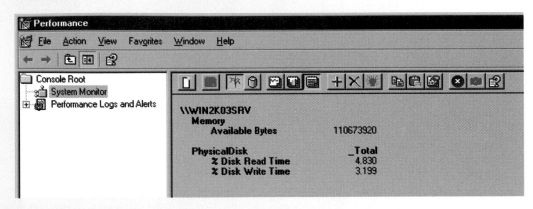

Click the View Graph button to return to our original view. Since we aren't getting much information from our Available Bytes counter, we might as well get rid of it. Click the entry for Available Bytes in the legend pane at the bottom of the console. To delete it, either press the DELETE key or click the Delete button on the toolbar. Feel free to try tracking other counters for other performance objects, if time permits. Close the Performance Console and the Search window when you are finished.

Using Performance Logs and Alerts

As powerful as System Monitor is, it still requires you to observe the monitoring process first hand, and the graph provides only a relatively brief interval of time. The Performance Console also offers **performance logs**, which can be used to record and store longer monitoring sessions, and alerts, which can be used to notify you when certain conditions are met.

Counter Logs and Trace Logs

The two types of logs offered by the Performance Console are distinctly different. On the one hand, **counter logs** track information in much the same way as System Monitor does, through the use of performance object counters. These logs can be recorded and

Try This!

Using Task Manager to Analyze the Impact of Common Tasks

System Monitor can provide much more in-depth information than Task Manager. Because of that, it can give you a more detailed picture of the impact of your most commonly used programs. Try this:

1. Launch the Performance Console and add two or three additional counters to the default counter set already present in System Monitor. Choose your counters from the Memory, PhysicalDisk, and/or Processor performance objects. Make use of the Explain button to learn more about the counters before choosing them.

2. Launch a commonly used program and then switch back to System Monitor and observe the impact of that program.

3. Repeat the process for two or three more programs.

4. Which programs had the greatest impact? Which counters were most affected for each program?

Baselines

The problem with taking measurements is that most are pretty relative. For example, is four feet tall for a person? It certainly is if you're a toddler, but not if you're a player in the NBA! In the same way, our measurements of server performance aren't of much use unless we first have some idea of what is normal. We need a standard to measure against. A common term for this standard is a baseline.

System Monitor, Task Manager, and other monitoring tools can be used to create baselines. However, since the baseline is supposed to be the standard against which we compare later measurements, it is important that we take the baseline measurements under the right conditions. If we establish our baseline at 3:00 in the morning when no one is using the server, then any activity at all during the workday is going to look extremely high.

Most experts recommend that baseline measurements for just about anything need to reflect low, high, and normal conditions rather than just one measurement, even if it is an average. What good is it to know that the yearlong average temperature in Las Vegas is 67 degrees when it's an average of 91 in July and 46 in January! Or better yet, when it's 90 during the day and only 50 at night!

then reviewed at a later time using System Monitor. **Trace logs**, on the other hand, do not make use of counters, but rather record particular events, and cannot be viewed without the aid of a third-party application. Because of this, our focus will be on the use of counter logs.

Counter logs are created in System Monitor by clicking the Performance Logs and Alerts entry in the left pane, right-clicking Counter Logs in either pane, and choosing New Log Settings. After you give the log a name, the dialog box depicted in Figure 9.13 appears. From the General tab, you can choose to add the complete counter set for a particular performance object by clicking the Add Objects button, or you can choose individual counters by clicking the Add Counters button. Adding counters is done in exactly the same fashion as it is in System Monitor. The General tab also allows you to set the sampling interval and, if necessary, to enter an account name and password under which to run the log. However, for most counter logs, this is not necessary.

The Log Files tab of the settings dialog box depicted in Figure 9.14 allows you to modify the naming convention, location, and data type of the log file. You can even add a comment, if you so desire. The Schedule tab shown in Figure 9.15 allows you to control when the log starts and stops recording and even allows you to specify the action to take after the log is closed. For example, you can automatically begin another log or even execute a command.

Once a counter log has been configured and has recorded data for a while, it can be stopped, opened, and reviewed in System Monitor by clicking the View Log Data button. Once the log has been loaded, you add counters from the log to the graph just as you would if you were doing real-time monitoring. This allows you to collect data on multiple counters and yet pick and choose which results you want to view. You can even control the time range you wish to view from the total capture period.

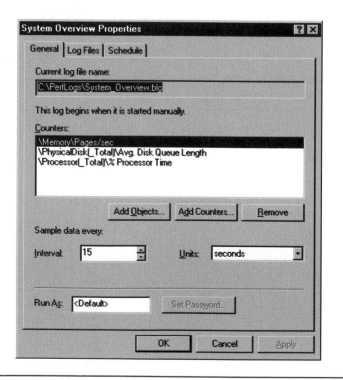

● **Figure 9.13** The General tab of a counter log's settings dialog box

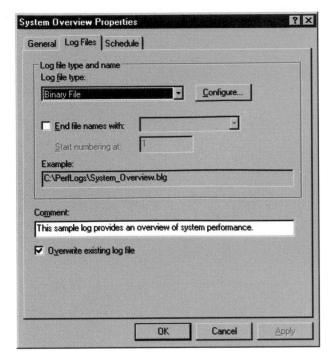

● **Figure 9.14**   The Log Files tab of a counter log's settings dialog box

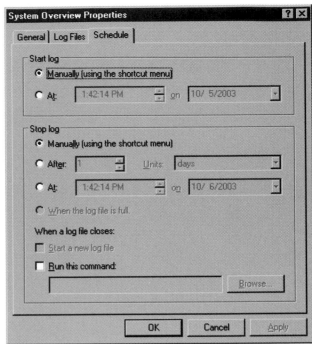

● **Figure 9.15**   The Schedule tab of a counter log's settings dialog box

Step-by-Step 9.3

Creating a Counter Log

Counter logs are a fantastic tool for monitoring a server without requiring the administrator to actually be present during the monitoring period. Through the creation of such logs, it is easier to collect data over longer periods of times, which can be useful for spotting certain performance trends. Keep in mind that the logs themselves can have some impact on server performance, so it is best to limit the number of counters and the amount of time the logs run to avoid creating server slowdowns. In

this Step-by-Step, you will create a relatively simple counter log, let it run for a brief time, and then view the results using System Monitor.

To complete this Step-by-Step, you will need

■ A properly configured Windows Server 2003 Domain Controller

■ Access to an administrator-level account on the computer

Step 1

Open the Performance console, if it is not already open, and double-click the Performance Logs and Alerts entry in the left pane. This will open that level of the hierarchy and also display the links to the two logs and the alerts in the right pane. Right-click Counter Logs in either pane and choose New Log Settings to open the New Log Settings dialog box. Name the log **Test Counter Log** and click OK to open the settings dialog box for the new log.

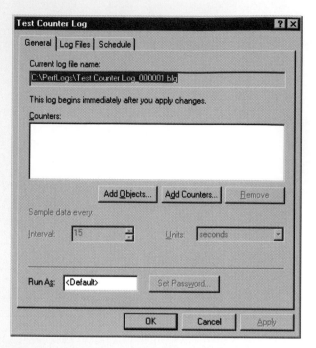

Step 2

Click the Add Objects button to begin the selection of the performance object to monitor. By monitoring an entire performance object, you are actually monitoring all of its counters at once. Although this can be very convenient when it comes time to analyze the data, you should consider monitoring only select counters when possible to minimize the load on the server. Since this log will run for only a short time, choosing an entire set of counters will not have a negative impact. In the Add Objects dialog box, click the option button labeled Use local computer counter objects and select Processor from the Performance objects list. Click the Add button and then click Close.

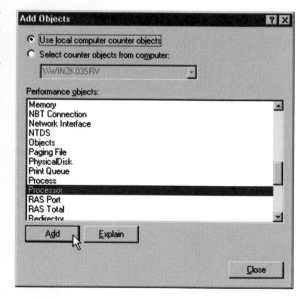

Step 3

Verify that **\Processor(*)*** appears in the counter list of the General tab. This indicates that all counter objects for all processors will be monitored. Change the Interval setting to **1** so that we can collect a relatively large number of data samples in a relatively short time. Normally, the sampling interval is increased to longer periods as you monitor for longer periods. Since we are going to monitor for only about a minute, taking one sample a second should not cause any problems.

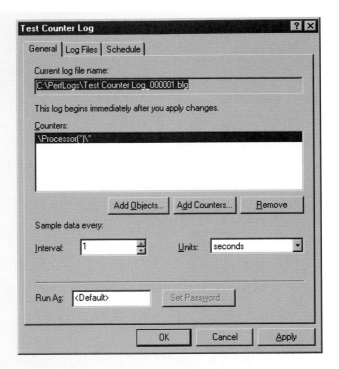

Step 4

Click the Log Files tab to view the file type and naming convention for this log file. By default, the log file will be in binary format, which is just fine for viewing in System Monitor. However, other file formats are available for importing the resulting data into other programs, including database management systems and spreadsheets. Note, also, that the file's name will end with six digits, represented by "nnnnnn," and will begin with the number 1. This system is used to allow for the capture of multiple data samples under the same log file name. Each time you stop, and then restart, a log file, the file name will increment by 1. Thus, our first capture will be Test Counter Log_000001, while later captures using the same log would be Test Counter Log_000002, and so on. This system allows for up to 999,999 separate capture sessions under a single log name! I think that will probably be enough for just about anyone. Note that you can also enter a comment to further describe the log, if you so desire.

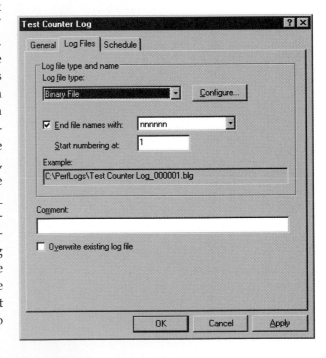

Step 5

Click the Schedule tab to check the schedule for this log. By default, a counter log begins capturing as soon as you finish configuring it and is terminated manually. You can choose whether to start and stop the log at a particular time and date or handle it manually. You can also choose to close the log when it is full, which requires you to configure the size of the log in the Log Files tab by using the Configure button. By default, logs will run until the drive runs out of space! Finally, this tab also allows you to dictate other actions to take when a log is closed, which include starting another log or executing a command. For now, we'll leave the default schedule in place. Click OK to close the dialog box and begin capturing. If you are prompted that the folder C:\ PerfLogs does not exist, simply click Yes to create it now.

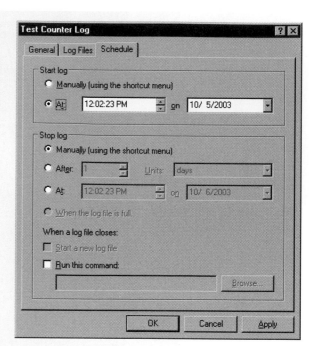

Step 6

Double-click the Counter Logs entry in either pane and you should see your log entry, along with a sample log created by the operating system. The icon for your log should be green, which indicates that it is currently started and running. You may adjust the column widths for the log name and other information to make them easier to read. Wait at least one minute to allow the log to capture a sufficient data sample. After a minute or so, right-click the icon for the log you created and choose Stop. After a moment, you should see the icon for your log turn red, indicating that the log has stopped.

Step 7

Return to System Monitor and click the New Counter Set button to clear the display and then click the View Log Data button. Verify that the Source tab of the System Monitor Properties dialog box is visible and click the option button labeled Log files. Click Add to open the Select Log File dialog box, which works just like a standard File Open dialog box. The Look in selection box should already be set to the perflogs folder, and you should see an entry for Test Counter Log_0000001. Select it and click Open to return to the System Monitor properties dialog box. Click OK to close the dialog box.

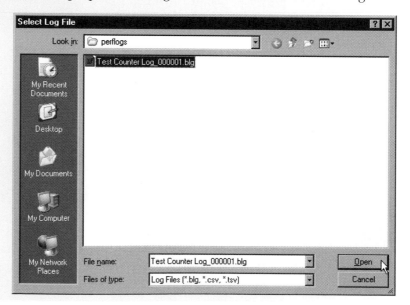

Tip: If the Select Log File dialog box is not displaying the perflogs folder, simply navigate to C:\PerfLogs.

Step 8

Even though we've opened the log file, we still need to select which counters to display in the same way that we selected counters when using System Monitor earlier. Click the Add button to open the Add Counters dialog box. You'll notice that only one Performance Object, Processor, is available because that is the only object we monitored. However, all of the counters for that object and all of their instances, if any, can now be added to the System Monitor display. For the purposes of this Step-by-Step, click the option button labeled All counters. Then click Add followed by Close. You should now see a rather crowded graph that represents all of the data you captured concerning the Processor object.

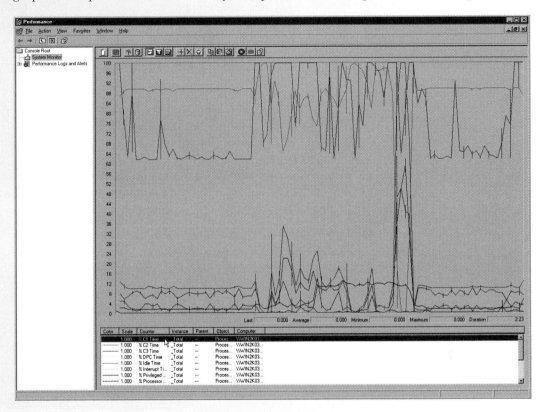

Step 9

When you've collected data over time, it can be useful to focus in on particular periods. Although the System Monitor graph does not display the actual capture times, it is possible to use the properties dialog box to navigate to certain times or ranges of time within the overall data sample. Right-click the graph and choose Properties from the shortcut menu. Click the Source tab to reveal the Time Range controls. At the bottom of the tab, you'll see a slider control with the beginning time and date of your capture listed at the top and bottom on the left side, and the ending time and date of your capture listed in the same locations on the right side. Grab either end of the slider and slide it toward the middle while observing the graph in the background. You may reposition the dialog box if you need to. You should notice that a thin, black, vertical line moves across the graph as you move the ends of the slider. This is useful for targeting an area where the graph is indicating a potential problem. However, this line may not show up if the server is running too many other programs. If you do not see the line, try deleting about half of the counters from the display and try again. You should be able to view ranges as small as a single second! When you are finished, close the System Monitor properties dialog box.

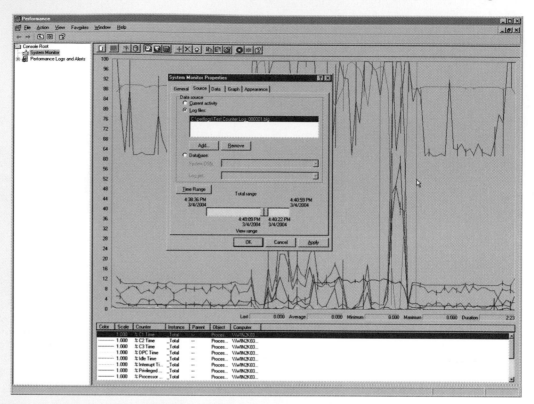

Step 10

Even though the counter log we created is currently stopped, it's probably not a good idea to leave it "lying around," since it was only for testing purposes. Remember, by default, a running log will run until the hard drive is full! To get rid of the log, simply click the Counter Logs entry in the left pane and then delete the log by either selecting it and using the DELETE key or by right-clicking it and choosing Delete from the shortcut menu. Interestingly enough, deleting the log does not delete existing log files. They are still available in the PerfLogs folder until manually deleted. You may delete the file, but since it is most likely less than one megabyte in size, you can safely leave it if you wish.

Using Alerts

Alerts are nothing more than automated alarms that are triggered when certain conditions are met. Alerts monitor counters for the various performance objects just like counter logs and are configured in much the same way. However, with alerts, you also specify a level for the counter at which to take action, and the action to take. Whereas System Monitor required your presence during monitoring and counter logs require you to open and view the log after the data is collected, it is possible to configure alerts to *tell* you when you need to get involved with a potential situation. However, to get alerts to do that, we've got to check on something first.

Have you received any "spam" in your e-mail inbox lately? How about pop-up windows as you browse the Internet? Yep, me too. Well, apparently the lovely folks who came up with those little intrusions in our lives got creative. They figured out a way to use a Windows server operating systems feature to disguise their messages. They used something called the **Messenger service** to make dialog boxes pop up that seem to be from the operating system, when they're really externally generated. As a result, Microsoft made a little change with Windows Server 2003: they disabled the Messenger service by default. That's not a huge problem most of the time, but we need that service running if we want to create alerts that can really "alert" us!

Windows Server 2003 depends on a great many services to do a great many things. In fact, by definition, a **service** is just a program or process that works with the operating system to support the activities of other programs and users. Services can be started, stopped, and otherwise managed through the Services console, which is depicted in Figure 9.16 and is accessible by clicking Start | Administrative Tools | Services. Although you normally don't have to work directly with services to any great extent, there are situations, like the one we're facing, where it's necessary. As part of the Step-by-Step that follows, we'll take a brief detour over to the Services console and discuss how to manage the behavior of services.

In certain rare situations, some server and network problems can be traced back to the failure of one or more services to run. In such cases, the services management techniques demonstrated in Step-by-Step 9.4 may also come in handy.

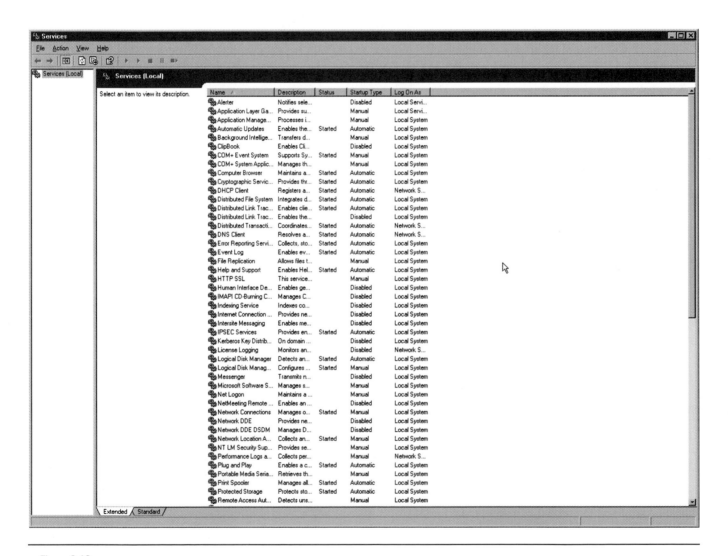

• **Figure 9.16** The Services Console

Configuring an Alert

Alerts are particularly useful when you are trying to establish how often a particular condition occurs. They can also be useful as warnings that certain potential problems may exist, such as insufficient bandwidth or memory. When you consider the number of counters that can be monitored, there's practically no limit to what an alert could be used for. In this Step-by-Step, we'll begin by reconfiguring the Messenger service so that the alert we create will be able to send a notification message to a particular computer on the network. We will then configure a simple alert for a situation we know will occur soon after it is set. In this way, we can explore both the configuration and the result of an alert.

To complete this Step-by-Step, you will need

- A properly configured Windows Server 2003 Domain Controller

- Access to an administrator-level account on the computer

| Step 1 | Open the Services console by clicking Start | Administrative Tools | Services. Note that the services are listed in alphabetical order by default and that the left-hand pane displays columns for Name, Description, Status, Startup Type, and Log On As. Scroll down the list and locate the entry for Messenger and note its status and startup type values. If status is blank and startup type is Disabled, then continue on to Step 2. If the service is currently started, go ahead and read the next step anyway so that you will know how to start a nonrunning service if you ever need to! |

Tip: Services rarely just stop on their own. However, quite a few services are disabled by default in Windows Server 2003 to save resources and/or enhance security. Additionally, it is occasionally necessary to stop and then restart a service that gets "stuck" or stops functioning correctly.

| Step 2 | Double-click the entry for the Messenger service to bring up its properties dialog box. Change the Startup type to Automatic and then click Apply. After a brief pause, the Start button should now be available. When it is, click it to start the service. A dialog box with a progress bar will appear briefly while Windows tries to start the service. When that dialog box disappears, you should note that the status of the service now displays as Started in both the properties dialog box and in the Services Console. When you've verified that the service is started, go ahead and close the dialog box and the Services console and go on to Step 3! |

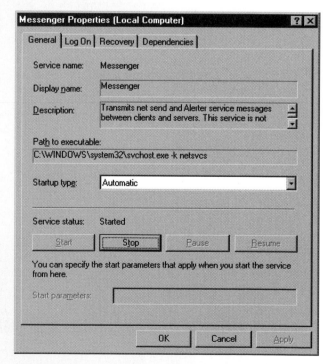

Step 3

If necessary, open the Performance Console and expand the left-pane entry for Performance Logs and Alerts. Right-click Alerts and choose New Alert Settings. Name this alert **Test CPU Usage Alert** and click OK to open the properties dialog box for the new alert.

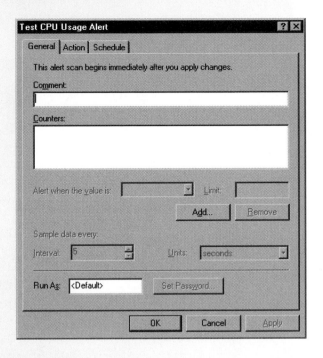

Step 4

Like counter logs, alerts allow you (through the General tab) to choose a counter to monitor, add a comment to the alert, and choose a sampling interval. Unlike counter logs, alerts also require that you specify a value relationship, which determines when the alert is sent. Additionally, alerts can monitor only specific counters, not entire performance objects. Of course, this only makes sense, since we have to specify a value and each counter is measured differently. Click the Add button to open the Add Counters dialog box. Select the option button for Use local computer counters, and keep the default performance object, Processor, and the default counter and instance, which is %Processor Time and _Total. Click Add and Close to return to the properties for the alert. Verify that \Processor(_Total)\%Processor Time appears in the Counters box. Enter **10** in the limit box to trigger the alert when the CPU usage reaches 10%. Leave the interval at five seconds.

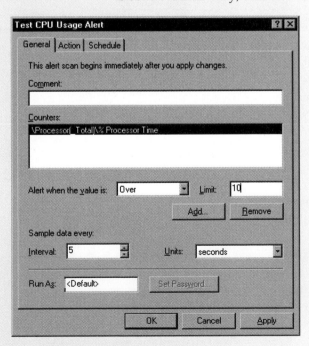

Tip: You'd likely never need to set an alarm for the %Processor Time counter, and if you did, you certainly wouldn't set it for only 10%! This counter regularly jumps from 1% to 100% and everywhere in between depending on what programs are currently running. However, it makes for an easy demonstration!

Click the Action tab. Note that, by default, the alert will make an entry in the application event log. Since we'll be looking at the event logs in the next section of this chapter, that's ideal for us! We can also choose to send a message to a specific computer, start a preexisting counter log, and/or execute a command. Check the second check box and enter your server's computer name in the text box.

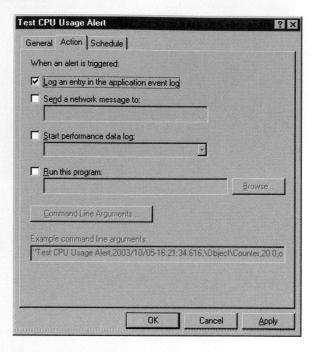

Tip: The Messenger service can be enabled through Services on the Administrative Tools menu. Just be sure, if it is enabled, that you watch for those fake messages!

Click the Schedule tab to view the available options. Like a counter log, an alert is scheduled by default to begin when it is first configured and end manually. However, you can also choose specific start and end times or start and stop it manually. Additionally, you can also set the alert to end after a specified number of seconds, minutes, hours, or days. To be on the safe side with our alert, set the scan to end after 10 minutes. That way, if we forget to delete it, we won't be bombarded with alert messages every time the CPU usage climbs over 10%! Note that there is an option to start a new scan as soon as the old one finishes. Leave that check box unchecked for now.

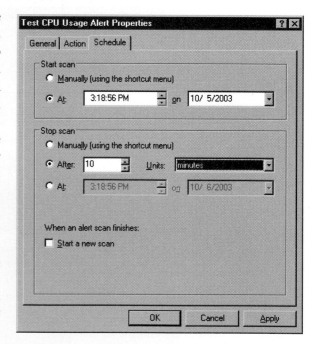

Click the OK button to close the dialog box and verify that your alert icon appears in the right pane and is green, which indicates that the alert is running. To ensure that the alert gets tripped, do a file search for a common word as we did several times earlier. Within a matter of seconds, perhaps even before you begin the file search, you should receive an alert from the Messenger service informing you that the alert threshold was exceeded. Once you see that, you can go ahead and delete the alert in the same way that we deleted the counter log earlier. If you don't delete it right away, I'm betting you'll get another reminder or two during the next ten minutes!

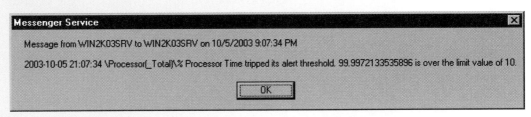

Monitoring Event Logs

Even without our active participation, Windows Server 2003 is constantly keeping tabs on a lot of what is going on with the server and the network. The **Event Viewer** console presents this collected information in the form of three or more **event logs**, which can be used to analyze problems and otherwise monitor overall performance. Let's take a look at what type of information the three basic event logs track.

The Application, Security, and System Logs

The actual number of event logs to be found in Event Viewer varies with the nature of the server. For instance, since our servers our configured as domain controllers, Event Viewer will include the Directory Service and File Replication logs. Since our servers are also configured to act as DNS servers, Event Viewer will also include a DNS server log. These logs are certainly important; however, the logs you'll spend the most time with are the logs found on every Windows Server 2003 computer: the application, security, and system logs.

The Application Log

The **application log**, as the name implies, contains events associated with various applications, including elements of the operating system itself. For instance, the alerts and counter logs we created earlier show up here as event entries during creation and at other times.

The events recorded in the application log are usually one of three types: Information, Warning,

Cross Check

System Monitoring Using the Performance Console

In our discussion of the Performance Console, we've covered three distinct tools. Take a moment to review what we've covered and answer the following questions:

1. What is the basic purpose of the System Monitor?
2. What is the basic purpose of a counter log?
3. What is the basic purpose of an alert?

or Error events, which represent exactly what you would expect. Information events merely communicate normal events that occurred with no problems. Even something as simple as completing the Windows Product Activation (WPA) process gets recorded as an Information event. A Warning event, on the other hand, indicates a situation that could become a problem, although it isn't one as yet. For instance, prior to activating Windows, several warning events will appear reminding you that you need to complete the process within a certain number of days. Finally, the Error events describe situations that need immediate attention. I've never tried it, because it would be a bit of a hassle, but I assume that failure to activate Windows within the allotted time period would probably turn up an error event. Of course, you wouldn't get to see the error, because you can't use Windows to do anything *but* complete the activation process at that point!

The Security Log

The **security log** is solely used to record two types of events: Success Audits and Failure Audits. These audit events are the result of monitoring, or auditing, the access of various objects including files, folders, and printers, as well as certain activities such as logons and logoffs. In Windows Server 2003, auditing is already enabled for several predefined types of events, which is a change from Windows 2000 where it was initially disabled.

The System Log

The **system log** is where the action really is. In this log you'll find every event of any significance, whether Information, Warning, or Error, that doesn't appear in some other log. Events may be associated with everything from printing a document to configuring IP addresses and more. If I'm looking for an event that I think may have been recorded by one of the logs, and I'm not sure where to look, I usually start with the system log!

Using the Event Logs

The first thing to remember about the event logs is that they do not have an unlimited capacity. That means that you cannot depend on any of the logs recording every event that ever happened since the day the server was first installed. However, Microsoft has made some significant changes with Windows Server 2003 to the default capacity of the logs and their behavior when that capacity is reached.

Under Windows 2000, each of the three primary logs had a default capacity of 512KB. This incredibly small default size meant that logs quickly reached capacity on busy servers. The logs were set to overwrite events when they became full, thus replacing the oldest events with newer events, but the default setting only allowed events older than seven days to be overwritten. As a result, logs left with their default settings on busy servers frequently reached their capacity, and then stopped logging and generated an error message because they could not overwrite any existing events.

Windows Server 2003 sets a default size for the three primary logs of 16MB, which is a heck of a change from the bad old days of Windows 2000. Additionally, the default overwriting behavior has been changed to allow the logs to overwrite events as needed. Not only has this eliminated the chance that the logs will stop logging events, it has provided a very large data set to work with on even the busiest of servers. However, it is still possible to set your own maximum log size for each of the three logs, with the ultimate maximum at 4GB. You can configure the log to overwrite events by age or to wait to be manually cleared when full. Truthfully, though, the new defaults practically eliminate the need to even mess with these settings.

The second thing to remember when working with event logs is that each event is described by a number of different fields, which can be used to filter the event log to show only a list of similar events or to "step through" the log, stopping at only certain events. These fields include the event type, source, category, date, and time, thus making it relatively easy to work with logs holding even hundreds of thousands of events. We'll take a look at this feature in Step-by-Step 9.5.

Step-by-Step 9.5

Monitoring Event Logs

Good system administrators know that checking the event logs on a regular basis is a good way to spot problems and potential problems that may not otherwise be apparent. Of course, the logs are also useful when you know a problem exists and you need to try to track down its source. Since the event logs can hold so much information, it is wise to gain some basic familiarity in techniques that make the data a little more manageable. In this Step-by-Step, we will use the application log and the event created from our alert in Step-by-Step 9.4 to practice filtering events, finding events, and reading event details.

To complete this Step-by-Step, you will need

- A properly configured Windows Server 2003 Domain Controller

- Access to an administrator-level account on the computer

Caution: This Step-by-Step assumes that you have completed Step-by-Step 9.4 and that the application log has not been cleared since its completion.

| Step 1 | Open the Event Viewer by clicking Start | Administrative Tools | Event Viewer. When the console opens, double-click Application in the left pane to display the application log. |

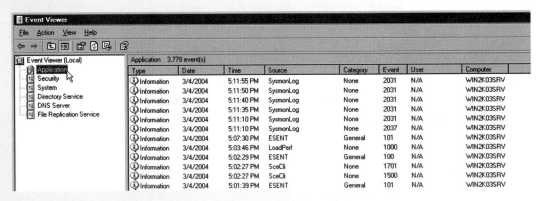

| Step 2 | Although the events associated with the alert from Step-by-Step 9.4 are likely listed at the top of the event log, we'll first try to locate them by creating a filter. Right-click Application in the left pane and select View | Filter to open the Filter tab of the Application |

Properties dialog box. Use the Event source selection list to choose the source for the alert event, which is SysmonLog, and click OK. Notice that only events with that source are now displayed and that the information bar above the column headings now states that this is a filtered view. To remove the filter, right-click Application in the left pane and choose View | All Records.

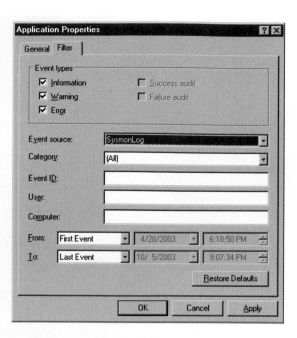

Step 3

The Find feature is useful for stepping through events in the log file in terms of their similarity in one or more characteristics. To open the Find dialog box, right-click Application in the left pane and click View | Find. You may have noticed that some or all of the events in the filtered view from Step 2 shared the same Event ID number. Every event has a unique ID number associated with it that can be useful for tracking down a particular type of event. Enter the Event ID number **2031** in the Event ID text box and click Find Next. If necessary, reposition the dialog box so that you can see which records get highlighted as you continue to click the Find Next button. By default, the Find Next button searches the list from top to bottom and asks you if you'd like to start again when you reach the end. However, if the event you are looking for is the first event at the top of the log, you will not find it with the Find Next button until you have started at the beginning again. You can also choose to search from bottom to top, if you so desire.

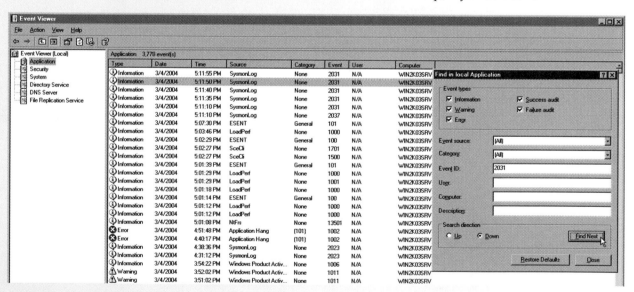

Step 4

Close the Find dialog box, and double-click one of the events with Event ID 2031. This opens the Event Properties dialog box, which displays all of the identifying information for the event and a description of what happened. Note that there are two arrow buttons for navigating to the next or previous event and a Copy button for copying the event information to the clipboard so that you can paste it into another document, such as an e-mail to tech support! Also note that some events, like this one, display a hyperlink in the description that can be used to obtain more information about events. Some events also display associated data in the section at the bottom of the dialog box. When you are finished working with the event logs, close all open dialog boxes and all open windows.

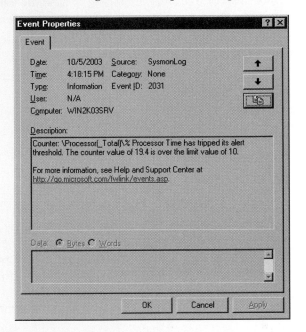

Chapter 9 Review

■ Chapter Summary

After reading this chapter and completing the Step-by-Step tutorials and Try This! exercises, you should understand the following facts about monitoring and managing server performance in Windows Server 2003.

Monitor the Server Using Task Manager

- Task Manager can be opened by right-clicking the taskbar and choosing Task Manager. You can also use CTRL-ALT-DELETE and click Task Manager in the Windows Security dialog box. You can also use CTRL-SHIFT-ESC or type **taskmgr** from the command line.

- The Applications tab in Task Manager lists the running applications and their status. It can be used to switch between tasks, to start new tasks, and to terminate unresponsive tasks.

- The Processes tab lists the currently running processes along with their CPU time and RAM. The Processes tab can be used to terminate a process or a process tree. You can right-click an application in the Applications tab and choose Go To Process to see which processes belong to which applications. You can also modify the priority of a running process in this tab.

- The Performance tab consists of graphic and numeric displays that detail the current and recent demands made on the server's CPU and memory resources.

- The Networking tab displays graphic and numeric information regarding the performance of the network interface card.

- The Users tab displays locally logged-on users and can be used to log users off or disconnect their session. This tab can also be used to send messages to logged-on users.

- Task Manager is useful for terminating frozen or improperly running programs. It is also useful for tracking down the reasons behind slow server performance.

Use the Performance Console for Server Monitoring and Alerts

- System Monitor is accessed through the Performance Console. It can be used to track counters and counter instances associated with a wide variety of performance objects.

- The information in System Monitor can be presented as a line graph, a histogram, or a report.

- Counter logs can be used to track the same information as System Monitor. Counter logs record the data over time for later viewing and analysis through System Monitor.

- Trace logs require the use of a third-party program to be read.

- Alerts monitor counters and are triggered when those counters reach certain predetermined levels. Alerts are recorded in the application log and may also be configured to send a message to a computer, run a performance log, or execute a command.

Monitor Event Logs

- The application log, as the name implies, contains events associated with various applications, including elements of the operating system itself.

- The security log is solely used to record Success Audits and Failure Audits, which are the result of monitoring, or auditing, the access of various objects, including files, folders, and printers, as well as certain activities such as logons and logoffs.

- The system log tracks a wide variety of system events.

- The event logs in Windows Server 2003 begin with a default maximum size of 16MB. This may be increased to as high as 4GB. By default, older events are overwritten by newer events when necessary.

- Event logs may be filtered, and events can be searched for in terms of a number of fields used to describe events.

Key Terms List

alerts *(280)*

application log *(285)*

commit charge limit *(263)*

commit charge peak *(263)*

commit charge total *(263)*

counter *(268)*

counter logs *(273)*

event logs *(285)*

Event Viewer *(285)*

handles *(262)*

instance *(270)*

Messenger service *(281)*

Performance Console *(268)*

performance logs *(273)*

performance object *(269)*

priority *(261)*

process *(260)*

process tree *(260)*

security log *(286)*

service *(281)*

system cache *(263)*

system log *(286)*

System Monitor *(268)*

Task Manager *(259)*

threads *(262)*

trace logs *(274)*

Key Terms Quiz

Use terms from the Key Terms list to complete the sentences that follow. Don't use the same term more than once. Not all terms will be used.

1. A process can consist of multiple _____s, which are the actual calculations being performed by the processor.

2. A counter may have more than one _____.

3. In order for alerts to send a message to a computer when triggered, the _____ must be running.

4. Success Audit and Failure Audit events are found in the _____.

5. System Monitor is found in the _____.

6. _____ is/are used by the operating system to keep track of resources such as open files or Registry entries.

7. In System Monitor, Processor is an example of a/an _____.

8. _____ require a third-party application to be read.

9. You can right-click an application in the Applications tab of Task Manager and choose Go To _____.

10. The security log can be found in the _____.

Multiple-Choice Quiz

1. Which of the following reduces the number of events displayed in an event log?

   a. Find

   b. Search

   c. Query

   d. Filter

2. The largest an event log may be is

   a. 512KB

   b. 16MB

   c. 4GB

   d. 16GB

3. The Messenger service is _____ by default in Windows Server 2003.

   a. Disabled

   b. Started

   c. Enabled

   d. Stopped

4. In Task Manager, the initials PF stand for

   a. Process flow

   b. Page file

   c. Processor focus

   d. Page finds

5. System Monitor offers _____ different views.

   a. 2

   b. 3

   c. 4

   d. 5

6. Counter logs are saved in

   a. C:\Documents and Settings

   b. C:\PerfLogs

   c. C:\SysmonLog

   d. C:\NetmonLogs

7. When System Monitor is first opened, it is already monitoring _____ counters.

   a. 4

   b. 3

   c. 2

   d. 1

8. In System Monitor, a column chart-type display is called a

   a. Histogram

   b. Bar chart

   c. Report

   d. Line graph

9. Which of the following is *not* created in the Performance Console?

   a. Alert

   b. Counter log

   c. Event log

   d. Trace log

10. Which of the following keyboard shortcuts will bring Task Manager up with no other action needed?

   a. ALT-SHIFT-ESC

   b. CTRL-SHIFT-ESC

   c. CTRL-ALT-DELETE

   d. CTRL-ALT-ESC

11. The button in the Add Counters dialog box that helps you learn about the different counters is labeled

   a. Explain

   b. Description

   c. Purpose

   d. Definition

12. Which of the following does not allow you to choose multiple counters to monitor?

   a. System Monitor

   b. Counter log

   c. Alert

   d. They all allow multiple counters for monitoring.

13. The events generated by alerts can be found in which event log?

   a. Application log

   b. Security log

   c. System log

   d. All of the above

14. How many event logs are present on *all* Windows Server 2003 servers?

   a. 1

   b. 3

   c. 5

   d. 6

15. When, by default, are events overwritten in Windows Server 2003 event logs?

   a. After seven days

   b. Never

   c. When the log is full

   d. When the server is rebooted

■ Essay Quiz

1. Your new trainee is having trouble understanding the concept of an *instance* in System Monitor. Explain the concept.

2. You need to reboot the server, and your boss, who is in the building across the street, is still logged on. What tool discussed in this chapter may come in handy in this situation, and what are two ways it might help?

3. Your supervisor recently discovered the wonders of the System Monitor. She would like you to start monitoring every counter for every performance object. Explain to her why this is not a good idea.

4. Explain when you would use a counter log.

5. Describe a situation in which you would create an alert.

Lab Projects

• Lab Project 9.1

Pick two counters each from the Memory, PhysicalDisk, and Processor performance objects. Do not pick counters that were discussed in the chapter. Research these six counters and, in your own words, write a description of what they measure and why you would want to monitor them.

• Lab Project 9.2

Find four counters from at least two different performance objects that would be ideal candidates for an alert. Explain why you would configure an alert for these counters and what value you would choose to trigger the alert. Do not use counters discussed in the chapter or the counters from Lab Project 9.1.

• Lab Project 9.3

Review your System event log at the end of each day for the next week. Make note of the most common events you see. Based on your observations, answer the following questions:

1 What Error events did you observe? Do they indicate a need for any particular action on your part?

2 What Warning events did you observe? Do they indicate potential problems or temporary conditions?

3 Were the Information events of any use? If so, how would they be helpful?

From Here to There: Remote Installation of the Windows XP Professional Client

"Progress is made by lazy men looking for easier ways to do things."

—Robert Heinlein

In this chapter, you will learn how to:

- **Configure a server for Remote Installation Services**
- **Configure Remote Installation Services**
- **Perform a remote installation of Windows XP Professional**
- **Create an image from a reference computer**

Since a server isn't of much use unless there are clients connected to it, it's likely that, sooner or later, you'll need to get involved in installing desktop operating systems and configuring client computers. In the "bad old days," this meant hours upon hours of running from computer to computer with OS installation disks in hand. As one of the "lazy men" mentioned in the opening quote, I always felt there must be an easier way. Fortunately, Windows Server 2003 offers Remote Installation Services, which, with just a little preparation, lets us lazy folk sit back and let the server do all the hard work. That's what I call progress!

In this chapter, we will begin by adding Remote Installation Services to our Windows Server 2003 computer. Once we've got that configured, we will then use the server to create a file set that can be used to install Windows XP Professional on client machines. After we run through an actual remote installation with that file set, we'll also take a look at how a Remote Installation Server can be used to create customized installations, based on the configuration of a reference computer.

Configuring a Server for Remote Installation Services

Remote Installation Services (RIS) allows you to install client operating systems over the network at need. Of course, this makes initial OS installations easier, but RIS servers actually do much, much more. However, before we can start to work with this nifty little labor saver, there are a few requirements we need to consider and some preparatory steps we need to take. Let's take a quick look at some of the things RIS can do for us, and then we'll discuss those requirements and preparations.

Remote Installation Services Function and Requirements

RIS works in one of two ways. In one mode, RIS can be used to create an image of an operating system installation CD. In a second mode, RIS can image a client machine's existing installation of an OS, any installed programs, and any configuration settings. In both modes, the resultant image can be installed on client machines over the network and customized to reduce the amount of interaction needed on the part of the user. We'll discuss the details of these two modes of operation in greater depth a little later in this chapter.

To use RIS on a network, at least one server needs to have the Remote Installation Service installed, which makes it an RIS server. The service is not installed by default. The reason for this is that several requirements must first be met before RIS can be used. As usual, these requirements fall into two categories: hardware and software.

> An image is nothing more than a fancy type of copy that copies not only files, but also the hierarchical structures and relationships of the files as they existed on the source the image was made from. That means that an image, whether of a CD or a hard disk, can essentially behave just like that original disk.

RIS Hardware Requirements

The hardware requirements for an RIS server go just a bit beyond those required by the server operating system itself. In addition to those minimum requirements, it is also necessary to have sufficient hard drive space on which to store the operating system images RIS creates. Microsoft recommends at least 4GB of space; however, this amount is heavily dependent on the number of images you create, as you might imagine. If you need to create only one or two images, even a 2GB volume would do. More important, images cannot be saved to either the boot or system volume, which for most servers means the C: drive. In fact, Microsoft recommends that RIS images be stored on their own volume, which must be formatted with the NTFS file system. Of course, a network interface card (NIC) is also necessary (the faster the better!), which isn't much of a problem for a server. However, there cannot be more than one NIC installed, which may be the case if the server is acting as a router for the network. In such cases, a member server may be configured to take on the RIS server role.

> The RIS server should ideally be located within the same network segment as the clients it is supposed to serve. If the clients have to go through a router to connect to the RIS server, you need to make a whole slew of configuration changes to both the router and the server to make the process work. Trust me when I tell you that this is more pain than it's worth. If necessary, consider placing RIS servers locally on each server segment that needs them.

How RIS Conserves Disk Space

When you're talking about creating images from the installation CDs for operating systems, you're talking about a significant amount of hard drive space! Of course, Microsoft does recommend using a dedicated volume of at least 4GB, but even then the number of images would normally be limited to about six, which really isn't that much. However, RIS uses a nifty little technology, with a truly awesome name, to keep things under control.

Installing RIS also installs and activates the **Single Instance Store Service (SIS)**, which includes a smart bit of code called the **SIS groveler agent**, or groveler for short. Now, outside of the computer world, a groveler is a pitiful person who goes crawling around acting humble and servile. In the case of RIS, the groveler is certainly crawling around beneath our notice and serving us, but it should be proud of what it does because it's really quite cool!

Groveler crawls around the RIS volume and inspects the files it finds. When it thinks it has found duplicate files, it compares them carefully in several ways to make sure they are exact duplicates. If it determines that they are, it puts a new copy of the file in a special folder called the **SIS Common Store Folder** on the RIS volume. Next, the groveler deletes the duplicate files from where they were located and replaces them with a pointer, called the **reparse point**, to the new location of the file.

The really great thing about SIS and the groveler agent is that the various Windows versions you create images from *do* have a ton of duplicate files. Because of that, the groveler can have a huge impact on the amount of space that gets used by multiple images. See, I told you the groveler should be proud of itself!

RIS Software Requirements

All versions of Windows Server 2003, with the exception of Web Edition, can be configured to act as RIS servers, as can all versions of Windows 2000 Server. However, it is also necessary that Active Directory, DNS, and DHCP be installed and running on the network. This doesn't mean that the RIS server has to be the domain controller, DNS server, or DHCP server. In fact, if the RIS server is going to see heavy use, it's probably a good idea to use separate servers to avoid potential performance issues. However, the technology behind RIS requires the other services to work its magic. Fortunately for us, our servers should be just fine, due to our activities in earlier chapters.

> I should also mention that RIS requires a TCP/IP-based network. However, since TCP/IP is really the de facto standard for Microsoft networking, it's usually a given that the requirement is met.

Try This!

Authorizing a Server

If we were not installing RIS on an already-authorized DHCP server, we would have to authorize it after installation. Let's take a look at how you would authorize an RIS, or any other, server. Try this:

1. Log on to your server as the administrator.

2. Click Start | Administrative Tools | DHCP.

3. Right-click DHCP at the top of the left pane and choose Manage authorized servers from the shortcut menu.

4. If you needed to add an authorized server, you would click the Authorize button and then enter the IP address of the server. That's all there is to it!

5. Close all open dialog boxes and windows.

Additional Considerations

If RIS is installed on a server that is not currently acting as a DC, or DNS or DHCP server, it is also necessary to **authorize** the server to provide RIS services to the network. This step is really just a security measure to help the administrator manage the servers. It's necessary because pretty much anyone with local access to the server can install the RIS service, but only the administrator can authorize it, thus allowing it to function. This way, the administrator has direct control over how many RIS servers are created and how they function.

Installing Remote Installation Services

The actual process of installing RIS on a server is really quite simple. However, this is also a good time to create a new volume for the images we will be creating later, if one does not already exist. We will begin this Step-by-Step by creating and formatting a new simple volume on one of our dynamic disks and then proceed with the RIS installation.

To complete this Step-by-Step, you will need

■ A properly configured Windows Server 2003 Domain Controller

■ Enough unallocated space on one dynamic disk to create at least a 2GB simple volume

■ Access to an administrator-level account on the computer

Step 1　Open the Computer Management tool. To do this, click Start | All Programs | Administrative Tools | Computer Management. When the Computer Management console opens, maximize the window, if necessary. Using the left pane, click Disk Management. (You may have to first click the plus sign to the left of Storage, if Disk Management is not visible.)

Step 2　To create a simple volume, right-click the unallocated space of a drive with at least 2GB of remaining space and choose New Volume. When the New Volume Wizard dialog box appears, click Next.

Step 3　Verify that Simple is selected and click Next. If necessary, adjust the amount of space to be used for the simple volume, but make sure that at least 2000MB are allocated. Click Next.

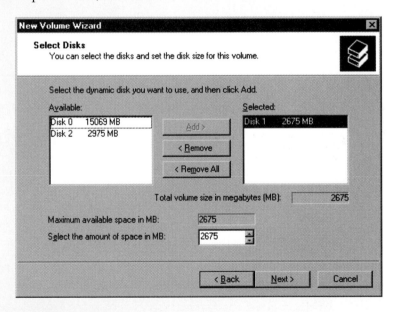

Step 4　Choose a drive letter for the new volume (I'm using "R" for my example) and click Next. Verify that the volume will be formatted using NTFS and enter the volume label **RIS**. Click Next and then Finish, and wait for the new volume to be completely formatted, which may take five minutes or more, depending on the drive.

Step 5　Once the new volume is formatted, we can continue with our installation of RIS. Close the Computer Management console and click Start | Control Panel | Add or Remove

Programs. When the dialog box opens, click Add/Remove Windows Components in the left pane.

Step 6

When the Windows Components Wizard dialog box appears, scroll down until you see the entry for Remote Installation Services. Click the check box to check it and click Next. If you are prompted for the installation files, insert the Windows Server 2003 CD or point the wizard to the network share where they can be found.

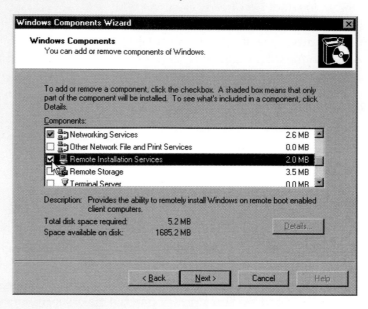

Step 6

When Windows is done configuring the component, click Finish and then click Yes when prompted to restart the computer. When the computer restarts, log back on with an administrator account.

■ Configuring Remote Installation Services

After RIS is installed, it needs to be configured. This configuration not only prepares the service for use, it also takes you through the creation of the first operating system **flat image**, which is simply a virtual copy of the installation CD that, for all intents and purposes, acts just like the original. The actual process is simple, but it can take a half an hour or more to actually create the flat image. However, as simple as the process is, there are a few aspects we should discuss beforehand.

Operating System Considerations

When choosing the operating system to use for our first RIS image, there are some constraints that we

---

✓ Cross Check

Installing RIS

In our discussion of the Remote Installation Service, we've discussed a number of hardware and software requirements that must be met in order for the service to function. Take a moment to review what we've covered and answer the following questions:

1. What hardware preparations must be made before installing RIS?

2. What other services must be running on the network?

---

need to keep in mind. On the one hand, RIS is not capable of creating flat images from just any operating system, nor is it limited to only those traditionally installed on client machines. On the other hand, we need to be sure we maintain compliance with any applicable licensing agreements.

Keep in mind that a flat image is only one of the two possible images that can be created by RIS. That's why we keep emphasizing the term "flat." The creation of the different images, and their purposes, differ a bit, as will become clear when we discuss the other alternative at the end of the chapter.

Supported Operating Systems

A common misconception is that RIS can be used only to install client operating systems. While that was true when RIS was first introduced with Windows 2000, in Windows Server 2003 it can also be used to also install several different server operating systems. You'll find that this is a bit more important with the other image type we'll be discussing at the end of the chapter, but it can be helpful when setting up new member servers or domain controllers if you don't feel like hauling around the CDs and sitting through every step of the installation process!

Another point of confusion concerns which operating systems flat images can be made from. For instance, RIS cannot make an image of Windows 98, which was more of an issue under Windows 2000 Server, because that was still a common choice for a client operating system. However, since Windows 98 was never a *good* choice for a client operating system, it makes sense not to encourage its use by supporting it through RIS!

For client-level operating systems, RIS supports flat images for Windows 2000 Professional and Windows XP Professional. Windows XP Home is not supported, since it really isn't capable of fully joining a domain-based network, which was the same problem Windows 98 had. On the server side, RIS supports flat images for both Windows 2000 Server and Advanced Server and Windows Server 2003 Web, Standard, and Enterprise Editions (both 32- and 64-bit.) Windows Server 2003 Datacenter is not supported in any version, for reasons that aren't entirely obvious but most likely have to do with the size and complexity of that edition of the OS.

Licensing Considerations

It's important to remember that just because you don't have to carry CDs around doesn't mean you don't have to worry about licensing anymore. Although operating systems like Windows XP and Windows Server 2003 will do their best to keep you honest with Microsoft Product Activation, some people tend to get forgetful about licenses when using RIS to install Windows 2000 products. Try very hard not to be one of those people! The potential for fines, and even jail time, isn't worth it.

From a convenience standpoint, Microsoft offers several different volume licensing packages to accommodate the need to purchase

Try This!

Microsoft Licensing Plans

Staying in compliance with the terms of your software licensing agreements is serious business, to both businesses and individuals. The issue becomes more complex in networked environments where it is necessary to accommodate the need for hundreds, or even thousands, of licenses for products like operating systems and office suites. Microsoft maintains a web site that discusses the various licensing plans it offers businesses that need to license their products in volume. Try this:

1. Point your browser to http://www.microsoft.com/licensing/.

2. Click the link labeled Volume Licensing Overview. Read the information and then click your Back button to return to the preceding page.

3. Which licensing plan would be appropriate for your school or place of business?

large numbers of licenses for both client and server operating systems. In the case of those products that do use a product activation key, it is even possible to get a **Volume Licensing Key (VLK)**, which is a single key usable with multiple installations of the volume-licensed product. This saves you from having to manually enter the product activation key with each installation by allowing you to make it part of the unattended installation answer file. A relatively new feature even allows you to encrypt the information and set an expiration date on the VLK to prevent unauthorized installations. We'll add a single-use product key to an answer file later in the chapter, so you can see how this is done.

Step-by-Step 10.2

Configuring RIS and Creating a Windows XP Professional Flat Image

Since Windows XP Professional is really the ideal client operating system in a Windows Server 2003 network, we are going to use that OS to create our first flat image. However, the process is essentially the same whether you are creating an image for Windows XP, Windows 2000, or Windows Server 2003. If a copy of Windows XP Professional is not available, you can run through this exercise by using your Windows Server 2003 CD to create the flat image.

To complete this Step-by-Step, you will need

- A properly configured Windows Server 2003 Domain Controller

- A properly licensed copy of Windows XP Professional, or other supported OS

- Access to an administrator-level account on the computer

Caution: This Step-by-Step will take at least one-half hour to complete, if not longer! Be sure that sufficient lab time exists before beginning!

Step 1

Click Start | Administrative Tools | Remote Installation Services Setup to launch the Remote Installation Services Setup Wizard. Take a moment to read the requirements for successful installation and use of RIS. The PXE boot ROM requirement for client computers at the bottom of the list is necessary only when we use an image to install an OS to a client computer. We will be discussing this requirement in the next section of this chapter. Click Next to continue.

Step 2

The second dialog box is used to enter the path to the folder where the image files will be stored. The folder should, ideally, be named **RemoteInstall** and should be located on the volume you created in Step-by-Step 10.1. Change the path, if necessary, and click Next to continue.

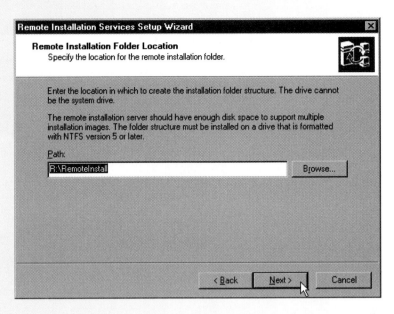

Step 3

The third dialog box allows you to choose whether or not to activate the service upon completion of the wizard. Additionally, you can choose to respond only to known computers, which are computers that have an existing computer account in Active Directory. For the purposes of this exercise, check both check boxes and then click Next to continue.

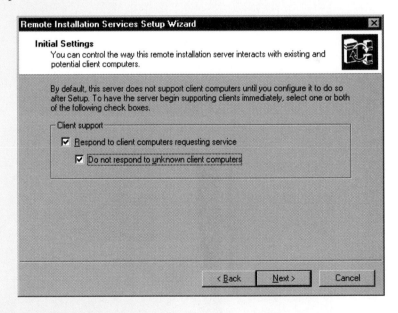

Step 4

If necessary, modify the path to the installation files so that it points to the Windows XP Professional installation files. These files can be either on a CD or on a network share. The default will be your first CD drive, which means the default will usually be correct. Place your Windows XP CD into the drive. If the Welcome to Windows screen appears, click Exit to close it. Click Next to continue.

Step 5

Enter the name of the folder in which the image files should be stored. The default is acceptable, but I tend to rename mine to indicate the OS the image is for. In this case, I would enter **WINDOWSXPPRO**. The user never sees this folder, and you rarely have to access it, so it isn't a big deal if you don't rename it. Click Next to continue.

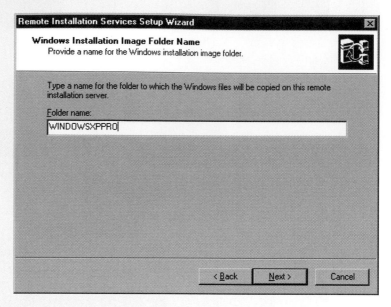

Step 6

You'll notice that the Friendly description and Help text already contain entries appropriate to whatever OS you are creating an image for. Although you can certainly change these if you like, there really isn't any reason to at this point. If you later create other images for the same OS, perhaps with different answer files or configuration settings, it might be necessary to make a change. Click Next to continue.

Step 7

Verify your settings and then click Finish. From here it's just a matter of waiting for the files to be copied over and the image to be created. You may want to grab a bite to eat and grab a good book (like this one!) because you're in for a wait of up to a half-hour or more. When the process is complete, click Done and then remove the OS CD from the drive.

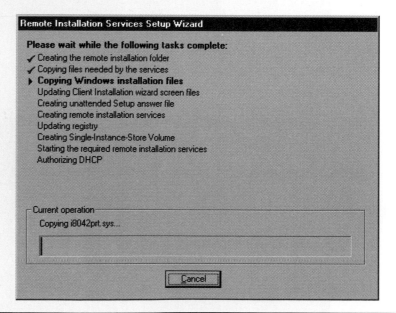

Additional RIS Configuration Settings

After RIS is installed and the first image is created, we can also make additional configuration choices that make the process even easier for the user of the client machine. Unfortunately, you have to do a bit of digging to find these settings, but it's worth the effort! Some of the settings are part of the group policy for the domain, or OU, that the client computers belong to while others are accessed as part of the properties of the RIS server. However, the two groups of settings work hand-in-hand.

Group Policy Settings

We've mentioned from time to time in earlier chapters that group policies allow a system administrator to standardize a number of different aspects of how users and computers experience the network. Chapter 11 is, in fact, dedicated to the use of group policies. However, we do need to take a bit of an advanced look at the topic in this chapter because several of the RIS settings we need to discuss are set as group policies. Keep in mind that there can be many different group policies in force at any one time. For instance, there is a default domain policy and there can also be separate policies for individual OUs. For the purposes of our lab experience, we will deal with the default domain policies, thus applying our choices to the entire domain.

Although there are many ways to edit group policies, the easiest way to access the default domain policy is through Active Directory Users and Computers. From that console, simply right-click the domain in the left pane and choose Properties. From there you just click the Group Policy tab, select the Default Domain Policy, and click the Edit button, as illustrated in Figure 10.1. This opens up the Group Policy Object Editor console for the default domain policy. Don't worry if I lost you there; we'll be doing this together in the next Step-by-Step! Once the Group Policy Object Editor is open, you can find the additional settings for RIS by following the path shown in Figure 10.2: User Configuration | Windows Settings | Remote Installation Services. Double-click the icon in the right-hand pane for Choice Options to open the Choice Options Properties dialog box you

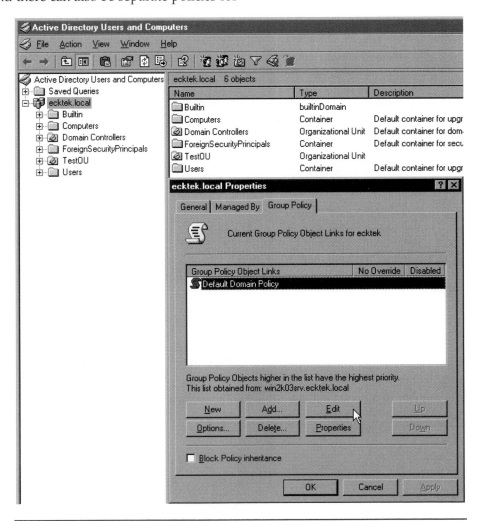

• **Figure 10.1** Editing the Default Domain Policy through the domain properties in Active Directory Users and Computers

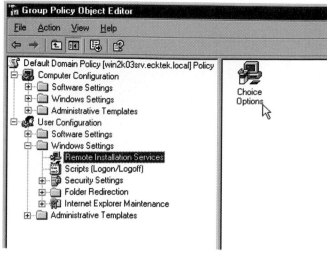

- **Figure 10.2**   The location of the RIS Choice Options in the Group Policy Object Editor console

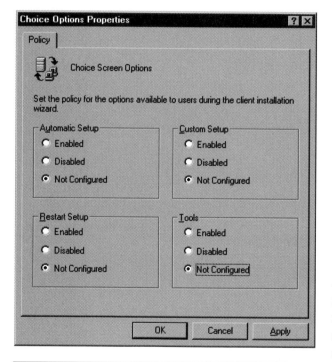

- **Figure 10.3**   The Choice Options dialog box

see in Figure 10.3, which offers settings for Automatic Setup, Custom Setup, Restart Setup, and Tools. Each of these options can be set to Enabled, Disabled, or Not Configured. Enabled and Disabled, of course, mean just what they say, while Not Configured means that the option's setting will be whatever it is for the parent object. For instance, if an OU has all of its options set to Not Configured, but the domain the OU is in has them set to Enabled, the options will be enabled in the OU. Let's take a look at what each of these options actually does.

Automatic Setup   Enabling Automatic Setup is supposed to enable RIS to automatically set both the computer name and the location (OU) for client computers. That means that RIS should be able to create a new computer account for a client and name it automatically. I say "supposed to" and "should" because approximately one week before this was written, Microsoft announced that an error prevented Windows XP Professional computers from joining Windows Server 2003 domains during unattended installations. That means that, for now at least, even if we enable this setting we're still going to have to **prestage** the client computers we want to be able to use RIS and enable our users to join them to the domain. We prestage a computer by creating the computer account ahead of time as a managed computer. We'll still enable this setting because Microsoft is working on the issue, but for now it won't actually create or name the computer accounts for us. It's too bad really; it's a neat feature!

Custom Setup   Custom Setup is simply the opposite of Automatic Setup. Since we're going to be prestaging the client computers and we want to minimize user interaction, we'll disable this setting.

Restart Setup   The Restart Setup option is one I usually enable, since it allows users to continue an aborted installation from where it left off. Of course, this is necessary only in rare cases where the network goes down or the power goes out in the middle of the installation, but better safe than sorry, right?

Tools   Enabling Tools makes it possible for users to access certain tools through RIS even if their computer has no installed OS. Perhaps it's a form of micromanagement, but I typically don't enable this option. There isn't that much a user should really need to fix when using RIS, and I'd rather address any problems in person, rather than depending on the user to fix them. However, the option is there if you want to use it!

Server Property Settings

Once a server has been made into an RIS server, a new tab, called Remote Install, is available from the server's properties dialog box in Active Directory.

As you can see in Figure 10.4, this tab allows us to modify the client support settings we made during the installation of RIS. For instance, by unchecking the Respond to client computers requesting service option, we can effectively turn RIS off if we don't want clients to have access to it. We can also use the Verify Server button to test the server's operation and the Show Clients button to view any clients that have used the RIS server. However, the most important button here is the Advance Settings button, which opens the dialog box shown in Figure 10.5. Let's take a look at what the three tabs of this dialog box allow us to do.

New Clients   The New Clients tab allows you to configure the automatic naming and location of the computer accounts RIS creates when automatic setup is enabled. Well, it would if that feature was working! The pull-down box you see in Figure 10.5 allows you to choose from some preset options for the name of the computer account, like first name, last name, or user name. As you can see, the default option bases the name on the user name of the user. However, you can also click the Customize button to open the dialog box shown in Figure 10.6. Here you can use a variety of codes to create your own template for computer names. Since we need to prestage client computer accounts, this feature won't do much for us right now.

Images   The Images tab shown in Figure 10.7 allows you to manage the actual RIS images, and even create new images. From here you can access the properties of an image, which, as you can see in Figure 10.8, displays a variety of information about the image, allows you to adjust the permissions on the image files, and allows you to modify the description and help text associated with the image. It's even possible from here to associate an existing image with a new answer

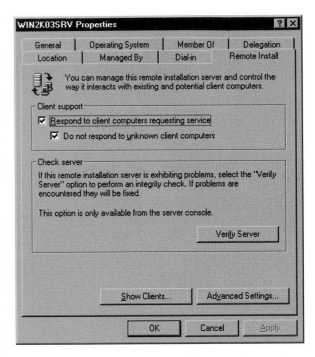

• **Figure 10.4**   The Remote Install tab of a RIS server's properties dialog box

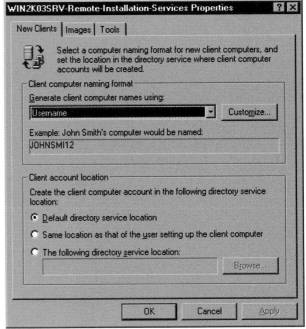

• **Figure 10.5**   The New Clients tab of the advanced settings dialog box for an RIS server

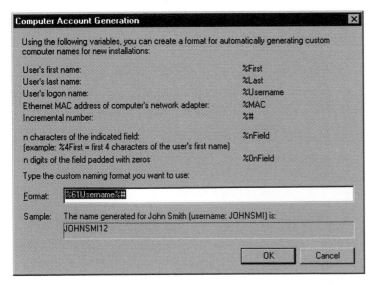

• **Figure 10.6**   Computer Account Generation dialog box

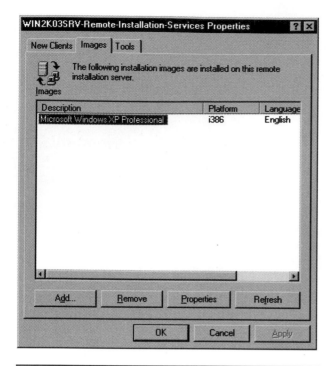

● **Figure 10.7** The Images tab of the Remote Installation Services Properties dialog box

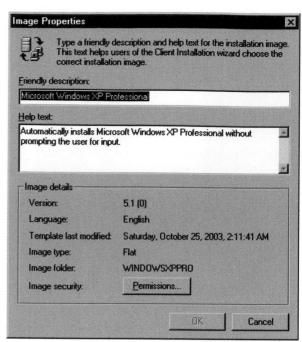

● **Figure 10.8** The Image Properties dialog box

file, essentially providing another version of an image with different installation choices dictated by the answer file.

Tools If troubleshooting tools are installed on the RIS server, they can be managed from this tab. By default, none are. However, as I mentioned earlier, when no OS is installed there's rarely much need for diagnostic and repair tools on the part of the user.

Step-by-Step 10.3

Advanced RIS Configuration

RIS won't be much of a labor saver if clients have trouble using it and end up calling the system administrator constantly for help. If we take the time to take advantage of some of the more advanced RIS settings, we can minimize the possibility that users will get stuck while trying to perform an RIS installation. That means we have more time and our users are happier and more productive. That's what

I call a win-win situation! We'll still need to prestage the client computer accounts, but we'll wait to do that until the next Step-by-Step.

To complete this Step-by-Step, you will need

- A properly configured Windows Server 2003 Domain Controller with RIS installed

- Access to an administrator-level account on the computer

Step 1

Open Active Directory Users and Computers by clicking Start | Administrative Tools | Active Directory Users and Computers. In the left pane, right-click the name of the domain and choose Properties.

Step 2

In the properties dialog box, click the Group Policy tab. Select the Default Domain Policy and click the Edit button. This will open the Group Policy Object Editor.

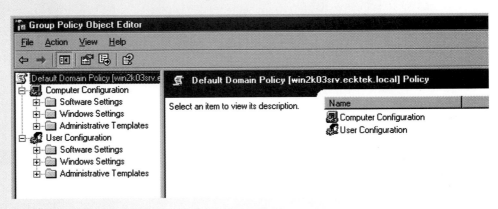

Step 3

Under User Configuration, click the plus sign next to Windows Settings in the left pane and then select the entry for Remote Installation Services. Double-click Choice Options in the right pane to open the Choice Options Properties dialog box.

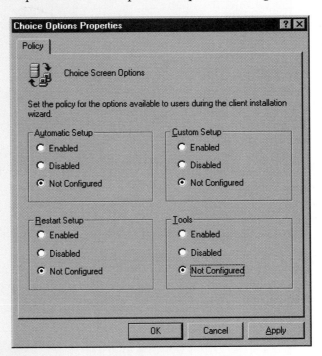

Step 4

Enable Automatic Setup and Restart Setup and disable Custom Setup and Tools. In other circumstances you might well make other choices, but for our purposes we want to set up the simplest, least interactive installation experience possible. That's the type of installation that stands the least chance of causing confusion or difficulty for our users at the client computers. Even though Automatic Setup won't create computer accounts yet, we'll leave it enabled for when it's fixed. Click OK to close the dialog box and then close the Group Policy Object Editor window and the properties dialog box for the domain.

Step 5

Click the Domain Controllers container in the left pane. Right-click the name of your server in the right pane and choose Properties. When the properties dialog box opens, click the Remote Install tab.

Step 6

We don't really need to make any changes to the configuration settings you will find in this dialog box, but we can take a look around. Begin by clicking the Verify Server button. When the Check Server Wizard dialog box appears, click Next and wait for the verification to finish, which usually takes only a few seconds, if that. If any problems are found, check with your instructor. You may need to reinstall RIS. Otherwise, click Finish and then Done.

Caution: If you click Cancel instead of Finish, you will pause the Remote Installation Service and clients will not be able to use it. If you think you may have done this, simply verify the server again and be sure to click Finish and Done when the process is complete.

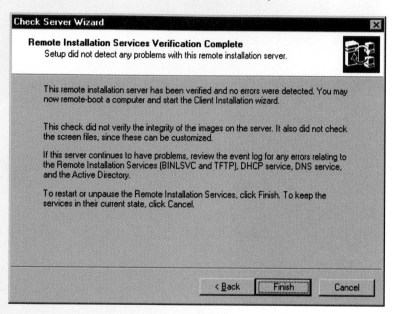

Step 7

Click the Advanced Settings button to display the Remote Installation Services Properties dialog box and the New Clients tab. Without making any changes, try pulling down the selection list labeled Generate client computer names using. You may also click the Customize button to explore those options. Since we will prestage the client computer accounts, these settings will have no effect for now. Click OK twice to close the two dialog boxes and then close Active Directory Users and Computers.

 Cross Check

Configuring RIS

After we got RIS installed, we made a number of configuration adjustments to modify the way it works. Take a moment to review what we've discussed and answer the following questions:

1. What configuration options were available through Choice Options in the Group Policy Object Editor?

2. What configuration options were available through the Remote Install tab of the server's properties dialog box?

■ Performing a Remote Installation of Windows XP Professional

It'd be a real waste to go through all the work we've done to prepare a flat image of Windows XP Professional and not use it to install the OS to a client computer. However, before we can do the actual installation, there are just a few things we need to get straight in terms of the client requirements and preparations.

RIS Client Requirements

The obvious requirement for installing an OS image to a client computer using RIS is that the client must meet the minimum system requirements for the OS. That part's easy, right? However, the trickier problem is making sure that the computer can access the RIS server even if no OS is installed. The secret to that little stunt lies with the NIC.

PXE-Enabled NICs

The term **Preboot Execution Environment (PXE)** describes a technology that works in conjunction with NICs to enable a computer to essentially boot from the network even when no operating system is present on the local hard drive. On computers that support PXE, it's possible to configure the NIC as a boot device, just as is normally done with the CD drive, hard drive, and floppy drive. On machines configured to use the NIC in this way, pressing the F12 key when prompted causes the computer's NIC to request a connection to the network and download specialized booting and configuration files. Thus PXE provides an ideal way to take a client computer with no OS and connect it to an RIS server to download and install one.

There are a few potential problems when attempting to use PXE to connect to an RIS server. The most obvious of these is that PXE has only been around since 1998 and there are still some relatively new computers, especially cheaper models, that don't support it at all. In such cases, you might be able to upgrade the NIC and the motherboard's BIOS to support PXE. However, in most cases, you just won't be able to use PXE at all. It is possible to make a boot disk that substitutes for PXE, but it supports only 32 models of NICs. Chances are pretty slim that it will work considering the number of different NICs out there! However, if you do need to create one, use the program **rbfg.exe**, which is located in R:\RemoteInstall\Admin\i386, where R is the remote install volume you created earlier. The dialog box you see in Figure 10.9 leads you right through the process in a matter of seconds.

Another issue when trying to use PXE, assuming the client computer supports it, is that the computer may not be configured to boot from the NIC at all. In such a case, consult the computer's documentation for directions on how to access the CMOS setup utility. Although every CMOS setup is different, if the motherboard's BIOS supports booting from the NIC, there should be a setting to move the NIC to the head of the boot order. After the new OS has been installed, simply rerun the setup and

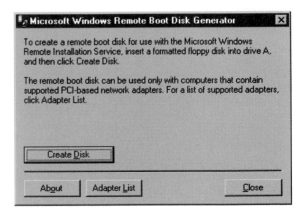

• **Figure 10.9** The Microsoft Windows Remote Boot Disk Generator

remove the NIC from the boot order. Even when the NIC is first in the boot order, it's still normally necessary to press F12 to actually boot from the network, so if you forget to remove it from the boot sequence, it will eventually default to the next boot device.

Prestaging a Computer Account

As we've already mentioned, we need to prestage our client computer, which means we need to create a computer account for it as a managed computer. Managed computer accounts require that we enter the Globally Unique Identifier (GUID) of the NIC in the computer. On most modern computers, the GUID is located on a sticker somewhere on the computer. However, as with anything, there are exceptions. For instance, the system I'm using in my lab seems to lack that lovely little sticker, so I had to get tricky!

If you have trouble finding the GUID, you could try booting the machine after you've moved the NIC to the head of the boot sequence. In most cases, after a brief pause, the NIC's MAC address and GUID will be displayed on the screen as it tries to boot from the network. As soon as you see this, press the PAUSE key on your keyboard, which will stop the boot process, and write down all 32 characters as carefully as you can. Don't bother with the hyphens; Windows doesn't want them when we create the account. However, do make sure you can read your own handwriting. Mine's so bad I misread three different characters the first time I tried to create the account! We'll use this GUID in the next Step-by-Step to create the managed computer account.

The Product Key

There's one last thing we need to do if we want to make the RIS installation as automated as possible, and that's to provide the OS with its product key so that the user doesn't have to type it in. In cases where you are using a single license copy of an OS, this step isn't necessary, because you can use the product key only once, legally, and making it a part of the RIS installation process takes at least as long as it would to type it in during the installation. However, in those cases where a company has purchased a volume license to an OS along with a Volume Licensing Key (VLK), the VLK is usable by each copy that is installed. By making the VLK a part of the automated installation, we assure that our users won't need to interact with the installation at all, after it's started, until it's time to log on to the new OS.

To allow RIS to fill in the product key automatically, we need to add it to the answer file for the image we will be installing. This answer file, which by default is named **ristndrd.sif**, is located in R:\RemoteInstall\Setup\English\Images*yourfoldername*\i386\templates, where R is the letter of the RIS volume and *yourfoldername* is the name of the folder to which you saved the image. Simply use Notepad to open this file, locate the [UserData] section, and add the line ProductID=*XXXXX-XXXXX-XXXXX-XXXXX-XXXXX*, with your product key in place of the Xs as shown in Figure 10.10. Save the file and you're good to go!

The "sif" extension associated with answer files stands for "setup information file," which makes a lot of sense!

```
ristndrd.sif - Notepad
File  Edit  Format  View  Help
[data]
floppyless = "1"
msdosinitiated = "1"
OriSrc = "\\%SERVERNAME%\RemInst\%INSTALLPATH%\%MACHINETYPE%"
OriTyp = "4"
LocalSourceOnCD = 1
DisableAdminAccountOnDomainJoin = 1

[SetupData]
OsLoadOptions = "/noguiboot /fastdetect"
SetupSourceDevice =
"\Device\LanmanRedirector\%SERVERNAME%\RemInst\%INSTALLPATH%"

[Unattended]
OemPreinstall = no
FileSystem = LeaveAlone
ExtendOEMPartition = 0
TargetPath = \WINDOWS
OemSkipEula = yes
InstallFilesPath =
"\\%SERVERNAME%\RemInst\%INSTALLPATH%\%MACHINETYPE%"
LegacyNIC = 1

[UserData]
FullName = "%USERFIRSTNAME% %USERLASTNAME%"
OrgName = "%ORGNAME%"
ComputerName = %MACHINENAME%
ProductID=w2h3w-g6tyk-tf9tc-pkt6b-pwrym

[GuiUnattended]
OemSkipWelcome = 1
OemSkipRegional = 1
TimeZone = %TIMEZONE%
AdminPassword = "*"


[Display]
```

• **Figure 10.10**   Adding the ProductID entry to an answer file

Installing an OS to a Client Machine Using RIS

Actually using RIS is really very simple, once you've configured everything correctly! Just be sure, before starting this Step-by-Step, that the client computer you are going to install Windows XP Professional on is compatible and prepared. It needs to be compatible in that it supports PXE as well as the other system requirements for Windows XP Professional. It needs to be prepared in that the NIC has been moved to the head of the boot order *and* you've verified that nothing important will be lost when the OS is installed. Keep in mind, an RIS installation completely wipes any existing information off the client computer's hard drive. Because of that, be sure you have your instructor's approval before beginning this exercise. Also keep in mind that this is an OS installation. As such, the process will probably take a minimum of 30–45 minutes to complete, depending on the speed of the network. However, your interaction should be needed for only the first 5 minutes or so and at the end.

To complete this Step-by-Step, you will need

- A properly configured Windows Server 2003 Domain Controller with RIS installed

- A client computer compatible with Windows XP Professional. This computer must have a PXE-enabled NIC installed. The NIC should be the first device in the boot sequence for the client computer.

- The GUID for the client computer's NIC

- A network connection between the client PC and the server that does *not* cross a router. A simple connection through a hub will do fine

- The product activation key for the copy of Windows XP Professional from which the flat image was made

- Access to an administrator-level account for the domain

Step 1

Since we need to prestage the client computer, we need to begin at the server. Open Active Directory Users and Computers by clicking Start | Administrative Tools | Active Directory Users and Computers.

Step 2

For this exercise, we will create the computer account in the Computers container. Right-click the container in the left pane and choose New | Computer.

Step 3

Enter **RISTEST** for the computer's name. Click the Change button so that we can make sure even non-administrator accounts will be able to join the computer to the domain. Enter **domain users** in the text box; then click OK and then Next to continue.

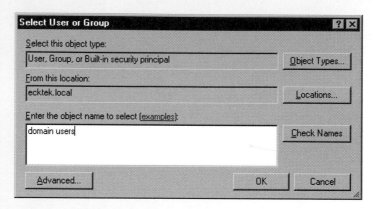

Step 4

Check the check box for This is a managed computer and enter the GUID in the text box. Case does not matter, but do not use hyphens. Windows will add the hyphens and enclose the number in a set of curly braces {} later. You could type it like that yourself, but it's extra keystrokes and I'm lazy, remember? Click Next to continue. If you can't click Next, check your GUID. You're either missing a character or two or have extra characters.

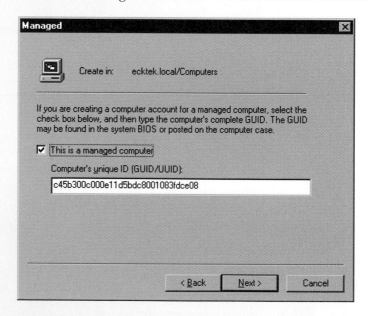

Step 5

You can either allow the computer to use any RIS server or assign it to one in particular. On larger networks, you can use this setting to help balance the load among several RIS servers. In our lab, the default, which is any server, will do just fine. Click Next and then Finish.

| Step 6 | While we're still on the server, let's go ahead and add the product key to the answer file for our image. Open Notepad by clicking Start | All Programs | Accessories | Notepad. |

| Step 7 | Click File | Open. Navigate to your RIS volume. Open the following folders in order: RemoteInstall | Setup | English | Images | *yourimagefolder* | i386 | templates. Choose All Files from the Files of Type selection list. Double-click ristndrd.sif to open it. |

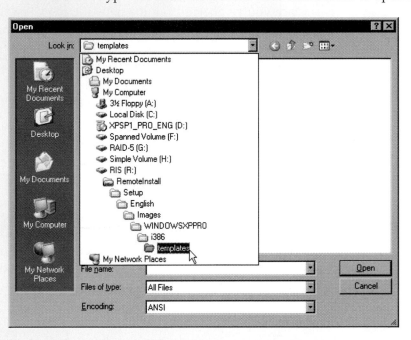

| Step 8 | Locate the [UserData] section of the file. Add the line **ProductID=XXXXX-XXXXX-XXXXX-XXXXX-XXXXX** to the end of this session. Save and close the file. |

Step 9

Now that the account is set up and the answer file is edited, turn on the client machine and watch for the prompt to press F12 to boot from the network. If you miss it, just turn the computer off and back on to try again. It is frequently hard to see the prompt the first time if the monitor has not yet warmed up. If you're still having trouble, try just tapping the F12 key every few seconds as the computer boots. That will usually catch it for sure.

Step 10

Once you've booted from the network, the Client Installation Wizard opening screen should appear. This is the program used by RIS to enable the client machine to copy over the necessary files for installing the OS image. Read the information and press ENTER to continue.

Step 11

Enter the username and password of a domain account. Use TAB to move between the fields and press ENTER when you're done.

Step 12

Choose Automatic Setup and press ENTER. Read the warning about all of the hard drive's data being deleted and then press ENTER again to continue.

Step 13

Read the summary screen and press ENTER when you're ready. From here, it's mostly a matter of waiting until the computer prompts you to log on to Windows XP. After about 10 minutes, the setup program will reboot the computer to go from text mode to graphics mode, but even that doesn't require your intervention. The entire process should take between 30 and 45 minutes.

Step 14

When the client computer finally boots into Windows XP, press CTRL-ALT-DELETE to log on. Click the Options button and change the Log on to a selection list to show the domain of the server. Log on with the same account you used to start the RIS process. Congratulations! You performed your first RIS installation! Go ahead and log back off for now. We'll need to log on as a domain administrator in the next Step-by-Step.

■ Creating an Image from a Reference Computer

As you might recall from way back at the beginning of this chapter, RIS can actually create two types of images. Flat images, which we've been working with, are great for automating the installation of OSs to client machines, but they don't do much more than that. However, our other option allows us to go much further in customizing the image and essentially allows us to clone one computer to many others so that they all have the same setup.

RIPrep Images

A **RIPrep image** is so named because it's created by the **Remote Installation Preparation Wizard**. Unlike a flat image, a RIPrep image is not based on the installation CD for an OS. A RIPrep image is

---

☑ Cross Check

Installing a Flat Image on a Client Computer

As we discussed the process of using RIS to install a flat image on a client computer, we introduced some new terms and concepts. Take a moment to review the material and then answer these questions:

1. What is PXE and what is its purpose in terms of RIS?

2. What does it mean to prestage a client? What information is necessary to be able to do so?

prepared from a client computer, called a **reference computer**, which becomes the model for all computers that then use the RIPrep image. The idea is that you install the OS on the reference computer, along with any applications you'd like your client computers to have, make any necessary configuration changes, and then create a RIPrep image that can be used to duplicate the setup on other computers.

The really nifty thing is that these other computers do *not* have to be identical to the reference computer. The Remote Installation Preparation Wizard removes any information from the image that's particular to the reference machine. As long as the destination clients have a **hardware abstraction layer (HAL)** that's compatible with the HAL of the reference computer, the image will install. Of course, that begs the question: what's a HAL?

The Hardware Abstraction Layer (HAL)

The HAL is part of the operating system that lets the OS interact with the computer's hardware in an "abstract," or general, way. For example, the HAL lets the OS talk to the video card as "the video card" in general terms rather than as a "NeoVisionTek Ultra XGA SupraMag Xti25000 Model 38c Revision B" video card. Okay, I made that one up, but you get the idea: being able to deal with the hardware on a more general basis can be more efficient than trying to communicate individually with each piece of hardware on its own terms.

Both the OS and device drivers initiate calls to, or communicate with, the HAL. In fact, it works as sort of an intermediary between the two.

The good news is that there are only a few different HALs out there that we have to worry about. That means that matching them up so that we can use RIPrep images isn't that hard. The four basic HAL types are Programmable Interrupt Controller (PIC) HAL; Advanced Configuration and Power Interface (ACPI) PIC HAL; Advanced Programmable Interrupt Controller (APIC) HAL; and the Advanced Configuration and Power Interface (ACPI) APIC HAL. In addition, the APIC HAL and the ACPI APIC HAL each have a uniprocessor version and a multiprocessor version. It really doesn't matter what the difference between each of these HAL types is. All we need to know is that if we create a RIPrep image on a computer that uses one type, what other HAL types will support that image? Of course if the image is installed on a computer that uses the same HAL as the reference computer, there's no problem. However, there are also some cross-compatibilities, which are listed in Table 10.1.

Table 10.1	HAL Compatibilities for RIPrep Images
Images Created on Computers with a. . .	**. . .Can Be Used on Computers with. . .**
Programmable Interrupt Controller (PIC) HAL	Same All other HALs are compatible
Advanced Configuration and Power Interface (ACPI) PIC HAL	Same Uni- and multiprocessor ACPI APIC HALs
Advanced Programmable Interrupt Controller (APIC) HAL—uniprocessor	Same ACPI APIC uniprocessor HALs
Advanced Programmable Interrupt Controller (APIC) HAL—multiprocessor	Same APIC uniprocessor HALs
Advanced Configuration and Power Interface (ACPI) APIC HAL—uniprocessor	Same
Advanced Configuration and Power Interface (ACPI) APIC HAL—multiprocessor	Same ACPI APIC uniprocessor HALs

Table 10.2   HAL Versions and Corresponding Original Filenames

HAL Version	Original Filename
Programmable Interrupt Controller (PIC) HAL	hal.dll
Advanced Configuration and Power Interface (ACPI) PIC HAL	halacpi.dll
Advanced Programmable Interrupt Controller (APIC) HAL—uniprocessor	halapic.dll
Advanced Programmable Interrupt Controller (APIC) HAL—multiprocessor	halmps.dll
Advanced Configuration and Power Interface (ACPI) APIC HAL—uniprocessor	halaacpi.dll
Advanced Configuration and Power Interface (ACPI) APIC HAL—multiprocessor	halmacpi.dll

To find out which HAL your computer is using, find the **hal.dll** file, which is located in the System32 subfolder of your Windows folder. Right-click the file, choose Properties, click the Version tab, and select the Original File name. The list of original filenames, and the HALs they represent, are listed in Table 10.2.

Operating System Considerations

RIPrep images support the same operating systems as flat images, with one exception: you cannot create a RIPrep image from Windows Server 2003 64-bit Enterprise Edition. For your review, I've summarized the OS support for both types of images in Table 10.3.

Table 10.3   RIS Image Support for Various Operating Systems

Operating System	Images Supported (Flat and/or RIPrep)
Windows Server 2003 64-bit Enterprise Edition	Flat Only
Windows Server 2003 Enterprise Edition	Both
Windows Server 2003 Standard Edition	Both
Windows Server 2003 Web Edition	N/A
Windows XP Professional	Both
Windows 2000 Advanced Server	Both
Windows 2000 Server	Both
Windows 2000 Professional	Both

Step-hy-Step 10.5

Creating a RIPrep Image of a Reference Computer

The process of installing from a RIPrep image is not appreciably different from using a flat image. However, the process of creation does differ in a few significant ways, which makes it worthwhile that we try making one for ourselves. Although RIPrep images are usually created from preconfigured reference machines with programs installed and configuration changes made, those things do not change the method for creating the image, so we will forgo them for now. Of course, if you like, you may certainly try installing a few applications before

creating this image and then try using the image to set up a client on your own!

To complete this Step-by-Step, you will need

- A properly configured Windows Server 2003 Domain Controller with RIS installed

- A client computer with Windows XP Professional installed. The client computer from the preceding Step-by-Step would be ideal.

- A network connection between the client PC and the server that does *not* cross a router. A simple connection through a hub will do fine.

- The product activation key for the copy of Windows XP Professional installed on the reference computer

- Access to an administrator-level account for the domain

Caution: This Step-by-Step will take at least one-half hour to complete, if not longer! Be sure that sufficient lab time exists before beginning!

Step 1

Use the administrator account for the domain to log on to the server from the client computer. RIPrep images can be created only from the client and only by an administrator.

Step 2

Click Start | Run. Enter the command ***yourservername*\reminst\admin\ i386\riprep.exe**. Click OK.

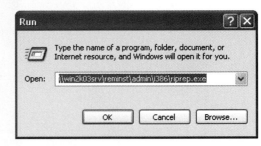

Step 3

When the Remote Installation Preparation Wizard starts, read over the text and then click Next to continue. Confirm that your RIS server's name appears in the next dialog box and then click Next again.

Step 4

Enter a name for the folder that will hold the RIPrep image. The name really doesn't matter, but I usually try to make it descriptive. In this case, I used **XPRIPREPTEST** so that I'd remember that this was just a test image. Click Next to continue.

Step 5

Fill in the Friendly description and Help text boxes however you like. Since this is a simple test image, I entered **Windows XP Professional RIPrep Image Test** and **This is a test** for mine. However, remember that, for a real image, this information is important because it is what the client sees when they are choosing which image to install when there are more than one. Click Next to continue when you are finished.

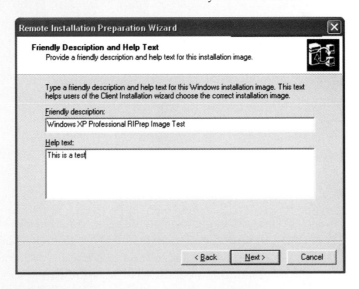

Step 6

The wizard will display a list of services that must be stopped before it can continue. Click Next and it will stop each of the services automatically. Once it is done, simply keep clicking Next to move through the summary and completion screens until the process actually begins. Eventually, after 15–20 minutes, the client computer will shut down.

This actually completes the building of the image, but we have some work left to do at the client to prepare it either for continued use or for building additional images. The nature of the RIPrep image creation process sort of requires us to "reset" the reference computer.

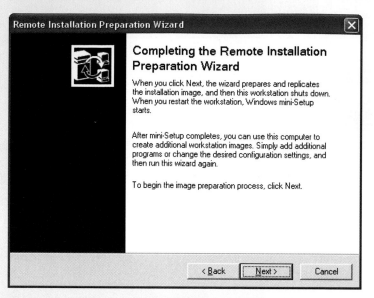

Step 7

Turn the client computer back on. After a minute, or so, a mini-setup for Windows XP will begin. When the Windows XP Setup Wizard appears, click Next to continue.

Step 8

The first two steps of the mini-setup ask you to accept the license and the regional and language settings. After moving through those two screens, you'll be asked to enter your name and the name of your organization. Enter at least your name and then click Next to continue.

Step 9

Enter the product key and click Next to continue. Setup will then suggest a computer name, which you can accept, and ask you to enter and confirm a password for the Administrator account. This is the password for the local administrator account, not an account on the domain. This password does *not* need to follow the complexity requirements Window Server 2003 demands. Enter and confirm the password and then click Next to continue.

Step 10

Modify the date and time settings to match your locale and click Next to continue. After a brief pause, the wizard will ask you to choose your networking settings. Click Next to accept the default Typical settings.

Step 11

The next step gives you the opportunity to join either a workgroup or a domain. Choose domain and enter the name of your domain. You will be prompted to enter a user name and password of an account authorized to join the computer to the domain. Enter the user name and password of an administrator-level account on your server and click OK. Be prepared to wait a minute or two while the computer is joined to the domain. The client computer may seem frozen, but it isn't.

Step 12	When prompted, click Finish to complete the wizard and restart the computer. When the computer reboots, you'll be greeted by the Network Identification Wizard. Click Next to continue.
Step 13	Enter the user name of your personal user account in the domain and the name of your domain and click Next to continue. In the following step, you're asked to choose the access level for the account. Your choices are Standard user, Restricted user, or Other. Leave the default option, Standard user, selected and click Next and then Finish. This will give your domain account permission to access resources on the local computer.
Step 14	Log on to the domain using your personal domain account to verify that the client computer is working properly. Shut down when you are finished.

Installing from a RIPrep Image

Because of the time involved, and the similarity to installing from a flat image, we aren't going to walk through the process of installing from a RIPrep image. However, there is one small point of difference that you should be aware of.

You'll recall that, in order to completely automate the process of installing from a flat image, we edited the ristndrd.sif answer file to include the Product Key. For RIPrep images, we can do the same thing, but we have to work with a different file. The answer file for RIPrep images is **riprep.sif**, and like the answer file for flat images, it is located in *R*:\RemoteInstall\Setup\English\Images*yourimagefolder*\i386\Templates, where *R* is the letter of your RIS volume and *yourimagefolder* is the name of the RIPrep image folder. Although the name of the file is different, it gets modified in the same way: simply add the line ProductID=*XXXXX-XXXXX-XXXXX-XXXXX* to the [UserData] section and save the file. From there, you're good to go!

Cross Check

RIPrep Images

In spite of their obvious similarities, RIPrep images are quite different in both their creation and their application from flat images. Take a moment to review what we've covered and answer the following questions:

1. How is the creation of a RIPrep image different from the process used to create a flat image?

2. What is the purpose of RIPrep images? How is that different from the purpose of flat images?

Inside Information

RIS Limitations

Now that you've had a chance to work with RIS, it's a good time to talk briefly about some of its limitations. As with anything, there are a few areas where RIS may not meet your expectations, or your needs. Here's a partial list of those limitations:

- *RIS can support only about 75 simultaneous client connections per RIS server.*

- *RIS cannot be used with wireless network cards, a limitation that becomes increasingly problematic as more and more businesses shift from desktops to portable computers.*

- *RIS cannot be used to duplicate a domain controller and may not completely duplicate a fully configured server.*

- *RIS cannot work with encrypted files, nor can it duplicate file and folder security settings.*

- *RIS cannot be used to upgrade an existing OS. That must be done manually or through other methods.*

■ Chapter Summary

After reading this chapter and completing the Step-by-Step tutorials and Try This! exercises, you should understand the following facts about installing, configuring, and using Remote Installation Services in Windows Server 2003.

Configure a Server for Remote Installation Services

■ RIS allows images of either operating system installation CDs or existing client machines with installed programs and configuration settings. These images can then be installed on other client computers over the network.

■ Microsoft recommends that RIS servers maintain a separate volume for images of at least 4GB in size formatted with the NTFS file system.

■ All versions of Windows Server 2003, with the exception of Web Edition, can act as RIS servers. All versions of the Windows 2000 server operating system were also able to act as RIS servers.

■ RIS requires that the network have Active Directory installed and that DNS and DHCP be running on at least one server.

■ RIS servers need to be authorized through DHCP if the server is not already authorized as a DHCP server.

Configure Remote Installation Services

■ As part of the process of configuring RIS, the first flat image is created. A flat image is an image of an operating system's installation CD.

■ RIS supports flat images for all editions and versions of Windows Server 2003, with the exception of the Datacenter Edition, and all server versions of Windows 2000. Windows XP Professional and Windows 2000 Professional are also supported.

■ All images still require proper licensing. Volume licensing is available and may include a Volume Licensing Key (VLK) to ease the creation of answer files for unattended installations.

■ RIS options available through the Group Policy Object Editor include Automatic Setup, Custom Setup, Restart Setup, and Tools. Each of these options can be enabled, disabled, or not configured.

■ The Remote Install tab of the server's properties dialog box can be used to verify the server, show the RIS clients, or access advanced settings.

■ The Advanced settings dialog box of the RIS server allows configuration of the client computer's account name and location, image management, and tool management.

Perform a Remote Installation of Windows XP Professional

■ Clients of an RIS server should have PXE-enabled NICs that allow them to boot from the network. In rare cases, a boot disk created with the rbfg.exe utility may allow non-PXE clients to use RIS.

■ Clients with PXE-enabled NICs must have the NIC moved to the head of the boot sequence to be able to boot from the network.

■ Prestaging a client computer is accomplished by creating a managed computer account for the client prior to using RIS to install an image. To create a managed computer account, you need the GUID for the NIC in the client computer.

■ Adding the Product Key to the ristndrd.sif answer file allows client computers to install a flat image over RIS with no user intervention.

Create an Image from a Reference Computer

■ An RIPrep image is created from an existing reference computer by the Remote Installation Preparation Wizard. A RIPrep image may include installed software and configuration settings from the reference computer.

■ The client machine that installs from a RIPrep image must have a HAL that is compatible with that of the reference computer.

■ The HAL allows the operating system to communicate in an abstract, or general, way with the computer's hardware.

■ RIPrep images are not supported by the 64-bit version of Windows Server 2003 Enterprise Edition.

- Installing from a RIPrep image is similar to installing from a flat image. However, the answer file is riprep.sif, instead of ristndrd.sif.

■ Key Terms List

authorize *(296)*
flat image *(298)*
hal.dll *(316)*
Hardware Abstraction Layer (HAL) *(315)*
Preboot Execution Environment (PXE) *(309)*
prestage *(304)*

rbfg.exe *(309)*
reference computer *(315)*
Remote Installation Preparation Wizard *(314)*
Remote Installation Services (RIS) *(295)*
reparse point *(296)*
RIPrep image *(314)*

riprep.sif *(319)*
ristndrd.sif *(310)*
Single Instance Store Service (SIS) *(296)*
SIS Common Store Folder *(296)*
SIS groveler agent *(296)*
Volume Licensing Key (VLK) *(300)*

■ Key Terms Quiz

Use terms from the Key Terms list to complete the sentences that follow. Don't use the same term more than once. Not all terms will be used.

1. The answer file for a flat image is _____.

2. We _____ a computer when the account is created prior to using RIS.

3. If an RIS server was not already a DHCP server, it is necessary to _____ it through the DHCP console.

4. A RIPrep image is an image of a _____.

5. When installing a RIPrep image to a client computer, the client must have a _____ that is compatible with the reference computer.

6. If you have to make a boot disk for a non–PXE enabled NIC, use the _____ utility.

7. The groveler creates a _____ to point the way to the SIS Common Store Folder for duplicate files.

8. _____ is the answer file for an image based on a reference computer.

9. Groveler is part of the _____.

10. In order to boot from the network, the client computer's NIC must support the _____.

■ Multiple-Choice Quiz

1. Where do you place the ProductID= entry in an answer file?
   a. [SetupData]
   b. [Unattended]
   c. [UserData]
   d. [GuiUnattended]

2. How many NICs are currently supported by the boot disk created with rbfg.exe?
   a. All
   b. 32

   c. 12
   d. Depends on the client machine

3. Which file do you check the properties of to determine a computer's supported HAL?
   a. halacpi.dll
   b. halapic.dll
   c. halaacpi.dll
   d. hal.dll

4. Which key do you press to boot from the network?

   a. F1

   b. F12

   c. F8

   d. F11

5. A GUID is a hexadecimal number that is _____ characters long.

   a. 64

   b. 32

   c. 24

   d. 12

6. PXE was introduced in

   a. 1995

   b. 1998

   c. 2000

   d. 2003

7. The New Clients tab of the RIS Advanced Properties dialog box bases computer names on _____ by default.

   a. User name

   b. First name, last name

   c. Last name, first name

   d. GUID

8. Answer files are inside the _____ folder.

   a. images

   b. templates

   c. i386

   d. English

9. RIS can support about _____ simultaneous connections.

   a. 25

   b. 50

   c. 75

   d. Depends on the capacity of the network

10. RIS cannot create an image of

    a. Windows 2000 Server

    b. Windows 98

    c. Windows XP Professional

    d. Windows 2000 Advanced Server

11. RIPrep images cannot be created from a computer running

    a. Windows Server 2003 Enterprise Edition 64-bit

    b. Windows XP Professional

    c. Windows Server 2003 Web Edition

    d. Windows 2000 Advanced Server

12. RIS was first introduced in

    a. Windows Server 2003

    b. Windows 2000 Server

    c. Windows NT

    d. Windows 98

13. You authorize a server through

    a. Active Directory Users and Computers

    b. DHCP

    c. DNS

    d. Group Policy

14. Which of the following is *not* necessary for RIS to be installed and function?

    a. PXE

    b. Active Directory

    c. DNS

    d. DHCP

15. Microsoft recommends that the RIS volume be at least _____.

    a. 8GB

    b. 6GB

    c. 4GB

    d. 2GB

■ Essay Quiz

1. Your supervisor is concerned that once RIS is installed, there's no way to stop clients from using it and the network will become saturated with RIS traffic. Explain at least two ways that you can prevent this.

2. Explain the benefits of using flat images, as you understand them.

3. Explain the benefits of using RIPrep images, as you understand them.

4. A user with a known PXE-enabled computer can't seem to boot from the network. Explain two possible reasons for this.

5. Explain how RIS tries to minimize the disk space used by images.

Lab Projects

• Lab Project 10.1

Research two or three providers of computers that would be appropriate choices for client machines on a network. Focus on whether or not the computers they are offering come with NICs that support PXE. Check at several different price levels to see if such cards are available at all levels or only in higher-priced machines. Are PXE-enabled NICs available in consumer-level machines, or just computers intended for business customers? Report your results to the class and your instructor.

• Lab Project 10.2

For this project, use the client computer you installed the flat image on in the chapter. Install one or more applications on the computer. Create a RIPrep image of this reference computer. After the image is complete, connect your client computer to another student's server, and vice versa. Try installing their customized RIPrep image on your client. Report your success, and any difficulties, to the class and your instructor.

• Lab Project 10.3

For this project, use the RIPrep image you created from your client computer in Lab Project 10.2 to restore your client to its original state. You may leave the installed programs alone or uninstall them as your instructor directs.

The Best Policy: Managing Computers and Users Through Group Policy

"Dogbert: I'm going back to my old job as a network systems administrator.
Dilbert: Why?
Dogbert: I'm attracted by the potential for reckless abuse of power."

—SCOTT ADAMS

In this chapter, you will learn how to:

- **Explain the capabilities of group policy**
- **Manage security using group policy**
- **Manage users' environments using group policy**
- **Manage group policy implementation and interaction**

When it comes to managing the way users experience a network, nothing comes close to the level of power offered by group policies. Through group policies, we can change numerous settings that affect the security of our network; the ability of users to access files, programs, and services; and even the nature of the user's desktop environment while using client computers.

In this chapter, we will introduce some of the more commonly used aspects of group policies. We will begin by taking a closer look at just what group policies can do and how they are applied. Once we're familiar with the basics, we'll try our hand at controlling security settings and the user's environment by modifying some group policy settings for our domain. Finally, we'll take a look at how to manage the actual implementation of group policy and the interaction of multiple group policies and test the group policy settings we modified.

Understanding the Capabilities of Group Policy

As we've mentioned from time to time in earlier chapters, group policy allows administrators to create a customized collection of configuration settings that can be applied to domains, sites, OUs, and even individual computers. Each unique collection of settings is called a **group policy object (GPO)** and each GPO is linked to its **scope of management (SOM)**, which is the domain, site, OU, or computer to which the GPO applies.

Some policies are created automatically. For instance, every computer running Windows Server 2003, Windows XP, or Windows 2000 has a **local policy** that affects only that machine. When Active Directory is installed, a **default domain policy** is created to handle the overall policies for the domain and a **default domain controllers policy** is created to manage settings for any DCs in the domain. The default domain policy is linked to the domain itself, while the default domain controllers policy is linked to the domain controllers OU.

Administrators can edit existing GPOs or create new ones to modify desired settings. In this section, we'll take a look at the tools administrators use to create and edit GPOs, discuss the basic settings categories we can work with, and create a new GPO. Later in the chapter, we'll modify some of the settings of this new GPO and then see how to implement it and manage the interaction between it and the existing GPOs.

> We'll work with a new, blank GPO in this chapter so that we can easily reverse our changes when we're finished by removing the link to it.

Group Policy Tools

The most commonly used tool for working with GPOs is the **Group Policy Object Editor** shown in Figure 11.1. Like many of the administrative tools in Windows Server 2003, the Group Policy Object Editor is a snap-in for the Microsoft Management Console (MMC). Windows Server 2003 automatically creates two specialized MMC consoles when Active Directory is installed for dealing with some of the settings for the default domain and default domain controllers policies. These consoles are accessed through the Administrative Tools menu. However, these consoles provide access to the security policies for only those GPOs, not the entire collection of settings.

There are actually several methods for accessing the Group Policy Object Editor. One method is through the properties of the SOM the GPO is linked to. For instance, to work with the GPO for the domain, you can access the domain's properties through Active Directory Users and Computers. From there, as shown in Figure 11.2, you can use the Edit button on the Group Policy tab to open the Group Policy Object Editor for the selected GPO. This method is also useful for managing existing GPOs, which we'll take a look at later in this chapter.

Another method for working with GPOs is to create a new Group Policy Object Editor console, which we'll be

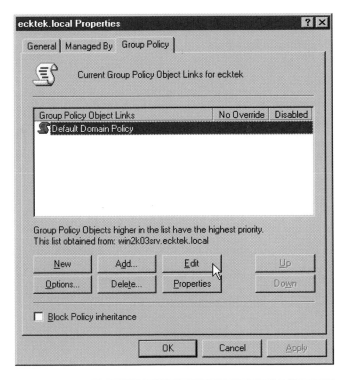

● **Figure 11.1**   The Group Policy tab of the Domain Properties dialog box

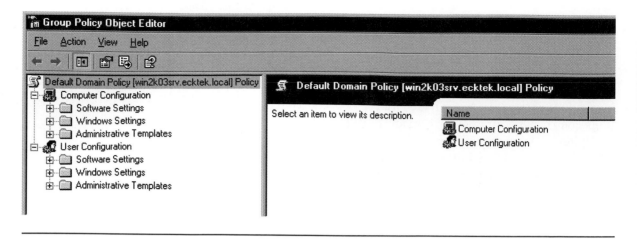

● **Figure 11.2**   The Group Policy Object Editor Console

The Group Policy Object Editor console is the only method for accessing the local computer policy. However, this policy rarely needs to be edited in a networked environment.

If you would like to download and try the GPMC, simply go to http://www.microsoft.com/windowsserver2003/gpmc/default.mspx and follow the links to download and install the utility. However, wait to do so until the end of this chapter.

doing in the next Step-by-Step. This method adds the Group Policy Object Editor snap-in to the Microsoft Management console and allows you to choose to edit an existing GPO or to create a new one.

The newest tool for working with GPOs is the **Group Policy Management Console (GPMC)**, shown in Figure 11.3. The GPMC provides a single, unified interface for managing all aspects of all existing group policies within the domain and also provides tools for analyzing, and controlling, the interaction of multiple policies. However, GPMC is *not* actually part of Windows Server 2003. It is an additional tool that can be downloaded at no charge from Microsoft's web site. However, all actual policy editing is still done through the Group Policy Object Editor, with the difference that the editor is launched directly from within the GPMC. Additionally, installing the GPMC disables the Group Policy tab of the properties dialog box for domains, sites, and OUs. As such, it can be sort of confusing for those administrators who are already familiar with group policy from working with Windows 2000. For these reasons, we're not going to focus on GPMC in this text. However, it is a nifty tool and worth a look once you're comfortable with the more traditional methods for managing GPOs. Consider giving it a try after you finish this chapter.

Try This!

Opening the Group Policy Object Editor from the Command Line

The command **gpedit.msc** can be used to easily open the Group Policy Object Editor for the local computer from the command line. Try this:

1. Click Start | Run.

2. Enter the command **gpedit.msc** and click OK.

3. Browse through the local computer policy. Close the console when you are finished.

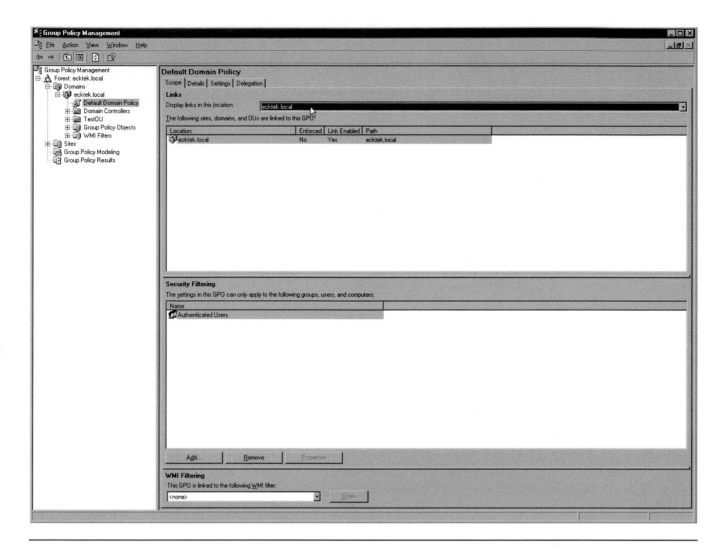

• **Figure 11.3**   The Group Policy Management Console

Group Policy Settings Categories

The bad news is that we can't discuss each and every one of the possible group policy settings; there are just too many! However, we can take a look at the general setting categories and get an idea of what types of settings they contain. Then, a bit later in the chapter, we'll take a closer look at some of the more commonly used settings.

You may have noticed in Figure 11.2 that the GPO settings are divided into computer configuration and user configuration settings. As the names imply, **computer configuration settings** focus on controlling aspects of the computer and its operating system, regardless of who the user is, while **user configuration settings** do the same for users, regardless of what computer they are using. The computer configuration settings are applied during the computer's boot process, prior to the appearance of the CTRL-ALT-DELETE prompt. The user configuration settings are applied after the user logs on and their account is validated.

Both computer configuration and user configuration settings are further divided into three subcategories, which are software settings, Windows settings, and administrative templates. Let's take a look at these subcategories and how they differ between computer and user configuration.

Software Settings

The **software settings** category is pretty darned simple. There's only one setting, for both computer and user configuration, called software installation, which does exactly what the name says it does! The software installation setting allows you to automatically deploy new software to either computers or users through the use of the **Windows Installer service** and a special file called a package.

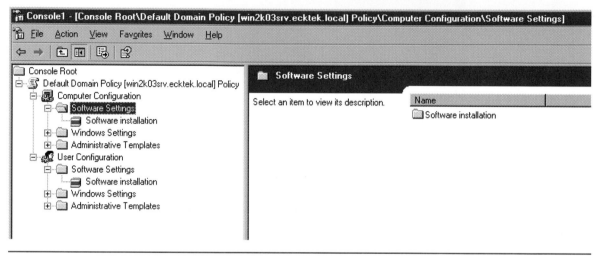

• Software Settings in the Group Policy Object Editor

A **package** is simply a file with the extension .msi, which includes the directions needed to properly install a software application. In many cases, the package file is provided by the software vendor, but it is also possible to create your own .msi files. When you deploy software using the software installation setting in group policy, the .msi file guides the client computer through the installation with little or no interaction needed from the user.

With the software installation feature of group policy, it is a relatively easy matter to roll out new software packages to select segments of the domain, without the need to dash from desktop to desktop with a load of installation CDs.

Windows Settings

The computer configuration **Windows settings** are used to configure startup and shutdown scripts and a whole slew of security settings. The scripts can be used to automate virus scans, maintenance programs, backups, or any number of other tasks that need to be run during either the startup or shutdown process. The security settings, some of which we will examine in detail in just a bit, provide extensive control over everything from how users log on to what programs they can run.

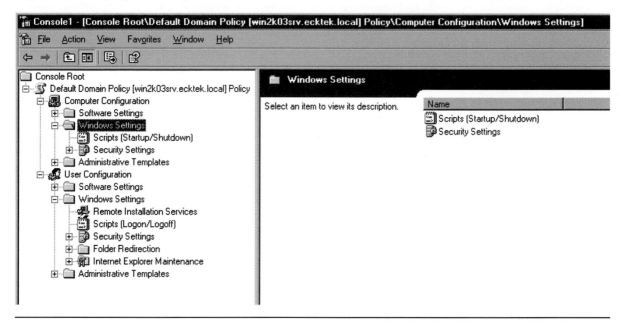

• Windows Settings and First Level Containers in the Group Policy Object Editor

The user configuration Windows settings also provide access to scripts, for when users log on and log off, and security settings, but far fewer security settings than those available under computer configuration. If you think about it, that makes a lot of sense. Security settings need to be applied to the computer *before* the user has logged on to be effective. Additionally, the user configuration Windows settings can be used to modify the behavior of RIS, as shown in Chapter 10, redirect several user folders to network locations, and perform a variety of maintenance tasks on Internet Explorer.

Administrative Templates

Although they vary, the **administrative templates settings** for both computer and user configuration allow for changes to the operating system's Registry. These settings can be used to change the desktop, modify the logon procedure, and even remove items from the Start menu or Control Panel. Remember earlier when I said there were just too many policy settings to discuss them all? Well, at last count, the administrative templates settings alone numbered 745! In fact, 200 of those settings are brand new for Windows Server 2003 and Windows XP. Now, remember our opening quote: it's possible to get a little power-mad with all these possibilities! However, these settings really can help improve the user's experience when they're used properly. You'll see what I mean a bit later when we explore a few of these settings in more detail.

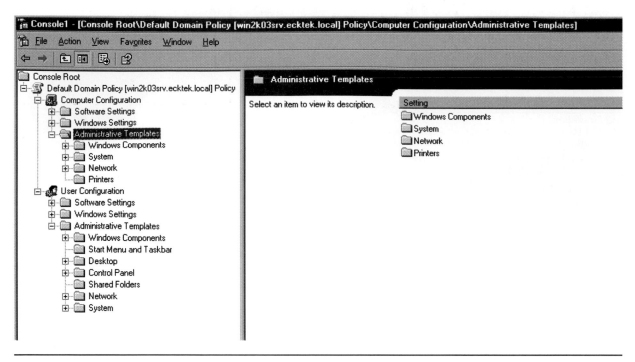

• Administrative Templates First Level Containers in the Group Policy Object Editor

Creating a New Group Policy Object and Opening the Group Policy Object Editor

Before we move on to discuss the various GPO settings, it makes sense to go ahead and create a new GPO, which will also open the Group Policy Object Editor so that you can "poke around" a bit. By creating a new GPO, we can easily try out different settings without worrying about permanently changing the existing policies. Once we have the policy created and the editor open, we'll save our console settings so that we can easily reopen it later when we need to.

To complete this Step-by-Step, you will need

- A properly configured Windows Server 2003 Domain Controller

- Access to an administrator-level account on the computer

Step 1
Click Start | Run and enter **mmc**. Click OK to open the Microsoft Management Console.

Step 2
Click File | Add/Remove Snap-in and click the Add button to open the Add Standalone Snap-in dialog box.

Scroll down the list and select Group Policy Object Editor. Click Add to open the Select Group Policy Object dialog box. We'll use this dialog box to create our new GPO. Click Browse.

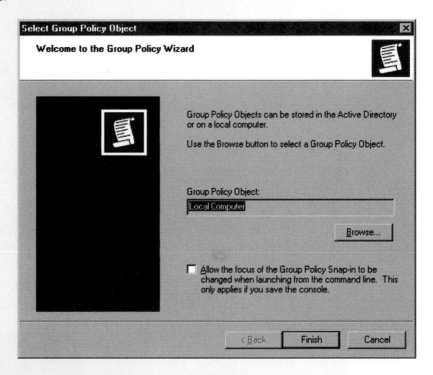

Click the middle of the three buttons to the right of the Look in selection list. This is the Create New Group Policy Object button. Name the new GPO **TestGPO** and click OK, Finish, Close, and OK in that order to close all remaining dialog boxes.

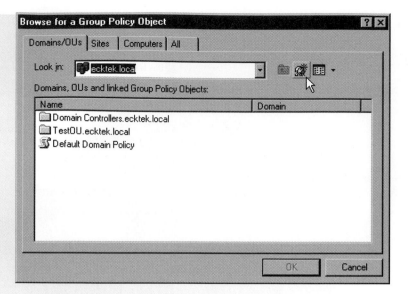

Step 5

Maximize both the console window and the inner snap-in window. Open the levels of the hierarchy until you can see at least the first level of containers under both computer configuration and user configuration. Adjust the width of the left pane so that you can see each of the entries in the hierarchy.

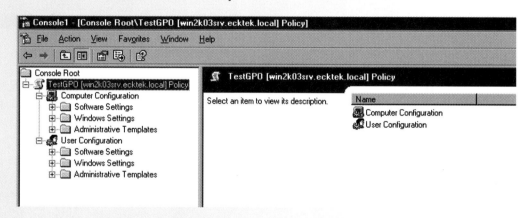

Step 6

Click File | Save. Click the Desktop button on the left side of the Save As dialog box. Name the console **TestGPO** and click Save. There will now be an icon on your desktop that you can use to reopen this console at need. You may leave the console open for now, if you will be continuing on into the next section of the chapter.

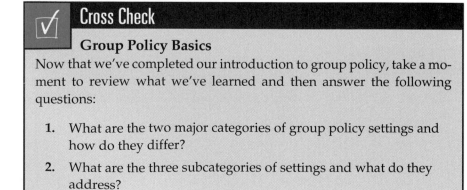

Cross Check

Group Policy Basics

Now that we've completed our introduction to group policy, take a moment to review what we've learned and then answer the following questions:

1. What are the two major categories of group policy settings and how do they differ?

2. What are the three subcategories of settings and what do they address?

Managing Security Using Group Policy

Some of the most important, and most commonly used, settings offered by Group Policy are those that deal with different aspects of security for the network. The importance of these settings is demonstrated by the fact that the two preconfigured Group Policy Object Editor consoles created by the installation of Active Directory *both* deal with the security settings of their respective GPOs. Let's delve a little deeper into what the some of these security settings are, before we jump in and make some adjustments of our own.

 Keep in mind that the default setting values we will be discussing are those of the default domain policy GPO. The GPO you created in Step-by-Step 11.1 has no settings configured at this time.

Security Settings

Although security settings can be found under the Windows settings category for both computer and user configurations, the most commonly used settings are those associated with computer configuration. Of these, the most commonly used are the account policies.

Account Policies

Account policies include password policies, account lockout policies, and Kerberos policies. Of the three, Kerberos policies rarely need to be modified. Kerberos security authenticates user accounts when users log on and allows them to request services from the server without further authentication. It is very rarely necessary, or desirable, to change Kerberos settings. However, both password policies and account lockout policies are frequently modified to either enhance or relax account security measures.

Password Policies   The **password policies** settings determine the rules for password creation and expiration. They are listed, with their default domain policy values, in Table 11.1. The most commonly changed settings are the maximum password age and the minimum password length. Some administrators shorten the age and increase the length to tighten security. When taken in conjunction with the password complexity requirements policy, this can be very effective. The enforce password history policy prevents users from recycling the same passwords over and over again. The default value of 24 is actually the maximum. Minimum password age is used to limit how often users can change their passwords. This prevents users from bypassing the history setting by quickly changing their password enough times to bypass the remembered passwords. The last setting, store passwords using reversible encryption, should not be used. It saves passwords in a form that is really no more secure than plain text, which greatly decreases security, as you can imagine! This setting exists only to provide compatibility for some applications that need to access the user's password for authentication. Fortunately, such programs are pretty rare.

Account Lockout Policies   Table 11.2 lists the **account lockout policies** and their default values. These policies control what happens when a user attempts to log on to an account with an incorrect password. By default, Windows Server 2003 does not lock users out of their accounts, regardless of how many failed attempts are made to enter a password. Administrators

Table 11.1	Password Policies and Their Default Domain Policy Settings
Policy	**Default Domain Policy Setting**
Enforce password history	24 passwords remembered
Maximum password age	42 days
Minimum password age	1 days
Minimum password length	7 characters
Passwords must meet complexity requirements	Enabled
Store passwords using reversible encryption	Disabled

Table 11.2	Account Lockout Policies and Their Default Domain Policy Settings
Policy	**Default Domain Policy Setting**
Account lockout duration	Not Defined
Account lockout threshold	0 invalid logon attempts
Reset account lockout counter after	Not Defined

who wish to enhance security, and prevent the guessing of passwords, configure the **account lockout threshold** for the number of attempts they wish to allow. When those attempts are used up, the **account lockout duration** controls how long that account will be made unavailable. The last setting, **reset account lockout counter after**, determines the time period during which attempts will be tracked. For instance, if it is set for five minutes, and the threshold is set to three, three failed attempts during five minutes will lock the account out for the amount of time specified by the account lockout duration setting.

Software Restriction Policies

Software restriction policies are one of the new features of Windows Server 2003, and a welcome one to many administrators. Through these policies, it is possible to block the running of specific programs or block the execution of programs in an entire directory. What's really neat about this feature is that it can be used to protect against e-mail viruses. By blocking the execution of programs for the folder the e-mail application stores attachments in, you can make it much less likely that a user will be able to open a virus-laden file. Of course, this isn't perfect protection; you should still have antivirus software running on all computers, but it is an added safety measure.

Software restriction policies can also target specific programs that have not even been installed yet. This is done by blocking the Registry entry for that program. When a user tries to install the software, the Registry entry for the application is recognized and the program is blocked.

Modifying Security and Software Restriction Policies

The procedure for making changes to the various policy settings of a GPO is pretty simple. However, the actual settings vary quite a bit, depending on what policy is being altered. In this Step-by-Step, we'll make some changes to a few of the policies we've just discussed. Later on, we'll test them out and see how they work.

To complete this Step-by-Step, you will need

- A properly configured Windows Server 2003 Domain Controller
- The new GPO created in Step-by-Step 11.1
- Access to an administrator-level account on the computer

Step 1

If necessary, reopen the TestGPO console. Open Computer Configuration | Windows Settings | Security Settings | Account Policies | Account Lockout Policy. We'll test out the security settings by setting up a brief lockout we can test later on.

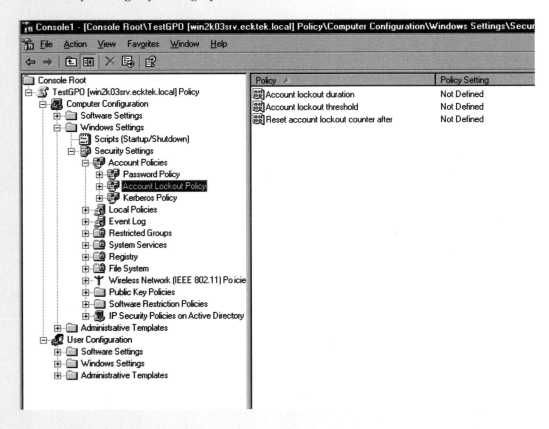

Step 2

Double-click the Account lockout duration policy to open its properties dialog box. Check the box to define the policy and set the time to 1 minute. Click OK. A dialog box will appear that informs you that the lockout threshold has been set to 5 tries and the reset time has been set to 1 minute. Click OK again and both dialog boxes will close.

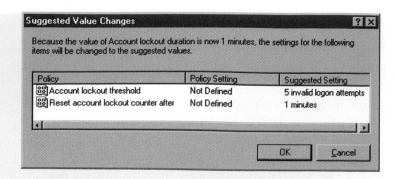

Step 3

Since 5 unsuccessful tries is a little excessive for our experiment, double-click the Account lockout threshold policy and change the setting to 1. Click OK.

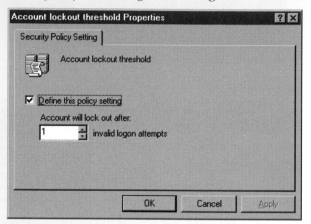

Step 4

Right-click the Software Restriction Policies container and choose New Software Restriction Policies from the shortcut menu. Right-click the Additional Rules container (in either pane) and choose New Path Rule.

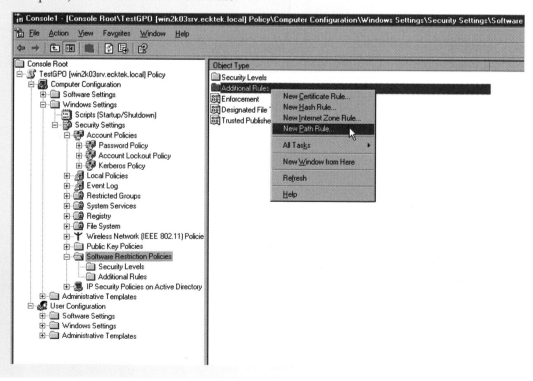

336

| Step 5 | We're going to temporarily block the Windows Server 2003 Calculator application. Type **C:\windows\system32\calc.exe** in the Path text box. Make sure the security level is set to Disallowed and click OK. You may leave the console open if you will be continuing to the next section of the chapter. If you do close the console, you will be prompted to save changes. Doing so simply saves your current place in the hierarchy in the left pane. |

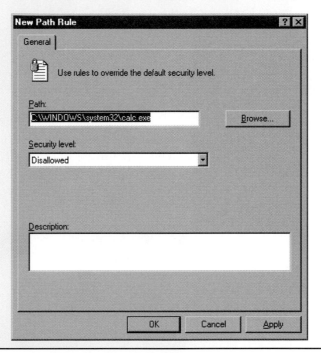

☑ **Cross Check**

Group Policy Security Settings

Now that we've gotten the chance to work with some of the group policy security settings, take a moment to review the material and answer the following questions:

1. What settings are found under password policies? What are their defaults?

2. What settings are found under account lockout policies? What are their defaults?

■ Managing Users' Environments Using Group Policy

As we've already mentioned, the group policy administrative templates settings provide extensive control over the functioning of the operation system and its components for both computer configuration and user configuration. These settings come from five administrative template files, named System.adm, Inetres.adm, conf.adm, Wuau.adm, and Wmplayer.adm. Table 11.3 lists the template files with their descriptions and the number of settings each provides under both computer configuration and user configuration. As you can see, the lion's share of the 745 policies come from the System.adm template, which controls the overall operating system settings.

Table 11.3	Policy Settings Breakdown for the Group Policy Administrative Templates		
Administrative Template	**Description**	**Computer Configuration Policies**	**User Configuration Policies**
System.adm	System settings	261	335
Inetres.adm	Internet Explorer settings	8	86
conf.adm	NetMeeting settings	32	N/A
Wuau.adm	Windows Update settings	N/A	4
Wmplayer.adm	Windows Media Player settings	5	14

The Group Policy Object Editor makes dealing with the administrative templates a little easier by dividing their many settings into categories, most of which are further subdivided as appropriate. Table 11.4 shows the names of the categories and whether they are found under computer configuration and/or user configuration.

Table 11.4	Administrative Templates First-Level Categories and Where They Are Found
First-Level Category	**Computer or User Configuration?**
Windows Components	Both
Start Menu and Taskbar	User Configuration
Desktop	User Configuration
Control Panel	User Configuration
Shared Folders	User Configuration
Network	Both
System	Both
Printers	Computer Configuration

Try This!

Download a Complete Administrative Templates Reference

Microsoft offers a comprehensive reference of all 745 administrative template policy settings in the form of an Excel workbook. If you have access to Microsoft Excel and an Internet connection, try this:

1. Point your browser to `http://www.microsoft.com/downloads/`.

2. Enter **Group Policy Settings Reference** in the keywords text box and click Go.

3. Click the Group Policy Settings Reference for Windows Server 2003 link.

4. Follow the instructions on downloading and using the reference.

Scenarios for Using Administrative Template Settings

In order to understand why you might want to use some of the administrative template settings, it might help to consider some realistic scenarios for their use. I can personally attest to the fact that each of these scenarios is realistic, since they've all happened on networks I administered! For each situation, we'll look at a particular administrative template policy that should help.

The Case of the Missing Taskbar

Although it's becoming less common, now that people tend to be more computer-literate, I can just about guarantee one or two complaints about missing or misplaced taskbars every time a new batch of students enroll. It's perfectly understandable, since prior to Windows XP it was all too easy to inadvertently move the taskbar or shrink it down to nothing. However, it's a frustrating problem for the user, and fixing it does take time away from other administrative tasks.

The Lock the Taskbar policy, which is located in User Configuration | Administrative Templates | Start Menu and Taskbar, fixes this problem handily. By enabling this setting, users are prevented from moving or resizing the taskbar. Additionally, the Prevent changes to Start Menu and Taskbar Settings policy, found in the same location, can be used to prevent the user from accessing the properties dialog box for these elements. This eliminates the chance that a user will choose Autohide for their taskbar, and then wonder why it keeps disappearing!

The Case of the Questionable Wallpaper

It's unfortunate, but it's true; people sometimes put things on their desktop that really shouldn't be there. From an employer's standpoint, allowing inappropriate materials to appear on the monitors of the company's computers can present a real liability issue. It's been my experience that merely *asking* people to use good judgment when choosing their wallpaper works only about 95 percent of the time. It's the 5 percent that will kill you!

One way to solve this problem involves the use of three policies found in User Configuration | Administrative Templates | Desktop | Active Desktop. The first two settings are Enable Active Desktop and Prohibit Changes. These turn Active Desktop on and prevent the user from changing the desktop configuration. The third setting, Active Desktop Wallpaper, allows the administrator to choose a specific image file to use as wallpaper under Active Desktop. Of course, this does limit the freedom of expression for the users, but it also helps limit legal bills!

The Case of the Fiddler

No, the Fiddler isn't one of the villains from the old Batman TV show. I'm talking about the user who is constantly playing with the various Control Panel settings. In most cases, this person doesn't mean any harm; they're merely trying to fine-tune the operation of the computer to their liking. However, as I'm sure you know, some of those Control Panel settings can be dangerous if you don't know what you're doing!

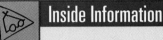

Inside Information

An Appropriate Level of Control

It's possible, using administrative templates, to almost completely control the look, feel, and function of the operating system on users' client machines. However, you should be judicious in just how much control you exert.

Most people find that personalizing their work environment is an important part of feeling comfortable and being productive on the job. That includes everything from pictures on the desk and potted plants to Windows wallpaper. When you actively prevent people from expressing themselves, it tends to lessen their motivation and, thus, their productivity.

The best time to use most of these policy settings is when client computers are shared by multiple users. These settings then prevent one user from making changes that interfere with another's ability to use the computer. When each user has their own computer, I advocate leaving as much control as is feasible in the hands of the users.

To foil the Fiddler, we need to go to User Configuration | Administrative Templates | Control Panel. The Prohibit access to the Control Panel setting does exactly what it says it does: it removes the Control Panel from the Start menu, removes the Control Panel folder from Windows Explorer, and prevents the user from otherwise running Control.exe, which is the actual Control Panel applet. If this seems too drastic, it's also possible to selectively choose which parts of the Control Panel the user can access with the Show only specified Control Panel applets policy. However, that one takes a bit more time to configure. Sometimes it's better to lock everything down and leave configuration changes to the administrators and technicians.

Step-by-Step 11.3

Modifying the Administrative Template Policies

Administrative template policy settings are modified in much the same as the security and software restriction policies we worked with in Step-by-Step 11.2. However, you do have to dig around a bit more to find them! We'll make a few final policy modifications to our new GPO in this Step-by-Step and then apply it and test its effects in the next section of the chapter.

To complete this Step-by-Step, you will need

- A properly configured Windows Server 2003 Domain Controller
- The new GPO as modified in Step-by-Step 11.2
- Access to an administrator-level account on the computer

Step 1

If necessary, reopen the TestGPO console you created earlier. Our first task is to modify the taskbar policies. Open User Configuration | Administrative Templates | Start Menu and Taskbar and double-click the Lock the Taskbar policy. Click Enabled and OK. Do the same for the Prevent changes to Taskbar and Start Menu Settings policy.

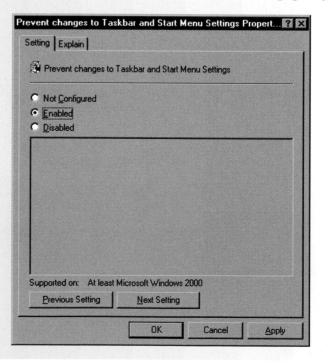

Step 2

Open User Configuration | Administrative Templates | Desktop | Active Desktop. Enable both the Enable Active Desktop and Prohibit changes policies. Double-click the Active Desktop Wallpaper policy. Click Enabled and enter the path shown in the first example in the middle of the dialog box, **C:\windows\web\wallpaper\home.jpg**, in the Wallpaper Name text box. Click OK.

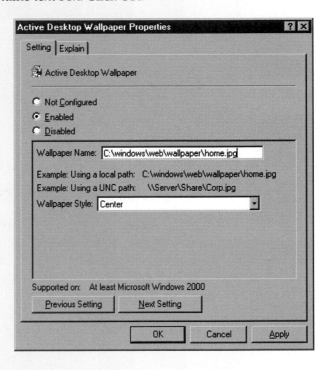

Step 3

Open User Configuration | Administrative Templates | Control Panel. Double-click the Prohibit access to the Control Panel policy and click Enabled. That will lock out the Control Panel, once we apply our new GPO. Click OK. You can close the console when you are done. Save the changes when prompted.

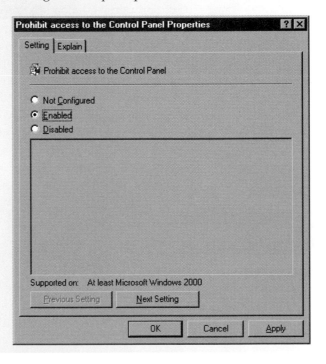

■ Managing Group Policy Implementation and Interaction

There's a reason we haven't tried out our new GPO yet; one of our settings won't work! The reason has to do with how GPOs are implemented and how multiple policy sets interact with each other. By default, new GPOs have a scope of management (SOM) of the whole domain. However, the domain already has an existing policy, the default domain policy, and one of our settings, the account lockout threshold, is in conflict with the existing policy. To understand the solution to this problem, we need to understand how GPOs are applied.

How Group Policy Is Applied

When more than one group policy is linked to an SOM, such as a domain, it's actually relatively easy to control their interaction. The Global Policy tab of the properties dialog box for the domain (or site or OU) lists the linked policies, as demonstrated in Figure 11.4. Policies that are higher in the list take priority over policies that are lower in the list. That means that the TestGPO policy has a lower priority than the default domain policy. That's a problem because the default domain policy has the Account lockout threshold enabled at 0 attempts, which means no lockouts will occur. Since the Account lockout policies in the two GPOs conflict, the higher-priority GPO wins out, which means no lockouts! All we have to do to fix this is move the TestGPO entry to the top of the list!

You should also know that GPOs are inherited, which means that an OU in a domain inherits the effects of any GPO applied to the domain itself. Unfortunately, inherited policies don't show in the list of linked policies. However, we can block against any inherited policies, if we like, by clicking the Block Policy inheritance button you see at the bottom of Figure 11.4. It's not foolproof; there are ways to keep inheritance from being blocked, as we'll see next, but it does block inheritance in most situations.

While we're talking about what we can do with the Group Policy tab, we might as well take a look at some of our other options. You'll notice in Figure 11.4 that there are an Options button and a Properties button along

By default, GPOs are applied in the following order: local, site, domain, OU. When there is a conflict between policies, the last applied policy takes priority over earlier policies.

with New, Add, Edit, and Delete. The functions of those last four are pretty obvious, but what about Options and Properties? Let's take a look.

Group Policy Object Options

The Options button opens the dialog box shown in Figure 11.5. As you can see, our two options are No Override and Disabled. The No Override option is actually another way of addressing the problem we have with the conflicting Account lockout settings. Checking it would prevent any other settings from taking a higher priority. It also prevents inheritance from being blocked, which is what I meant earlier when I said that blocking was not foolproof. However, since you have to set the No Override option manually, that's usually not a problem.

The Disabled option does exactly what it says. Disabling a GPO link keeps its settings from being applied at all. This is sometimes done when working on a new GPO to prevent problems as you are changing settings.

Group Policy Object Properties

The General tab of the properties dialog box for a GPO link, as shown in Figure 11.6, allows you to selectively disable either the computer configuration settings or the user configuration settings. Of course, you could also disable both, but that's essentially the same as disabling the GPO link using the options dialog box.

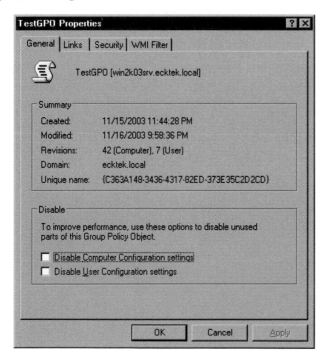

• Figure 11.6   The General tab of the GPO Properties dialog box

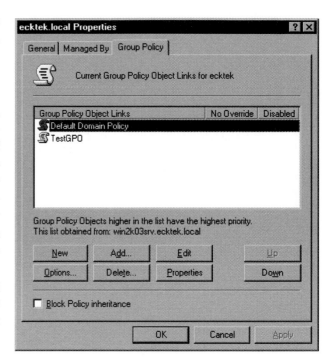

• Figure 11.4   The Group Policy tab of the Domain's Properties dialog box

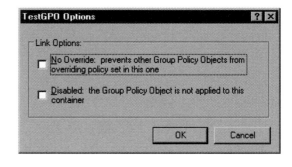

• Figure 11.5   The Group Policy Object Options dialog box

The Security tab is used to adjust who has access to the GPO. However, access usually doesn't need to be adjusted. The WMI Filter tab can be used to selectively apply policies based on group membership, but its use is a bit beyond the scope of this text.

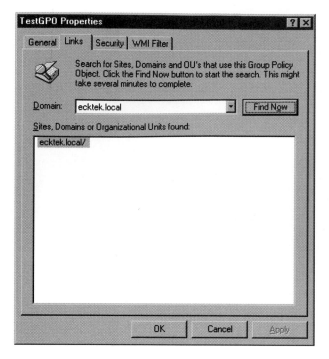

• Figure 11.7   The Links tab of the GPO Properties dialog box

The Links tab, shown in Figure 11.7, offers a Find Now button that will search for and display the sites, domains, and OUs to which the GPO is linked. However, it displays only those that are linked directly, not those that are inheriting the policy, so keep that in mind.

Analyzing Group Policy Interactions

In spite of the various management techniques we've just discussed, it can still be difficult to figure out exactly what policies are going to be in effect for any one part of the network once you're dealing with more than just the default domain policy. Fortunately, Windows Server 2003 offers a tool to help us figure it all out!

Resultant Set of Policy (RSoP)

Resultant Set of Policy (RSoP) is a group policy tool that analyzes all of the policies that apply in a particular situation and reports on the final effective, or resultant, policy. RSoP takes into consideration the priorities of GPOs, inheritance, inheritance blocking, and every other pertinent factor that leads to that final effective policy application.

RSoP can be run through Active Directory Users and Computers, for domains and OUs, or from Active Directory Sites and Services, for domains and sites. In some cases you have a choice between running RSoP in one of two modes: planning mode or logging mode. In planning mode, the effect of the policies is simply simulated on the server. In logging mode, RSoP can actually be used to remotely query the policies affecting a computer or user account that is currently logged on to the network. Of the two, planning mode is probably the most commonly used. It's also the only mode available when running RSoP for the domain.

Step-by-Step 11.4

Using RSoP and Modifying Group Policy Priority

Before we can test the GPO we've been working on, we need to fix the problem that will prevent our security settings from being effective. In this Step-by-Step, we'll use RSoP to identify the problem. Then we'll change the priority of the new GPO and run RSoP a second time to verify that it worked. Finally, we'll test the policy we've been working on throughout the chapter.

To complete this Step-by-Step, you will need

- A properly configured Windows Server 2003 Domain Controller

- The new GPO as modified in Step-by-Step 11.3

- Access to an administrator-level account on the computer

- A client computer running Windows XP that is joined to the domain. The computer we set up in Chapter 10 is ideal.

Step 1

Open Active Directory Users and Computers. Right-click the name of your domain in the left pane and choose All Tasks | Resultant Set Of Policy (Planning) to open the RSoP Wizard.

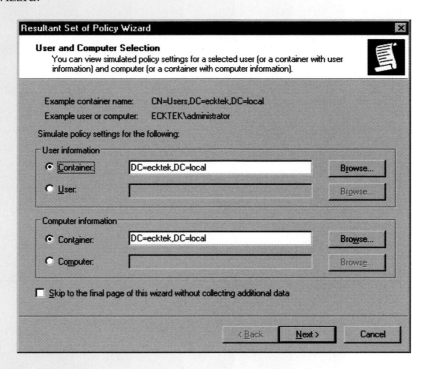

Step 2

The RSoP Wizard is highly customizable, with many options available to further modify the simulation. However, we only need a relatively simple analysis. Click the check box labeled Skip to the final page of this wizard without collecting additional data and click Next.

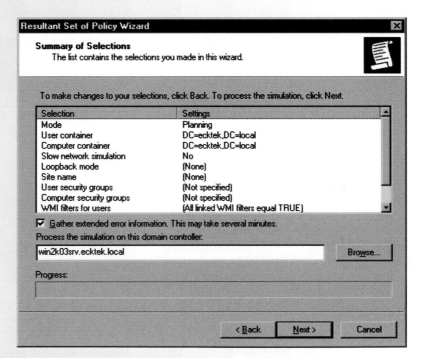

Step 3

When the summary screen appears, click Next and wait a few seconds for the process to complete. When the final dialog box of the wizard appears, click Finish. In a second or two, a Resultant Set of Policy console will open that looks very much like the Group Policy Object Editor.

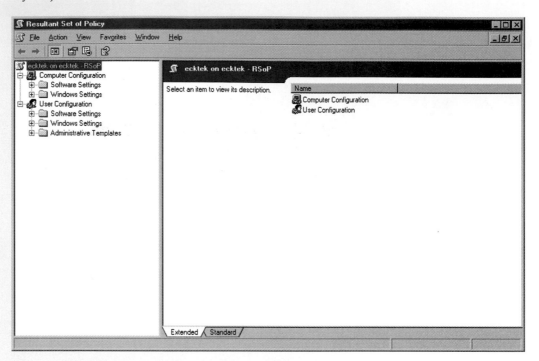

Step 4

Open Computer Configuration | Windows Settings | Security Settings | Account Policies | Account Lockout Policy. Note that, in the right pane, the setting for Account lockout threshold is set to 0 invalid logon attempts and that the source is the Default Domain Policy GPO. Close the RSoP console without saving changes.

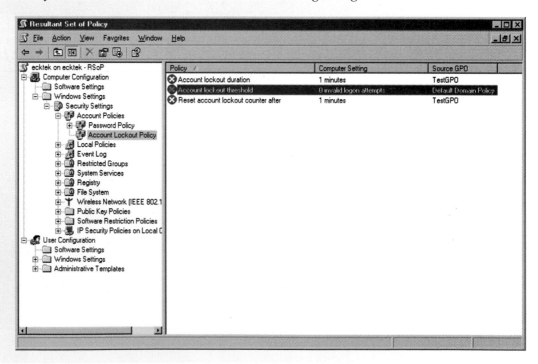

Step 5

In the Active Directory Users and Computers console, right-click the name of your domain and choose Properties. Click the Group Policy tab. Click Down to move the Default Domain Policy to the bottom of the list and click OK. Now TestGPO has a higher priority than the Default Domain Policy.

Step 6

Do Steps 1–3 again to re-open the RSoP console. Open Computer Configuration | Windows Settings | Security Settings | Account Policies | Account Lockout Policy. Note that now the setting for Account lockout threshold is set to 1 invalid logon attempts and that the source is now TestGPO. Close the RSoP console without saving changes. Leave the Active Directory Users and Computers console open.

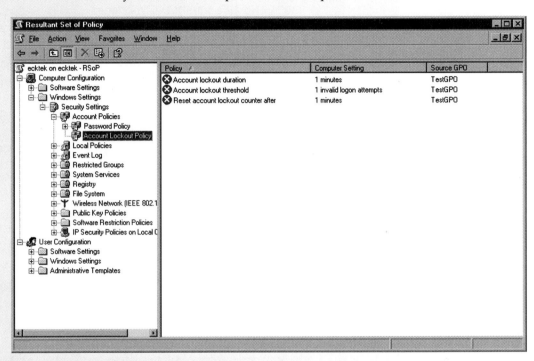

Step 7

Group policy is updated about every five minutes on domain controllers and about every 90 minutes on client machines. To ensure that our policy is active, we are going to force an update. Click Start | Run. Enter **gpupdate** and click OK.

Step 8

Start the client computer. When prompted to log on, do so using an incorrect password. Click OK when the error message appears and quickly try again with another incorrect password. You should receive a Logon message stating that your account has been locked out. Wait at least one minute and then log on using your correct password.

Step 9

When the desktop appears, you should see the home.jpg wallpaper. Right-click an empty spot on the desktop and choose Properties. Read the Restrictions message and then click OK.

Step 10

Right-click the taskbar and choose Properties. You should see the same message as in Step 9. Click OK.

Step 11

Click Start and note that Control Panel is missing from the Start menu.

Step 12

Try to open the Calculator applet by clicking Start | All Programs | Accessories | Calculator. A different error message will appear that informs you that a software restriction policy is keeping this program from running. Click OK. Shut down the client computer and return to the server.

Step 13

In Active Directory Users and Computers, right-click the name of your domain and choose Properties. Click the Group Policy tab. We are going to delete our GPO to return our network to its original state. Select TestGPO and click the Delete button. You have a choice between merely removing the link and removing the link and deleting the policy object. Choose to remove the link so that you can continue to experiment with TestGPO later. Click OK and then click Close. You may now close Active Directory Users and Computers.

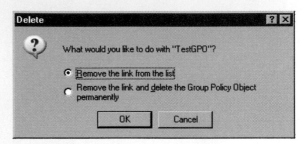

Step 14

Run **gpupdate** again as you did in Step 7. After it has run, restart the client computer and retest each of the things we looked at in Steps 9–12. You should still see the home.jpg wallpaper, but you should now be able to change it. The wallpaper remained because it was the last wallpaper the client computer was told to use. All other aspects of the client computer should be back to normal. When you are finished exploring, you may shut the system down.

☑ Cross Check

Managing the Implementation of Group Policy Objects

Now that we've discussed the techniques for managing multiple GPOs, take a minute to review what we've covered and answer the following questions:

1. How do you stop the inheritance of GPOs?

2. How do you run RSoP?

■ Chapter Summary

After reading this chapter and completing the Step-by-Step tutorials and Try This! exercises, you should understand the following facts about managing computers and users through group policy in Windows Server 2003.

Explain the Capabilities of Group Policy

■ A group policy object (GPO) is a collection of configuration settings that can be linked to a domain, a site, an OU, or even individual computers, which is its scope of management (SOM).

■ The installation of Active Directory automatically creates a default domain policy linked to the domain and a default domain controllers policy linked to the domain controllers OU.

■ The most commonly used tool for working with GPOs is the Group Policy Object Editor, which is a snap-in for the Microsoft Management Console (MMC).

■ The Group Policy Management Console (GPMC) is a new, downloadable, tool from Microsoft for working with GPOs. However, it still depends on the Group Policy Management Console for the actual editing of GPOs.

■ Group Policy settings are divided into computer configuration and user configuration settings. Each is further subdivided into software settings, Windows settings, and administrative templates.

■ Software settings can be used to install software applications through the use of package files and the Windows Installer service.

■ The computer configuration Windows settings are used to configure startup/shutdown scripts and security settings.

■ The user configuration Windows settings are used to configure logon/logoff scripts and security settings.

■ The administrative template settings provide 745 different Registry settings that alter the configuration of the operating system and its components.

Manage Security Using Group Policy

■ The most commonly used security settings are found under computer configuration. They include account policies and software restrictions.

■ Account policies include password policies, account lockout policies, and Kerberos security policies.

■ Software restriction policies can be used to prevent certain applications from running or to prevent the running of applications from a particular folder.

Manage Users' Environments Using Group Policy

■ The five administrative templates files are System.adm, Inetres.adm, conf.adm, Wuau.adm, and Wmplayer.adm.

■ Administrative templates policies can be used to reduce problems for both users and administrators by limiting what can be done with the operating system.

Manage Group Policy Implementation and Interaction

■ GPOs with a higher priority take precedence over lower-priority GPOs when there is a policy conflict. This priority can be adjusted.

■ GPOs are inherited. Policy inheritance can be blocked as long as the GPO is not set to No Override.

■ GPOs can be disabled completely, or you can selectively disable either the computer or user configuration settings.

■ Resultant Set of Policy (RSoP) is a tool for analyzing the effect of all applicable policies on a particular domain, site, OU, computer, or user.

■ Key Terms List

account lockout duration *(334)*

account lockout threshold *(334)*

account lockout policies *(333)*

administrative templates
settings *(329)*

Authentication Service (AS) *(334)*

computer configuration
settings *(327)*

default domain controllers
policy *(325)*

default domain policy *(325)*

Group Policy Management
Console (GPMC) *(326)*

group policy object (GPO) *(325)*

Group Policy Object Editor *(325)*

Kerberos security *(334)*

local policy *(325)*

package *(328)*

password policies *(333)*

reset account lockout
counter after *(334)*

scope of management (SOM) *(325)*

software restriction policies *(334)*

software settings *(328)*

Ticket Granting Service
(TGS) *(334)*

Ticket to Get Tickets (TGT) *(334)*

user configuration settings *(327)*

Windows Installer service *(328)*

Windows settings *(328)*

Resultant Set of Policy
(RSoP) *(344)*

■ Key Terms Quiz

Use terms from the Key Terms list to complete the sentences that follow. Don't use the same term more than once. Not all terms will be used.

1. _____ authenticates users once and uses a system of tickets to eliminate the need for services to re-authenticate in order to provide services.

2. The newest tool for working with group policy objects is _____.

3. A group policy object is linked to its _____.

4. The number of times you can unsuccessfully enter your password is determined by the _____.

5. _____ can be used to prevent users from executing e-mail attachments and potentially spreading computer viruses.

6. You can use _____ to analyze the end result of the application of multiple GPOs.

7. Although the security policy settings appear in two places in the Group Policy Object Editor, most changes are made under the _____ category.

8. The Windows Installer service makes use of _____ files that have the extension .msi.

9. The most common tool for working with GPOs is _____.

10. Each computer has its own _____.

■ Multiple-Choice Quiz

1. There are _____ administrative template files.

   a. 745

   b. 200

   c. 12

   d. 5

2. The relationship between a GPO and its SOM is called a

   a. Link

   b. Connection

   c. Inheritance

   d. Policy

3. If you want to be sure that a GPO has been applied, you can run the command
   a. gpedit
   b. gpupdate
   c. rsop
   d. gpmc

4. The default number of remembered passwords in the default domain policy is
   a. 45
   b. 1
   c. 7
   d. 24

5. A weakness of the new Group Policy Management Console is
   a. It has to be installed from the installation CD.
   b. It cannot directly edit GPOs.
   c. It isn't out yet.
   d. It must be purchased as part of the Windows Server 2003 support pack.

6. You cannot block inheritance of a GPO in which of the following situations:
   a. The GPO has its computer configuration settings disabled.
   b. The GPO is linked to an OU.
   c. The GPO has No Override set.
   d. The GPO is linked to the domain.

7. Newly created GPOs have an automatic link to the _____ in which they were created.
   a. Domain
   b. Site
   c. OU
   d. Local computer

8. Which of the following administrative templates has the most policy settings?
   a. conf.adm
   b. Inetres.adm

   c. System.adm
   d. Wuau.adm

9. How many of the administrative template policy settings are new for Windows XP and Windows Server 2003?
   a. 300
   b. 200
   c. 261
   d. 335

10. Which of the following is *not* a first-level category under computer configuration or user configuration?
    a. Software Settings
    b. Windows Settings
    c. Security Settings
    d. Administrative Templates

11. What is the default domain policy setting for account lockout threshold?
    a. 0
    b. 1
    c. 3
    d. 5

12. Which GPO is *not* created automatically?
    a. Default domain policy
    b. Default client policy
    c. Local policy
    d. Default domain controller policy

13. Which password policy should never be used?
    a. Minimum password length
    b. Passwords must meet complexity requirements
    c. Store passwords using reversible encryption
    d. Enforce password history

14. Which administrative templates first-level category appears under computer configuration but not under user configuration?

    a. Network

    b. Desktop

    c. Control Panel

    d. Printers

15. Which administrative templates file offers the fewest policy settings?

    a. conf.adm

    b. Inetres.adm

    c. System.adm

    d. Wuau.adm

■ Essay Quiz

1. You recently used group policy to prohibit access to the networking settings on the client computers. A few users have asked you why you did this. Explain your rationale.

2. The account lockout settings we used in the chapter were not realistic. Explain what the problem would be with using those settings.

3. Your boss has suggested that you use the administrative templates to lock down and limit changes to client computers as much as possible. Give several reasons why this might not be a good idea.

4. Explain the difference between computer configuration and user configuration policy settings.

5. A single computer, not joined to a domain, has only a local computer policy. Under what type of circumstances might you want to make changes to the policy settings for that computer? What types of changes might you make?

Lab Projects

• Lab Project 11.1

Develop at least three more scenarios similar to those in the text where administrative templates policy settings may be useful. Clearly explain the scenario and identify the policy or policies you think would be helpful. Explain your rationale and be sure to discuss any possible problems that might arise from implementing these policy changes.

• Lab Project 11.2

Create a new GPO that implements your policy changes from Lab Project 11.1. Use RSoP to check your GPO before testing it out on the client computer. Test your GPO and troubleshoot any problems, such as policy conflicts, that may arise. Be sure to remove the link to the new GPO after you have finished your testing.

• Lab Project 11.3

With your instructor's permission, go to http://www.microsoft.com/windowsserver2003/gpmc/default.mspx and download and install the GPMC. Go to http://www.microsoft.com/windowsserver2003/gpmc/gpmcwp.mspx and download the GPMC white paper, which is a technical reference on using this new tool. Run GPMC by clicking Group Policy Management from the Administrative Tools menu. Using the program's help file and the GPMC white paper, explore the utility. Report on whether or not you found the utility easy to learn and adapt to. Be sure to mention any advantages or disadvantages you noted in GPMC in comparison to the Group Policy Object Editor.

When you are finished, you can uninstall the GPMC from the Add or Remove Programs applet in Control Panel.

From There to Here: Server Management Using Remote Desktop for Administration

"It's not the hours you put in your work that counts, it's the work you put in the hours."

—Sam Ewing

In this chapter, you will learn how to:

- **Describe Remote Desktop for Administration concepts**
- **Configure and create a Remote Desktop connection**
- **Manage Remote Desktop connections**

The job of managing a network frequently requires trips away from the server room to work on client computers. However, many of those tasks also require access to the server, and its operating system, in order to set up accounts or make other configuration changes. As you might imagine, running back and forth between server and client is not only an ineffective way to get things done, it's also pretty irritating and time-consuming! Fortunately, Windows Server 2003 comes with Remote Desktop for Administration, which is a tool that allows us to save time and effort by accessing the server and its OS from pretty much anywhere we like.

In this chapter, we'll begin by discussing the major benefits of Remote Desktop for Administration. We'll then learn how to configure a remote connection from a Windows XP Professional client to a Windows Server 2003 server. Finally, we'll learn how to manage remote connections from the server.

■ Describing Basic Remote Desktop for Administration Concepts

If administering the network were my only job where I work, I guess I could probably spend most of my time in the server room so that I'd have ready access when configuration changes had to be made and computer and user accounts had to be managed. At least I'd get to play a lot of FreeCell, right? However, like many administrators in small companies, I find that taking care of the network and the client computers is only part of my job. As such, it's par for the course that, when I need to work on the server, I'm nowhere near the server room and it's pretty inconvenient to run up there and still try and get the rest of my work done. That's why I absolutely love the topic of this chapter. It's the best thing to happen to Windows since FreeCell (but don't tell my mother I said so, she's a FreeCell addict!). However, before we take a look at some of the benefits this little gem has to offer, let's talk about the Windows Server 2003 component that makes it all possible.

The **Terminal Services** component of Windows Server 2003 is responsible for allowing interactive logons to the server's operating system from remote locations. In simpler terms, it allows a user to access the server, its operating system, its hardware, and its installed applications just as if they were logged on to the server locally. Terminal Services provides this ability through two different modes: **Terminal Server** and the topic of our chapter, **Remote Desktop for Administration**. Although Remote Desktop for Administration is our primary focus, let's first take a quick look at what the Terminal Server mode does.

Benefits of Terminal Server

In Terminal Server mode, Terminal Services makes it possible for many users to simultaneously log on to the server from remote machines and run applications. These remote connections, or **sessions**, can be established from a wide variety of devices, including those not running Windows. This mode is frequently used to allow for centralized management and configuration of applications, or to allow underpowered and non-Windows clients to access and use software that requires Windows and/or processing power beyond what the client computer can provide.

 In Windows 2000, the equivalent of Windows Server 2003's Terminal Server mode of Terminal Services was known as Application mode.

A server running in Terminal Server mode can provide users of cheaper, relatively limited computers, which are sometimes referred to as **thin clients**, the full power and functionality of applications installed at the server. Since the applications run from the server, rather than on each client, they get the full benefit of the server's typically more powerful processor and more plentiful RAM. Additionally, since the software is installed only at the server, both application management and security become much easier. Just imagine how much easier it is to apply a program update to one computer instead of hundreds, and you'll see what I mean!

The problem with Terminal Server mode is that it requires the purchase of additional expensive licenses for each user who will be accessing the server using this mode. The last time I checked, a five-pack of these licenses ran about $750! At that rate, to use Terminal Server mode where I work would require an additional investment of somewhere around $30,000!

To be fair, that cost can sometimes be offset by the savings from buying cheaper client computers, but that isn't the right decision for all businesses.. Unfortunately, since these licenses *are* required in order to work with Terminal Server mode, it's unrealistic for us to explore it further in this text. However, the overall experience and concept is pretty much the same in the mode we will cover, so I think you'll get the idea!

Benefits of Remote Desktop for Administration

Unlike Terminal Server mode, Remote Desktop for Administration provides for only two simultaneous connections to the server and does not require the purchase of any additional licenses. This makes sense in that the basic purpose of Remote Desktop for Administration is to give administrators the ability to manage servers and networks from practically anywhere. To be honest with you, that's enough to make me happy! However, a more detailed look into some of its specific benefits may help you understand why I'm such a fan.

Ease of Use

You really couldn't ask for an easier method for accessing the server's desktop than what Remote Desktop for Administration offers; it's just a matter of a couple of clicks and entering the name of the server you want to connect to. From there, you log on to the server just as you would if you were sitting in front of it and go to town! By default, the server's desktop appears in full-screen mode and works exactly as it normally does. When you need to switch back and forth to the client desktop, you can either minimize the session or display it in a window.

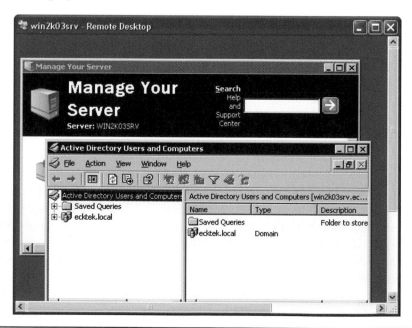

• A Windowed Remote Desktop for Administration Session in Windows XP

Access from Many Operating Systems

Both Windows XP and Windows Server 2003 have the client software for connecting to Remote Desktop for Administration sessions installed by default. The client is called **Remote Desktop Connection (RDC)** and can be found at Start | All Programs | Accessories | Communications. However, the options don't stop there. As you can see in Table 12.1, the list of supported operating systems is pretty comprehensive.

I find it pretty amazing that it's possible to connect to, and administer, a Windows Server 2003 server using everything from the first version of Windows to integrate networking (Windows for Workgroups) up through the competition's operating system (Macintosh OS). Additionally, with support for **Windows CE**, which is the version of Windows used by many handheld devices, it's even possible to access the server from the palm of your hand! Of course, the other side of that coin is that it makes it pretty difficult to escape your job, but the benefit is that you can do your job from just about anywhere, which brings us to our next benefit.

Table 12.1	Operating Systems for Which a Remote Desktop Connection Client Is Available
Operating System	
Windows for Workgroups	
Windows 95	
Windows 98	
Windows Me	
Windows NT	
Windows 2000	
Windows XP Home Edition and Professional	
Windows Server 2003 All Editions	
Windows CE 2.11	
Windows CE.NET	
Macintosh OS	

• The Remote Desktop Connection Dialog Box in Windows XP

Access from Many Locations

Remote Desktop connections are not limited solely to those computers physically connected to the network. In fact, access isn't even limited to computers connected locally to the LAN. RDC and Remote Desktop for Administration support connections over LANs, dial-up, and even **virtual private network (VPN)** connections made through the Internet! Again, while this might make taking a break from work a bit more difficult, it sure comes in handy when the other alternative is crawling out of bed at 3 A.M. and driving to work to fix a server problem!

The Windows CE Remote Desktop Connection client is normally provided by the manufacturer of the handheld device.

Low Resource Overhead

It might surprise you to learn that connecting to a server using Remote Desktop for Administration has little effect on the server's performance beyond the impact of performing the same management tasks locally. This is because the only data that needs to be exchanged between the client and the server consists of the input actions of the mouse and keyboard at the client and the display information from the server. In fact, this is one of the reasons why Remote Desktop for Administration connections can even be made over very low bandwidth conditions, such as a dial-up connection.

A VPN connection is a highly secure connection between two or more computers or networks that allows the participating machines to interact as if they were on the same physical LAN.

⚠ Microsoft even makes a point of mentioning that something as simple as a floppy disk left in a drive could stop a remote server from successfully restarting after a reboot!

Remote Desktop for Administration Limitations

Never fear, Remote Desktop for Administration's limitations aren't really all that bad. In fact, they're not even weaknesses or flaws, but merely some constraints you should be aware of before using it. They're important because there are a few situations where, if you aren't aware of them, they could cause you a bit of trouble.

Reboot with Caution

The Remote Desktop for Administration experience is so much like being there, you very well may forget that you aren't! Therein lies a problem. Although, in most cases, management tasks that require a server reboot aren't a problem, since you just reconnect when the server restarts, there are some cases where things can go awry.

I had one case where some recently installed printer software caused an error message to appear after every reboot. Until that message was cleared, the server would not respond to client machines in any way. Unfortunately, I forgot one day and used Remote Desktop for Administration to perform a service pack installation, followed by a reboot. Suffice it to say that when I realized about 20 minutes later that the server had still not come back up, I felt a bit embarrassed because I realized what I had done!

In general, a good policy is probably *not* to reboot the server from a Remote Desktop for Administration session unless it is both absolutely necessary and you are 100 percent sure that the reboot will go off without a hitch. Even then, I'd still check to be sure that everything comes back up all right, rather than waiting 20 minutes as I did!

Security Risks

I really shouldn't have to say this, but I will. When you're dealing with a technology that allows people to access your server remotely, security must always be a primary concern. By default, the local machine policy for a server allows remote logins to the server only from members of the Administrators group, which makes sense when you think about the whole purpose of Remote Desktop for Administration. In reality, the only thing you really have to do to maintain security is to maintain the security of the administrator accounts you'll be using to access the server remotely. That means using strong passwords and, in some cases, using an account name other than "Administrator."

The benefit to using a different administrator account name is that it makes it even more difficult for malicious users to gain access to the server. Not only do they have to obtain the password, they also have to figure out what the name of the administrator account is! Of course, the real protection is still the password, but every little bit helps, right?

Limited Connections

Although Remote Desktop for Administration gives complete access to the server's operating system, it was not intended for use in running general applications. Otherwise, you wouldn't need Terminal Server mode and those expensive licenses I mentioned earlier! As we've already said, there can be only two simultaneous connections to the server. However, that's not too rough of a limitation. After all, connections are limited to administrator accounts anyway, and don't they say that too many cooks spoil the soup? Where it becomes a problem is when administrators leave sessions active, thus blocking out other administrators who may need access. Fortunately, as we'll see a bit later, there are configuration settings and management techniques to address this problem.

Disabled by Default

The last thing that could trip you up in trying to use Remote Desktop for Administration is that it is disabled by default at the server. However, fixing this is a matter of a few quick clicks to get into the System Properties dialog box and enable it, so it's not that big a deal. Unless, of course, you forget to do it, in which case you won't be creating any remote connections!

Of course, the reason why Remote Desktop for Administration is disabled initially is for increased security. By requiring you to intentionally enable it, there's little chance that you won't know it's enabled. However, I'd also like to point out a key advantage to this so-called limitation: this is an extremely simple way of locking the system down for those times when you want to make sure no one can access the system remotely. But why would you want to do that? Well, the answer is pretty simple.

You've got to remember that Remote Desktop for Administration really does give you complete access to the server's OS, which is a good thing, as I've been saying. However, what if you're working on the server locally and someone else is connecting remotely? As long as your actions aren't in conflict, there's no problem with that. In fact, it can be a good way to divide the work between two administrators. The problem arises when two administrators are working at cross-purposes. Perhaps one is trying to perform a backup while another is trying to delete a bunch of older files. It's a good idea, when working at the server on something critical, to temporarily disable remote access so that this doesn't happen. Just remember to re-enable it when you're done!

Cross Check

Remote Desktop for Administration

Now that we've had a chance to discuss Remote Desktop for Administration concepts, take a moment to review the material and answer the following questions:

1. What are the benefits of Remote Desktop for Administration?
2. What are the limitations of Remote Desktop for Administration?

Enabling Remote Connections to Windows Server 2003

Before we can start configuring and creating connections to use Remote Desktop for Administration, we have to enable remote connections at the server. Keep in mind that this feature is always disabled by default. Also remember that it is sometimes a good idea to disable remote connections when performing sensitive work at the server to prevent possible conflicts.

To complete this Step-by-Step, you will need

- A properly configured computer with Windows Server 2003 installed
- Access to an administrator-level account on the computer

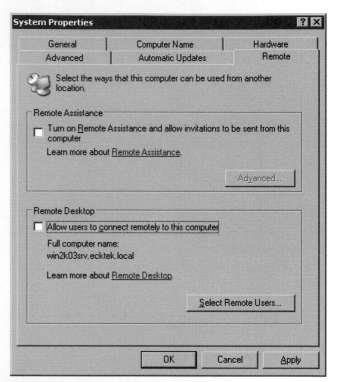

Step 1	At the server, click Start and then right-click My Computer and choose Properties. Click the Remote tab.

Step 2	Place a check in the box labeled "Allow users to connect remotely to this computer". When you do so, a Remote Sessions dialog box will appear telling you that accounts must have passwords to be able to access the computer remotely and reminding you that the proper communication port must be available if the server is behind a firewall. Click OK to close the Remote Sessions dialog box.

Step 3	Before clicking OK to close the Systems Properties dialog box, note that there is a Select Remote Users button. Keep in mind that the local policy for the server will prevent anyone who is not a member of the administrators group from gaining remote access. This button, therefore, doesn't serve much purpose unless you intentionally alter that policy. However, on Windows XP machines, this button can be used to add users to the Remote Desktop Users group, which can then access the Windows XP desktop. Click the OK button to close the dialog box.

Configuring and Creating a Remote Desktop Connection

As I indicated earlier, actually creating a connection is as simple as a couple of clicks and entering the name of the machine you want to connect to. However, there are a variety of options you can configure for each connection, which offer refinements to how the connection works.

Remote Desktop Connection Options

The Remote Desktop Connection options are available by clicking the Options button in the Remote Desktop Connections dialog box. Recall that you open the Remote Desktop Connections dialog box by clicking Start | All Programs | Accessories | Communications | Remote Desktop Connection. The options are divided into five tabs, which are General, Display, Local Resources, Programs, and Experience. Let's take a look at what each offers.

General Options

As you can see from Figure 12.1, the General options tab lets you enter the logon settings, including the computer name, user name, password, and domain. Although it is possible to check the box to save your password, I don't recommend it, as it presents far too much of a security risk.

Additionally, the General options tab allows you to save your preferred settings or load a saved configuration file. This is useful if you connect to several different servers and wish to use different settings for each. By configuring the settings for each and then saving them to a different file, you can easily access them later. Saved settings are saved locally in a **Remote Desktop protocol file** with an .rdp extension in the user's local My Documents folder. The default settings file, Default.rdp, is stored there as well but as a hidden file.

There is one potential problem you should be aware of with this tab. If you attempt to pull down the Computer drop-down list and select Browse for more, you'll be presented with a dialog box where you're supposed to be able to choose from a list of available computers. Unfortunately, unless Terminal Services has been installed on the server in its other mode, Terminal Server, you cannot use this method to select a computer. However, you can either type the computer's name or its IP address and that will work just fine!

Display Options

The most obvious choices on the Display options tab, shown in Figure 12.2, are those for screen size, or resolution, and color depth. Regardless of your client's screen size and resolution, moving the Remote desktop size slider the whole way to the right will take the display to full screen, which is the default. To be honest with you, there's very little reason not to work in full screen, since a windowed display may require you to use both horizontal and vertical scroll bars to move around the desktop.

> With one small exception, which we'll mention when we get to it, the options settings for Remote Desktop Connection are the same in both Windows XP and Windows Server 2003.

> Remote Desktop Connection does not require a domain-based network. This feature can also be used between computers in a workgroup.

● **Figure 12.1** The General options tab of the Remote Desktop Connection dialog box

As far as the colors setting goes, I usually don't worry about it, since I'm rarely working with graphically oriented applications at the server. Besides, as we'll see later, the server limits the colors to no more than 16-bit by default, so you can only go lower, not higher, without changing that setting at the server. That's okay, though, 16-bit is plenty good enough to play a few hands of FreeCell!

What isn't so obvious is the little check box at the bottom of this tab that says Display the connection bar when in full screen mode. Trust me on this one: leave this checked on! When this is on, a small yellow **connection bar** appears at the top of the remote display at all times. This bar displays the name of the machine you are connected to and a standard set of window control buttons. From here you can minimize or window the remote desktop, which does come in handy at times. However, the most important thing about the connection bar is that it reminds you that you are dealing with the remote machine. Don't think you'll ever get confused? Believe me, it's easy to do! On numerous occasions while working with Remote Desktop for Administration, I've lost my bearings and forgotten which desktop I was working with. In such cases, the connection bar is a lifesaver!

Local Resources Options

The Local Resource options tab, shown in Figure 12.3, lets you control the interaction between the remote session and your local peripherals. For instance, you can control whether or not sounds from the remote session play at the client computer and whether or not common keyboard shortcuts at the client are sent to the remote system. By default, any sounds from the remote computer will play at the client, and keyboard shortcuts, for the most part, will be sent as long as the display is full screen. I say "for the most part"

• **Figure 12.2** The Display options tab of the Remote Desktop Connection dialog box

• **Figure 12.3** The Local Resources options tab of the Remote Desktop Connection dialog box

because the CTRL-ALT-DELETE keyboard combination is always reserved for the client machine, rather than the remote machine. Remember that you can open the task manager in the remote session by right-clicking the taskbar and choosing it from the shortcut menu.

The bottom section of this dialog box allows you to control the handling of local drives, printers, and serial ports. For instance, by default, any local printer (connected to the client computer) is available to the remote machine for use. That means you can easily print to the local printer any information you may need to retain from the remote session. As you might imagine, that can come in handy. Otherwise, you might find yourself unable to print to a location near you. If necessary, you can also make local drives and serial ports available to the remote session. I sometimes find it necessary to do this with my drives, but rarely have cause to redirect my serial ports. Devices that have been made available to the remote session are said to be **redirected** or **mapped**. Of the two terms, I prefer "mapped," since the process is similar in concept to the way a network folder is mapped as a local drive at a client computer.

Programs Options

The Programs option tab, shown in Figure 12.4, simply allows you to assign certain programs to run upon establishing the remote connection. For instance, an administrator might want to run some sort of network monitoring package during any remote session to keep tabs on the health of the network. To be totally truthful, I've never found much use for this option, but it's nice to know that it's there!

• **Figure 12.4**   The Programs options tab of the Remote Desktop Connection dialog box

> Redirected devices are identified by the name of the client machine that established the session.

Inside Information

Clipboard Mapping

In addition to the ability to redirect local devices such as printers and drives to the remote session, Remote Desktop for Administration also provides **clipboard mapping***, which means that information, including files, can be copied and pasted between both the local client machine and the remote server session.*

Although clipboard mapping may not sound like a big deal, it can be a huge time saver. In many cases, I've found that the ability to copy and paste text and files between my local machine and my remote session has made it much easier to make configuration changes, troubleshoot problems, or transfer data. I frequently use this feature to copy and paste everything from error messages to scripts, which comes in handy, since my typing isn't the best!

● **Figure 12.5** The Experience options tab of the Remote Desktop Connection dialog box

Bitmap Caching is similar to the caching of images performed by Internet Explorer. Bitmapped images that are displayed on the remote desktop are saved in a temporary folder on the client machine where they can be retrieved quickly if needed again. This is always enabled, since it can only speed up the overall connection.

Experience Options

I know it sounds like a cliché to say "last but not least," but in the case of the Experience options tab, it's an appropriate description. As you can see in Figure 12.5, the default setting for the speed of a remote connection is Modem (56 Kbps), which simplifies the display of the remote desktop by eliminating several aspects of the normal desktop "experience." Now, menu animations, seeing the contents of windows while dragging them, and the desktop background aren't the most important things in the world, but if you have a faster connection, you might as well get the whole ball of wax, right? In this tab, you can either manually choose which aspects of the desktop you'd like to see or, by choosing the appropriate connection speed, let Windows choose them for you. On the other hand, if you notice that your remote connection seems to lag a bit, you can disable as many of these options as you like to try and improve the performance, without losing any real functionality. The available speed settings, and their corresponding experience settings, can be found in Table 12.2.

Another reason why the Experience options tab is certainly not "least" even though it is "last" is that it is the only tab that is different in Windows Server 2003 than it is in Windows XP. The difference is a single check box that appears at the bottom of the dialog box in Windows Server 2003 that says Reconnect if connection is dropped. For obvious reasons, when working with remote connections from a Windows Server 2003 computer, this is a good option to have turned on. As such, it is on by default. However, there might come a time when you'd rather not have Windows automatically reconnect, so, if you like, you could disable it. There's a good chance that this little feature will eventually make its way into Windows XP through some sort of update, but it hasn't happened yet. Fortunately, it's usually not much of a problem, at least over LAN connections.

Table 12.2	Connection Speeds and Experience Settings for Remote Desktop Connections				
Connection Speed	**Desktop Background**	**Show Contents of Window While Dragging**	**Menu and Window Animation**	**Themes**	**Bitmap Caching**
Modem (28.8 Kbps)	OFF	OFF	OFF	OFF	ON
Modem (56 Kbps)	OFF	OFF	OFF	ON	ON
Broadband (128 Kbps–1.5 Mbps)	OFF	ON	ON	ON	ON
LAN (10 Mbps or higher)	ON	ON	ON	ON	ON

Configuring a Remote Desktop Connection

Although you can certainly connect to a remote computer by just entering its name or IP address and clicking Connect in the Remote Desktop Connection dialog box, it isn't a bad idea to make sure that all of your connection settings are configured properly first. In this Step-by-Step, we'll make just a few changes to our configuration and then establish a remote connection to the desktop of our server from the client computer we set up back in Chapter 10.

To complete this Step-by-Step, you will need

- A properly configured computer with Windows Server 2003 installed and remote connections enabled
- The client computer set up in Chapter 10
- A LAN connection between the client and the server
- Access to an administrator-level account on the server

Step 1

At the Windows XP client computer, click Start | All Programs | Accessories | Communications | Remote Desktop Connection. When the Remote Desktop Connection box appears, click Options.

Step 2

On the General options tab, enter the name or IP address of the computer you wish to connect to, the administrator account user name, and the administrator account password. If necessary, verify that the domain name is correct.

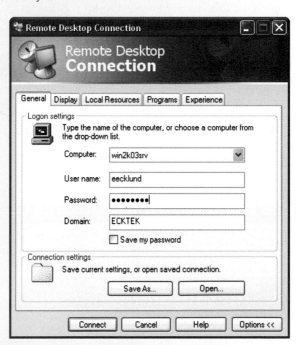

Step 3

Click the Display options tab and verify that the Remote desktop size slider is at full screen and that there is a check in the check box to display the connection bar while in full screen.

Step 4

Click the Local Resources options tab and check the box for Disk drives under local devices. Verify that remote computer sounds will be brought to the local computer and that

Windows key combinations will be sent while in full screen mode. We'll leave printers checked even though you probably haven't installed any on this lab client.

Step 5

Click the Experience options tab and choose your connection speed from the drop-down list. Note which options are selected based on your choice.

Step 6

Click the Connect button and read the Remote Desktop Connection Security Warning. Note that the warning concerns the fact that we've made our drives accessible to the remote machine, which could expose us to viruses, as well as other hazards. However, since we're essentially connecting to ourselves, I think we can trust us. Don't you agree? Click OK to dismiss the warning dialog box.

You should now be at the Windows Server 2003 desktop in full screen mode! Note the connection bar at the top of the screen. The push-pin icon on the left allows you to "un-pin" it so that it will hide itself when not in use. If the connection bar is hidden, just place your mouse pointer at the top middle of the display to bring it back up. You can, of course, also use the connection bar to minimize or window the remote desktop as needed. Take a few moments to explore the environment. It should feel just like you're sitting in front of your server!

Open Notepad and then click File | Save As. Pull down the Save in box and look for your local drives. They will appear as *C on Name*, where *Name* is the name of your client computer. Cancel out of the Save As dialog box and close Notepad.

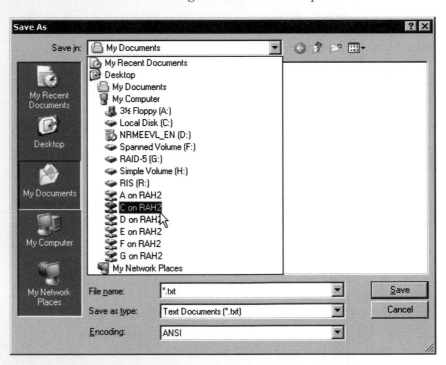

Leave the session open if you will be continuing on into the next section of the text. If you need to stop here, simply perform a logoff just as you would if you were sitting at the server. You will then be returned to your client desktop.

You can also disconnect a session by clicking Start | Shut Down and choosing Disconnect from the pull-down selection list for what you want the computer to do. However, since you can inadvertently shut the server down using this method, I don't recommend it!

Using Remote Desktop for Administration Sessions

Well, as you can see, getting connected to a server through Remote Desktop for Administration is actually pretty easy. However, there are a few additional things you should keep in mind, which aren't covered by the configuration options and procedures we've discussed so far. We still have to talk about how to end a session and an alternative way of starting one.

Ending a Remote Desktop for Administration Session

One important thing to remember is that how you end a session is probably more important than how you start one. Recall that there is a limit of two remote sessions when using Remote Desktop for Administration. If another administrator is logged on to one of the remote sessions and you end the session you are working on by using Start | Log Off, any running programs or processes will end (for your session) and that session will be freed up for someone else to use. This is referred to as ending a session. On the other hand, if you close the Remote Desktop Window, without logging off, your running programs and processes will continue to run and your session will remain unavailable to other administrators. This is referred to as disconnecting a session. When you reconnect, you will be reconnected to your running session. Think of closing the window as walking away from the computer, instead of logging off. It has the same effect.

Both methods of leaving a session are correct, depending on your needs. If you are finished working with the server and you have no tasks running, using the log off approach makes sure that the session is freed up for another administrator to use. However, if you've just started tasks that are going to take a while to run, such as monitoring programs or virus scans, you can simply shut the connection, which leaves the session running with any active tasks, and return to it later when they are finished. Just keep in mind that the session will not be available for anyone else to use. This sometimes presents a problem if administrators get into the habit of ending sessions by simply closing the window, thus locking everyone out. We'll take a look at how to free the sessions up from the server in the next session, but the best solution is training the administrators to end their sessions the correct way, according to their needs.

Connecting to Session 0

Some programs are written in such a way that they have trouble communicating with the type of Remote Desktop for Administration session we've learned how to create so far. Those programs communicate, through dialog boxes, messages, and alerts, only with **session 0**, which is also known as the **console session**. Regardless of what you call it, the console session is simply the session that is running locally at the server, as opposed to the two remote sessions supported by Remote Desktop for Administration. It is possible to work with programs that interact only with the

Cross Check

Configuring and Creating a Remote Desktop Connection

Now that we've had a chance to configure and use a Remote Desktop Connection, take a moment to review the material and answer the following questions:

1. What Remote Desktop Connection options change with the speed of connection?

2. What are the two basic ways of closing a session at the client? How are they different?

console session only from a remote connection, but to do so, you have to connect in a slightly different way so that your remote session will be treated as the console session.

There are actually a couple of different ways to connect to the console session, but the easiest is from the command line using the Run dialog box. The command **mstsc.exe /console** will bring up the same Remote Desktop Connection dialog box we've been dealing with, but when the connection is made, the server will treat it as session 0. There's no visible difference in the actual connection, or the RDC dialog box, but any dialog boxes or alerts sent to session 0 will appear in the remote connection, as they should.

You don't usually have to worry about connecting to the console session, especially when you're working with the operating system's built-in utilities and programs. However, keep this technique in mind in case you ever do run into a case where a program isn't working properly, and give it a try. Sometimes it's just the thing.

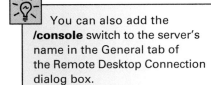

You can also add the **/console** switch to the server's name in the General tab of the Remote Desktop Connection dialog box.

We'll see in the next section that there is a way, from the server, to tell if a remote session has been connected as session 0.

■ Managing Remote Desktop Connections

In addition to customizing connection settings, there are a number of management tasks that can be performed at the server in relation to Remote Desktop for Administration. Administrators can customize connection settings at the server for all users or individual users. Administrators can also manage and interact with the current sessions of remote users. Let's take a look at the management tools that make it all possible and some of the more common configuration settings and management options they offer.

Modifying Sessions Settings at the Server

Session settings for all users can be configured at the server by using the **Terminal Services Configuration** console, which is found in Administrative Tools and is displayed in Figure 12.6. From this console, you can work with the properties of the connection protocol and the settings of the server itself. Note that there is also a column that identifies which session each connection is using. This is the one place you can tell if a remote session is acting as session 0, the console session.

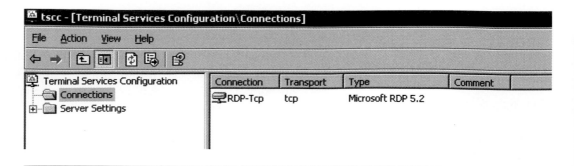

● **Figure 12.6** The Terminal Services Configuration Console

The connection type used by Terminal Services for Remote Desktop for Administration is the **RDP-Tcp**, which stands for remote desktop protocol-transfer control protocol. By modifying the properties of this connection, using the Client Settings tab of the properties dialog box shown in Figure 12.7, it is possible to modify most of the same options we were working with when we configured the options for the Remote Desktop Connection. This is sometimes done to eliminate certain options, such as drive mapping, to increase security.

Additionally, we can use the Sessions tab of the properties dialog box, shown in Figure 12.8, to place time limits on active sessions, idle sessions, and disconnected sessions. An **active session**, as the name implies, is one in which the user is actively performing tasks. It's rarely a good idea to put an actual limit on an active session, since it's obviously being used, but it can be done. An **idle session**, of course, is one in which there is no activity. Setting time limits on idle sessions is sometimes a good idea, since it is always possible that someone might begin a session and then forget about it, which could cause other administrators to be unable to connect. A **disconnected session** is one that is still running, but from which the user has disconnected by closing their remote desktop connection without logging off. As you recall, exiting a session without logging off keeps the session running and keeps anyone else from being able to access one of the two available sessions. This is a problem because the default behavior is that disconnected sessions *never* time out! If you find that people consistently disconnect from sessions without logging off, thus ending the session, you may want to place a time limit on disconnected sessions to free them back up again. Just be careful not to set the limit on disconnected sessions too low, since there are times when sessions are disconnected intentionally with processes and programs still running.

Once you've chosen your time limits for the various session types, you can also choose whether sessions that are broken or exceed their limits should be disconnected or ended. Unlike disconnected sessions, a session that is ended is actually reset, which means that all programs and processes end and the session is once again available for use by someone else. Although that's usually a good option for idle sessions, you should be cautious in ending disconnected

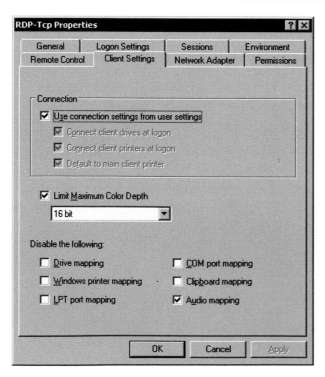

● **Figure 12.7** The Client Settings tab of the RDP-Tcp Properties dialog box

Introduction to Windows Server 2003

or active sessions too quickly. In general, I suggest placing no limits on active sessions, relatively short limits on idle sessions (15–30 minutes), and fairly generous limits on disconnected sessions (2–3 hours.) Although this may still result in occasional lockouts, it provides enough time for most processes that might be running during a disconnected session to complete. However, these limits will certainly vary depending on the nature of the work environment, and the real key is training administrators to end sessions when they are finished by logging off rather than leaving them disconnected when they don't need to be.

If you do have a problem with one particular user, you can open the Active Directory Users and Computers console and use the Sessions tab of the user's account properties dialog box, as shown in Figure 12.9, to modify settings that apply only to them. In fact, this is sometimes the best way to deal with a single forgetful administrator without penalizing the others. I know from personal experience I've been tempted to change these settings for one administrator on my network at work; unfortunately, he's the boss and might not like it very much. I guess I'll just have to keep training him!

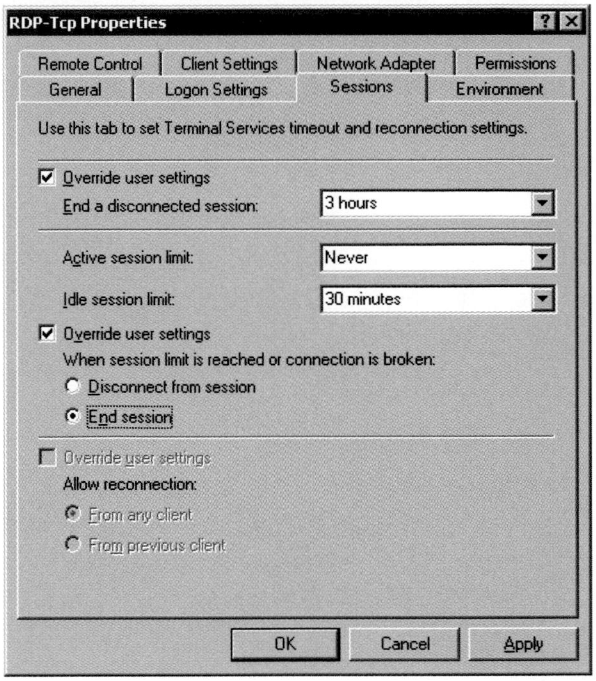

Managing Current Sessions

The Sessions tab of the **Terminal Services Manager** console, which is shown in Figure 12.10, is the tool to use if you need to monitor the sessions currently in use and, when necessary, disconnect or end them. This console allows you to disconnect active or idle sessions, thus leaving their programs and

• **Figure 12.8**   The Sessions tab of the RDP-Tcp Properties dialog box

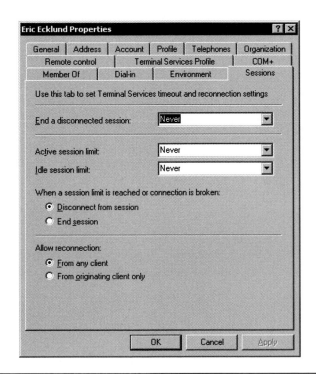

• **Figure 12.9**   The Sessions tab of a user account properties dialog box

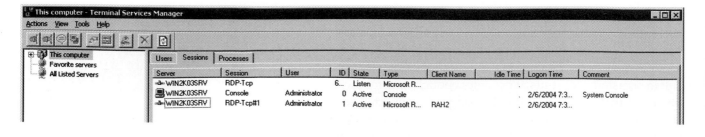

processes running. It can also be used to reset any connection, which ends it and frees the session back up for someone else to use. It can also be used to send messages to the user of a session, which is a nice gesture if you're about to disconnect or reset them! It's even possible to reconnect a disconnected session from the server, which comes in handy if you just disconnected the wrong person!

Step-by-Step 12.3

Configuring and Managing Remote Desktop for Administration Sessions from the Server

Even though the intent of this Step-by-Step is to make modifications from the server, we're going to continue to work through our Remote Desktop Connection we created in Step-by-Step 12.2. After all, what better proof that our connection lets us work with the server just as if we were sitting in front of it! After we've taken a look at some of the configuration changes we can make, we'll send the client computer a message from the server and then reset the session through the remote connection.

To complete this Step-by-Step, you will need

- A properly configured computer with Windows Server 2003 installed and remote connections enabled

- The client computer set up in Chapter 10

- A LAN connection between the client and server

- Access to an administrator-level account on the server

| Step 1 | If your Remote Desktop Connection is no longer open, reopen it. It is not necessary to make any changes to the basic configuration when you do this; simply enter the server's name and then log on to the server when prompted. |

| Step 2 | Click Start | Administrative Tools | Terminal Services Configuration. Maximize the console. Click the Server Settings container in the left pane to display the available options in the right pane. It is not normally necessary to modify these options, but there are some cases where it helps to restrict users to only one session in order to conserve the available sessions. |

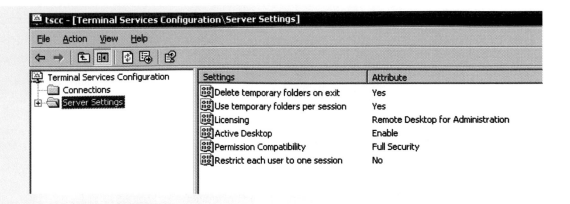

Step 3

Click the Connections container in the left pane and then right-click the RDP-Tcp connection in the right pane. Choose Properties and click the Client Settings tab. Note that connection settings are normally left up to the user. However, color depth is limited to 16-bit by default. Both this and the disabling of the audio mapping help conserve bandwidth.

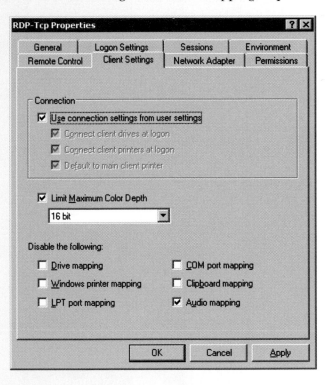

Step 4

Click the Sessions tab. Check the first check box, labeled Override user settings. Pull down the selection list for ending a disconnected session and note the available options. These suggested times are just that; suggested. You can actually enter any time interval you like, up to 49 days, 17 hours. Simply enter the limit as *X days Y hours Z minutes.* Try entering **15 days 20 hours 5 minutes**, as shown in the next illustration, and click Apply. Once you are sure your entry was accepted, change the entry back to Never, uncheck the check box, and click Close. You will see a message that the changes you made will not effect the currently active session. Click OK to clear the message.

Step 5	Close the Terminal Services Configuration console. Click Start	Administrative Tools	Terminal Services Manager. Maximize the console and click the Sessions tab in the right pane. Locate the session with your user name in the User column. Right-click the name of the server for your session where it appears in the Server column in the same row and choose Send Message. Enter a message to yourself and click OK. When your message appears on the screen, click OK to clear it. 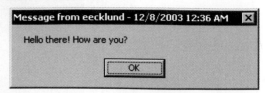
Step 6	Right-click the name of the server for your session again and choose Disconnect to disconnect your session. Click OK to confirm. After the session closes, reopen it from the client computer. Note that the session opens up right where you left off because it was only disconnected, not reset. 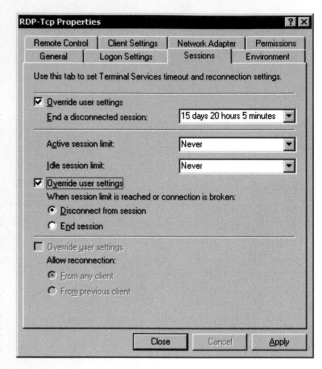
Step 7	Right-click the name of the server for your session again and choose Reset. Click OK to confirm. After the session closes, reopen it from the client computer. Note that this time your session is entirely new and all open windows from the previous session are closed. When you are finished, click Start	Log Off and click Log Off to end the session.

☑ Cross Check

Managing Remote Desktop for Administration Sessions at the Server

Now that we've had a chance to work with a few of the server-side settings and management tasks for Remote Desktop for Administration, take a moment to review the material and answer the following questions:

1. What mapping settings are available through Terminal Services Configuration that were not available through Remote Desktop Connection options?

2. What is the difference between disconnecting a session and resetting a session?

Chapter 12 Review

■ Chapter Summary

After reading this chapter and completing the Step-by-Step tutorials and Try This! exercises, you should understand the following facts about using Remote Desktop for Administration to remotely manage a Windows Server 2003 server.

Describe Basic Remote Desktop for Administration Concepts

- Remote Desktop for Administration is a feature of Terminal Services that can be used by administrators to create remote connections to the server, called sessions.

- Remote Desktop for Administration is easy to use and is supported by many operating systems. Connections can be established over dial-up, LAN, or VPN connections.

- Since Remote Desktop for Administration sends only keyboard and mouse input from the client and only displays data from the server, it has a very low resource overhead.

- Administrators should avoid rebooting a server while using Remote Desktop for Administration, as there is no way to troubleshoot a failed boot from a remote location.

- Remote Desktop for Administration does open a server up to increased security risks. Administrators must take care to guard the passwords to their accounts, use strong passwords, and consider changing the name of the administrator account.

- Remote Desktop for Administration supports only administrator accounts by default and allows for only two simultaneous connections.

- Remote Desktop for Administration access to a Windows Server 2003 computer is disabled by default. It can be enabled through the Remote tab of the System Properties dialog box.

Configure and Create a Remote Desktop Connection

- The General options tab of the Remote Desktop Connection dialog box allows you to enter the machine's name or IP address, as well as your user name, password, and domain. Settings can be saved as a Remote Desktop protocol file from this tab, and existing .rdp files can be loaded from here.

- The Display options tab allows you to control the remote desktop size and colors. You can also choose whether or not the connection bar should be displayed while in full screen mode.

- The Local Resources options tab allows for the redirecting, or mapping, of local resources to the remote session. Drives, printers, and serial ports are all devices that can be mapped or redirected.

- The Programs options tab can be used to launch programs upon establishing a remote session.

- The Experience options tab is used to select your connection speed. Various aspects of the desktop experience are enabled or disabled according to the selected speed.

- Closing a Remote Desktop for Administration session by logging off ends the session and all programs or processes associated with it. The session is then available for use by another user.

- Closing a Remote Desktop for Administration session by choosing Disconnect from the shutdown dialog box or by closing the Remote Desktop Connection screen disconnects the session but leaves all programs and processes running. If the user connects again later, they will connect to the same session.

- Session 0, also known as the console session, is the session that occurs locally at the server. To connect to session 0, use the /console switch either after the machine name or IP address in Remote Desktop Connection or after the command mstsc.exe in the Run dialog box.

Manage Remote Desktop Connections

- The Terminal Services Configuration console is used to modify the properties of the RDP-Tcp connection protocol. From the Client Settings tab of the RDP-Tcp Properties dialog box, limitations can be placed on the options available for use by the client machines in the Remote Desktop Connection dialog box.

- The Sessions tab of the RDP-Tcp Properties dialog box can be used to put time limits on active sessions, idle sessions, and disconnected sessions. When the time limit is exceeded or the connection is interrupted, you can choose to either disconnect or end the session.

- The Sessions tab of the Terminal Services Manager console can be used to monitor sessions, disconnect sessions, reset sessions, and send messages to client machines connected to a session.

■ Key Terms List

active session *(370)*
clipboard mapping *(363)*
connection bar *(362)*
console session *(369)*
disconnected session *(370)*
idle session *(370)*
mapped *(363)*
RDP-Tcp *(370)*
redirected *(363)*

Remote Desktop Connection (RDC) *(357)*
Remote Desktop for Administration *(355)*
Remote Desktop protocol file *(361)*
session *(355)*
session 0 *(369)*
Terminal Server *(355)*
Terminal Services *(355)*

Terminal Services Configuration *(369)*
Terminal Services Manager *(371)*
thin client *(355)*
virtual private network (VPN) *(357)*
Windows CE *(357)*

■ Key Terms Quiz

Use terms from the Key Terms list to complete the sentences that follow. Don't use the same term more than once. Not all terms will be used.

1. The _____ is normally displayed at all times when the Remote Desktop Connection display is in full screen mode.

2. An _____ is one in which there is no activity from the user.

3. Remote Desktop Connection supports _____, which makes it easy to exchange data and files between the local and remote computers.

4. Remote Desktop Connections use the _____ connection protocol.

5. The console session is also known as _____.

6. Both Windows XP and Windows Server 2003 have _____ installed by default.

7. Remote Desktop for Administration is one of two modes of _____ operation.

8. A _____ may still be running programs and processes even though the user is no longer connected.

9. A Remote Desktop Connection can be established through a LAN, via a dial-up connection, or over a _____.

10. _____ can be used at the server to send a message to a client machine connected to a session.

■ Multiple-Choice Quiz

1. The maximum number of connections supported by Remote Desktop for Administration is
   a. 2
   b. 10
   c. 25
   d. Dependent on the amount of RAM installed in the server

2. What is the maximum time limit you can place on a disconnected session?
   a. 17 days 5 hours
   b. 30 days 12 hours
   c. 49 days 17 hours
   d. 3 days 0 hours

3. The switch to connect to session 0 is

    a. /mstcs

    b. /0

    c. /root

    d. /console

4. Which options tab in Remote Desktop Connection is used to set the speed of the connection?

    a. General

    b. Experience

    c. Programs

    d. Local Resources

5. The chapter suggests that while using Remote Desktop for Administration, administrators should avoid

    a. Logging off

    b. Copying and pasting

    c. Rebooting

    d. Running antivirus scans

6. The extension of the files used to save settings in Remote Desktop Connection is

    a. .rdc

    b. .msr

    c. .rdp

    d. .mmc

7. If an administrator logs off the remote session, the session is

    a. Ended

    b. Disconnected

    c. Idle

    d. Reserved

8. Which Windows keyboard shortcut is *not* redirected to the remote session?

    a. CTRL-ALT-BREAK

    b. ALT-TAB

    c. CTRL-ALT-DELETE

    d. CTRL-C

9. Which console can be used to set session timeouts for an individual account?

    a. Terminal Services Manager

    b. Terminal Services Configuration

    c. Group Policy Editor

    d. Active Directory Users and Computers

10. What is the default timeout for a disconnected session?

    a. Never

    b. 1 day

    c. 2 days

    d. 3 days

11. What is the default upper limit on colors for Remote Desktop Connections in Windows Server 2003?

    a. 8-bit

    b. 16-bit

    c. 24-bit

    d. 32-bit

12. Which of the following is *not* a choice for connection speed on the Experience tab of the Remote Desktop Connection dialog box?

    a. Modem (28.8 Kbps)

    b. Modem (33.6 Kbps)

    c. Modem (56 Kbps)

    d. Broadband (128 Kbps–1.5 Mbps)

13. Which of the following devices is redirected by default in the Local Resources tab of the Remote Desktop Connection dialog box?

    a. Audio

    b. Drives

    c. Printers

    d. Serial ports

14. What is the default size of the Remote Desktop Connection display for the remote desktop?

    a. Full screen

    b. 1024×768

    c. 800×600

    d. 640×480

15. Which option on the Experience tab of the Remote Desktop Connection dialog box should almost always be on?

    a. Show contents of window while dragging

    b. Menu and window animation

    c. Bitmap caching

    d. Themes

1. Your boss is concerned that enabling remote access for Remote Desktop for Administration carries too much security risk. Explain some ways you can minimize the exposure.

2. Your boss still isn't convinced that Remote Desktop for Administration is worth taking the risk. Explain some of the benefits to the organization of enabling this technology.

3. You finally got permission to start using Remote Desktop for Administration on your network. What should you warn the other administrators about before they start using it?

4. One of your fellow administrators constantly leaves all of her sessions disconnected. Explain to her when she should disconnect and when she should end a session.

5. Under what circumstances would you disable remote access to the server temporarily?

Lab Projects

• Lab Project 12.1

Describe three different, specific, scenarios where you can imagine Remote Desktop for Administration improving an administrator's ability to perform a task. Be as specific as possible.

• Lab Project 12.2

Create a list of the "Ten Commandments" for using Remote Desktop for Administration that you would distribute to all administrators that would be using remote sessions. Focus on best practices, potential trouble spots, and security issues. Your list may exceed ten items if necessary.

• Lab Project 12.3

If you administered the network at your school or place of business along with several colleagues, what settings would you choose for timeouts of active, idle, and disconnected sessions? Explain your rationale.

The number in parentheses that follows each definition is the chapter in which the term is explained.

access control entry (ACE) Term for each individual user or group entry on the access control list (ACL) of a resource. (8)

access control list (ACL) The list of users and groups to whom permissions have been granted or denied for accessing a particular resource. (8)

account lockout duration Account lockout policy that controls how long a locked-out account will be made unavailable. (11)

account lockout threshold Account lockout policy that controls the allowed number of failed attempts prior to locking out an account. (11)

account policies Security settings policies that include password policies, account lockout policies, and Kerberos policies. (11)

Active Directory The directory service that manages the database of objects that make up a Microsoft domain. (1, 4)

active session A Terminal Services session in which the user is actively performing tasks. (12)

administrative templates settings Collections of group policy settings that allow for changes to the operating system's Registry. (11)

alerts A feature of the Performance console that allows for the creation of automated alarms that are triggered when certain conditions are met. Alerts may be configured for each of the counters the System Monitor is capable of monitoring. (9)

American Registry for Internet Numbers (ARIN) The Regional Internet Registry (RIR) responsible for allocating IP addresses within North America as well as a portion of the Caribbean and North Africa. (3)

answer file A text file used by Windows setup or remote installation services that provides the answers to installation and configuration questions. The default answer file is unattend.txt. (2)

application log The event log that contains events associated with various applications. (9)

attended installation An installation during which the user interactively responds to prompts by the Windows setup program for information and configuration options. (2)

authenticate To verify the identity of a user. This is typically done by matching a given account name with the password entered by the user. (1)

Authentication Service (AS) Service used by Kerberos security to authenticate a user account through Active Directory during logon. (11)

authorize The act of enabling a Windows Server 2003 server to provide a particular service to the network. (10)

Automated System Recovery (ASR) backup set A feature of Windows Backup that creates a set of disks that contain backups of all essential system files and settings including a bootable diskette that can be used to restore the backed-up files. (6)

basic disk A physical disk divided into from one to four partitions, which become the underlying structure for storing data on the disk. All four partitions can be primary partitions, each of which is treated as a single drive letter. One of the four partitions may be an extended partition, which is further subdivided into multiple logical drives. (6)

Classless Inter-Domain Routing (CIDR) A scheme for allocating IP addresses that makes use of variable-length subnet masks, as opposed to the three fixed masks of the older class-based system. (3)

clean installation An installation of an operating system on a computer hard disk that has been wiped clean of any previous operating system or data. (2)

client A computer that receives services from a server in a client/server network. (1)

client/server network A network that consists of one or more central computers, called servers, that provides services and access to resources to the rest of the computers connected to the network, which are called clients. (1)

clipboard mapping A feature of Terminal Services that allows the copying and pasting of information between the client and the server. (12)

clustering Linking multiple servers together in such a way that they can share the processing and/or network communications load. (1)

commit charge limit A statistic displayed on the Performance tab of Task Manager that displays the total amount of memory available by combining both the page file and the physical memory. (9)

commit charge peak A statistic displayed on the Performance tab of Task Manager that indicates the maximum amount of demand placed on the page file since Task Manager was run. (9)

commit charge total A statistic displayed on the Performance tab of Task Manager that indicates the amount of virtual memory currently in use. (9)

computer account An Active Directory object that represents a unique computer within the domain. (5)

computer configuration settings Group policy settings that focus on controlling aspects of the computer and its operating system, regardless of who the user is. (11)

connection bar A small yellow bar that appears at the top of the display in a full-screen Remote Desktop connection displaying the name of the remote computer and a set of window control buttons. (12)

console session In Terminal Services, the session that is running locally at the server. Synonymous with the term session 0. (12)

contact An Active Directory object that represents the contact information for an individual from outside the network. (5)

container An Active Directory object that can contain other objects. Containers are represented in Active Directory using variations on the folder icon. (5)

contiguous namespace A logical network structure, common to trees in Microsoft networking, in which all domains share the same root domain name. For instance, the domains peru.ezeranch.com, venezuela.ezeranch.com, and mexico.ezeranch.com all exist in a contiguous namespace. (4)

counter A statistic that can be tracked by System Monitor relating to the performance of some piece of hardware, software process, or operating system component. (9)

counter logs A feature of the Performance console that tracks performance object counters over time in a file so that they can be reviewed later using System Monitor. (9)

critical update An update to the operating system that addresses a security flaw or problem that could result in serious data loss or system failure. (2)

default domain controllers policy Group policy settings applied to any domain controller within a domain. This policy is created automatically when Active Directory is installed. (11)

default domain policy The overall group policy settings for a domain. This policy is created automatically when Active Directory is installed. (11)

defragment The process of rearranging the data stored on a hard disk so that all of the pieces of individual files are as close to adjacent to each other as possible. (6)

demote To remove the domain controller role from a server, converting it into either a member server or stand-alone server. (4)

disconnected session A Terminal Services session that is still running, but from which the user has disconnected by closing their remote desktop connection without logging off. (12)

disjointed namespace A logical network structure, common to forests in Microsoft networking, in which domains do not share the same root domain name. For instance, the domains peru.ezeranch.com and east.ezesteaks.com exist in a disjointed namespace. (4)

disk image A computer file that represents an exact duplicate of a hard disk and its contents. An image can be used to create an exact copy of that hard disk on another machine. (2)

distinguished name (DN) A name that fully identifies an Active Directory object and its place within the domain. An example is CN=WIN2K03SRV,CN= Servers,CN=Home,CN=Sites,CN=Configuration,DC= ezeranch,DC=com. (5)

distribution group An Active Directory object whose purpose is to group together computer accounts, user accounts, and group accounts, solely for the purposes of sending e-mail messages and not for the setting of access permissions. (5)

domain The basic logical structure of a Microsoft network. Domains are created and managed through Active Directory in Windows Server 2003 and Windows 2000. In Windows NT, domains are created and managed by the Security Accounts Manager (SAM) database. (1)

domain controller (DC) A server upon which Active Directory has been installed, which is then used to administer the network and its objects. (4)

domain functional level A configuration setting for Windows Server 2003 domain controllers that determines the features available within the Active Directory domain. The choice of domain functional level is limited by the presence of domain controllers running earlier operating systems such as Windows 2000 or Windows NT. (4)

domain local group A group scope that allows for access to resources only within the domain in which the domain local group account was created. Domain local groups may contain other domain local groups from the same domain and computer accounts, user accounts,

global groups, and universal groups from any trusted domain. (5, 8)

domain name The name of the Active Directory domain, which may either take the form of an Internet DNS name, such as ecktek.com, or a purely internal name, such as ecktek.local. (4)

domain name system (DNS) The system for assigning names to networks and computers that can then be associated with registered IP addresses. (4)

domain name system (DNS) service The Windows Server 2003 service responsible for resolving DNS names into IP addresses. (3)

dots per inch (dpi) Measurement of the print resolution of a printer. (7)

dotted decimal A form for expressing IP addresses that consists of four decimal numbers, ranging from 1 to 255, each separated by a period. The IP address 192.168.2.1 is one example. (3)

downgrade An installation of a less powerful edition of a new operating system over an existing installation of a more powerful edition of an older operating system. (2)

driver update An update to the software programs used by the operating system to communicate with various pieces of hardware within or attached to the computer system. One of the categories of updates found on the Windows Update web site. (2)

dynamic disk A disk that makes use of volumes, rather than partitions, for dividing the physical disk into discrete storage areas. (6)

dynamic IP address An IP address that is assigned by a dynamic host configuration protocol (DHCP) server. A dynamic IP address may change from time to time as its lease on the address expires. (3)

effective permissions The overall effect of all combined NTFS permissions inherited from group membership or applied to the user or group account directly. The ability to analyze effective permissions is a new feature to Windows Server 2003. (8)

event logs A feature of some versions of Windows that uses log files to track a variety of events relating to the system, security, applications, and other areas of operation. (9)

Event Viewer　The utility used to view and work with event logs. (9)

extended partition　A partition on a basic disk that can be further subdivided into logical drives. Each basic disk can have only one extended partition. Extended partitions are not bootable under Microsoft operating systems. (6)

extended volume　A volume that is actually an extension of an existing simple volume on the same disk. (6)

fault tolerance　The ability of a piece of hardware or software to survive normally catastrophic events. (6)

file allocation table (FAT)　The file system used by earlier versions of Windows and MS-DOS and still available as an alternative file system for newer Windows operating systems. Also the name of the actual record of files and their locations on hard disks that are formatted with this file system. (1)

file system　The system used by an operating system for naming, storing, and retrieving files on a hard disk. (1)

first-layer domain　In an Active Directory domain, the first child domains under the root domain. For instance, peru.ecktek.com is a first-layer domain of ecktek.com. (4)

flat image　A virtual copy of the installation CD for an operating system to be installed using RIS that, for all intents and purposes, acts just like the original. (10)

Folder Redirection of My Documents　A feature of Windows Server 2003 that allows redirection of users' My Documents folder on client machines to a centralized location on a server. (1)

forest functional level　A configuration setting for Windows Server 2003 domain controllers that determines the features available within the Active Directory forest. The choice of forest functional level is limited by the domain functional level of the domain controllers within the forest. (4)

formatting　The process of preparing a hard disk partition to hold data by placing the file system and its organizational structures on the drive. (2)

forward lookup zone　A list of external DNS servers to which requests for DNS names from outside the domain are sent. By default, a forward lookup zone is configured to query one or more Internet root servers to begin the process of resolving external DNS names. (3)

fragmented　Term used to describe a hard disk on which the pieces of individual files are spread across the disk rather than stored adjacent to each other. (6)

fully qualified domain name (FQDN)　A form of a computer's DNS name that indicates both the name of the computer and the domain to which it belongs. The name rah2.ecktek.com is an example of a fully qualified domain name that identifies the computer, rah2, on the domain, ecktek.com. (3)

global catalog (GC)　A directory database hosted on one of the domain controllers in a tree or forest that keeps track of a few key pieces of information for each network object within the tree or forest. Used to help locate network objects between domains without the need to fully replicate the Active Directory database of each domain. (4)

global group　A group scope that can be given permissions for only the domain in which it was created but that can obtain permissions for access in other domains in the forest by joining the domain local groups of those domains. Global groups may contain other global groups, computer accounts, and user accounts only from their own domain. (5, 8)

group account　An Active Directory object that represents a grouping of computer or user accounts for the purpose of access permission assignment or communication. (5)

group policy　A feature of Windows Server 2003 that allows administrators to apply collections of settings to all members of a domain or an OU. Group policy settings can be used to control everything from Registry settings at client computers to user rights and software restriction policies. (5)

Group Policy Management Console (GPMC)　A new tool introduced in Windows Server 2003 for more easily managing group policy object settings. Although the GPMC is not included with Windows Server 2003, it can be downloaded easily from Microsoft's web site. (4, 11)

group policy object (GPO)　Term used to describe each unique collection of group policy settings. (11)

Group Policy Object Editor The most commonly used administrative tool for working with group policy objects. (11)

group scope Term used to describe the extent of access potentially provided for by membership in a group. The three group scopes are domain local, global, and universal. (5, 8)

hal.dll The dynamic link library file used by Windows Server 2003 to represent the actual Hardware Abstraction Layer file provided by the manufacturer of the computer's motherboard. The hal.dll file is located in the System32 subfolder of the Windows folder. (10)

handles A statistic displayed on the Performance tab of Task Manager that represents all the resources, such as open files or entries in the Registry, that are currently being used by the CPU. (9)

Hardware Abstraction Layer (HAL) Part of the operating system that lets the OS interact with the computer's hardware in an "abstract," or general, way. (10)

Hardware Compatibility List (HCL) The tool of choice for Windows XP, Windows Me, and Windows 2000 for checking hardware compatibility for those operating systems. (2)

Hot Add Memory A feature of Windows Server 2003 that supports the adding of additional RAM to a running server without the need to reboot. This feature must also be supported by the server hardware. (1)

idle session A Terminal Services session in which there is no activity. (12)

inheritance Term that describes the implicit granting of access permissions to users and/or groups through their membership in groups that have been explicitly granted those permissions. (8)

instance Term used to describe a performance object counter when there is more than one "thing" that the counter applies to. An example would be the %Processor Time counter on a computer with multiple processors. The unique counter for a particular CPU would be one instance of the %Processor Time counter. (9)

Internet Assigned Numbers Authority (IANA) The ultimate authority for the allocation of IP addresses on a global basis. The IANA allocates IP addresses to lower-level Internet registries that then allocate addresses to actual networks. (3)

IP host name The segment of an IP address that identifies the individual computer on a network. Represented by the part of the IP address, in binary, that corresponds to the 0's of the subnet mask. (3)

ipconfig A useful Windows utility for displaying the status and configuration settings of a computer's network interface cards. (3)

IPv6 An IP addressing scheme that makes use of 128-bit addresses and provides over four million unique addresses for each square meter of the entire Earth's surface. (3)

Kerberos security The security system used by Windows Server 2003 to authenticate users and grant them access to resources. (11)

lease The duration during which a client that is assigned an IP address by a DHCP server is permitted to retain that IP addresses. Prior to the expiration of a lease, the lease can be renewed. After a lease has expired, the client must renegotiate a new lease and, in the meantime, the originally leased IP address may be reassigned to another client. (3)

local policy Group policy settings that apply only to the local computer. (11)

local print devices Term describing printers that are physically connected to one of the ports on a computer when being accessed from that computer. (7)

logical drive Subdivisions of a single extended partition on a basic disk, each of which is referred to by a single drive letter. (6)

logical printer In Windows Server 2003, a term for the software interface between the operating system and the actual printing device. (7)

mapped Term that refers to devices that have been made available to the remote session when using Remote Desktop Connection. Synonymous with the term redirected. (12)

member server A server that belongs to an Active Directory domain but is not a domain controller. (4)

Messenger service Service used to send performance alerts. It is disabled by default in Windows Server 2003. (9)

Microsoft Management Console (MMC) A standardized console interface for working with a variety of administrative tools called snap-ins. (1)

Microsoft Product Activation (MPA) An approach to reducing the piracy of Microsoft software that requires users to activate the software through Microsoft within a certain number of days after installation. In the case of Windows, the product can be activated only on a single computer system, thus eliminating the value of pirated copies. (2)

mirrored volume A volume on a dynamic disk that is an exact, real-time copy of a volume on another dynamic disk. Mirrored volumes provide fault tolerance without decreasing performance. (6)

mounted volume A volume on a dynamic disk that is associated with an existing folder rather than being assigned a drive letter. Such volumes are accessed by users as if they were folders. (6)

multimaster replication The process used by Active Directory to continuously synchronize the Active Directory database on all domain controllers within a domain to ensure that the information on each is up-to-date. (4)

name resolution The process of translating DNS or NetBIOS names into IP addresses and vice versa. (3)

namespace The logical area within Active Directory in which names are resolved. (4)

nesting The practice of making groups of a particular scope members of other groups of the same scope—For instance, making a domain local group a member of another domain local group. In general, nesting should be kept to a minimum, as it can make troubleshooting access-related problems difficult. (8)

.NET A Microsoft initiative for a technology that will allow a wide variety of devices easier methods for connecting and communicating. Microsoft's intent with this initiative is to expand the sharing of data beyond traditional computer networks to include cell phones, personal digital assistants, and other web-ready devices. (1)

Network Address Translation (NAT) A technology that allows a router, or other network device, with a public IP address to "stand in" for computers on the network using private IP addresses. NAT avoids the potential conflict of having IP addresses within a network duplicate IP addresses outside the network and helps conserve limited public IP addresses. (3)

Network Basic Input/Output System (NetBIOS) An older networking system used by earlier versions of Windows such as Windows 98 and Windows NT. (3)

network print devices Term describing printers that are accessed over a network connection. (7)

nonremote print device A printer that is accessed by a computer without the intervention of a server. (7)

NT File System (NTFS) The file system introduced in Windows NT that offers distinct advantages over the older, FAT file system. NTFS offers folder and file-level access permissions and, in later versions, file encryption. (1)

NTFS permissions Access permissions for files and/or folders that are part of the NTFS file system. (8)

open file backup A feature of Windows Server 2003 that allows even files that are currently in use by either the system or users to be copied by backup programs. (1)

organizational unit (OU) Logical network structures used to subdivide a domain into more manageable parts. Each OU can have its own group policies applied to it, and the administrative control of OUs can be delegated to ease the workload on the administrator of the domain. (4)

ownership An Active Directory concept that refers to the account that has the ability to control permissions on the object and grant permissions to others. The account that creates an object initially has ownership of that object. (8)

package A file containing installation instructions used to remotely install applications on client computers in conjunction with the Windows Installer Service. (11)

pages per minute (ppm) Measurement of the speed of a printer's output. (7)

parallel port A 25-pin, D-shaped female port used to attach a printer or other parallel device to a PC. (7)

parity-information stripe The additional blocks of information written to a RAID-5 volume that can be used to re-create any data lost from a hard disk failure. (6)

partition A discrete portion of a hard disk that is used as the underlying structure for the storage of data on that disk. A partition must be formatted with a file system before data can be stored on it. (2)

password policies Group policy settings that determine the rules for password creation and expiration. (11)

peer-to-peer network A network with no central server in which each computer on the network can act as both client and server to the others. (1)

Per Device or Per User licensing A Windows Server 2003 licensing mode that requires a single client access license for every potential user or device that might connect to the server but puts no limit on the simultaneous number of connections to the server. (2)

Per Server licensing A Windows Server 2003 licensing mode that is based on the total number of concurrent connections to a particular server with no regard to the users or devices that make those connections. The default licensing mode of Windows Server 2003 is Per Server licensing with five concurrent connections. (2)

Performance Console Administrative tool used to access System Monitor, counter logs, trace logs, and alerts. (9)

performance logs Log files, including counter logs and trace logs that can be used to track System Monitor performance object counters over time. (9)

performance object Term used to describe a unique element of hardware, software, or the operating system that may be measured by one or more counters in System Monitor. (9)

permissions A setting or collection of settings that determine the type and extent of access a user or computer may have for a particular resource. (1)

physical printer A Windows Server 2003 term sometimes used to describe the actual printing hardware so as to differentiate it from the logical printer. Also known as a print device or simply printer. (7)

Preboot Execution Environment (PXE) A technology that works in conjunction with NICs to enable a computer to essentially boot from the network even when no operating system is present on the local hard drive. (10)

prestage Preparing a client computer to use RIS by creating the computer account ahead of time as a managed computer. (10)

primary partition A partition on a basic disk that is assigned a single drive letter and may be bootable. (6)

print device A Windows Server 2003 term sometimes used to describe the actual printing hardware so as to differentiate it from the logical printer. Synonymous with the terms physical printer and printer. (7)

print queue The collection of documents being held by the print spooler waiting to print. (7)

print server A server-classed computer connected to multiple printers for the purposes of making those printers available to network clients. (7)

print spooler The software that accepts the documents that are to be printed and stores them until the printer is ready for them. (7)

printer A Windows Server 2003 term sometimes used to describe the actual printing hardware so as to differentiate it from the logical printer. Synonymous with the terms physical printer and print device. (7)

printer permissions Access permissions applied to shared print devices. (8)

printer pooling Technique of treating several identical printers as a single logical printer for the purposes of distributing print jobs among the printers that make up the pool. (7)

priority When used in relation to printers, priority refers to the setting controlling which logical printer prints first. When used in relation to print jobs, priority refers to the setting controlling which print job prints first. When used in relation to running processes, priority refers to the setting that controls which process has first call on the computer and operating system's resources. (7, 9)

process   Term used in Task Manager to describe an executable program currently running on the computer. (9)

process tree   A collection of related processes. (9)

promote   Describes the process of converting a standalone or member server into a domain controller through the installation of Active Directory. (4)

protocol   A set of rules and standards for network communications between computers and/or networks. (3)

publish   The act of creating an Active Directory object that represents a shared resource such as a folder or printer. (5)

RAID   Acronym that stands for "redundant array of inexpensive (or independent) disks." (6)

RAID-5 volume   A volume that uses three or more dynamic disks to provide both increased performance and fault tolerance through striping data and the use of a parity-information stripe. (6)

rbfg.exe   The utility used to create a boot disk for non-PXE-enabled client computers so that they can access an RIS server. (10)

RDP-Tcp   Acronym for remote desktop protocol-transfer control protocol, which is the connection type used by Terminal Services for Remote Desktop for Administration. (12)

redirect print jobs   The process of reassigning the port associated with a logical printer for the purposes of sending print jobs intended for one print device to another. (7)

redirected   In printing, a term that refers to moving print jobs from one logical printer to another. In Terminal Services, a term that refers to devices that have been made available to the remote session when using Remote Desktop Connection. When used in reference to Remote Desktop Connections, it is synonymous with the term mapped. (7, 12)

reference computer   A client computer used as the basis of a RIPrep image. (10)

relative distinguished name (RDN)   A simple form of an object's name that uniquely identifies it relative to its place in the Active Directory hierarchy. (5)

Remote Desktop Connection (RDC)   The client software in Windows XP and Windows Server 2003 used to create and configure connections to Remote Desktop for Administration. (12)

Remote Desktop for Administration   A Terminal Services mode that allows administrators to connect to the server from remote locations. (12)

Remote Desktop protocol file   File used to save customized settings for Remote Desktop Connections. (12)

Remote Installation Preparation Wizard   The utility used to create RIPrep images of reference computers. (10)

Remote Installation Services (RIS)   Service that allows client computers to be set up over the network. (10)

remote print device   A printer that is accessed by a computer with the intervention of a server. (7)

reparse point   A pointer used by the Single Instance Store groveler agent when it deletes duplicate files. The pointer redirects programs to the SIS Common Store Folder, which is the new location of the file that was duplicated. (10)

reset account lockout counter after   Account lockout policy setting that determines the time period during which consecutive failed logon attempts will be tracked and compared to the account lockout threshold setting. (11)

Resultant Set of Policy (RSoP)   A group policy tool that analyzes all of the policies that apply in a particular situation and reports on the final effective, or resultant, policy. (11)

reverse lookup zone   Used by a DNS server to resolve a DNS name from an IP address. (3)

RIPrep image   A Remote Installation Services image created from a reference computer. (10)

riprep.sif   The answer file used in conjunction with RIPrep images. (10)

ristndrd.sif   The answer file used in conjunction with flat images. (10)

root domain   The first domain created in the first tree of a forest. (4)

root servers   Public DNS servers that assist in the resolution of external domain names by pointing requests toward the DNS server responsible for the top-level domain that name belongs to. (3)

router   A network device used for connecting two different networks, such as a LAN and the Internet, together. Frequently provides Network Address Translation (NAT). (3)

scalable   A term that refers to the ability of something, such as a network operating system, to grow to meet increasing demands. (1)

schema   The set of attributes, both required and optional, that describe a network object within an Active Directory domain. (4)

scope   The range of addresses to be allocated by a DHCP server. (3)

scope of management (SOM)   Term used to describe the domain, site, OU, or computer to which a group policy object is applied. (11)

second-layer domain   A child domain of a first-layer domain. For example, sales.peru.ezeranch.com is a second-layer domain of peru.ezeranch.com, which is a first-layer domain of ezeranch.com, which is the root domain. (4)

Security Accounts Manager (SAM)   The Windows service in Windows NT that was responsible for maintaining the database of all network objects within a domain. The SAM was replaced by Active Directory in Windows 2000 Server. (1)

security group   A group account that is used to assign permissions for access of resources within the network. (5)

security ID (SID)   A unique identifier associated with each security principal that is used by the operating system to identify that security principal. (5)

security log   The event log that contains Success and Failure audit events. (9)

security principal   An Active Directory object, such as a computer account, user account, or group account, that can be given access permissions to network resources.

Each security principal is uniquely identified by the operating system by its security ID. (5)

server   A central computer that provides services and access to resources to other computers on the network. (1)

service   A program or process that works with the operating system to support the activities of other programs and users. (9)

service pack   A collection of many different updates, improvements, and sometimes additions to the operating system that is released after extensive testing. One of the categories of updates found on the Windows Update web site. (2)

session   In Terminal Services, term used to describe remote connections to the server. (12)

session 0   In Terminal Services, the session that is running locally at the server. Synonymous with the term console session. (12)

Shadow Copies of Shared Folders   A feature of Windows Server 2003 that allows users to retrieve previous versions of files saved to network shares without administrator intervention. This feature stores file revisions with every file write, allowing users to select exactly which version of a file they wish to restore. (1)

share permissions   Access permissions applied to shared folders. (8)

shares   A term used to describe resources, such as folders or printers, that have been made accessible, or shared, to the rest of the network. (1)

simple volume   A volume on a single dynamic disk that provides no increased performance or fault tolerance but can be expanded through the use of extended volumes on the same disk or spanned volumes across different disks. (6)

Single Instance Store Service (SIS)   Service that conserves disk space on an RIS server by minimizing the duplication of files between multiple images. (10)

SIS Common Store Folder   The folder used by the Single Instance Store Service (SIS) to store copies of deleted duplicate files. (10)

SIS groveler agent The component of the Single Instance Store Service (SIS) responsible for scanning for duplicate files, deleting them, and replacing them with a reparse point that indicates the new location of the file. (10)

site An Active Directory structure that uses subnets to segment the domain by connectivity speed. (4)

snap-in Term used to describe an administration tool that can be added to the Microsoft Management Console (MMC). (5)

software piracy The illicit copying and/or distribution of software beyond the terms of the manufacturer's license agreement. (2)

software restriction policies A new feature of Windows Server 2003 group policies that makes it possible to block the running of specific programs or block the execution of programs in an entire directory. (1, 11)

software settings A category of group policy settings for both users and computers that contains the software installation settings. (11)

spanned volume A volume that uses up to 32 dynamic disks to create larger volumes. Such volumes do not improve performance and actually decrease fault tolerance, since the loss of one disk destroys the whole volume. (6)

special permissions A highly customizable set of access permissions for files and/or folders on an NTFS-formatted volume. (8)

stand-alone server A server that is not a domain controller and does not belong to an Active Directory domain. (4)

static IP address An IP address that has been manually configured and does not change. (3)

striped volume A volume that uses identically sized segments of up to 32 dynamic disks to create a larger volume with improved performance. Such volumes decrease fault tolerance, since the loss of one disk destroys the whole volume. (6)

strong password A password that is difficult to guess. Strong passwords typically use a combination of upper- and lowercase letters, numbers, and symbols and avoid the use of proper names and words that can be found in a dictionary. (2)

subnet mask Used to mask off the part of an IP address that identifies the network from the part that identifies the individual machines on the network. 255.255.255.0 is one common example of a subnet mask. (3)

symmetric multiprocessing (SMP) A technology that allows a computer to run more than one processor simultaneously. (1)

system cache Memory used to hold the contents of files that are currently open by the operating system. (9)

system log The event log that contains events associated with the operating system. (9)

System Monitor Administrative tool accessible through the Performance console used to monitor the performance of hardware, software, and operating system components. (9)

Task Manager Utility used to manage running applications and processes and monitor a variety of key resource statistics regarding CPU, RAM, and virtual memory utilization. (9)

Terminal Server A Terminal Services mode that allows users to connect to the server for the purposes of running applications installed on the server using the server's CPU, RAM, and other hardware. (12)

Terminal Services The component of Windows Server 2003 responsible for providing users and computers remote access to the server's operating system either for the purposes of running applications or for remote administration of the server and the network. (5, 12)

Terminal Services Configuration An administrative tool used to configure a variety of server and protocol settings for Terminal Services connections. (12)

Terminal Services Manager An administrative tool used to monitor and manage connected Terminal Services sessions. (12)

thin client A relatively inexpensive and low-powered computer that is used to run applications from the server using the Terminal Server mode of Terminal Services. (12)

threads The subcomponents of a process that are performing calculations in the CPU. (9)

Ticket Granting Service (TGS) Kerberos component that grants a ticket to an account requesting a particular service that is then used by that service to authenticate the account. (11)

Ticket to Get Tickets (TGT) Ticket issued to an account by the Kerberos Authentication Service (AS) indicating that the account has been authenticated. Also known as Ticket Granting Tickets. (11)

trace logs Performance logs used to record the occurrence of specific events. A third-party viewer is required to view trace log data. (9)

Transmission Control Protocol/Internet Protocol (TCP/IP) The network communications protocol suite used by the Internet and Microsoft networks. (3)

tree A logical network structure that consists of a hierarchy of two or more domains that share a contiguous namespace. (4)

two-way, transitive trust The trust that exists by default between domains in a tree. The trust is two-way in that each domain is trusted by and trusts each other domain. The trust is transitive in that if one domain trusts another, it also trusts all other domains trusted by the other. (4)

unattended installation An installation that depends on an answer file for responses to the setup program's prompts and configuration options rather than on the interactive input of the user. (2)

universal group A group scope that can be given access to resources within any domain in the forest. Universal groups may contain other universal groups, global groups, computer accounts, and user accounts from any domain in the forest. (5, 8)

upgrade installation An installation of an operating system over a previously installed copy of an earlier operating system that preserves system settings and installed applications. (2)

USB port A small, rectangular port used to connect printers, and a variety of other devices, to a PC. A single port can support high-speed transfer of data to up to 127 devices. (7)

user account An Active Directory object that represents a unique user. (5)

user configuration settings Group policy settings that focus on controlling aspects of the user, regardless of what computer they are using. (11)

user principal name (UPN) A name that identifies both a user and the domain to which their account belongs. A simple example of a UPN is an e-mail address, such as eecklund@ecktek.com. (5)

virtual private network (VPN) A highly secure connection between two or more computers or networks that allows the participating machines to interact as if they were on the same physical LAN. (12)

volume The discrete areas of storage on a dynamic disk that are assigned either drive letters or associated with an empty folder. (6)

Volume Licensing Key (VLK) A single product key usable with multiple installations of a volume-licensed product. (10)

weak password A password that is relatively easy to guess. (2)

Windows Backup A utility included with some versions of Windows for backing up data stored on hard disks to floppy disks or tape drives. (6)

Windows CE The version of Windows designed to run on portable devices such as personal digital assistants (PDAs). (12)

Windows Installer service Service used to remotely install applications to client computers from the server. (11)

Windows Internet Name Service (WINS) The service responsible for resolving NetBIOS names into IP addresses. (3)

Windows Server Catalog The online tool for checking the compatibility of both hardware and software with Windows Server 2003, Windows XP, and Windows 2000. (2)

Windows settings A category of group policy settings for both users and computers that are used to configure startup and shutdown scripts, logon and logoff scripts, and security settings. (11)

Windows Update An online tool that checks for and installs updates to the operating system. Windows Update can be customized to automatically download and install upgrades or to merely notify the user that new upgrades are available. (2)

Windows Upgrade Advisor A utility included on the Windows Server 2003 installation CD that can be used to check a system for compatibility with the operating system before the installation is begun. (2)

workgroup The Microsoft term for a peer-to-peer network. (1)

zone name Identifies the domain or portion of a domain for which a DNS server is responsible. Used by the DNS server to determine which name requests are internal and which are not. (3)

A

Access control problems, troubleshooting, 252–253
Access to resources using groups, 232–257
Account delegation, 156
Account lockout counter, resetting, 334
Account lockout duration, 334
Account lockout policies, 333–334
Account lockout threshold, 334
Account lockout threshold Properties dialog box, 336
Account policies, 333
ACE (access control entry), 242, 250
ACL (access control list), 242
ACPI APIC HAL, 315
ACPI PIC HAL, 315
Activating Windows Server 2003, 57
Active Directory, 9, 109
    adding a shared folder to, 246
    benefits of, 115–116
    creating domains by installing, 118–130
    domain names vs. DNS domain names, 113
    domain-based network, 94
    dragging and dropping items in, 117
    extends interoperability, 116
    features in Windows Server 2003, 115–118
    GPMC, 117
    improved user interface, 117
    installing on a stand-alone server, 120–126
    new features of, 117–118
    planning the installation of, 118–120
    renaming domains, 117–118
    simplifies management, 115–116
    strengthens security, 116
Active Directory consoles, running from the command line, 144

Active Directory Domains and Trusts console, 138–130, 144
Active Directory installation, testing, 126
Active Directory Installation Wizard
    completing, 126
    Create New Domain screen, 122
    Database and Log Folders screen, 123
    Directory Services Administrator Password Restore Mode screen, 125
    DNS Registration Diagnostics screen, 124
    Domain Controller Type screen, 121
    NetBIOS Domain Name screen, 123
    New Domain Name screen, 122
    Permissions screen, 125
    Shared System Volume screen, 124
Active Directory object management, 154–164
Active Directory objects, 137–143
    caution when deleting, 154
    contacts, 141
    creating with Active Directory Users and Computers, 143–154
    creating common, 150–154
    names of, 138–139
Active Directory Service, 115
Active Directory Sites and Services, 144
Active Directory Users and Computers, 136–169, 312
    adding a shared folder, 246
    Advanced Features option, 146
    creating objects with, 143–154
    default containers, 148–150
    description bar, 148
    Detail view, 147
    domain properties in, 303
    interface, 144–148
    managing objects with, 154–164

moving and editing objects in, 159–164
navigating the hierarchy, 148
saving a view, 148
sorting the display, 148
toolbar buttons, 148
window, 9, 144–145
window panes, 145
Active partition, 171
Active session, explained, 370
Adams, Scott, 324
Add Counters dialog box, 270–271
Add Mirror dialog box, 184
Add Objects dialog box, 276
Add or Remove Programs, 87
Add Printer Wizard, 207–211, 221
completing, 211
Install Printer Software screen, 210
Local or Network Printer screen, 208
Name Your Printer screen, 211
Select a Printer Port screen, 209
Welcome screen, 207
Add Standalone Snap-in dialog box, 331
Add Standard TCP/IP Printer Port Wizard, 209, 221
Additional Drivers dialog box, 214
Addressing, 74–80
Addressing scheme, 75
Addressing system, 74
Administration. *See* Active Directory Users
and Computers
Administrative template first-level categories, 338
Administrative template policies, modifying, 340–341
Administrative template settings, 329–330,
339–340, 342
Administrative templates (Group Policy), 329–330,
338–340, 342
Administrator group permissions, 243
Administrator password, 46
Administrator password for Restore Mode, 120, 125
Administrator-level accounts, multiple, 148
Advanced Security Settings dialog box, 246–249, 253
Advanced TCP/IP Settings dialog box DNS tab, 99
Alert icon, 285
Alert Properties dialog box
Action tab, 284
General tab, 283
Schedule tab, 284

Alerts, 280–285
configuring, 282–285
deleting, 285
to send notification messages, 282
All Programs, on the Start menu, 55
Answer files, 39
for RIPrep images, 319
for unattended installations, 37–38
APIC HAL, 315
Application log, 285–289
Application processes hogging server
resources, 260
Application Properties dialog box Filter tab, 288
Applications, viewing processes associated
with, 260
Applications tab (Task Manager), 259, 266–267
ARIN (American Registry for Internet Numbers),
78, 83
AS (Authentication Service), 334
ASR (Automated System Restore) backup set, 187
Attended installation, 37, 39, 48–54
Authorizing a server to provide RIS, 296
Automatic addressing, TCP/IP and, 46
Automatic Private IP Addressing, 80
Automatic Update (Windows Update), 63–64
Available Bytes counter, 272–273

■ B

Backing up files, 18
Backing up and restoring a volume, 189–193
Backup hardware, 186
Backup methods, 193
Backup Progress dialog box, 192
Backup or Restore Wizard, 188, 189–193
Backup or Restore screen, 190
Backup Type Destination and Name
screen, 191
Items to Back Up screen, 191
What to Back Up screen, 190
What to Restore screen, 192
Backup software, 187
Backups (*see also* Windows Backup)
advantages of tape drives for, 187
scheduled, 188
Baselines (baseline measurements), 274

Basic disks
  capabilities and limitations of, 171
  converting to dynamic disks, 173–175
  vs. dynamic disks, 171–173
Binary basics, 75
Binary IP address, 77
Binary number system, 75
Binary-to-decimal conversion, 79
Bitmap Caching, explained, 364
Bits (binary digits), 77
Boot loader, 171
Boot manager, 171
Booting from the network, 314
Browse for a Group Policy Object dialog box, 332
Builtin container, 149

■ C

CAL (Client Access License) license packs, 44
CD image, 295
CDs, backing up to, 186
Change permission, 243, 245
Check Disk Simple Volume dialog box, 194
Check Server Wizard dialog box, 308
Choice Options Properties dialog box, 303–304, 307
CIDR (Classless Inter-Domain Routing), 79
Class-based IP addresses, address ranges for, 79
Class-based scheme for allocating IP addresses, 78
Clean installation, 40
Client computer
  installing a flat image on, 314
  prestaging, 304, 310, 312
Client configuration for DHCP, 101
Client Installation Wizard, 314
Client requirements for RIS, 309–311
Client Settings tab of RDP-Tcp Properties dialog box, 370, 373
Client/server networks, 5–6, 8
Clipboard mapping, explained, 363
Closing frozen or improperly running programs, 265
Closing a misbehaving program, 259
Clustering, 13
CMOS setup, 309–310
Command prompt window, opening, 81
Commit charge, 260, 263
Commit charge limit, 263

Commit charge peak, 263
Commit charge total, 263
Computer Account Generation dialog box, 305
Computer account properties, 155–156
Computer account Properties dialog box, 155
  Delegation tab, 156
  Dial-in tab, 156
  General tab, 155
  Location tab, 156, 160
  Managed By tab, 156, 161
  Member Of tab, 156, 164
  Operating System tab, 155
Computer accounts (computers), 47, 137–139
  creating, 151–152, 312
  prestaging, 304, 310, 312
Computer configuration settings
  (Group Policy), 327
Computer Management console, 174–175, 179, 184–185
Computer Management tool, 174–175, 179, 184–185, 297
Computer Name and Administrator Password screen, 53
Computer Name Changes dialog box, 45
Computers container, 149, 312
Concurrent connections, setting number of, 45
Configure a DNS Server Wizard, 97, 99
Connection bar (on remote display), 362
Connection properties, changing, 82–83
Connectivity, of Windows Server 2003, 16
Console session, explained, 369
Contacts (Active Directory), 141
Containers
  default, 148–150
  hierarchy of, 145–146
  opening, 146
Contiguous namespace, 111
Control Panel settings, prohibiting access to, 339–341
Convert command, 119
Convert to Dynamic Disk dialog box, 174
Copy backup, 193
Counter log Settings dialog box
  General tab, 274, 276–277
  Log Files tab, 274–275, 277
  Schedule tab, 274–275, 277–278

Counter logs, 273–280
  creating, 275–280
  deleting, 280
Counters (in System Monitor), 268–273
  adding, 270
  monitoring multiple, 272
CPU monitoring, 265–266
CPU requirements for Windows Server 2003
  Datacenter Edition, 20
  Enterprise Edition, 20
  Standard Edition and Web Edition, 19
CPU time, 266–267
CPU Usage, 262, 265–267, 283
CPU Usage alert, 283
CPU Usage column chart, 262
CPU Usage History line chart, 262
Critical updates, 60, 62
CTRL-ALT-DELETE, 55, 259, 314, 327, 363

D

Daily backup, 193
DC (domain controller), 109
  domain functional level of, 233
  more than one on the network, 109–110
  server promoted to, 109
  when to add a second, 120
Decimal-to-binary conversion, 79
Default domain controllers policy, 325
Default domain policy
  editing, 303
  explained, 325
Default-First-Site-Name, 114
Definitions of terms used in this book, 379–388
Defragmenting a drive, 196
Deploy.cab file, 39
Developer tools (.NET), 16
Device license, 44
Device Settings tab (printer), 212
DHCP (Dynamic Host Configuration Protocol), 46, 82
  benefits of, 86
  client configuration, 101
  configuring, 89–90
  installing, 87–88
  setting up, 85–93
DHCP lease, 89–90

DHCP lease duration, 89
DHCP lease length, 90
DHCP MMC snap-in, 90, 100
  Address Pool, 93
  with new scope, 92
  Scope Options, 93
DHCP scope
  activating, 92
  adding, 89–93
  default gateway, 90
  deleting, 93
  DNS and WINS settings, 90
  excluded IP addresses, 89
  exclusion ranges for, 93
  IP address range and subnet mask, 89
  name and description, 89
  options, 93
  Router properties, 93
  test scopes, 93
DHCP server, 82, 85
  authorizing to provide RIS, 296
  configuring DNS, 96–100
  configuring WINS options, 100
  setting up, 86
DHCP services, 82
Differential backup, 193
Directory Permissions dialog box (Windows NT), 7
Disconnected session, 370
Disjointed namespace, 113
Disk errors, 194
Disk image, 40
Disk quotas, 10
Disk space, how RIS conserves, 295–296
Distribution group, 233
DN (distinguished name), 138
DNS configuration, 94
DNS (Domain Name System), 87
  configuring, 95–100
  installing, 87–88, 119–120
  setting up, 94–101
  vs. WINS, 94–95
DNS domain names, 110–111, 113, 119
DNS lookup zones, 95
DNS management snap-in, 96
DNS Registration Diagnostics screen, 124
DNS root domains, 113
DNS server configuration, testing, 101

DNS servers, 94
 configuring, 96–100
 forward lookup zone, 95
 forwarders, 99
 running more than one, 94, 100
DNS settings, 83
DNS zones
 creating, 96
 forward and reverse, 96
 naming, 95, 97–98
Domain account, 47
Domain controller type, setting, 121
Domain Controllers container, 149
Domain functional level of domain controller, 233
 default, 127
 raising, 127–130
Domain Guests group, 150
Domain local account to represent shared folder, 238
Domain local group, 142, 233, 235–236
 with access to resources, 235
 creating an ACE for, 250
 global group as member of, 241
 joining global groups to, 236
 scope and membership rules, 233
Domain names, 110, 119
 checking on the status of, 111
 DNS vs. Active Directory, 113
 finding the IP addresses behind, 80
 internal, 110
 in other countries, 113
 registering, 111
Domain properties, in Active Directory Users and Computers, 303
Domain Properties dialog box Group Policy tab, 325, 343
Domain.msc command, 144
Domains, 108, 109–111
 creating by installing Active Directory, 118–130
 in a disjointed namespace, 113
 function of, 109
 joining, 318
 registering, 98
 renaming, 117–118
 servers in, 119
DOS program, 1
Dotted decimal notation, 76–77
Downgrades, 41

Dpi (dots per inch), 213
Drive device letters
 for a new volume, 297
 reserved, 172
Driver updates, 60, 63
Drivers
 installing additional, 214
 for older operating systems, 216
Dsadd group command, 242
Dsa.msc command, 144
DSPs (Datacenter Support Providers), 13
Dsquery computer command, 126
Dsquery server command, 126
Dssite.msc command, 144
Duplexing, of mirrored volumes, 177
DVDs, backing up to, 186
Dynamic disk volumes. *See* Volumes
Dynamic disks
 advantages of, 172
 vs. basic disks, 171–173
 best practices for using, 179
 converting basic disks to, 173–175
 creating volumes on, 179–185
 when to use, 172–173
Dynamic IP addresses, 82

■ E

Eastwood, Clint, 232
Effective permission, 249, 253
Error events, 286
Evaluation versions of Windows Server, grace period for, 57
Event ID number, 288
Event information, copying to the clipboard, 288
Event logs, 285–289
 analyzing trends in, 286
 explained, 285
 fields in, 287
 monitoring, 285–289
 saved as text files, 286
 using, 286–287
Event Properties dialog box, 288–289
Event Viewer, 285–289
 Find feature, 288
 opening, 287

Events in the application log, types of, 285–286
Everyone group, 112, 243
Ewing, Sam, 354
Experience tab (RDC), 364, 366
Explain Text dialog box, 271
Extended partitions, 171–172
Extended volumes, 176, 182–183

▪ F

Failing disks (with mirrored volumes), 194–195
FAT (file allocation table) file system, 6, 43
Fault tolerance, 172
File
    ownership of, 248–249
    restoring a previous version of, 18
File access, managing, 242–252
File backup, 18
File encryption in Windows 2000, 10
File permissions, 246–247
File system, 6, 42–43
Files currently executing, viewing, 260
Find dialog box (Event Viewer), 288
First-layer domains, 112
Flat images, 298–302
    creating, 300–302
    installing on a client computer, 314
Folder access, managing, 242–252
Folder level permissions by user account
  (Windows NT), 7
Folder locations, 119
Folder permission inheritance, 247–248
Folder permissions, 246–248
Folder Redirection of My Documents, 17–18
Folders (*see also* Shared folders)
    creating and sharing, 244–245
    ownership of, 248–249
ForeignSecurityPrincipals container, 149–150
Forest functional level
    default, 127
    raising, 127–130
Forests, 112–113
    of domains in a disjointed namespace, 113
    linking, 113
Forward lookup zone (on DNS server), 95–96

Forwarders (external DNS servers), 99
FQDN (fully qualified domain name), 94
Fragmentation, 195–196
F12, to boot from the network, 314
Full Control permission, 243

▪ G

Gall, John, 136
Gateway configuration, 93
Gateway setting, default, 83
GC (global catalog), 112
Global groups, 142, 233–236, 241
    for holding user accounts, 235
    joining to domain local groups, 236
    scope and membership rules, 234
Global security group, creating, 238
Glossary of terms used in this book, 379–388
Gpedit.msc command, 326
GPMC (Group Policy Management Console),
  117, 326–327
Group accounts (groups), 141–142, 233–241
    adding from the command line, 242
    adding objects to, 241
    best practices, 234–237
    creating and managing, 237–241
    Effective permission for, 249
    granting Change permission to, 245
    need for, 236–237
    types of, 233
    using to access resources, 232–257
Group management common tasks, 237
Group membership, checking, 253
Group nesting, 233, 253
Group Policy, 303
    administrative templates settings, 329–330
    capabilities of, 325–332
    computer configuration settings, 327
    how it is applied, 342–344
    managing, 342–348
    managing computers and users with, 324–353
    managing security with, 333–337
    security settings, 333–337
    software restriction policies, 334–337
    software settings, 328

user configuration settings, 327
user environment management, 337–342
Windows settings, 328–329
Group Policy administrative templates, 338
Group Policy interactions, analyzing, 344
Group policy object (GPO), 325
creating, 330–332
options, 343
properties, 343–344
Group Policy Object Options dialog box, 343
Group Policy Object Properties dialog box
General tab, 343
Links tab, 344
Group Policy Object Editor MMC snap-in, 303–304, 307
console, 326, 328–330, 332
opening, 325–326, 330–332
Group Policy priority, changing, 344–348
Group policy settings, for RIS, 303–304
Group policy settings categories, 327–330
Group Policy tab of Domain Properties dialog box, 325, 343
Group Policy tools, 325–327
Group Policy Wizard, 331
Group Properties dialog box
General tab, 239–240
Member Of tab, 240
Members tab, 240
Group scope, 141, 233–234, 240
Groveler, explained, 296
Guest account, 150
GUID (Globally Unique Identifier), 62, 152, 310

H

HAL compatibilities for RIPrep images, 315
HAL (hardware abstraction layer), 315
HAL types, 315
HAL versions and original file names, 316
Hal.dll file, 316
Handles, 262
Hard disk image, 295
Hard disk partitions. *See* Partitions
Hard drive space requirements for Windows Server 2003
Datacenter Edition, 21

Enterprise Edition, 20
Standard Edition and Web Edition, 20
Hardware for backing up, 186
Hardware compatibility, checking, 29–36
Hardware incompatibility, reasons for, 29
Hardware RAID, 178
Hardware requirements for a RIS server, 295
Hardware requirements for Windows Server 2003
minimum, 21
recommended, 21
HCL details, 34
HCL (Hardware Compatibility List), 31–34
searching, 33–34
vs. Windows Server Catalog, 34
Heinlein, Robert, 294
Hexadecimal, 77
Hill, Napoleon, 108
Hosts, on the network, 77
Hot Add Memory, 13
128–bit addresses, 77

I

IANA (Internet Assigned Numbers Authority), 78
IANA reserved IP addresses, 79
Idle session, explained, 370
Image, creating from a reference computer, 314–319
Image Properties dialog box, 306
Imaged installations, 40
Images tab (RIS server Properties dialog box), 305–306
Incremental backup, 193
Information events, 286
Inheritance, 235, 247–251
Initial password, 46, 140
Installation plan for Windows Server 2003, 47–49
Installation planning sheet, 49
Installation problems
can't install, 64–65
CD drive in not bootable, 64–65
troubleshooting, 64–66
unsupported upgrade path, 64
Installation of Windows Server 2003, 28–73
attended, 37, 39, 48–54
choosing a method, 37–40

post-installation problems, 65–66
preparing, 40–48
resuming failed, 65
system requirements, 19–21
testing, 55–57
unattended, 37–39
upgrade vs. clean, 40–41
Installing Active Directory
and creating domains, 118–130
planning, 118–120
on a stand-alone server, 120–126
testing the installation, 126
Installing a printer, 203–211
Installing from a RIPrep image, 319
Installing RIS, 297–298
Installing Windows components, 87–88
Instance, explained, 270
Internet communications protocol, 75
Internet Protocol (TCP/IP) Properties dialog box,
    83–85
Internet root servers, explained, 95
Interrupts/Sec counter (System Monitor), 271
IP address allocation, class-based scheme for, 78
IP addresses, 75–80
    configuring static, 83–85
    finding, 80
    IANA reserved, 79
    masking off, 77–78
    private, 79–80
    public, 78–79
    ranges of for class-based, 79
    ranges of for private, 80
    requesting from ISP or ARIN, 83
    scarcity of, 86
    unique, 76
IP addressing, dynamic vs. static, 82
IP addressing scheme, private, 79–80, 83
IP host names vs. NetBIOS names, 94
Ipconfig command line utility, 81
Ipconfig report, 81
IPv4 addresses, 77
IPv4 (Internet Protocol version 4), 76–77
IPv6 addresses, 77
IPv6 (Internet Protocol version 6), 76–77
ISP (Internet service provider), 78, 83

K

Kakuzo, Okakura, 258
Kerberos security, 334
Kernel memory information, 263

L

Lease (DHCP), 89–90
Lease duration (DHCP), 89
Lease length (DHCP), 90
License packs, 44
Licensing, 44
Licensing considerations of RIS, 299–300
Licensing mode, setting, 45
Licensing Modes screen (Windows Setup), 45
LIR (Local Internet Registry), 78
Local administrator account password, 318
Local Area Connection Properties dialog box,
    82, 84
Local logon limitations, 154
Local policy, explained, 325
Local print devices, 203–205
Local Resources tab (RDC), 362–363, 366
Locally connected printer, installing, 206–211
Log On to Windows dialog box, 55
Logging on to Windows Server 2003, 55–56
Logical network structures, 115
Logical printer, 203
Logical structure of a network, 108–115
Logon names, logical, 139–140
Logon prompt, 55
Logs, 285–289
    overwriting events as needed, 286–287
    sizing, 287
    types of, 273
Lookup zones (DNS), 95
LPT (Local Printer Terminal), 203

M

Manage Documents permission, 251
Manage Printers permission, 251

Manage Your Server window, 56
Manageability of Windows Server 2003, 15
Managed computer accounts, 310
Managed dialog box, 312
Mapped remote session, explained, 363
Member server
    explained, 118
    purpose of, 119
Memory performance object counters, 272
Memory status, viewing, 263
Memory Usage setting, 267
Messenger service, 281–282
Messenger service Properties dialog box, 282
Microsoft licensing plans, 299
Microsoft Networking, 108–135
Microsoft Product Activation, 299
Mirrored volumes, 177
    breaking the mirror, 195
    creating, 184
    duplexing, 177
    failing disks with, 194–195
    removing the mirror, 195
MMC (Microsoft Management Console), 9, 143, 268
Mounted volumes, explained, 172
MPA (Microsoft Product Activation), 56–57
Multifunction printers, 204
Multimaster replication, 109–110
Multiple forest networks, 113
Munro, Hector Hugh, 74
My Computer, on the Start menu, 55
My Documents, folder redirection of, 17–18

■ N

Name resolution, explained, 94
Namespace
    contiguous, 111
    disjointed, 113
    explained, 110
    root domain of, 110
NAT (Network Address Translation), 80
Nested OUs, 114
Nesting of groups, 233
.NET
    explained, 16–17
    techologies behind, 17

NetBIOS Domain Name screen, 123
NetBIOS flat name space, 94
NetBIOS (Network Basic Input/Output System)
    names, 94, 119
Network Adapter History, 263
Network administration. See Active Directory
    Users and Computers
Network communication problem, 266
Network communications protocol, 75
Network Connections menu, 84
Network installations, 39
Network logical structure, 108–115
Network physical structure, 114–115
Network print devices, 204–205
Network printer, trouble printing to, 225
Network printing, 202–231
Network services and protocols, configuring,
    74–106
Network settings, 46–47
    Custom settings, 46
    Typical settings, 46
Network Setup dialog box (Windows for
    Workgroups 3.11), 2
Network shares, creating, 244
Networking, 108–135, 263–264
Networking Services dialog box, 87–88
Networking Settings screen (Windows Setup), 54
Networking tab of Task Manager dialog box,
    263–264, 266, 268
Networks
    growth in size and complexity of, 234
    purpose for, 232
New Clients tab (RIS server properties dialog box),
    305, 308
New Object - Computer dialog box, 151–152
New Object - Group dialog box, 238–239
New Object - User dialog box, 153
New Path Rule dialog box, 337
New Scope Wizard, 89–93
    Add Exclusions screen, 91
    Configure DHCP Options screen, 92
    IP Address Range screen, 91
New Volume Wizard
    Assign Drive Letter or Path screen, 181
    completing, 182
    Format Volume screen, 181
    Select Disks screen, 180, 183, 185
    Select Volume Type screen, 180

New Zone Wizard, 96
    Dynamic Update screen, 98
    Zone Name screen, 98
NICs (network interface cards), 263, 295
    GUIDs of, 310
    PXE-enabled, 309–310
NIR (National Internet Registry), 78
Nonremote print device, 205
Nonremote printer, installing, 206–211
Nontransitive trusts, 112
Normal backup, 193
Notepad, saving a file in, 367
NTFS (NT File System), 6, 42–43
NTFS permissions, 242, 246–251
    setting, 249–251
    share permissions and, 246, 248–249, 252–253
    standard permissions, 246–247
    verifying inheritance of, 250
NTFS5, 9–10
NTFS4, 10

O

Object management, 154–164
Object properties, 154–159
OEMs (original equipment manufacturers), 14
Offline printers, user intervention for, 225
One-way trusts, 112
Open dialog box, 313
Open file backup, 18
Operating systems
    drivers for older, 216
    flat images made from, 299
    product key, 310–311
    support for older, 120
    Windows versions as, 1
Optical media, backing up to, 186, 188
Orphan processes, terminating, 265
OU properties, 158–159
OU Properties dialog box
    COM+ tab, 159
    General tab, 159
    Group Policy tab, 159
    Managed By tab, 159
OUs (organizational units), 113–114, 142
    creating, 154

    nested, 114
    reflecting the structure of the organization, 114
Ownership, of a file or folder, 248–249

P

Parallel cable length limitations, 204
Parallel ports, 203
Partitioning, 42
Partitions, 42
    creating, 51
    deleting, 51
    extended, 171–172
    formatting, 42, 51–52
    listing existing, 51
    primary, 171
Password aging, default, 153
Password policies, 333–334
Passwords, 44
    administrator, 46
    complexity requirements, 140
    initial, 46, 140
    for local administrator account, 318
    for Restore Mode, 120, 125
    for shared folders, 4
    strong, 45–46
    weak, 46
Peer-to-peer networking, 2–4, 8
Per Device or Per User licensing, 44
Per Seat licensing, 44
Per Server licensing, 44
PerfLogs folder, 280
Performance
    monitoring and managing, 258–293
    volumes that improve, 176–177
Performance Console
    log types, 273
    server monitoring with, 268–285
Performance logs and alerts, 273–285
Performance object, explained, 269
Performance object to monitor, choosing, 276
Performance problems
    post-installation, 65–66
    storage-related, 195–196
Performance tab (Task Manager dialog box),
    262–263, 265–267

Permission Entry dialog box, 246, 248
Permissions (*see also* NTFS permissions;
   Share permissions)
      allowed or denied individually, 247
      applying directly to user accounts, 237
      assigning, 250
      effective, 249, 253
      inheritance of, 247–251
      over shared folders, 242–243, 245
      precedence of least restrictive, 253
      setting at Active Directory installation, 125
      tracking, 253
Permissions tab of Advanced Security Settings
   dialog box, 247
PF Usage, 267
PF Usage column chart, 262
PF Usage History line chart, 262
Physical memory status, 263
Physical printer, defined, 203
Physical structure of a network, 114–115
PhysicalDisk performance object counters, 271
PIC HAL, 315
PIN (personal identification number), 46
Policy settings. *See* Group Policy
Pooling printers, 219–222
Pop-up windows, 280
Ports, setting for printers, 215–216, 222
Post-installation problems, 65–66
Ppm (pages per minute), 213
Pre-installation decisions, 47
Prestaging a client computer, 304, 310, 312
Previous version of a file, restoring, 18
Primary partitions, 171
Print device properties, configuring, 212–218
Print devices
      configuring and sharing, 212–218
      explained, 203
Print job priorities, changing, 224
Print jobs
      managing, 218, 222–224
      pausing/canceling/restarting, 223, 225
      redirecting, 222–223
      scheduling, 224
      shortcut menu for, 223
Print permission, 251
Print processor, 217

Print queue, 217
Print servers, 204–206
      dedicated, 206
      for local print devices, 205
Print spooler, explained, 217
Printer access, managing, 242–252
Printer availability, 216
Printer cable length limitations, 203
Printer configuration and management, 202–231
Printer drivers
      for older operating systems, 216
      updating, 216
      use of incorrect, 226
Printer object (Active Directory), 143
Printer permissions, 218, 251–252
Printer pool, creating, 220–222
Printer pooling, 219–222
Printer priority, 216
Printer problems, troubleshooting, 225–226
Printer Properties dialog box
      Advanced tab, 216–218
      Device Settings tab, 212
      General tab, 212–213
      Ports tab, 215–216, 222
      Security tab, 218, 251
      Sharing tab, 213–215
Printer status, 219
Printers, 203
      connection options, 203–205
      data handling options, 205–206
      installing, 203–211
      logical, 203
      managing, 218–222, 242–252
      multifunction, 204
      physical, 203
      sharing, 214–215
Printers and Faxes dialog box, 215
Printing defaults, setting, 217–218
Printing problem of nonsense characters, 225–226
Printing speed, resolution and, 213
Priority of processes, 261
Private IP address ranges, 80
Private IP addresses, 79–80
Private IP addressing scheme, 79, 83
Process priority, 261
Process tree, 260

Processes
    ending, 260, 265, 267
    explained, 260
    number of running, 260
    terminating orphaned, 265
    that are using large amounts of CPU time, 266
Processes associated with an application, viewing, 260
Processes tab of Task Manager, 260–262, 265–267
Processor object
    data captured concerning, 279–280
    monitoring, 276–280
Processor time and memory
    allocating, 261
    %Processor Time counter, 270, 283
Product activation, 56–57
Product key, 300, 310–311
Product Key screen (Windows Setup), 53
ProductID entry
    adding to an answer file, 311
    changing in ristndrd.sif file, 313
Programs, terminating, 267
Programs tab (RDC), 363
Properties, 303
Properties dialog boxes, 155
    Security tab, 246, 250–251
    Sharing tab, 244–245
Protocol for network communications, 75
Protocol suite, 75
Public IP addresses, 78–79
Public networks distributed using classes, 78
Publish, explained, 143
PXE (Preboot Execution Environment), 309
PXE-enabled NICs, 309–310

■ Q

Queue, defined, 217

■ R

RAID, concept of, 178
RAID levels, 178
RAID (Redundant Array of Inexpensive/Independent
    Disks), 177
RAID-5 volumes, 177–185

Raise Domain Functional Level dialog box, 129
Raise Forest Functional Level option, 129
Raise Forest Functional Level warning, 130
RAM requirements of Windows Server 2003, 20–21
Rbfg.exe utility, 309–310
RDC client for older OSs, 358
RDC dialog box
    Display tab, 361–362
    Experience tab, 364, 366
    General tab, 361, 365
    Local Resources tab, 362–363, 366
    Programs tab, 363
RDC options, 361–364
RDC (Remote Desktop Connection), 357
    configuring, 361–369
    managing, 369–372
    Security Warning, 367
    speeds and experience settings for, 364
RDNs (relative distinguished names), 138
RDP-Tcp, 370
RDP-Tcp Properties dialog box
    Client Settings tab, 370, 373
    Sessions tab, 371, 374
Read permission, 242
Realtime priority of a process, 261
Recovery Console, starting from installation CD, 43
Redirected devices, 363
Redirected remote session, 363
Ref.chm help file, 39
Reference computer
    creating an image from, 314–319
    creating a RIPrep image of, 316–319
    explained, 315
Regional and Language Options screen
    (Windows Setup), 52
Registering a domain, 98, 111
Reliability of Windows Server 2003, 15, 177–178
Remote Desktop for Administration, 354–378
    access from many locations, 357
    access from many OSs, 357
    basic concepts, 355–360
    benefits of, 356–357
    disabled by default, 359
    ease of use, 356
    in full screen or windowed view, 368
    limitations of, 358–359
    limited connections, 359

low resource overhead, 357

rebooting the server and, 358

security risks, 358–359

server management using, 354–378

Remote Desktop for Administration sessions, 368–369

configuring and managing, 372–374

connecting to session 0, 368–369

ending, 368

in Windows XP, 356

Remote Desktop Connection dialog box (Windows XP), 357

Remote Desktop connections, 264

Remote Desktop protocol file, 361

Remote Install tab (RIS server Properties dialog box), 305

Remote Installation Preparation Wizard, 314. *See also* RIPrep

Remote print device, 206

Remote Sessions dialog box, 360

Remote tab of System Properties dialog box, 360

Reparse point, 296

Resolution and printing speed, 213

Resource records, 98

Resources

sharing of organizational, 232

tracking, 253

using groups to access, 232–257

Resources being used by a program, recovering, 265

Restore Mode administrator password, 120, 125

Restore Progress dialog box, 193

Restoring a previous version of a file, 18

Reverse lookup zone, 95–96

Review and install updates link, 61

RIPrep, 314–319

RIPrep image, 314–319

answer file for, 319

HAL compatibilities for, 315

installing from, 319

operating system considerations, 316

RIPrep image of a reference computer, creating, 316–319

Riprep.sif file, 319

RIR (Regional Internet Registry), 78

RIS client requirements, 309–311

RIS configuration, 298–308

advanced, 306–308

OS considerations, 298–300

RIS image support for various operating systems, 316

RIS imaging, 295, 316

RIS installation wipes client's hard drive, 311

RIS (Remote Installation Services), 294–323

Automatic Setup, 304

configuring a server for, 295–298

Custom Setup, 304

function and requirements, 295–296

group policy settings for, 303–304

hardware requirements, 295

how it conserves disk space, 295–296

installing, 297–298

licensing considerations, 299–300

limitations of, 319

Restart Setup, 304

server property settings, 304–306

software requirements, 296

supported operating systems, 299

TCP/IP network requirement, 296

Tools option, 304

RIS server, 295

RIS server Properties dialog box

Images tab, 305–306

New Clients tab, 305, 308

Remote Install tab, 305

Tools tab, 305–306

RIS Setup Wizard, 300–302

Folder Location screen, 301

Initial Settings screen, 301

Welcome screen, 300

Windows Installation Image Folder screen, 302

Ristndrd.sif file, 310, 313

Ristndrd.sif file [UserData] section, 313

Root domain of a namespace, 110, 113

Router, 80, 83, 93

Router configuration, 93

RSoP console, 346–347

RSoP (Resultant Set of Policy), 344–348

RSoP Wizard

Summary of Selections screen, 345

User and Computer Selection screen, 345

Run dialog box, 317

■ S

Saint-Exupery, Antoine de, 1
SAM (Security Accounts Manager), 5–6
Save As dialog box, 367
Scalability, 12
Scheduled backups, 188
Scheduling print jobs, 224
Schema, 112
Scope (DHCP). *See* DHCP scope
Second-layer domains, 112
Security
    managing with Group Policy, 333–337
    of Windows Server 2003, 15
Security groups, 141
    for controlling access to resources, 233
    types of, 141–142
Security log, explained, 286
Security risks of Remote Desktop for Administration, 358–359
Security settings (Group Policy), 333–337
Security tab
    of printer Properties dialog box, 218, 251
    of Properties dialog boxes, 246, 250–251
Select Columns dialog box, 263–264
Select Group Policy Object dialog box, 331
Select Groups dialog box, 162–163, 241
Select Log File dialog box, 278–279
Select User or Contact dialog box, 161
Select User or Group dialog box, 312
Select Users/Contacts/Computers/Groups
    dialog box, 241
Separator page (in printing), 217–218
Server name, 44–46
Server operating systems, support for older, 120
Server property settings (RIS), 304–306
Server-class computers, 20
Servers in a domain, 119
Service packs, 60, 62
Services
    defined, 281
    stopping and restarting, 282
Services console, 281–282
Services management, 281
Session settings, configuring at the server, 369–371
Session 0, explained, 369

Sessions
    explained, 355
    managing current, 371–372
Sessions tab of RDP-Tcp Properties
    dialog box, 371, 374
Sessions tab of Terminal Services Manager, 371–372
Sessions tab of user account Properties
    dialog box, 371
Setup information file (SIF), 310
Setup Manager, 39
Shadow copies of shared folders, 18
Shadow Copy, 18
Share permissions, 242–245
    combining, 243
    and NTFS permissions, 246, 248–249, 252–253
    setting, 244–245
Share Permissions tab of Permissions
    dialog box, 245
Shared folder object (Active Directory), 143
Shared folders, 143, 242–246
    adding to Active Directory, 246
    domain local account to represent, 238
    on a peer-to-peer network, 4
    Permissions dialog box for, 242
    permissions over, 242–243
    shadow copies of, 18
Shared printer, 213–215
Shared resource access, troubleshooting, 252–253
Shared resources, 232, 252–253
Shared System Volume screen, 124
Share-level permissions by user account
    (Windows NT), 6
Sharing tab of Properties dialog boxes, 244–245
Shutdown button, access to when logging on, 55
SID (security ID), 137
Simple volume, 175–176
    creating, 180–182, 297
    creating a backup of, 189–193
    space to be used for, 297
Simple Volume Properties dialog box, 194
Single-use product key, 300
SIS Common Store Folder, 296
SIS groveler agent, 296
SIS (Single Instance Store) service, 296
Sites, 114–115
Smart clients (.NET), 16

SMP (symmetric multiprocessing), 12
Software piracy, 56
Software restriction policies, 18–19, 334–337
Software Restriction Policies container, 336
Software settings (Group Policy), 328
SOM (scope of management), 325, 342
Spanned volumes, 176, 183
Special permissions, 218, 246–247, 252–253
Special printer permissions, 252
Speed of Windows Server 2003, 15
Spooled, defined, 217
Stand-alone server
    explained, 118
    installing Active Directory on, 120–126
Standard permissions (NTFS), 246–247, 251
Standard printer permissions, 251
Start menu, My Computer and All Programs on, 55
Static IP addresses, 82–85
Storage
    management complexity factors, 170
    managing, 170–201
    troubleshooting, 194–196
    using volumes to manage, 175–185
Storage-related performance problems, 195–196
Striped volumes, 177, 183
Strong passwords, 45–46
Structure of a network
    logical, 108–115
    physical, 114–115
Subnet masks, 77–78
    default, 83
    entered automatically, 85
    variable-length, 79
Subnetting, 77–78
Suggested Value Changes dialog box, 336
System cache, 263
System compatibility report, 31
System log, explained, 286
System Monitor, 258, 264, 268–273
    interface, 268–271
    monitoring multiple counters, 272
    searching in, 271
System Monitor console, modifying, 272
System Monitor counters, 268–273
System Monitor Properties dialog box Source tab, 279–280
System Monitor toolbar buttons, 269–270

System Properties dialog box Remote tab, 360
System requirements for Windows Server 2003, 19–21
    Datacenter Edition, 20–21
    Enterprise Edition, 20
    minimum, 19–21
    recommended, 21
    Standard Edition and Web Edition, 19–20
SYSVOL folder, 119

◼ T

Take Ownership permission, 249
Tape drives for backup, advantages of, 187
Task Manager, 258
    analyzing the impact of tasks, 265
    layout and features of, 259–264
    opening, 259, 266
    server monitoring using, 259–268
    status bar, 260
    warning about terminating a process, 267
Task Manager button, 259
Task Manager dialog box
    Applications tab, 259, 266–267
    Networking tab, 263–264, 266, 268
    Performance tab, 262–263, 265–267
    Processes tab, 260–262, 265–267
    Users tab, 264
Taskbar, locking, 339–340
Taskmgr command, 259
Tasks
    analyzing the impact of, 265
    ending unresponsive, 259
    switching between, 259
TCO (total cost of ownership), 19
TCP/IP configuration, verifying, 81
TCP/IP (Transmission Control Protocol/ Internet Protocol), 75
    and automatic addressing, 46
    basic concepts of, 75–81
    configuring, 82–86
Terminal Server, 355–356
Terminal Services, 158, 264, 355
Terminal Services Configuration, 369–370, 373
Terminal Services Manager console Sessions tab, 371–372

Terminating programs, 265, 267
Terms used in this book, glossary of, 379–388
Testing network, 62
TestOU container, 239
TGS (Ticket Granting Service), 334
TGT (Ticket to Get Tickets), 334
Thin clients, explained, 355
32–bit addresses, 77
Threads, 262
Time slices, assigned to running processes, 261
Tolkien, J.R.R., 28
Trace logs, 274
Transistors, 75
Transitive trusts, 112
Tree-like organizational structure diagram, 113
Trees, 111–113
Trusts, 111–112
Two-way transitive trusts, 111–112

Remote Control tab, 158
Sessions tab, 158, 371
Telephones tab, 157
Terminal Services Profile tab, 158
User accounts (users), 139–140
    applying permissions to directly, 237
    creating, 152–153
    effective permission for, 249
    global groups to hold, 235
    logging off or disconnecting, 264
    sending messages to, 264
User configuration settings (Group Policy), 327
User environment management (Group Policy), 337–342
User license, 44
User logon name, 152
Users container, 150
    in Detail view, 147
    initial contents of, 150
Users tab of Task Manager dialog box, 264

U

Unattended installation, 37–39
    vs. attended, 39
    benefits of, 38
    problems and solutions, 38–39
Universal group scope and membership rules, 235
Universal groups, 142, 233–236
Update categories (Windows Update), 60–63
Updates, reviewing and installing, 61
Updating Windows Server 2003, 58–64
Upgrade vs. clean installation, 40–41
UPNs (user principal names), 138–139
USB cable length, 203
USB (Universal Serial Bus) ports, 203
Use Printer Offline, 219
Use Printer Online, 225
User account properties, 156–158
User account Properties dialog box
    Account tab, 157
    Address tab, 157
    COM+ tab, 158
    Environment tab, 158
    General tab, 156–157
    Organization tab, 158
    Profile tab, 157

V

Video card, 315–316
Virtual memory use, viewing, 260
VLK (Volume Licensing Key), 300, 310
Volume label, descriptive, 181
Volume Licensing, 299
Volume licensing packages, 299
Volume Shadow Copy, 187
Volumes
    backing up and restoring, 189–193
    creating, 297
    creating on dynamic disks, 179–185
    defragmenting, 196
    drive letter for, 297
    explained, 172
    extended, 176, 182–183
    formatting, 181
    mirrored, 177, 184, 194–195
    RAID-5, 177–185
    simple, 175–176, 180–182
    space to be used for, 297
    spanned, 176, 183
    striped, 177, 183

that grow, 175–176
   that improve performance, 176–177
   that improve reliability, 177–178
   types of, 178
   using to manage storage, 175–185
VPN connection, 357
VPN (virtual private network), 357

■ W

Wallpaper, preventing changes to, 339, 341
Warning events, 286
Weak passwords, 46
Welcome to Windows logon prompt, 55
Whois utility, 111
Windows, history of, 1–11
Windows Active Directory. *See* Active Directory
Windows Backup, 186–193. *See also* Backup
   or Restore Wizard
      backup methods, 193
      backup options, 186–187
      features of, 187–188
      pros and cons of, 188–189
      volume backup and restore, 189–193
Windows Calculator, 79
Windows CE, Remote Desktop Connection for, 357
Windows components, installing, 87–88, 298
Windows Components Wizard, 87–88, 298
Windows Explorer, 244
Windows folder, 119
Windows Installer service, 328
Windows Licensing Agreement, 50
Windows NT, 4–8
      administration of, 7
      Microsoft support for, 7
      security risks of, 7
      setting folder-level permissions, 7
      setting share-level permissions, 6
      versions of, 5
Windows NT Server 4.0 Splash screen and
   logon prompt, 5
Windows Remote Boot Disk Generator, 309
Windows Security dialog box, 259
Windows Server Catalog, 31–32, 34–36
Windows Server 2003
   activating, 57

Active Directory features, 115–118
   authorizing to provide RIS, 296
   configuring for RIS, 295–298
   configuring session settings, 369–371
   enabling remote connections, 360
   evaluation copy of, 13, 57
   evolution of, 1–11
   installing Active Directory on, 120–126
   logging on to, 55–56
   logs that overwrite events, 286–287
   management, 354–378
   monitoring using Performance Console,
      268–285
   monitoring using Task Manager, 259–268
   new and improved features of, 15–19, 58
   performance monitoring and managing,
      258–293
   performance slowdown, 265–266
   promoting to DC, 109
   storage management complexity factors, 170
   updating, 58–64
   viewing current configuration, 81
   viewing who is currently logged on, 264
Windows Server 2003 Datacenter Edition, 13–14
   High Availability Program, 13
   minimum requirements, 20–21
   recommended requirements, 21
Windows Server 2003 Enterprise Edition, 12–13
   minimum requirements, 20
   recommended requirements, 21
Windows Server 2003 family, 11–14
Windows Server 2003 family server products, 12
Windows Server 2003 family updates, 60, 62–63
Windows Server 2003 installation. *See* Installation
   of Windows Server 2003
Windows Server 2003 Standard Edition, 12
   minimum requirements, 19–20
   recommended requirements, 21
Windows Server 2003 Web Edition, 14
   minimum requirements, 19–20
   recommended requirements, 21
Windows settings (Group Policy), 328–329
Windows Setup
   Computer Name and Administrator
      Password screen, 53
   Licensing Modes screen, 45
   Networking Settings screen, 54

Regional and Language Options screen, 52
Welcome screen, 50
Your Product Key screen, 53
Windows Task Manager. *See* Task Manager
Windows 2000, 8–11
    Application mode, 355
    ease of use and interface concerns, 10
    editions of, 9
    file encryption in, 10
    Full Control to Everyone group, 243
    primary logs default capacity, 286
Windows 2000 Server, 8
Windows 2000 Server logon prompt, 8
Windows Update, 58–61
    Automatic Update settings, 63–64
    automatically download and install, 63–64
    configuring, 63–64
    download updates and notify before
      installing, 63
    notify before downloading, 63
    privacy policy, 62
    Scan for updates, 59
    update categories, 60–63
Windows Update Privacy Statement, 62
Windows Update web site, 59
Windows Upgrade Advisor, 29–32

Windows for Workgroups, 1–4
    Network Setup dialog box, 2
    with Network window open, 2
    versions of, 2
Windows for Workgroups 3.11 Splash screen, 1
Windows XP Professional client, 294–323
Windows XP Professional flat image, creating,
    300–302
WINS options, configuring in DHCP Server, 100
WINS (Windows Internet Name Service), 87
    vs. DNS, 94–95
    installing, 87–88
    setting up, 94–101
Workgroup
    explained, 3
    joining, 318
WPA (Windows Product Activation) process, 286
Write permissions, 247

■ Z

Zones (DNS)
    creating, 96
    forward and reverse, 96
    naming, 95, 97–98

INTERNATIONAL CONTACT INFORMATION

AUSTRALIA
McGraw-Hill Book Company
Australia Pty. Ltd.
TEL +61-2-9900-1800
FAX +61-2-9878-8881
http://www.mcgraw-hill.com.au
books-it_sydney@mcgraw-hill.com

CANADA
McGraw-Hill Ryerson Ltd.
TEL +905-430-5000
FAX +905-430-5020
http://www.mcgraw-hill.ca

**GREECE, MIDDLE EAST, & AFRICA
(Excluding South Africa)**
McGraw-Hill Hellas
TEL +30-210-6560-990
TEL +30-210-6560-993
TEL +30-210-6560-994
FAX +30-210-6545-525

MEXICO (Also serving Latin America)
McGraw-Hill Interamericana Editores
S.A. de C.V.
TEL +525-1500-5108
FAX +525-117-1589
http://www.mcgraw-hill.com.mx
carlos_ruiz@mcgraw-hill.com

SINGAPORE (Serving Asia)
McGraw-Hill Book Company
TEL +65-6863-1580
FAX +65-6862-3354
http://www.mcgraw-hill.com.sg
mghasia@mcgraw-hill.com

SOUTH AFRICA
McGraw-Hill South Africa
TEL +27-11-622-7512
FAX +27-11-622-9045
robyn_swanepoel@mcgraw-hill.com

SPAIN
McGraw-Hill/
Interamericana de España, S.A.U.
TEL +34-91-180-3000
FAX +34-91-372-8513
http://www.mcgraw-hill.es
professional@mcgraw-hill.es

**UNITED KINGDOM, NORTHERN,
EASTERN, & CENTRAL EUROPE**
McGraw-Hill Education Europe
TEL +44-1-628-502500
FAX +44-1-628-770224
http://www.mcgraw-hill.co.uk
emea_queries@mcgraw-hill.com

ALL OTHER INQUIRIES Contact:
McGraw-Hill Technology Education
TEL +1-630-789-4000
FAX +1-630-789-5226
http://www.mhteched.com
omg_international@mcgraw-hill.com

LICENSE AGREEMENT

THIS PRODUCT (THE "PRODUCT") CONTAINS PROPRIETARY SOFTWARE, DATA AND INFORMATION (INCLUDING DOCUMENTATION) OWNED BY THE McGRAW-HILL COMPANIES, INC. ("McGRAW-HILL") AND ITS LICENSORS. YOUR RIGHT TO USE THE PRODUCT IS GOVERNED BY THE TERMS AND CONDITIONS OF THIS AGREEMENT.

LICENSE: Throughout this License Agreement, "you" shall mean either the individual or the entity whose agent opens this package. You are granted a non-exclusive and non-transferable license to use the Product subject to the following terms:

(i) If you have licensed a single user version of the Product, the Product may only be used on a single computer (i.e., a single CPU). If you licensed and paid the fee applicable to a local area network or wide area network version of the Product, you are subject to the terms of the following subparagraph (ii).

(ii) If you have licensed a local area network version, you may use the Product on unlimited workstations located in one single building selected by you that is served by such local area network. If you have licensed a wide area network version, you may use the Product on unlimited workstations located in multiple buildings on the same site selected by you that is served by such wide area network; provided, however, that any building will not be considered located in the same site if it is more than five (5) miles away from any building included in such site. In addition, you may only use a local area or wide area network version of the Product on one single server. If you wish to use the Product on more than one server, you must obtain written authorization from McGraw-Hill and pay additional fees.

(iii) You may make one copy of the Product for back-up purposes only and you must maintain an accurate record as to the location of the back-up at all times.

COPYRIGHT; RESTRICTIONS ON USE AND TRANSFER: All rights (including copyright) in and to the Product are owned by McGraw-Hill and its licensors. You are the owner of the enclosed disc on which the Product is recorded. You may not use, copy, decompile, disassemble, reverse engineer, modify, reproduce, create derivative works, transmit, distribute, sublicense, store in a database or retrieval system of any kind, rent or transfer the Product, or any portion thereof, in any form or by any means (including electronically or otherwise) except as expressly provided for in this License Agreement. You must reproduce the copyright notices, trademark notices, legends and logos of McGraw-Hill and its licensors that appear on the Product on the back-up copy of the Product which you are permitted to make hereunder. All rights in the Product not expressly granted herein are reserved by McGraw-Hill and its licensors.

TERM: This License Agreement is effective until terminated. It will terminate if you fail to comply with any term or condition of this License Agreement. Upon termination, you are obligated to return to McGraw-Hill the Product together with all copies thereof and to purge all copies of the Product included in any and all servers and computer facilities.

DISCLAIMER OF WARRANTY: THE PRODUCT AND THE BACK-UP COPY ARE LICENSED "AS IS." McGRAW-HILL, ITS LICENSORS AND THE AUTHORS MAKE NO WARRANTIES, EXPRESS OR IMPLIED, AS TO THE RESULTS TO BE OBTAINED BY ANY PERSON OR ENTITY FROM USE OF THE PRODUCT, ANY INFORMATION OR DATA INCLUDED THEREIN AND/OR ANY TECHNICAL SUPPORT SERVICES PROVIDED HEREUNDER, IF ANY ("TECHNICAL SUPPORT SERVICES"). McGRAW-HILL, ITS LICENSORS AND THE AUTHORS MAKE NO EXPRESS OR IMPLIED WARRANTIES OF MERCHANTABILITY OR FITNESS FOR A PARTICULAR PURPOSE OR USE WITH RESPECT TO THE PRODUCT. McGRAW-HILL, ITS LICENSORS, AND THE AUTHORS MAKE NO GUARANTEE THAT YOU WILL PASS ANY CERTIFICATION EXAM WHATSOEVER BY USING THIS PRODUCT. NEITHER McGRAW-HILL, ANY OF ITS LICENSORS NOR THE AUTHORS WARRANT THAT THE FUNCTIONS CONTAINED IN THE PRODUCT WILL MEET YOUR REQUIREMENTS OR THAT THE OPERATION OF THE PRODUCT WILL BE UNINTERRUPTED OR ERROR FREE. YOU ASSUME THE ENTIRE RISK WITH RESPECT TO THE QUALITY AND PERFORMANCE OF THE PRODUCT.

LIMITED WARRANTY FOR DISC: To the original licensee only, McGraw-Hill warrants that the enclosed disc on which the Product is recorded is free from defects in materials and workmanship under normal use and service for a period of ninety (90) days from the date of purchase. In the event of a defect in the disc covered by the foregoing warranty, McGraw-Hill will replace the disc.

LIMITATION OF LIABILITY: NEITHER McGRAW-HILL, ITS LICENSORS NOR THE AUTHORS SHALL BE LIABLE FOR ANY INDIRECT, SPECIAL OR CONSEQUENTIAL DAMAGES, SUCH AS BUT NOT LIMITED TO, LOSS OF ANTICIPATED PROFITS OR BENEFITS, RESULTING FROM THE USE OR INABILITY TO USE THE PRODUCT EVEN IF ANY OF THEM HAS BEEN ADVISED OF THE POSSIBILITY OF SUCH DAMAGES. THIS LIMITATION OF LIABILITY SHALL APPLY TO ANY CLAIM OR CAUSE WHATSOEVER WHETHER SUCH CLAIM OR CAUSE ARISES IN CONTRACT, TORT, OR OTHERWISE. Some states do not allow the exclusion or limitation of indirect, special or consequential damages, so the above limitation may not apply to you.

U.S. GOVERNMENT RESTRICTED RIGHTS: Any software included in the Product is provided with restricted rights subject to subparagraphs (c), (1) and (2) of the Commercial Computer Software-Restricted Rights clause at 48 C.F.R. 52.227-19. The terms of this Agreement applicable to the use of the data in the Product are those under which the data are generally made available to the general public by McGraw-Hill. Except as provided herein, no reproduction, use, or disclosure rights are granted with respect to the data included in the Product and no right to modify or create derivative works from any such data is hereby granted.

GENERAL: This License Agreement constitutes the entire agreement between the parties relating to the Product. The terms of any Purchase Order shall have no effect on the terms of this License Agreement. Failure of McGraw-Hill to insist at any time on strict compliance with this License Agreement shall not constitute a waiver of any rights under this License Agreement. This License Agreement shall be construed and governed in accordance with the laws of the State of New York. If any provision of this License Agreement is held to be contrary to law, that provision will be enforced to the maximum extent permissible and the remaining provisions will remain in full force and effect.